For

TIMOTHY E. KNUDSEN
(1955 1973)

"I am a Christian. I am not afraid to die."

Acknowledgements

The following essays and bibliography contain slightly revised versions of their original published form. All are reprinted with the permission of their publishers. All rights reserved.

"Calvinism as a Cultural Force," in *John Calvin: His Influence in the Western World*. W. Stanford Reid, editor. Grand Rapids: Zondervan, 1982, 13-29.

"Apologetics and History," in *Life Is Religion*. Henry Vander Groot, editor. St. Catherines: Paideia Press, 1981, 119-133.

"Roots of the New Theology," in *Scripture and Confession*. John Skilton, editor. Philadelphia: Presbyterian & Reformed, 1973, 247-273.

"Analysis of Theological Concepts: A Methodological Sketch," in *Westminster Theological Journal*. 40, Spring, 1978, 229-244.

"May We Use the Term Theonomy?" in *Theonomy: A Reformed Critique*. William S. Barker & W. Robert Godfrey, editors. Grand Rapids: Zondervan, 1990, 15-37.

"The Transcendental Perspective of Westminster's Apologetic," in *Westminster Theological Journal*. 48, Fall, 1986, 223-239.

"Progressive and Regressive Tendencies in Christian Apologetics," in *Jerusalem and Athens*. Robert Geehan, editor. Philadelphia: Presbyterian & Reformed, 1971, 275-298.

"Crosscurrents," in *Westminster Theological Journal*. 35, Spring, 1973, 303-314.

ROOTS AND BRANCHES:

THE QUEST FOR MEANING AND
TRUTH IN MODERN THOUGHT

ROBERT KNUDSEN

ROOTS AND BRANCHES: THE QUEST FOR MEANING AND TRUTH IN MODERN THOUGHT

With an introduction by

William Edgar

Edited By Donald Knudsen

Paideia Press
2009

Published by
The Reformational Publishing Project, and
PAIDEIA PRESS LTD
Grand Rapids, MI USA
www.reformationalpublishingproject.com

Scriptural citations are taken from the NIV
unless otherwise stated

ISBN 978-0-88815-206-0

Book design by K. J. Hollingsworth,
Typeface, Linotype Palatino, Adobe Garamond

"Symbol and Reality in Nicolas Berdyaev," in *Westminster Theological Journal*. 24, November, 1961, 38-47.

"The Ambiguity of Human Autonomy and Freedom in the Thought of Paul Tillich," 4-part series in *Philosophia Reformata*. 32 (1967) 55-67, 33 (1968) 32-44, 34 (1969) 38-51, 37 (1972) 3-25.

"Transcendental Motives in Karl Jaspers' Philosophy," in *Philosophia Reformata*. 34 (1969) 122-133.

"Rudolf Bultmann," in *Creative Minds in Contemporary Theology*. Philip E. Hughes, editor. Grand Rapids: Eerdmans, 1966, 131-162.

"Transcendental Method in Dooyeweerd," in *Anakainosis*. I/3, April, 1979, 2-8.

"The Religious Foundation of Dooyeweerd's Transcendental Method," in *Contemporary Reflections on the Philosophy of Herman Dooyeweerd*. D.F.M. Strauss and Michelle Botting, editors. Lewiston, Queenston, Lampter: Edwin Mellen Press, 2000, 271-285.

"Dooyeweerd's Philosophical Method," mimeographed lecture delivered at Annual Philosophy Conference, Wheaton College, Wheaton, IL, Oct. 13, 1962.

"Philosophia Reformanda: The Idea of Christian Scientific Endeavor in the Thought of Herman Dooyeweerd," in *Reflections on the Philosophy of Herman Dooyeweerd*. Mimeographed text, Westminster Theological Seminary, 1968.

Bibliography Of The Writings Of Robert D. Knudsen, in *Westminster Theological Journal*. 58, Spring, 1996, 111-121.

FOREWORD

A central focus of Robert D. Knudsen's writings is the idea of the word of God, as this is manifested in the 'law' or structure by which all things are properly made. "Blessed is the man ... his delight is in the law of the LORD, and on his law he meditates day and night" (Psalms 1: 2). Not that law here becomes a thing unto itself, but is rather understood as the way by which something has been rightfully made, as from the beginning, and by which it can also continue in its being on the right path in the light of the Word.

One of my father's favorite Saturday afternoon traditions was to work out in the backyard. There was a right way to put in the new pine trees, and there were less than 'right' ways to do so. My father worked in the blazing sun of the Philadelphia summer afternoon in the knowledge that the right way to plant trees was to do so thoroughly. One should set up all ingredients carefully and with due measure. Care should be maintained for drainage, for exposure to variations in the landscaping. In this process, one analyzes the situation in depth, that is, from top to bottom, and works carefully through the project in its entirety.

It has been mourned that my father could not edit and prepare for publication an anthology of his writings. But, we as a family know that he has gone to be with his own Father, in whose hands there is everlasting comfort and joy. So the Knudsen family has rejoiced in the opportunity to complete this work on behalf of the memory of the earthly father that we so deeply admired and loved.

None of the Knudsen sons had a hand in the decision to dedicate this volume to the memory of our brother, Timothy, who passed away many years ago. Our mother came to this decision. We as a family thank our mother, Ali, for her many years of selfless devotion to us and to many others in the community.

This community definitely includes students, staff, and faculty at Westminster Theological Seminary, without whose support over the past years this effort in re-publication might have become pointless.

Many thanks are due specifically to Dr. William Edgar, professor of apologetics at Westminster. He has written a wonderful introduction to this volume. I realize that the idea for this anthology was his from the start, but also that any editorial oversights that might still remain in this anthology are not of his responsibility and doing.

The main text in its entirety has been re-edited simply because, for one thing, it has been digitalized prior to publication. This is a far cry from what my father once did on Saturday evenings in writing with his pen and paper.

Editorial corrections have been made and incorporated into this new text in good faith. The emphasis on faithfulness to both the original documents and to current language and style has been maintained.

Many thanks are due to Kerry Hollingsworth and to the Reformational Publishing Project of Grand Rapids, Michigan for the actual publishing opportunity.

Donald Knudsen   Steven Knudsen
Lafayette Hill, PA   Morgantown, West Virginia
Easter Sunday, 2009

Introduction To The
Robert D. Knudsen Anthology

Philosophy in the Reformed tradition is like a good wine. With the years it ripens, adding depth, intricacy, bouquet, and when the time comes to use it, proves strong and venerable. The principal vineyard from which this particular school of thinking issues comes from the Netherlands. The vines themselves originate in Calvin's Geneva. The Reformer believed that the world was the Lord's, and that every realm of life belonged to him. Thus, he rejected the autonomy of human action in God's world, while at the same time implicitly endorsing a certain kind of secularization. That is, he believed that God was directly sovereign over every area, every institution, and thinking itself, a sovereignty not always mediated by the church. To put it another way, Calvin rejected any sacred-secular dichotomy. Instead, he affirmed the need for a differentiated society, one in which various professions, callings and institutions would develop their own proper relationship to God's revelation.

The kind of progressive Calvinistic philosophy espoused in the present anthology is rooted in the Reformation's understanding of the Lordship of Christ over every area of life. This tradition blossomed again in a remarkable way in the 19th century, particularly in the Netherlands. In the setting of the great revival of religion in Holland, men like Guillaume Groen van Prinsterer and Abraham Kuyper developed a social philosophy based on their conviction that the motive of Creation-Fall-Redemption provides the only framework which can provide meaning for our world. Thus, there is an order of creation from which we may derive structural norms for these callings and institutions. True, there has been a radical fall, which has corrupted the entire world. Sin has also corrupted the thought process. So the direction of things has been stained with sin. But not the structures themselves, which remain in force. As Christ governs the world for the purpose of its redemption, creation is affirmed, and enhanced. Philosophy has its rightful part to play in this world.

To put this in terms of biblical theology, progressive Calvinism affirms the ongoing value of the cultural mandate, expressed in Genesis 1:26-31. Because mankind is made after God's image, and because God commanded the human race to go into all of creation and have proper, loving dominion over the world, history has meaning. The fall did not abrogate this arrangement. Rather, because of God's grace in Christ, the cultural mandate is enhanced and deepened. The so-called great commission, the command to go into all the world and make disciples of the nations (Matthew 28:16-20), is now the redefined version of the cultural mandate. So, history now works toward the increasing unfolding of the creation, yet in an administration of grace. Making disciples includes submitting every area of life to the Lordship of Christ. While we deeply desire individuals to be saved, and to begin their journey to the new heavens and the new earth, we see them as called to particular tasks during their short lives. The same holds for institutions. And it holds true for philosophy as well.

Robert Donald Knudsen (1924-2000) was born and raised in Oakland, California. He obtained his undergraduate degree from the University of California at Berkeley in 1944. He then studied at Westminster Theological Seminary, where he earned the Bachelor of Divinity in 1947. His higher education took him to the University of Basel, to Union Theological Seminary in New York, and to the Free University of Amsterdam, where he obtained the PhD in 1958, with a dissertation on "The Idea of Transcendence in the Philosophy of Karl Jaspers." Among his other academic achievements, he was acquainted with Karl Barth, and was a teaching assistant for Paul Tillich. Professor Knudsen was an ordained minister in the Orthodox Presbyterian Church, and fairly active in denominational committees. And he taught apologetics at Westminster Theological Seminary for forty years, from 1955 to 1995, when he retired. He died in 2000, survived by his adored wife, Ali Mulder Knudsen, and three sons and families.

On a personal note, "Bob" was my Department Chair, and something of a father figure to me. He called me "William," and was always vigilant to the end that I would aspire to greater depth, to faithfulness, and to profundity in my work. He had a strong zeal for Westminster, and worked tirelessly so that the Seminary would stay strong in the Reformed faith. We worked as a team, and, though he was my senior in every way, Bob liked to herald the academic ideal of the "society of fellows," so that I never felt like a little person in the face of a giant.

In one way Robert Knudsen's career was undramatic. Some philos-ophers have become celebrities, well-known outside their otherwise secluded academic circles. One thinks of Isaiah Berlin, the legendary British liberal, historian of ideas, the intellectual giant whose writings were known well beyond academe. One might think of Luc Ferry, the French humanist philosopher who became Minister of Education and wrote best sellers on deep philosophical issues. Knudsen did not have such a public profile. Yet he worked steadily, methodically, faithfully, as a scholar and a churchman. No doubt his impact will be felt for a long time. He had a quiet influence on many leaders in the field of Reformed philosophy and other disciplines. His work indeed covered a wide vari-ety of intellectual subjects with integrity and depth, and the present volume is a veritable showcase of great scholarship within a Reformed understanding of the world.

Two particularly important influences on the author of the chapters in this anthology need to be mentioned. The first is Cornelius Van Til (1895-1987), who taught at Westminster from its founding, and continued there for close to fifty years. The pioneer of the apologetic approach known as presuppositionalism, Van Til had deep roots in the Kuyperian tradition. He believed that every part of life, particularly epistemology, were gov-erned by pre-conditions which informed their character. In order truly to confront an unbelieving worldview it was necessary to lay bare the deep structures of a particular view and to argue "transcendentally" in order to show "the impossibility of the contrary," or the untenability of non-Christian thought. Only when one begins with the self-contained God of the Bible, the "ontological Trinity," as he liked to call him, can one justify human thought and find value to live by. Van Til recognized Knudsen's talents as a student, as did other professors at the Seminary, and urged him to go to Holland in order to study the Amsterdam Philos-ophy in some depth. It was understood that he would eventually come back to associate himself with these men as their colleague. It is worth noting that when he did come to Philadelphia to teach, Knudsen was given to deliver classes in systematic theology as well as apologetics.

The second influence is Herman Dooyeweerd (1894-1977). He was the most influential of the Amsterdam philosophers. A law professor at the Free university of Amsterdam, he set forth what was known as the "tran-scendental critique of theoretical thought," which criticized the dogma of the "pretended autonomy of theoretical thought." Although the apol-ogetical implications of Dooyeweerd's thought have not yet fully been explored, there is plenty of potential for that to happen. And Knudsen began the process. Following Kuyper, Dooyeweerd believed that religion and faith were universal characteristics of all of humanity, made as the image of God. Knudsen embraced much of Dooyeweerd's approach, and attempted to blend it into the more theologically informed understanding of Van Til. This was not always easy. Indeed, it is fair to say that his career at Westminster involved attempts at reconciling the two visions, so close, and yet with important differences. As is well-known from various debates, both Dooyeweerd and Van Til accused each other of being "dogmatic" about their methods. Dooyeweerd had trouble with Van Til's idea of humans "thinking God's thoughts after him," based, as he conceived it, on Scriptural notions. He said, "Nowhere does the Bible speak of obeying the voice of God in terms of subjecting every thought to divine thought." Van Til, on the other hand, accused Dooyeweerd of an impossible restriction, which "definitely excluded the contents of biblical teaching as having the basically determinative significance for your method of transcendental criticism." Knudsen had the difficult job of mediating between these views, attempting to see the best face of each side.

In the present volume, entitled Roots and Branches: The Quest for Meaning and Truth in Modern Thought, Robert Knudsen draws deeply from all of these wells. Here, we are treated to the sharp and thorough analytical gifts inhabiting his spirit. In the first part, Knudsen delivers a penetrating understanding of the provenance of our current thought. He defends the worldview expressed above. Accordingly, our dedication to the task of obedience in our moment of history is not a side-bar in the unfolding historical process, nor a necessary evil on our way to heaven, but the privileged response to God's call in the historical process, a vocation appropriate to the culture God has given us here and now, rooted in the creation, and informed by a realistic view of sin, but also of a hopeful view of redemption. As he looks at figures and dates, we find Knudsen especially pointed as he discusses Immanuel Kant and Søren Kierkegaard. In the second part, he interacts with theological apologetics and the attending issues. His inaugural address, now an essay, "The Transcendental Perspective of Westminster's Apologetic," is something of a masterpiece, an apt summary of the genius of presuppositional apologetics. Finally, in the third section, we are treated to his ability to penetrate deeply into the core of some of the most important thinkers of the twentieth century, from Berdyaev, to Tillich, Jaspers,

Bultmann, and, of course, to Dooyeweerd himself. One or two of these essays are alone worth the price of admission!

We are deeply indebted to the Reformational Publishing Project for making these texts available to the general readership. And we express special thanks to professor Knudsen's son, Donald, for his meticulous care in making these texts available in such a clear and uniform manner. May these writings enhance our understanding of the contours of contemporary thought. And may they perpetuate the memory of one of God's most precious gifts, the extraordinary gentleman-scholar, Robert D. Knudsen. It is with humility and gratitude that we present these texts to a world which dearly needs their wisdom. We have here an astonishing vintage! Let us consume with gratitude and humility.

William Edgar
Professor of Apologetics
Westminster Theological Seminary, Philadelphia

CONTENTS

Part IV: An Assessment of Herman Dooyeweerd

PART ONE

THE ORIGINS OF
CONTEMPORARY THOUGHT

CALVINISM AS A CULTURAL FORCE

C alvin was a patron of modern human rights. In his thought he anticipated the modern republican form of government. He contributed toward the modern understanding of the relationship of natural and positive law. Fully abreast of the social and political movements of his time, he understood that the rise of the modern national state, the burgeoning of international trade, the development of the bourgeois class, and the vast expansion of the money market required a reassessment of the prohibition of lending money at interest. Calvin, furthermore, stood against the abuses of power in his time and wrestled with the problem of the right to revolt.

The impact of Calvin and Calvinism on modern Western culture has been well documented. This influence, it is acknowledged, has been great. Calvin and Calvinism take their places among the major forces that have molded our modern Western society.

Tracing these influences is important from a historical point of view. What has the influence of Calvinism been? Precisely how far has this influence extended? To assess Calvinism as a cultural force properly, however, it is necessary to penetrate to a deeper level of questioning. What is it about Calvinism that determines the peculiar fashion in which it relates to culture? What cachet does it impress on culture? In these respects how does it differ from other Protestant movements? Without having asked such questions one is scarcely in a position to inquire meaningfully into the extent of its influence. [1]

That focusing one's attention on the nature of Calvinism's impact is the more significant approach is clear when we bring to mind that any movement that has attained historical importance will have a corresponding cultural influence. That is indeed true of Calvinism. It is true as well, however, of Lutheranism, Anabaptism, Methodism, Puritanism, and the like. It is true of any movement, irrespective of the attitude it takes to culture. Even the anti-worldly stance of a broad segment of the confessing Christian church has a special kind of cultural influence, though it be a negative one. The withdrawal of Christians from what is called "cultural involvement" has itself a cultural impact. More important than the question of the extent of Calvinism's influence will be that of the quality of that influence.

In treating Calvinism as a cultural force, therefore, we do not have in mind a bare description, important as that might be, of the influence that Calvinism has exerted on our Western culture. Instead, we ask what it is about Calvinism that has established the character of this influence. Why is it that Calvinism has had a positive attitude toward culture and has been able to make constructive cultural contributions? Why indeed is it that this positive attitude belongs to the very genius of Calvinism, so much so that Calvin had in view not only a reformation in doctrine, in individual life, and in the life of the church, but also a transformation of all of culture in the name of Christ?

In answering these questions we may, for the sake of convenience, organize our thoughts around four major points: 1) that in Calvinism there is no dichotomy between Christianity and culture; 2) that because of its penetrating insight into the doctrine of creation, the universality of divine revelation, and the place of law, it is impossible for Calvinism, be it ever so important to keep intact the biblical doctrine of the Creator/creature relation, to think in terms of a simple, unqualified distinction between the divine and human spheres and activities; 3) that all of life, including culture, is theonomous, i.e., it has its meaning in its being subject to God and to His law; and 4) that the power of the sovereign Creator-God also embraces the course of history, so that one can discern God's revelation also in that which pertains most immediately to culture, namely, man's forming activity.

Calvinism's Positive Attitude Toward Culture

Calvin expressed his gratitude that at the same time that God again brought to light the gospel in its purity, He also brought into being a renaissance of the humanities. [2] It was Guillaume Budé who at the time of Calvin had sought to introduce into the French scene the humanistic learning that had arisen in the Italian Renaissance. He promoted a love for the liberal arts (*bonae litterae*) in contradistinction to the studies that prepared one to make a living (theology, law, medicine). [3] Calvin firmly agreed with Budé that the liberal arts were essential in forming man, in developing his humanity. Indeed, we find in Calvin a love for the liberal arts and a concern for training in them that in no way falls behind that of his humanistic contemporaries. One does not require many words, he said, to express how dear to us is the pursuit of the liberal arts. [4]

Calvin took a positive stance also toward rhetoric and the natural sciences. The influence of rhetorical theory on his theological method has been noted. In the introduction to his commentary on Thessalonians he acknowledges that he owes his humanistic learning and his method teaching (*discendi rationem*) to the well-known humanist Maturin Cordier. Like rhetoric, the natural sciences are gifts of God, created by Him for the use of mankind. [5] The final source of the true science of nature is none other than the Holy Spirit. [6] Calvin was, however, a stubborn opponent of the pseudo-science of astrology, which was enjoying a vogue in his time, even as it is in ours. [7]

The spiritual climate in which Martin Luther grew up was that of the mysticism of the late Middle Ages. Unlike Calvin and Melanchthon, he remained largely untouched by the renaissance of humanistic learning of his time. In contrast, Calvin early took to humanistic studies. As a test of his competence as a humanistic scholar, he produced his famed commentary on Seneca's *On Clemency (De Clementia)*. [8] Trained by the outstanding legal scholars of his time, Pierre de l'Estoile and Andrea Alciat, well conversant with the philosophy of classical culture, and himself a recognized humanistic scholar, Calvin manifested throughout his entire life a profound interest in, and mastery of, contemporary cultural developments. He continued to display an interest in man's humanity and in those good gifts of God, including art and music, that were able to contribute to its development. [9]

It is a mistake to suppose that Calvin's enduring interest in humanistic studies and in man's cultural development was a simple holdover from antedating his conversion to the evangelical faith. His concern for the humanities and for the human is too much bound up with his overall point of view to warrant such an interpretation. In fact, in a sense that must be well defined and carefully preserved from misunderstanding, Calvin may be called a "humanist." [10] Throughout his life he had a profound allegiance to what is human.

Indeed, Calvin turned his barbed criticisms against those whose humanism meant that they set themselves against the sovereignty of God, the authority of God's Word, the depravity of man, and the doctrines of grace. At age twenty-seven, in the famous letter that formed the introduction to his Institutes of the Christian Religion, he spoke out against humanism that did not share the evangelical doctrine. [11] Rather than against a Christian humanist such as Budé, he struck out at those who apotheosized the human self [12] and thought that realization of what is human can be attained only in presumed independence from God and from His revelation. Himself a humanist, Calvin rejected what was at the heart of the Renaissance idea of human personality, that man is the creative source of his own values and is therefore at bottom unable to sin. [13] If the humanities were dear to Calvin for their ability to develop human virtues, if the sciences were to be cultivated as good gifts of God, those must be opposed who thought that the arts and sciences might be employed as if they were sufficient to themselves. The thought was foreign to Calvin's mind that the arts and science could be free from religion (*non debere distrahi a religione scientiam*). [14]

One need not suppose that Calvin's attitude to what is human and to what belongs to human cultural achievement is without any need of correction. His positive attitude to them, however, is indigenous to his thought and has profound implications for the attitudes of those who call themselves Calvinists. It helps account for the way in which Calvinism acts as a cultural force.

For Calvin, unlike other leaders of the Reformation, there is no basic dichotomy between the evangel and the world, the gospel and culture. There was in his thought, at the same time, no simple, uncritical acceptance of the products of human genius. His attitude required that they be criticized as to the conception behind them and that they be subjected to the rule of Christ.

Calvinism On The Divine And The Human

Calvin confessed the absolute sovereignty of God. With the other Reformers he also confessed that by the grace of Christ the believer is related in his heart immediately to the sovereign God as He has revealed Himself in His Word. As we have already shown, this did not mean for Calvin that God's sovereign activity came to stand in a relation of indifference, or possibly even antithesis, to what is human and to what belongs to the realm of human cultural achievement. Calvin viewed God's activity in such a way as to avoid any such dualism. The God who sovereignly works in man's heart is the same God who has revealed Himself as the Creator of man and of human cultural values.

One who has a profound grasp of God's revelation of Himself as the Creator will understand that the divine and the human may not be conceived of as if they were on opposite ends of a spectrum, so that exalting the one would mean per se debasing the other. God is not honored by demeaning His creation, nor is His creation exalted by demeaning God. The creation is the expression of God's Creator-will. In its unspoiled state God called it good. He reveals Himself as being actively concerned with it. To glorify God one need not denigrate the creation; he need only carry out in it what answers to God's Creator-will for it.

If one has a profound understanding of the biblical revelation concerning creation, he will understand that what is at issue is not a mere emphasis on what is divine or what is human but whether or not what is human and what belongs to the sphere of human activity has been brought to conform to the will of God as expressed in His law. That is to say, he will see that what is at issue is whether they answer to what God desired for them from the beginning.

It is clear that the Reformation doctrine of the immediate working of God's grace through His Word in the human heart arose in opposition to the views that the human is a semi-autonomous sphere antecedent to the divine and that performing works by one's own natural powers serves as a necessary preamble to the working of grace. By the time Luther began to set forth his doctrine of justification by faith alone the nominalist William of Ockham, in whose logic he had been instructed by Trutvetter and Usingen, and whom he called his teacher (*magister meus*), [15] had already created a climate of thought uncongenial to the idea that nature is the preamble of grace. Ockham disallowed that anything outside the evangel might serve to judge it or act as a staging platform for God's gracious provision and for man's believing response. Luther was proud of belonging to the school of Ockham, whom he regarded as the head and the most clever of the scholastic doctors.

The nominalist position appeared to dovetail, furthermore, with his doctrines of grace. Nominalists taught God acts directly, addressing man with an absolute, sovereign demand, without room for an exercise of natural human powers of judgment, discrimination, or choice. They taught that divine grace is not the accompaniment, even if that is understood as the divine perfection, of human works. They taught that divine grace works immediately in man's heart, in indifference to, or even in contrast to, human accomplishment.

I do not wish to suggest that Luther's understanding of the doctrines of grace arose out of, or even depended on, this nominalist teaching. This understanding, I hold, came from his reading of the Scriptures. The Ockhamist tradition, however, provided a niche for it in its criticism of the view that nature is the preamble of grace. Once these doctrines had been discovered, furthermore, the nominalist teachings were able to affect their theological outworking and to determine the conception as to how the gospel relates to culture.

It is acknowledged that Luther's view of what is called the "two kingdoms" is deeply affected by nominalism. For the sphere of nature, he taught, the widely accepted Aristotelian concept of knowledge is sufficient. For religion, however, it is only revelation that is authoritative. Here human reason has to submit itself entirely to the Word of God. The natural understanding and its logic, limited as they are to the finite, are detrimental to theology, because they do not lead to faith but rather away from it.

The manner in which this nominalist tradition distinguished between the divine and the human has indeed a point of contact with the concrete verbal usage in the Scriptures. The Scriptures often speak of the activity of God and the activity of man in such a way as to set them diametrically over against each other. It is possible, however, to adopt a usage without having penetrated to the truth behind it. This, it would appear, was the case with the nominalistic understanding of the biblical teaching concerning God and man, which was thought to parallel that of grace and nature. It was inevitable that this tradition should affect the manner in which Luther developed his theology and conceived of the relationship between Christianity and culture.

Luther correctly holds forth for the evangelical doctrine of the immediate operation through the Word of God's sovereign grace. In Luther's thought, however, there is a very marked distinction between an inner sphere of divine, spiritual activity and an outer sphere of worldly ordinances. In line with the nominalist position, this outer sphere, in contrast to the inner, is regarded as formal and conventional. At the least, it stands to the spiritual realm in a relation of indifference. Human cultural activity, which belongs to this external sphere, is acceptable, as long as its standards are not thought to apply to the spiritual realm. There is no inner connection, however, between it and this spiritual realm. Spiritual activity affects the cultural, to use a metaphor, only as it effervesces and spills over into it. In comparison with the spiritual, human cultural activity must suffer.

Within this context, it is not surprising that Melanchthon, discovering in Luther's position no inner point of contact with culture and concerned with the foundations of theology and his practical program of university reform, moved farther and farther toward an uncritical acceptance of what came to him from the secular milieu. He accommodated his position more and more to that of Aristotle, who, he said, had developed the only scientific philosophy. [16] True to the Reformation doctrines of grace in his personal confession, Melanchthon accommodated himself nevertheless to secular culture in a fashion that was impossible for Calvin.

In Calvin's thought we find no such dualism. Indeed, for him there is no relatively autonomous sphere of human activity preceding the operation of God's grace. Moreover, there is no limitation of divine sovereignty as it operates in the human heart. In Calvin's thought, however, these attitudes combine with a profound understanding of the biblical doctrine of creation. God is the absolute, sovereign Creator and Sustainer of all things. There is nothing of which He is not the Creator and that is not subject to His Creator-will. All things, including those that are apparently the most trivial, are revelatory of Him. Furthermore His sovereign Creator-will embraces what is human and what belongs to the sphere of human achievement, the course of history and of cultural development. All of them are subject to His will, as expressed in His law.

In Calvin, therefore, we do not find a simple, across-the-board – what amounts to a logicistic – distinction between God and man, between what is divine and what is human activity. Indeed, one must honor to the full the biblical distinction between the Creator and His creation. It is, however, a profound understanding of this very biblical doctrine that preserves one from using the terms "God" and "man" *en bloc*, in the simple, unqualified way against which I am warning. This pitfall is avoided if one, with Calvin, thinks within the creation, under the horizon of God's revelation, in terms of the expression of God's Creator-will in His law.

Calvin saw that everything conformable to God's will as expressed in creation has God's approval. As he answers to God's creative purpose, man answers to what is his state of nature, to that which God at the creation declared to be good. Thus Calvin could embrace with enthusiasm the program of natural science to ferret out the secrets of God's universe. Thus too, he could accept freely the products of human genius that contributed to man's being man. Granted that these things were meaningless apart from religion; they were indeed meaningful with it. They were good gifts of God, imparted by the power of the Holy Spirit. To be sure, mankind is depraved at its heart because of sin, and culture has not developed without severe dislocations. Depravity is, however, contrary to nature. It is unnatural. What does not answer to God's Creator-will, what is not truly in conformity with His law, is an expression of that unnaturalness that has entered the world because of sin. This deformation, however, even though it is great, is not such as to have separated the world and its culture from God's purpose and plan. Nor is it such that the world no longer displays God's glory. God's good gifts are spread abroad, without any special favor to those who are of the household of faith. Truth, which is present by the influence of the Holy Spirit, must be embraced, therefore, wherever it is found. In spite of the depravity of man's heart, God has, by His common grace, kept embers burning of that which answers to His Creator-will. [17] Thus it is possible to understand that there are even brilliant accomplishments of the human spirit among those who have in their hearts little or no place for the teachings of the Word of God.

Calvin's view of the relation of God and man appears to be epitomized in his famous statement at the beginning of his Institutes, that there is a correlation between one's knowledge of God and his knowledge of himself (*Dei notitiam et nostri res esse coniunctas*). [18] The thought is that one knows himself truly only as he knows himself in the light of God and His revelation, with the corollary that if one knows himself truly he also knows God truly. It is not too much to draw from this correlation the thought that for man to be truly related to God religiously is to be truly related to himself and to be truly related to himself religiously is to be truly related to God.

As I understand the matter, Calvin's idea of the correlation between our knowledge of God and our knowledge of ourselves opened the way for him to meet what must have been for him a major problem, viz., that of relating the humanistic training he had received and for which he continued to have the greatest respect, to the truths of the gospel, which he embraced at his conversion. It expressed a point of view in which the danger of taking "God" and "man," the "divine" and the "human," *en bloc* had already been avoided. It allowed him, in a fashion that is truly conformable to Scripture teaching, to give full place to man's humanity and to his cultural achievements without detracting in the least from the honor and glory of God.

Calvin viewed man's humanity in its depth. Indeed, that depth-understanding was not guided by an idea of universal humanity such as that of the Renaissance, where man was thought to be autonomous personality, the creative source of his own values; instead, it was led by the revelation of God concerning His purpose in creation, the distorting effects of sin, and His provision for the redemption of man and his world. For Calvin it became possible to relate the idea of humanity to the religious antithesis portrayed in Scripture. The way was opened for the idea that man has his being in his relationship to God. Man is himself, is truly human, as he answers to what is his state of nature, to what he was created to be. [19] In this fashion it is possible to see that the *humanum* is realized not in autonomous isolation from God but in relation to him, and that sinful human autonomy, far from being the avenue to human self-realization, is itself a distortion of what is human.

Against this background it is clear that what is at issue is not a simple, relative emphasis or de-emphasis of man and the products of human activity. The issue is whether what man does and how he conceives himself conform to what God intended for him from the beginning in His sovereign Creator-will. It follows that any idea of man, of human activity, or of the products of that activity must be examined as to its religious root. Does man seek to express his humanity in conformity with the law of God, is he ready to acknowledge the unnaturalness attaching to everything human and to all human accomplishment because of sin, and is he prepared to depend in everything relating to himself and his activities on the redeeming grace of Christ and its restoring power?

From the vantage point we have now reached we are able to bring into sharper focus how Calvin's thought is "humanistic." His position does not require one, in the interests of God's glory and of the gospel of Jesus Christ, to negate or even to depreciate what is human. In fact, man's humanity may even be exalted without detracting from the honor of God. Interest in, and concern for, the *humanum* becomes humanism in a pejorative sense only when it is thought that man's center of gravity, as it were, resides in himself, in a presumed autonomy vis-a-vis his Creator. The latter kind of humanism, as we have noted, budded during the Renaissance and flowered at the time of the Enlightenment. To this kind of humanism Calvin reacted vigorously, as its exponents were attempting with every means at their disposal to defeat the cause of the Reformation.

CALVINISM ON THE RULE OF GOD THROUGH LAW

In the preceding we have ascertained that for Calvin God's sovereign Creator-will is without limitation. It penetrates everything, even those things that are apparently the most insignificant. Everything is revelatory of God, expressing in some way or other His majesty and glory. We have ascertained, furthermore, that this sovereign will of God is not understood apart from His revelation of Himself, apart from the expression of His will in His law, to which man and indeed the entire creation are subject. It is in line with Calvin's thought to say that man has his being in his responding to God's impartation of Himself in His revelation. Man is himself in freely responding to the call of God, in his obedience to God's sovereign will, which to be sure does not hem him in but serves as the medium within which he realizes himself. [20]

With this understanding, I turn to my third proposition: For Calvin, all of life, including what is loosely called "culture," is theonomous; that is, it has its being in its subjection to God and to His law.

What comes particularly into focus here is Calvin's view of law. If God, as the Creator, is above the law (*deus legibus solutus*), without anything outside of His own being that might limit Him, man and the entire cosmos with him are under the law, subject to it. For creaturely existence in its entirety, bounds are set up by the law of God. Apart from these bounds creaturely existence has no meaning.

Accordingly, the image that is brought to mind by Calvin's view of the divine sovereignty is not that of a despotic tyrant but that of a grand architect, a designation Calvin often applied to God. [21] When speaking of the creation, Calvin could easily refer to its architectonic, to its architecture, which is a revelation of the greatness and the goodness of God. The idea of creation brings with it for Calvin the idea of order, one in which everything is built up into a magnificent structure, a thing of beauty. [22]

This understanding makes it impossible to see in the Calvinistic idea of the sovereignty of God a sanction for any kind of unlimited human sovereignty. All creaturely existence is limited. Even though man may have authority sanctioned by God, it is bounded. Human sovereignty is always restricted to the bounds set for it.

These two facets, the all-penetrating character of God's Creator-sovereignty as He has revealed Himself in His Word and the boundedness of all creaturely existence, appear in the Reformation idea of calling.

Luther is credited with having brought about a Copernican revolution of the idea of calling as it was held in the Middle Ages. The idea of calling had been applied only to special areas, so-called "holy orders," for which a special consecration was needed. Indeed, the idea was rife that only monasticism was a true calling. Likewise, a life of spiritual contemplation was highly favored over an active life. [23] Recognizing that all of life as it reflects God's purpose is holy, Luther extended the idea of calling to embrace every legitimate activity of man.

The full impact of Luther's revolutionary conception can be felt, however, only if one escapes the kind of dualism he himself fell into with his distinction between an inner, spiritual realm and a sphere of external ordinances. Calvin, I have asserted, never shared such a dualistic view. Indeed, even as Luther did, he rejected the idea that nature is the preamble of grace and he held that God works immediately in the human heart through His Word; he was, however, untouched by the nominalist influences that affected the outworking of Luther's thought. His view, as I established in the preceding section, did not at all involve a depreciation of human cultural activity and human institutions. In Calvin the Reformation idea of calling was able to come to purer expression in its universal significance.

For Calvin, man's life in its entirety is understood as a response to the calling of God. Man is a covenant being. He has, as Luther put it, an assured rule according to which he is to live and die (*certa regula tum vivendi tum moriendi*). In every aspect of his life one is confronted with the sovereign God, before whom he must give an account of himself.

Indeed, the calling of God has this universal sense. The Reformation idea of calling does not come to full expression, however, apart from the idea that there are particular callings. The Reformation recovered the idea of the sanctity of all legitimate human activities. What is at stake, therefore, is not whether one enters a particular calling but whether in the sphere in which he is active he views his labor in the light of the divine call and serves God there with all his heart.

One of the keystones of Calvin's view of calling was his understanding that a great diversity of gifts has been given to people according to the sovereign will of the Spirit of God. Just as it is not a single ray of the sun that lightens the world, but all of the rays conjoin to perform their task, so God spreads His gifts abroad, in order to keep mankind in mutual interdependence. [24] Among men there is a diversity of gifts, leading to a diversity of functions. That one has a particular place and task presupposes that he has a calling to it. By accepting this place and its obligations one has an assured calling (*certa vocatio*). [25] One's vocation is an obedient answer to the divine calling. [26]

In this connection, Calvin employed another figure, that of the body. This he extended beyond the church to the family and to the state. [27] The worldly callings belong to the state. [28] The members of the state as well as of the church, with their diverse gifts, are united in a body, with mutually dependent functions. Thus Calvin developed what has been called an "organismic" view of the church, the state, the family, etc. [29]

The Reformation idea of calling, especially as it was developed by Calvin, leads to the idea that sanctity attaches to what are broadly called man's "cultural activities." Man's cultural activity is thought of as being in response to a divine call and as involving a divinely given cultural task. Thus man's cultural activity is theonomous, having its meaning only in response to God and to His law, which sets its bounds and establishes its meaning. This step, in effect, was already taken by Calvin.

Calvin discerned such an organic sphere in the family. The family is a creation ordinance founded by God. [30] It is an eternal and indestructible institution of God. [31] The head of the family in the narrow sense of the word, the husband, has been given special gifts of the Spirit. Because of those gifts, he has been entrusted with an authority, which he is called to exercise in the particular sphere within which he is placed. Within the family there is a special relationship of superordination and subordination. According to the divine arrangement, the husband is the head of the wife, in such a way, however, that he should care for her as he does for his own body. Indeed, he is to love her as Christ loved the church and gave Himself for it. On her part, the wife is to be subservient to her husband in the Lord, giving him the love and obedience he should have as her head. Over both husband and wife, however, is the head of all things, Jesus Christ. Both the husband and the wife are limited in their authority and activity. Their lives as a married pair come to fruition in their obedience to the law of God as it pertains to the sphere to which they are called.

Calvin's organismic view also came to expression in his idea of the state, in which he found in this regard an analogy with the family. [32] He related to the state also his idea of the diversity of mankind as to gifts and station. The state too is analogous to a body, in which the various members have their own place and function. In the state people are gathered together in an organic unity, with different stations of life and differing functions.

Over the state is the ruler. His authority, Calvin taught, is not derived first of all from the will of the people; it is given first of all by God. [33] The divine source of the authority of the magistrate resides in his having received the peculiar gifts of the Spirit for ruling. [34] Within the sphere of the state, therefore, there is an authority, a seat of power, that is divinely legitimated.

Calvin interacted with the ancient idea that the ruler is above the law because he is its source (*princeps legibus solutus*). Indeed, he allowed, the ruler is the source of the positive law that is binding within his territory. Calvin spoke in this sense of the ruler as the law personified (*lex animata*). [35] True to his conception in general, however, Calvin held that the authority of a ruler is limited. A ruler must himself submit to the positive law that holds within his territory. [36] Positive law, furthermore, is only one expression of law; besides it there is natural law, a law of nature,[37] which Calvin associated closely with fairness. Every positive law must express the principle of fairness. Apart from this it is void. [38]

What for Calvin is the meaning of natural law? The answer to this question is not a simple one. Like Luther and Melanchthon, Calvin had a warm appreciation for Roman law, which had been received widely and was interacting with current legal systems. He shared the distinction that the Roman jurist Quintilian made between the laws that have been given to everyone by nature, that is, natural right (*iustum natura*), and the laws that pertain to a folk or a people, in which context laws receive their formal juridical expression (*iustum constitutione*). [39] Calvin's openness to Roman law at this point, involving as it does a formal agreement with its idea that there is a law of nature, is in agreement with his attitude in general toward human cultural achievement and, more particularly, with his attitude toward the system of Roman law, into which he introduced very few corrections. That he accepted the idea of natural law does not mean, however, that he did not place it in a setting that would materially change its meaning. To hold a view of a law of nature, as Calvin did, was not to come into the camp of the Stoics, with their idea of universal reason, or into material agreement with Roman law, in its view of the origin and the meaning of natural law.

That Calvin could accept Roman law at all depended on his interpretation of its place in the providential plan of God, and that would
of necessity involve his having reinterpreted it, placing its distinctions
within the context of his understanding of Christian doctrine. Accepting it was agreeable to his idea that God had not allowed the world to
go to ruin because of sin but that He had preserved it by His common
grace. Calvin's acceptance of some kind of natural-law doctrine also
reflects his interpretation of the Scripture teaching concerning what is
understood "by nature" (*physei*) by those who are outside the pale of
God's special revelation, those who, unlike the Jews, have not received
the oracles (*ta logia*) of God. That these nevertheless do "by nature" the
things that are written in the law of God is, according to Calvin, to be
ascribed to the human sensibilities spread throughout mankind (*sensus
communis*), which reflect the divine will and which have been preserved
from annihilation by God's common grace. It follows that Calvin could
not think of the law of nature as a right inhering in a universal reason,
understood apart from the biblical message. The law of nature had to be
related to the order of creation, through which, in spite of the ravages of
sin, God continues to reveal Himself everywhere and at all times.

A ruler, then, who indeed for Calvin is the source of the positive laws
inscribed on the statute books of his territory, is subject to the law of
nature. According to Calvin, this law of nature is the rule and the goal
of all positive laws and is that which establishes their bounds. [40] A ruler
is subject, therefore, to a law whose authority far exceeds any laws that
he himself might generate. In the final analysis, he is subject to God,
who is the final source of all law and all authority.

Indeed, the respect Calvin had for the magistrate and for the gifts of
ruling was enormous. One is obliged to approach a ruler as one who is
endowed by the Spirit of God Himself with the remarkable gifts suited
for ruling. This human authority, however, sanctioned as it is by divine
authority, is always restricted, being bound to the limits of the calling
pertaining to the office of ruler.

Calvin's view of calling, whether it be to activity in the sphere of the
home, the state, teaching, or the church, always displays these two facets.
There is, on the one hand, the idea that all of life is response to the universal call of God, whose sovereign will embraces all things and whose
providence extends to every minutia of human existence. There is, on
the other hand, the companion idea that human response is channeled

by specific callings, so that each has his place and performs his function within a body.

It would remain for the great Dutch statesman and theologian Abraham Kuyper to draw together the threads of Reformed teaching and to develop the idea of "sphere sovereignty," or, as it has been called, "sovereignty in the individual spheres of life," that God, whose absolute sovereignty extends over all of life, has ordained various spheres of society, each of which has a derived sovereignty within its own orbit. [41] Calvin already understood, however, that there was a diversity of gifts and callings and that each had to be understood in relation to God and to His sovereign will. According to Calvin, as well as Kuyper, one might serve according to his peculiar gifts, his special capacities, in his own place, and be graced with the knowledge that he was engaged in fulfilling a particular calling of God.

Calvin's view of the diversity of callings established by God makes it imperative to reconstruct a widespread notion of modern times concerning the nature of culture and society. Up to this point I have used the word culture in a rather general and indiscriminate sense, without throwing into question the common usage of the term. According to this usage, culture is the general term denoting the order that has been brought into being by human agency. Culture is supposed to embrace everything that does not come ready-made as part of nature. Thus it is thought to include all language, all laws, all social conventions, etc.

For the greater part, when a contemporary introduces such a topic as "Christianity and Culture," he has in mind the word *culture* interpreted in this way. Culture, embracing all human contrivance and its products, is set in contrast to what belongs to the sphere of the divine. One introduces thereby a discussion of the relationship of Christianity, as being of divine origin, to what is the product of human contrivance in the widest sense of the word.

Calvin's view of nature and of natural law suggests that this view needs reconstruction. His view does not allow all law and all structure that is not just that of nature to be understood as a product of human contrivance. Human contrivance itself, on the contrary, has its meaning within the framework established by the divine ordinances, which it is beyond human prerogative to change.

Again, Calvin's view does not allow one to consider the divine and the human *en bloc*. Human activity is meaningful only within the bounds set by God's sovereign will expressed in His law. God's law constitutes the abiding framework for human activity, apart from which it loses its meaning. Human cultural activity, indeed all of culture, is theonomous, having its meaning in relation to God and to His law.

CALVINISM ON MAN'S CULTURAL ACTIVITY

Calvin lived in a time of ferment and change, in an age that he himself described in terms that were most unflattering. It was a time of innovations of thought, of profound social dislocations, and of religious conflict. In both the Renaissance and the Reformation there was not only a vivid awareness of returning to what had for a long time been obscured, a return to the sources (*ad fontes*), but also a consciousness that this return was to mark a new beginning, the emergence of a new age that would differ in marked degree from the one that had immediately preceded.

In the midst of such ferment it is not surprising that there also arose a sense of historical change. This awareness also gripped Calvin. His view of natural law did not prevent him from being supple with respect to the changes that were everywhere taking place around him. He knew that it is impossible to associate the will of God altogether with the existing order, for to do so would have been to sanction the forces of conservatism and of reaction. The assault characteristic of his time on well-established ideas and customs was not simply destructive and devoid of meaning. It is clear, however, that Calvin did not abandon everything to the forces of history, as our discussion of law has already shown us. That he embraced a doctrine of natural law would itself stand in the way of such an abandonment. He did not divorce his view of change from God or from His law in a fashion that would lead him down the path to revolution. Even though he was more restrained in his attitude toward them than was Luther, Calvin held in contempt those on the fringe of the Reformation who struck out with revolutionary fervor against what was established.

It is true, nevertheless, that Calvin had a sharp eye for the role of history. Furthermore, he was a modern person in the sense that he did not consider history simply the moving image of eternity. His refusal to limit the sovereign will of the Creator-God could not stop short of history. History, for Calvin, has meaning resident in itself. [42] History and historical change fall within the province of God's sovereign activity and carry out the purposes of His will. [43]

Did Calvin possess, then, a well-worked-out principle of historical change that would account for his giving prominence to history without falling, on the one hand, into a conservatism or, on the other hand, into a revolutionary stance? Did he have a clear notion of what it is that constitutes culture, so that he could see clearly how history and historical culture-formation have their place within the order of the cosmos as God has created it? He was indeed fully aware of what had been done in the past toward constructing a Christian view of history, having read the church fathers, including Augustine, who is the first to have developed what might be called a Christian philosophy of history. Indeed, he himself also developed a view of history. The answer to the above questions, however, must be in the negative. Calvin did not develop a philosophy of history in the technical sense of the word.

It is better to conclude that Calvin possessed a finely tuned sense of the attitude a Christian ought to have with respect to historical change, a sense that was schooled in his study of history, in his training, and especially in his profound grasp of biblical teaching.

It is significant on this score that before his conversion to the evangelical faith Calvin was already fully involved in what was one of the most powerful modernizing forces of his time, the humanistic renaissance. This had already made an important impact in Roman Catholic circles – witness the fact that the leading French humanist, Budé, was a Roman Catholic – and had influenced some of Calvin's closest associates. Calvin first established himself as a humanist. Only after that did he undergo the development that was to make him the grandest systematician of the Reformation. Having already planted his feet solidly in the modern world, Calvin's problem would not be how to enter modernity but how to relate himself and the new learning to the ancient truths of the gospel as they had again been brought to light by the Reformation and how to interpret the modern world in their light.

It must also not be forgotten that Calvin, in the interests of applying the truths of the gospel to life, was drawn into the practical arena. His principles did not have about them that air of unreality that attaches to ideal schemes that have little or no contact with actual life. There is in Calvin a healthful realism. It has been suggested that his principles had effect because he was in contact with real-life situations and was in a position to change them. [44]

We observe Calvin, for instance, attempting as much as was possible to replace canon law in Geneva with the principles of Roman law. [45] We see him, in cooperation with Marot, raising the level of appreciation for music in worship. [46] We see him entering the field of education, with the founding of the Academy in Geneva, and attempting to develop a truly Christian view of learning. [47] We find him, through his intense literary efforts, raising the level of the French language to unaccustomed heights. [48] In the introduction to his *Institutes of the Christian Religion* he addresses the king in a fashion reminiscent of that of the early apologists, pleading for the welfare of the true followers of the gospel, but stating also, in a fashion that related to the deepest concerns of the current political situation, that the true interests of the state are advanced only as there is true obedience to Christ and to the truths of His Word.[49] Truly, for Calvin, the Word of God was not to remain in the cloisters of the human heart. Its energies were to radiate out into the entire world, into all of life, including the domain of culture.

At bottom, however, it was because Calvin had penetrated so profoundly into the depths of the Christian world view that he was able to develop a proper sense of history and of its dynamics. That he had understood, as Augustine before him, the seminal meaning of the biblical doctrine of creation, that he acknowledged the sovereignty and the providence of God over all things, so that nothing escaped God's Creator-will, made it possible for him to see that this will extends also to history and to that which is central to history, man's forming activity, which is the heart of cultural development.

If one stands in the line of Calvin, it is not necessary to view human cultural activity in contrast to a presumed sphere of divine activity. Culture may be viewed as an aspect of human activity, indeed in distinction to nature, but not independent of the divine law, the divine plan, and divine calling. Human cultural activity may be viewed as a response to God's calling, even as all of life is, and may be judged as to whether it is carried out in accordance with His Creator-will. What is required is a reconstruction of the idea of culture, which views it within the context of divine revelation, the context within which it becomes meaningful. Human cultural activity, carried on in obedience to God's law is an expression of His will. It is in line with the thought of Calvin to say that what flows from cultural activity has a place in God's plan as it relates to the end of this age and the coming of a new heavens and a new earth.

REFERENCES

1. Writing in the 1930s, the outstanding Austrian Calvin scholar Josef Bohatec reported that the more recent Calvin scholarship had been attempting to determine what characterizes the Calvinistic world of thought as it relates to church, state, and society: "Geht das Interesse der neueren Forschung darauf aus, die Eigenart der calvinischen, auf die kirchliche, staatliche und soziale Wirklichkeit sich beziehenden Gedankenwelt zu bestimmen." Josef Bohatec, *Calvin's Lehre von Staat und Kirche: mit besonderen Berüchtsichtigung des Organismus-gedankens* (Breslau: Marcus, 1937), xiii.

2. Ed. Baum et al., *Corpus Reformatorum: Ioannis Calvini Opera quae Supersunt Omnia*, 7, 516. (Hereinafter referred to as Calvin, *Opera*.)

3. Josef Bohatec has explored in great detail Calvin's relationship to the French humanism of his time, more particularly to that of the acknowledged leader of the French Renaissance, Guillaume Budé. Josef Bohatec, *Budé und Calvin: Studien zur Gedankenwelt des französischen Fruhhumanismus* (Graz: Hermann Böhlaus, 1950). (Hereinafter referred to as *Budé und Calvin.*)

4. Calvin, *Opera*, 7, 516. Cf. Bohatec, *Budé und Calvin*, 121.

5. Ibid. 34, 304; 31, 94. Cf. *Bohatec, Budé und Calvin*, 264.

6. Ibid. 33, 577. Cf. Bohatec, *Budé und Calvin*, 264.

7. Ibid. 40, 554. Cf. Bohatec, *Budé und Calvin*, 270-80.

8. Ford Lewis Battles and Andre Malan Hugo, *Calvin's Commentary on Seneca's De Clementia: With Introduction, Translation and Notes* (Leiden: Brill, 1969).

9. Bohatec, *Budé und Calvin*, 467, 470.

10. Bohatec comes out boldly with the assertion "Calvin was a humanist" ("*Calvin war Humanist*"). Ibid., 472. He takes pains, however, to define carefully what he means here by "humanism" and to distinguish Calvin's humanism both from that of the Renaissance and from that of ancient culture. Cf., in particular, ibid., 472-483.

11. Cf. ibid., 127-41.

12. Ibid., 479.

13. Ibid., 265.

14. Calvin, Opera, 39, 251. Cf. Bohatec, *Budé und Calvin*, 254.

15. Wilhelm Risse, *Die Logik der Neuzeit. I: 1500-1640* (Stuttgart-Bad Cannstadt: Friedrich Fromann, 1964), 81.

16. Ibid. 82, 106, 120.

17. Calvin's idea of the law of nature, unlike that of the Stoics, does not rest

on a conception of a universal cosmic reason but is inextricably bound up with the biblical doctrine of creation and the created order of things. Thus Calvin has a place for the doctrine of God's "common" or "preserving" grace. Bohatec discusses extensively Calvin's view of the law of nature, relating it to the doctrine of creation and showing Calvin's use of the doctrine of common grace. Cf. Josef Bohatec, *Calvin und das Recht* (Graz: Hermann Bohlaus, 1934), 22-24, and passim.

18. Calvin, *Institutes*, I.1.1. Cf. Bohatec, *Budé und Calvin*, 243.

19. According to Calvin, Bohatec writes, man in his state of nature willingly subjected himself to the rational norms. Bohatec, *Budé und Calvin*, 352.

20. Calvin's idea of the humanum, in contrast to an idea of human autonomy, is manifest in his view that human freedom is not license but a freedom in obedience to God's law. "Die wahre Freiheit ist nicht Ungebundenheit, sondern Freitheit im Gehorsam, Freiheit unter dem Gesetz." Ibid. 473-74.

21. Léon Wencelius, *L'esthétique de Calvin* (Paris: Societé d'Edition 'Les Belles Lettres', n.d.), 30.

22. Wencelius closely associates Calvin's idea of beauty with order. In every description of beauty is found the notion of order. "La notion d'ordre se retrouve à chaque description de beauté. Tout chose belle est ordonnée en ellemême." Ibid. 46. "La création révèle Dieu ... grâce à sa beauté, c'est-à-dire grâce à son ordre merveilleux." Ibid. 40; cf. 34.

23. Bohatec, *Calvins Lehre von Staat und Kirche*, 638-39.

24. Calvin, *Opera*, 2, 252. Bohatec, *Calvins Lehre*, 640.

25. Bohatec, *Calvins Lehre*, 636.

26. "Der Beruf ist gehorsame Antwort auf den göttlichen Ruf." Ibid. 644.

27. Ibid. 647.

28. Ibid.

29. Bohatec is especially interested in showing that Calvin's idea of calling is intimately connected with this organismic view. "Die Eigenart des calvinischen Berufsgedankens wurzelt in seiner Einordnung in das Organismussystem." Ibid. 646.

30. Calvin, *Opera*, 28, 148.

31. Ibid. 52, 276. Cf. Bohatec, *Calvins Lehre*, 652.

32. Bohatec, *Calvins Lehre*, 653.

33. Ibid. 169, 171.

34. Ibid. 12.

35. Ibid. 37.

36. Ibid. 38.

37. Bohatec, *Calvin und das Recht*, 126.

38. Ibid. 97, 101, 106, 122, 127.

39. Ibid. 98f.

40. For Calvin, says Bohatec, natural law, which is virtually identical with the moral law, serves as the *ratio* of all written laws. Ibid. 97. "... das Natturrecht Regel, Ziel und Grenze der positiven Gesetze ist." Ibid. 101; cf. 106.

41. "Sphere-Sovereignty" (*Souvereiniteit in eigen kring*) is the title of the famous address delivered by Abraham Kuyper at the opening on October 20, 1880, of the Free University of Amsterdam, 3rd ed. (Kampen: Kok, 1930). Cf. Abraham Kuyper, Lectures on Calvinism (Grand Rapids: Eerdmans, 1931, 1943).

42. Bohatec, *Budé und Calvin*, 284.

43. Calvin, *Opera*, 39, 588. Cf. Bohatec, *Budé und Calvin*, 282.

44. Ibid. 298.

45. Bohatec, *Calvin und das Recht*, 121; cf. 211ff.

46. Cf. Wencelius, *L'esthétique de Calvin*, 225ff.

47. Cf. Bohatec, *Budé und Calvin*, 300ff.

48. Ibid. 263.

49. Cf. Andre Biéler, *La pensée économique et sociale de Calvin* (Geneva: Georg, 1961), 74ff., and passim.

APOLOGETICS
AND HISTORY [1]

Early modern philosophy was not oriented to history. The word was not "history" but the "power of   reason," and this reason was thought to be elevated above history. It was understood along mathematical lines and was endowed with creative capabilities. "Give us material," said René Descartes, the father of modern philosophy, "and we shall construct a world for you." [2] Reason, thought Descartes, was sufficient on its own to demolish the world and to build it up again by its own creative power. History did not dominate reason; instead, reason dominated history. Reason was supposed to interpret and guide history by means of its super-historical ideas.

The attitude of René Descartes toward the relationship of reason and history prevailed in early modern philosophy. A historical manner of thinking was introduced into modern thought by Giambattista Vico only in conscious opposition to the ideas of Descartes. [3]

Descriptions have often been given as to how the modern rationalistic spirit came to dominate theology, gradually replacing revelation with reason. This tendency came to expression in the movement called "deism," which is typified by the title of the book of Matthew Tindal (1656-1733), *Christianity as Old as the Creation* (1730). By this title Tindal did not mean to express only that the truths of Christianity were ancient and venerable, reaching back to the creation. For him "creation" and "reason" were virtually synonymous. That Christianity was as old as the creation meant for him that the truths of Christianity were simply a restatement of the truths of reason. According to many with deistic tendencies, Christianity had simply stated, at an earlier time and to a wider audience, the truths that reason of itself was able to discover. [4]

In response to the rationalistic challenge of deism, evangelical Christians attempted to establish a preserve for revelation, where reason could not trespass. Reason was limited, they said, unable to lay claim to the entire territory. It was difficult, however, for the evangelical to make his strategy work, because he had not found a way intrinsically to delimit reason. He was forced to stand by as more and more of his territory was conquered, as more and more truths of revelation were either abandoned altogether or were declared to be at bottom truths of reason.

An influential attempt to countermand the influence of deism was that of Bishop Joseph Butler (1692-1752), who is famous for his *The Analogy of Religion, Natural and Revealed, to the Constitution and Course of Nature* (1736).[5] Butler sought to turn the edge of deistic criticism by appealing to the deist's own faith in the order of nature, which for the deist was the order of reason. You criticize the truths of revelation, Butler said, but look around you at nature. It has difficulties analogous to those in the sphere of revelation, and yet you daily exercise faith in it. [6] Whatever difficulties there are in revelation, Butler argued, they are not sufficient to render it unreasonable for a rational man to vest his faith in it. [7]

In developing his argument, Butler divided the terrain, as was customary, into two parts, that of nature and that of grace. His reasoning with regard to the sphere of nature was typified by his argument for immortality. [8] During our lives, he reasoned, we observe that we undergo many transformations (childhood, youth, maturity, old age) without losing our identity. This experience establishes a presumption that our personal identity will continue on even beyond that transformation called "death," unless there is sufficient reason to the contrary. [9] Butler claimed that there was no evidence for such a reason. There are indeed difficulties, but these are not such as to render it unreasonable for a rational man to believe in an afterlife. Butler's approach was similar in the realm of grace. [10] You hear of the Christian doctrines concerning the Mediator, the need for grace, etc. These truths lie closer to your experience than you might suppose. There are analogies within our experience to the truths of Christianity. We observe, for instance, an analogy to the Christian doctrine of grace in the fact that one is not always forced to bear the full consequences of his errors. We find an analogy to the work of the Mediator in that one sometimes gives himself in the place of another. Whatever difficulties there may be with such Christian doctrines, they do not override the force of the analogies to them within our experience. The difficulties are not such as to make it unreasonable for a rational man to vest his faith in them.

It has often been described how David Hume (1711-1776) attacked the Butler-type apologetics. [11] Butler's argument rested on the possibility of forging a link between what lies within and what lies beyond our experience. Working within a sphere of thought obviously dominated by the mechanics of Isaac Newton, Butler had reasoned that momentum once established could reasonably be assumed to continue, according to the law of inertia, unless there was sufficient reason to the contrary. [12] Once having gotten a good start, one might reasonably expect to jump successfully from the one bank to the other. David Hume brought into question the possibility of forging such a link. There was no way of bridging the gap between what is within and what is beyond our experience, he argued, except by way of the idea of causality; but the idea of causality itself rests upon our customary experience and is valid only within that experience. It cannot serve to establish a link between our experience and what lies beyond it. [13] Furthermore, what truly underlies our attempt to fill in the gaps of our experience and to come up with the kind of world in which a Butler-type apologetics might work is an inclination of the mind. Hume took the inertia that Butler and others had discovered in the "external" world and transposed it to the mind. [14] It is only because of a "subjective" inclination, an "inertia of the mind," that we desire at all to reason from this world to another. The miracles, for example, which some peoples (i.e., primitive ones) take to be signs of supernatural intervention, arise as stories because of the needs of primitive imagination. Such stories satisfy curiosity and awaken an agreeable sense of wonder. They are not a result of reporting events in the outer world. [15]

The effects of Hume's reasoning on a Butler-type apologetics were grave. It took an argument from experience that was thought to be neutral and reinterpreted that experience in such a way that the argument became invalid.

In this situation apologetics was inclined to go in one of two directions if it was to find an alternative apologetical stance. There was a tendency, on the one hand, to retreat into a mere confession of Christian truth, without any attempt to do apologetics. One could even emerge with the idea that there is an incongruity between Christian confession and its presumed intellectual defense. In my own circles we call this attitude "fideism." [16] A different line of action, on the other hand, was to attempt to place apologetics upon a new foundation, one that would free it from criticisms like those advanced by David Hume. According to my best knowledge, it was the Scotsman James Orr (1844-1913) who initiated the latter trend, at least for the English-speaking world, drawing upon resources from the idealistic traditions in Germany and Britain. [17]

To illustrate this newer thinking, we must employ a different image. The image we have used before is that of someone who attempts to vault a stream (or perhaps a canal, as it is done in the Netherlands) with the aid of a pole. If his pole is long enough and if he can get a strong enough grip on it, all he must do is to establish sufficient momentum in order to jump safely to the opposite bank. We saw Hume argue against this view along the following line: "Yes, indeed, sir, that is nice; but I am sorry, sir, you don't have a pole and the other bank is in point of fact a product of your own imagination. We have enough to do simply to keep moving on this side of the stream!" The newer image we may employ, in order to visualize the approach of James Orr, is this: A surveyor comes and observes the near bank of the stream with utmost care. He observes that it is such that he can make sense of it with his surveying instruments. He then asks himself, reflecting upon what he has done, "What is it that makes this rational understanding possible?"

It is, as I have suggested, the latter route that James Orr took. Given our experience, what is it then, he asks, that lies at the very foundation of its possibility? [18] This kind of thinking is what is called "transcendental." [19] Am I incorrect in thinking of James Orr as the first, at least in the English-speaking world, to employ a transcendental method in apologetics?

Orr argued that to understand the world of our experience it is necessary to postulate certain axioms (presuppositions) drawn from the Christian world and life view. The first of those axioms is the God who has revealed himself in Jesus Christ. The second is the Biblical (Christian) doctrine of creation and of man. The third is the Christian view concerning the sin and disorder in the world. [20]

These presuppositions are postulates. As postulates they are not drawn simply from experience, as if we could take off from our experience of sense and rise to a transcendent, divine realm. But Orr does not regard these presuppositions as postulates, on the order of geometrical axioms, from which we might deduce the being of God not only but also that of the world and human existence.

If we simply begin with experience as something neutral, Orr understood, there is no way we can ascend to the absolute being of God. We are always left with something within our experience, with something finite. To this extent Hume was right. If, on the other hand, we seek to deduce the Christian doctrines of God, the world and man, and sin, we must proceed, Orr correctly observed, from a standpoint superior to them. But what is more ultimate than God himself, or more a beginning than his creation of the world and of all things in it?

We must first discover a point of departure that does not pretend to be neutral or seek to deduce from ultimate presuppositions, but one that presents us with the key to opening up the meaning of our experience. [21]

In my estimation, James Orr did not bring his program to an altogether satisfactory conclusion. I am convinced, nevertheless, that Orr hit upon insights suggestive of methods that are actually being used -- or that should be used in apologetics today -- if we are to give adequate place to the sovereignty of God and to the authority of his revelation.

Orr gained insight, for example, into what we might call the boundary character of the Christian starting point for thought. He was aware of the anomalies that arise for the human mind if it transgresses the boundary between what is immanent to the world, i.e., what is within the world, and what transcends it as its absolute origin.

In his book *The Christian View of God and the World* (1893), Orr reviewed some of the objections a simple-headed rationalism had urged against the idea of a God who transcends the world in infinite majesty. What was God doing before he created the world? Why did he create it just at one moment and not at another? I am certain that you have heard these and other questions like them. Wisely, like Augustine and Calvin, Orr refrained from attempting to answer such questions head on. Even asking them, he said, suggests that one is on the wrong track, that he has an erroneous idea of the relation between time and eternity. One should not seek to answer such questions but should reflect upon why it is that one should not even ask them, and upon the adequacy of his understanding of the boundary between God and man. [22]

Reflecting on the boundary, we can see that there is indeed a boundary idea which is itself not a product of our thinking nor which is even penetrable to our thinking, but which is necessary to that thinking if it is not to proceed in a wrong direction. Thus, any disturbance at the boundary will have repercussions within the limits of the boundary. Thus, too, in order to make it possible to survey the terrain adequately, one will have to obtain a proper idea of the boundary. If he fails in this all-important regard, his survey points will be off, and he will obtain a distorted picture of the terrain he is attempting to map out.

James Orr's position is, in my estimation, not quite so good as the one I have sketched here. His writings employ this transcendental method, however, or are at least so suggestive of it that I can honestly class James

Orr as a bona fide forerunner of the kind of apologetics I am describing.

A "bare-bones" description of this method might run as follows: Lose the handle on the true transcendence standpoint and you will no longer be able to obtain a unified view of the created cosmos. Your view of the cosmos will be driven in opposing directions. There will come into being contradictory viewpoints which do not truly belong to the cosmos in its created goodness but which are distortions of it.

This pattern comes to more or less clear expression in James Orr's argument for the Christian faith from history. [23] The Christian, Orr says, finds the central point of reference for his life and thought in the God-man, Jesus Christ, who is the crown of the revelation of God. If one refuses to place Jesus Christ at the center, there comes into play a process within history, unavoidable in its consequences, in which there is a descent from Christian conviction to bare humanism, from humanism to agnosticism, and from agnosticism to despair. [24]

It is characteristic of history, Orr said, to carry things to their extremes. [25] Thus, letting go of the Christ will lead to ever more dire consequences. One will be faced with ever more extreme choices, as the dialectic of history deepens. One will be faced, as we have said, first with the choice between Christ and humanism, then with the choice between Christ and agnosticism, and finally with the extreme choice between Christ and despair. [26] It is at this final point, at the nadir of despair, Orr said, that reason can again assert itself and begin its ascent again to the God-man Christ, in whom alone is the key to reason and meaning. [27]

Kindly note that this argument does not require one to rise above the boundary between God and man. It only requires that one have a proper idea of the boundary.

Kindly note also that this argument does not attempt a direct confirmation of the Christian position, of the centrality of Christ for life and thought. It assumes the Christian position as the proper starting point, as that in which there is the true idea of the boundary, the proper expression of the relation between God, man, and the cosmos. Lose hold of this transcendence point and a process will inevitably be set into motion within the world, within history, a process that is dialectical in character, leading to necessary choices between ever more extreme alternatives. That a departure from the Christian starting point leads inevitably to irrationalism and despair is taken as indirect proof of the validity of this starting point. A Christian view of the boundary, involving a view of the relation of immanence and transcendence, becomes the foundation for a presuppositional apologetics that uses an indirect method of proof for the Christian faith.

Orr's indirect method proof has allowed me to include him among the apologists who do not take a neutral position outside of the citadel of the Christian faith in order to defend it, but who mount a defense of Christianity while remaining solidly within its walls. [28] Accordingly, the defense of the Christian faith is not made to depend upon something outside of that faith, as if one required an "objective standard" in the sense of a neutral standard, a yardstick, if you will, that does not itself depend for its validity upon the Christian faith. Instead, the defense of the faith must proceed upon the standpoint of that faith itself. It must present the Christian position as the only one upon the foundation of which our experience is intelligible. Orr argued that it is only by taking Jesus Christ as one's starting point that one can avoid landing up in agnosticism and eventually in despair. For this reason it is possible to number Orr among those whom we today call "presuppositional apologists," even though we must register some disappointment with the way he carried on his argument.

James Orr was capable of mounting an argument from history because of developments that had taken place in current philosophy. He learned, to mention one, from the British philosopher Thomas Hill Green (1836-1882). [29] Green complained that British philosophy had gone to seed in David Hume. He sought to reconstruct it by drawing on the idealistic tradition represented by Immanuel Kant (1724-1804) and Georg W. F. Hegel (1770-1831). [30] Of the two it was Hegel who had carried to their end tendencies within the developing idealistic movement and had intimately connected Reason with the course of history. For Hegel history was the story of Reason (or Absolute Spirit) coming to self-awareness by way of a dialectical development. [31] That cannot be said of James Orr. There are points at which Hegel influenced Orr, however. The very fact that Orr used an argument from history as he did points to this influence. For it was particularly in Hegel that Reason was no longer identified, as in Descartes, with mathematical thinking, nor identified, as in the thought-sphere represented by Newton, with reasonable assumptions understood along the lines of a mechanical model; in Hegel, Reason became intimately associated with history, and history became the stage upon which Reason came to expression in its dialectical unfolding.

Orr agreed with Hegel that the totality, the point of concentration, of all meaning is rational. Reason, furthermore, leads to Jesus Christ. If Christ is not placed at the center, there is an inevitable fall into unreason and despair. [32]

We can learn, however, from respects in which Orr differed from Hegel. For the latter, despair was necessary to Reason. It was only as Reason passed through an entire series of way-stations of despair that it could come to itself, that is, attain complete self-consciousness. [33]

Even though there are similarities between him and Hegel, Orr takes a position here that Hegel would have rejected out of hand. According to Orr, Reason can pertain apart from despair. One descends into despair only as he rejects Christ and falls into the grip of a power that leads him from reason to unreason, from meaning to meaninglessness. What serves to trigger this necessary movement need not happen. One need not reject Christ. Furthermore, one may restore Christ to his rightful place and thus overcome the despair. Further still, at the nadir of despair, Reason can again take over and lead us again to meaningful existence. [34]

James Orr, as I have pointed out, is influenced by Hegel's idea of dialectic in history. Unlike Hegel, however, he uses dialectic only in a negative sense. The dialectic, the necessary development whereby one is gradually forced to decide between ever sharper antitheses, comes into being only when the true concentration point of meaning has been abandoned. It is a sign that the true transcendence point has been lost. Restore this true point of reference, and the dialectic disappears.

Now it is just this negative use of dialectic that I have singled out as a contribution on Orr's part to Christian apologetics. [35] Lose the true concentration point and you will of necessity fall into difficulties, the presence of which is an indirect proof of the validity of the true starting point. The centrality of Christ is testified to by the meaninglessness that issues upon rejecting him. I should certainly not suggest that we follow Hegel, for whom meaning was only in an encounter with meaninglessness. It is James Orr whom we say is an early advocate of a method employed by presuppositional apologetics.

How James Orr conceives of reason, however, leads to some difficulties. For him the fullness of meaning is rational. Its loss means unreason and despair. The necessary development leading from reason to unreason, however, must itself be an expression of some kind of reason (what one might call an "immanent logos"), a tendency that gets one in its grip.

Finally, reason must be thought of as the force that guides the mind of man, having seen the futility of unreason, to the fullness of meaning in Christ.

That Orr thinks of reason in these ways poses problems. If reason is that which is abandoned in the descent toward unreason, how can it also function as that which provides the framework of this descent itself? If it is the goal to which the process of history leads, how then can it function as the force that drives this process along? Hegel would certainly have objected to allowing these facets of reason to lie next to one another, as Orr left them. If Orr was to retain his purely negative use of dialectic, however, he could not draw these strands together in a universal rational process. The descent from reason to unreason could not be thought of as a constitutive part of the odyssey of reason leading to Christ. [36]

If reason is a universal force guiding the historical process towards Christ, however, would there not be an inclination to view the dialectic, itself part of the historical process, as making a positive contribution, and not only as providing a sign of the abandonment of reason for unreason? Understanding experience in the light of the postulate of sin and disorder would allow one to ascribe an exclusively negative meaning to dialectic, interpreting it as the result of a sinful rejection of the God-man. If one does this, however, can he think of the ascent to Christ as a tendency of universal human reason?

Another related question arises concerning Orr's view of history. Orr must think of history as that in which everything is driven to extremes -- a "reason" in history. It might be argued, on the contrary, that history is a great leveler.[37] The exalted ideals of men and women, their exalted personal ideals, are dissipated by the need to adjust to the historical situation, where compromise appears to be the rule rather than the exception, if one is to be effective and is not to isolate himself, depriving himself of historical power. Observations along this line were important, at least, for Hegel's philosophy of history.[38] In any case, it may be questioned that history, as by an inner law, brings everything to its purest expression.

To retain the force of Orr's apologetical reasoning, however, it is not necessary to make history carry the entire burden, making it display a kind of dialectical structure that is untrue to the actual course of events. We may view history within the broader context of God's creation, where it holds true that if you lose the handle of the true transcendence point, you are unable to see the cosmos in its true origin, its integrality, its coherence. You are bound to set up one aspect of the cosmos against another, making it impossible to establish the proper reference points to carry out your survey operation successfully.[39]

One might argue, in fact, that placing the entire burden on the historical is itself one-sided. It is a consequence of isolating one aspect of the created order of reality at the expense of others.[40]

We should attempt to place James Orr's apologetical insight, his negative use of dialectic, within a broader context. We observe that it is not only history but all of our experience that is dependent upon the light of God's revelation if we are not to fall into insoluble problems. We must see all of our experience in God's light if we are to gain a proper boundary idea and are not to fall into meaninglessness. But this observation leads us to take a closer look at Orr's view of the relationship between reason and revelation.

It is certain that James Orr gave an important place to reason. It is reason that we observe at work in the history of mankind, leading it ever higher, to ever higher insights. [41] What, then, of revelation? Orr's view of reason led him to make statements that differed very little from those of his predecessors. The Hebrew-Christian religion, which Orr regarded as the true one, taught for ages that God is one, an ethical and personal being with whom man has personal fellowship. These are insights which reason through the ages had slowly been approaching, moving ahead, often with short and uncertain steps, but always advancing towards the truth. [42] Because of his view of reason, Orr did not always escape, therefore, the deistic notion that revelation presents earlier and to a wider audience that which reason of itself is able to discover.[43]

Important to Orr's position as a whole is his view that reason at its apogee, at its high point, always rises above itself toward the infinite. [44] At the high point of reason there is the union of the finite and the infinite, the human and the divine. [45] This unity is manifested in Jesus Christ. [46] Indeed, for James Orr, Christ becomes the one towards whom reason leads, the one who is the embodiment of reason at its highest point of development. According to Orr, it was the great service of Idealism to point out the affinity between the divine and the human, something that Christianity had already long proclaimed in its message concerning Jesus Christ. [47] Because of his view of reason, Orr comes to think of Christ as the goal of a universal tendency in history towards participation in the divine. This contrasts with his own tendency to interpret all of experience in the light of Christian presuppositions.

His manner of thinking unfortunately allowed Orr to employ that kind of "foot-in-the-door" reasoning that we discover in earlier apologetes. You are familiar with the image of the door-to-door salesman, who first tries to get his foot in the door and then to get completely inside the house. Like many of his predecessors, Orr thought that if he could induce his opponent to go a certain distance with him, that opponent might well find it congenial to proceed yet further. A case in point is his refutation of the thought of a leading agnostic of his day, Herbert Spencer (1820-1903). Spencer, he reports, taught not only that we do not know God (*ignoramus*) but that, because of the intrinsic limitations of the mind, we cannot know him (*ignorabimus*). Inconsistent with his own agnosticism, Orr retorts, Spencer admits that there is an absolute, of which everyone is aware. If Spencer is inclined to proceed this far, what is to prevent him from proceeding further? It is, furthermore, only a step from thinking of the absolute as a being (ontological) to thinking of it as ethical will, and indeed only another step to thinking of it as personal identity.[48] All this parallels the upward course of reason, from being, to the ethical idea, to personality (spirit) as the fusion of the divine and the human.[49]

From the perspective we have gained, we may shed some light on Orr's argument from history. If one abandons the Christ, he abandons the One in whom is manifested the openness of the human to the divine, the God-man. If one then replaces that with humanism, namely, with the idea of man on his own, closed off hermetically from the divine, he is bound to go on from there to agnosticism and despair.

What we have pointed out concerning Orr's view of reason must affect our evaluation of his position. In spite of his presuppositional approach, Orr employed neutral ideas of reason which then supposedly became Christian ideas as they were extended to infinity.

In this connection I very often refer to Orr's definition of sin. One of his postulates, you will remember, was that of the sin and disorder in the world. What, then, does he understand by sin? For James Orr, sin is that which absolutely ought not to be.[50] Thus, by reason, we are able to obtain an idea of what is good, just as we can advance to the idea of God as an ethical being. We are able to arrive at the idea of sin when we have extended this ethical idea to infinity, as the expression of what ought to be absolutely or unconditionally.[51] Sin is the transgression of this ultimate norm. It is what absolutely, or unconditionally, ought not to be.

We have commended Orr for having attempted to erect an apologetic upon a Christian foundation. One ought to defend the Christian faith without taking a position outside of that faith. This is, at least, the tendency we observed in Orr's thinking. We also commended him for having developed a method in harmony with this idea, namely, what we have called a "negative use of dialectic." Because of his acceptance of a philosophy of human reason, however, we discerned a tendency in his thinking to miss opportunities offered by his better insights.

If he was to be true to his radical Christian intentions, Orr should not have thought of God's revelation as a vanguard after which reason marches, slowly perhaps and with stops and starts, but with sure progress toward the truths that revelation has broadcast earlier and to a wider audience. The relation to God and his revelation should not have been viewed as the capstone of a self-transcending reason; instead, every idea should have been examined as to what was already at work in it, as to the fundamental religious antithesis underlying it.

The latter approach requires that one explore in depth, that he penetrate beneath the surface of an idea, even one that might give the impression of being neutral, valid apart from the truth of the Christian faith.

Orr pointed in this direction when he explored the idea of the boundary. What idea of the boundary, of the relation of the Creator to the creature, is at work already in any view that confronts us? In his thinking, has one in reality transgressed this boundary, attempting to set something created in the place of God? As presuppositional apologists have pointed out, this is the pattern of human apostasy described by the apostle Paul in the first chapter of Romans.

Let me conclude by summarizing some of the consequences for apologetics of taking a position such as the one I have associated with James Orr's better insights. I speak negatively and then positively.

1. Faced with an apologetical situation, we do not first seek to establish contact with another and then seek to move in our thinking toward the Christian faith. We inquire, on the contrary, as to what is already at work in any position, including our own. That is to say, we inquire as to the presuppositions that are already at work.

2. Faced with any apologetical situation, we do not look for a common ground with an opponent. We understand that those who object to the Christian faith are themselves impelled by a faith and that this faith is based upon a religious commitment.

3. Faced with any apologetical situation, we do not stop short of pointing out this ultimate commitment. We penetrate, spiraling down to the religious motivation, in order to show that what is at work is a basic antithesis.

4. Faced with any apologetical situation, we do not only point to contradictions in another's thinking. We attempt to show that it is only by proceeding religiously according to the Biblical message that one can lay hold of the true transcendence standpoint and that one can obtain a view of the boundary from which God's creation, including man, can be seen as to its true origin, its true unity, and the true relationships of its aspects.

References

1. This essay is a revised form of a lecture delivered on November 30, 1979, at Trinity Theological College, Bristol, England.

2. As quoted by Herman Dooyeweerd, *The Secularization of Science*, translated with an introduction by Robert D. Knudsen (Memphis, 1979), 19.

3. See *The New Science of Giambattista Vico*, translated by Thomas Goddard Bergin and Max Harold Fisch (Ithaca, N.Y., 1948) and Robert D. Knudsen, History (Cherry Hill, N.J., 1976), 9.

4. Ernest Campbell Mossner, *Bishop Butler and the Age of Reason* (New York: 1936), 74ff., 77.

5. *The Works of the Right Reverend Father in God Joseph Butler* (Oxford, 1874), Vol. I.

6. Butler, 5.

7. Butler, 10, 11-12.

8. Butler, part I, chapter I, "Of a Future Life."

9. "There is in every case a probability, that all things will continue as we experience they are, in all respects, except those in which we have some reason to think they will be altered" (Butler, 15; see also 16, 21-22).

10. Butler, part II, "Of Revealed Religion"; see also 202-03.

11. See Mossner, 156-65. A more recent discussion is that of Anders Jeffner, *Butler and Hume on Religion: A Comparative Analysis* (Stockholm, 1966), including the literature lists, 21-24.

12. Butler, 11-12, 14-16.

13. David Hume, *A Treatise of Human Nature*, edited by L. A. Selby-Bigge (Oxford, 1928), Book I, part iii, section 2: " 'Tis only causation, which produces such a connexion....' "

14. See Herman Dooyeweerd, *A New Critique of Theoretical Thought*, I (Philadelphia, 1953), 291, 292, 297.

15. See Anders Jeffner, *Butler and Hume on Religion: A Comparative Analysis* (Stockholm, 1966), 112-25.

16. See Cornelius Van Til, *Christian-Theistic Evidences, In Defense of Biblical Christianity,* VI (Philadelphia, 1976), 34.

17. Van Til, 36ff.

18. James Orr, *The Christian View of God and the World,* tenth edition (Edinburgh, 1908), 103ff.; see also 94f.

19. Van Til speaks of the "high standard" set by Orr's use of transcendental method in apologetics (Van Til, 47).

20. Orr, lectures III, IV, and V.

21. "... a God capable of proof would be no God at all; since this would mean that there is something higher than God from which His existence can be deduced. But this applies only to the ordinary reasoning of the deductive logic. It does not apply to that higher kind of proof which may be said to consist in the mind being guided back to the clear recognition of its own ultimate pre-suppositions. Proof in Theism certainly does not consist in deducing God's existence as a lower from a higher; but rather in showing that God's existence is itself the last postulate of reason -- the ultimate basis on which all other knowledge, all other belief rests" (Orr, 94; see also Van Til, 47).

22. Orr, 129.

23. Orr, lecture II, "The Christian View and its Alternatives."

24. Orr applies the "method of appeal to history" (Orr, 43; see also 40f., 64f.).

25. Orr, 43; see also 45, 47, 48, 51, 53.

26. "History presents us with a series of alternatives" (Orr, 44; see also 44ff., 47ff., 51ff.).

27. "... I am at present concerned ... not to refute Pessimism, but rather to show how, as a first step in an upward movement back to Christ, by its own immanent dialectic it refutes itself ..." (Orr, 54; see also 64).

28. Robert D. Knudsen, "Progressive and Regressive Tendencies in Christian Apologetics," in Jerusalem and Athens, edited by E. R. Geehan (Philadelphia, 1971), 275-98; see also 280-83.

29. See Orr, 59, 104, 125.

30. G. W. Cunningham, *The Idealistic Argument in Recent British and American Philosophy* (New York: 1933), 42.

31. G. W. F. Hegel, *Phenomenology of Spirit,* translated by A. V. Miller (Oxford, 1977), 488-93; see also 591.

32. Orr, 63f., 215ff., 39, 40, 43ff.

33. "The self-knowing Spirit knows not only itself but also the negative of itself ..." (Hegel, 492, passim).

34. Orr indeed speaks of two movements in history, a downward one leading away from and an upward one leading to Christ. The pattern, however, is that of a trough, into which unbelief brings one, and out of which a straight-line ascent is possible, "retracting the stages of the earlier descent"

(Orr, 64). A simple descent and/or ascent would be rejected by full-blown Hegelianism as "abstract."

35. Knudsen, "Progressive and Regressive Tendencies," 281, 283, 291.

36. We have already stated that Orr's line of thought would be rejected as "abstract," indeed, as "undialectical," by consistent Hegelians. Had he taken the consistently Hegelian route, the descent to despair would have been far more than a warning signal that the true starting point had been abandoned. He would have had to include, as many contemporary theologians do, the shadow of unbelief together with the sunlight that streams from the God-man, Christ.

37. According to Hegel, anything sticking up out of history had to be mediated and included in the historical process.

38. Hegel's early moves to reconcile ideals and experience are traced by H. S. Harris, *Hegel's Development: Towards the Sunlight* (Oxford, 1972).

39. L. Kalsbeek, *Contours of a Christian Philosophy* (Toronto, 1975), 109ff.

40. Robert D. Knudsen, *History* (Cherry Hill, N.J., 1976), 38ff.

41. Orr, 95.

42. Orr, 87ff.

43. Christianity is "... really the higher truth which is the synthesis and complement of all the others ..." (Orr, 11; see also 12f.).

44. Orr, 113, 156ff.

45. Orr, 141, 244, 246.

46. Orr, 284.

47. Orr, 120f.

48. Orr, 80ff., 84, 86, 92.

49. Orr, 64f., 120f.

50. Orr, 171.

51. Orr, 166, 171.

ROOTS OF
THE NEW THEOLOGY

R ecent theologians are conscious of having brought something new into theology. That is so much the case that they call theirs a "new theology" in stark contrast to the old. The church, they say, must witness in our time to the grace that is in Christ Jesus. In this program a heavy accent must fall on the words "our time," for the times change, they believe, and no theology can be adequate to every age. Is their awareness a true one?

Considered from one point of view they have, let us admit, an excellent case. It can hardly be expected that the church will be able to frame its message exactly in the same terms for every age. That the times change is evident. Have we not been exposed in our time, for example, to an ever-increasing tempo of technological advance? Can we expect that the proclamation of the church can tower like a granite massif above this cataract?

We must not forget, however, the word of Scripture, "Lord, thy word is settled in heaven" (Psalm 119:89). The major question is not whether the church from time to time will vary the formulation of its beliefs to meet the challenges of a rapidly changing world. The fundamental question will always be whether the proposed modifications affect the very foundation of that upon which the church is built, the gospel of Jesus Christ.

When theologians step to the front with a "new" theology, one will always have to inquire as to its standing with respect to the gospel once and for all delivered to the saints. One will always have to ask whether its message and program are those that are set forth in the Scriptures themselves, or whether they root in a philosophical and theological soil that will poison the church and wither its branches. Our purpose is to throw light on these questions. We shall do so by exploring certain ideas that have prepared the soil in which the new theology has taken root.

THE ROOTS OF THE OLD LIBERALISM

The older liberal theologies issued from the collision of the historic Christian faith with the rationalistic humanistic faith that arose in the Renaissance and the Enlightenment. The supernatural Christianity of the Bible was pitted against a movement that criticized by means of Reason both the Bible and the faith that was built upon the Bible. The truths of the Scriptures were replaced by truths that were supposed to be derived from Reason or at least adequately supported by it. This conflict was dominant throughout the eighteenth century and extended into the nineteenth.

Early humanism had been captivated by the infinite possibilities open to man. Exploration and invention were opening new horizons. There seemed to be no final limits to the development of man's creative possibilities. Furthermore, the world appeared to reflect the inner boundlessness of man's spirit and to offer an unlimited terrain for the deployment of human capabilities.

The instrument of this conquest was Reason. It was to serve both as a means of breaking down the walls of the closed universe which had been inherited from the Middle Ages and as a means of building upon a new foundation, which it discovered in its own creative power. Thus the path would be opened to freedom and harmony.

In this enterprise Reason sought to harness the power of the new science that had arisen from the application by Galileo and others of mathematical thought to the world of nature. The world came to be viewed as a huge machine, governed by mechanical laws which could be discovered by science. Within the confines of this world-machine there was little place, however, for the bold conception of the human spirit that had captivated the minds of the early humanists. Instead, the human spirit, like the rest of nature, appeared to be dominated by a network of causes which ran their course in a mechanical and necessary way, irrespective of human ends. [1]

A reaction set in with Jean Jacques Rousseau. Man was supposed to be rational and free, he complained, but everywhere he was in bondage. With his science he had created a scaffolding of human institutions and conventions that were hemming him in and robbing him of his freedom. In the name of human dignity and worth Rousseau called man to forsake this conventional world and to return to the more original harmonies of nature.

It was the Königsberg philosopher, Immanuel Kant, who took up this challenge and put it in a more adequate form. Kant's philosophy still has a strong rationalistic cachet. In Kant, however, there was a revolt in the name of Reason against the earlier faith that the source of human freedom could be discovered in the scientific domination of nature. Reason still wore the badge of the preserver of human freedom and dignity; but now it had been distinguished from science, the weapon that it had earlier sought to employ in its struggle for freedom. Kant sought to provide a bulwark against the encroachment of the mechanical world-view of science by limiting science and human understanding to what could be experienced by the senses. The deeper ground of human freedom was now discovered in the independent, autonomous human will -- not the will as it looks to this or that goal to satisfy its human wants, but will as it sets for itself an absolute moral law. Kant held that it was as the autonomous will subjected itself to this moral law, itself what creative Reason had produced, that it first constituted itself a free moral agent.

Later German idealism broke through the confines of Kant's rationalism. It no longer sought the true human selfhood in terms of a general rule, a moral law. Instead, it considered the true rule of morality to be a reflex of the creative individuality of free personality. [2] Nevertheless, this later idealistic philosophy must still be understood as a further development of Kant's attempt to discover the locus of true human dignity and freedom in contrast to external nature. It is this later idealism which provided the background for the rise of the older liberal theology, as distinguished from modernism, which remained closer to the old-style rationalism or which wedded itself to some naturalistic philosophy, such as pragmatism.

Friedrich Schleiermacher, the father of modern theology, represented this post-Kantian idealism. With the insights it provided he tried to surpass both rationalism and supernaturalism by re-interpreting both. Religion was a matter of experience, but not of experience that was subject to the domination of theoretical thought. Religion was at bottom feeling, which transcended the realm of nature and was in this sense supernatural, a matter of grace. The idea of God was a reflex of this basic feeling. But these ideas of super-nature and of grace are understandable only within the framework of the Kantian distinction of nature and freedom. The theology of Schleiermacher can be understood only in the context of the struggle, which Kant also undertook, to discover a concentration point that would provide a ground for the human personality against the inroads of the ideal of science. For Schleiermacher the feeling of absolute dependence, which is at the heart of religion, is not supposed to be a feeling of a purely psychological nature.[3] It is a feeling of a more fundamental sort which is supposed to provide an absolute reference point for the human spirit. The finite world is at the disposal of the finite understanding, subject to its control. On the contrary, in the feeling of absolute dependence one is related to what is supposed to be a transcendent source that elevates him above the limits of the finite world.[4] It is therefore a mistake to think that when Schleiermacher referred to the feeling of absolute dependence, he had in mind a feeling of a purely subjective kind, with exclusively psychological qualities. It was supposed to be endowed with transcendental significance.[5] In it he sought to discover the final reference point for human freedom and worth against the loss of oneself in the confines of external nature.[6]

In the thought of the other fountainhead of liberal theology, Albrecht Ritschl, the Romantic feeling philosophy is replaced by a philosophy of moral freedom more directly in the line of Immanuel Kant. Ritschl's idea of a kingdom of free personality is dependent upon the Kantian idea of a pure willing, which subjects itself to an absolute standard of freedom, in contrast to an empirical willing, which is confined to nature.

Ritschl repudiates the orthodox conception, which views man as having been created in an original state of righteousness, as having received the divine command to obedience, as having fallen under the just condemnation of God, and as having the provision of salvation through the satisfaction of divine justice by the substitutionary atonement of Christ. From his standpoint this scheme is rejected as imposing general, rational categories of nature on the level of theology.[7] Theology has to do with the level of freedom. We are reconciled to God in Christ Jesus, a historical figure who assumes for our practical judgment the value of the divine; and we are given the task of building the ethical kingdom of God.

Here again there is a supposed triumph of the personality ideal. It is as Christ assumes for us absolute value, it is as we set for our willing the idea of the kingdom of God, that we rise above what can be understood in terms of nature. In Christ there is an absolute point at which there can be the realization of human dignity and freedom. The ideal of the kingdom of God is the triumph of free personality over the confines of nature.[8]

With all its variations liberal theology had a common root in the idealistic tradition. It set up an idea of free personality in contradistinction to a nature that was conceived in general, rational categories. In Schleiermacher the key is found in a pure feeling of dependence in contrast to psychological feeling, which pertains to nature. In Ritschl the key is pure willing, which sets for itself the idea of the ethical kingdom of freedom in contrast to willing that is only natural impulse.

In response both orthodoxy and neo-orthodoxy have charged the older liberalism with setting up ideals of personality and freedom of which Christ could only be the highest exemplar. Each from its own standpoint has accused the older liberalism of denying the uniqueness of Jesus Christ.

If one takes into account what we have said about the older liberalism, he cannot accept this objection without further qualification. In its modern form, as it has arisen in opposition to the science ideal, the personality ideal seeks a concentration point of human dignity and worth in contrast to nature. Post-Kantian idealism discovered this concrete point in the human spirit, in contrast to the general, rational categories of nature. Albrecht Ritschl, for instance, consciously attempted to discover such a point. He found it in the Christian community, for whose practical judgment Jesus Christ had the value of the divine. The testimony of this community was self-authenticating. It was impossible for one who stood outside of its communion to criticize or even to understand the Christian message. To understand one had to be involved.[9] For Ritschl this would be enough to establish the uniqueness of Jesus Christ, for it was the confession of Christ in his divine worth that stood at the center of the unique Christian community.

One would be able to come to this conclusion, however, only if he was able to agree that it was possible on an idealistic basis to reach a veritable concentration point. This existentialism has denied. From its standpoint the ideals of idealistic thought are themselves only general truths. Existential theologians are bound to conclude that the Christ of the older liberalism was only the exemplar, be it the highest one, of general truths which could be understood apart from him.[10]

The older liberalism did not survive the dissolution of the idealistic philosophy that provided its seedbed and the framework on which it could develop. Destructive influences converged on it both from biblical scholarship and from philosophy. Biblical scholarship began to see that the eschatological message of Jesus, which the older liberalism had sought to discard as a primitive, mythological form of expression in favor of the idea it expressed, was inseparable from Jesus' message as a whole. This threw in doubt the attempt to discover the essence of Jesus' message in purely ethical truths. Furthermore, the moral ideas themselves suffered at the hand of philosophy. The ideals, which had been thought to have a transcendent status, were depressed to the level of nature. Now they were thought to be explainable in terms of natural causes. No longer could they provide a key to the dignity and worth of the free human personality.

The breakdown of idealistic philosophy prepared the way for the newer forms of liberalism that have dominated the theological scene in our time. When we have sketched some of their foundation ideas, we shall have provided a framework for understanding the theological background out of which the newer trends of theology have emerged.

When the transition to contemporary theology has been described, it has been Søren Kierkegaard who almost uniformly has stood at the center of discussion. Without wishing to underestimate the tremendous impact that his conflict with the system of Georg Friedrich Hegel has made on the philosophy and theology of the twentieth century, we would suggest that the roots of the ideas we are to explore go back into the history of idealistic thought itself.

There are particularly three closely related areas that we shall examine as harbingers of the newer philosophy and theology: 1) the genesis of the idea of the transmoral, as a key to the supposed conquest of the philosophy of will and as a means for the contemporary reintroduction of the doctrines of sin and of divine grace; 2) the historicness (*Geschichtlichkeit*) of human existence and even of being itself; 3) the idea of truth as historic (*geschichtlich*) event.

THE TRANSMORAL

The practical philosophy of Immanuel Kant was moralistic in the sense that it rooted human freedom and personality in a transcendent willing, an ethical freedom. This ethical philosophy required a distinction between empirical will and intelligible will, between a willing on the psychological level and a pure willing which constituted human personality as free personality. It demanded that it be possible for an idea to rise unambiguously above the confines of nature.

Subsequent to Kant, however, the ethical life of man as a whole becomes incorporated in nature. All human willing is then understandable in terms of socio-psychological laws of origin and development. In the pattern that develops in the conflict of the personality ideal against the science ideal, it is regarded to be a matter of human convention, without any possible employment as a concentration for human dignity and worth. It is this conception of will that predominates in existential philosophy and theology. This accounts for the fact that they seek the ultimate ground of meaning beyond the level of will, in what is transmoral.

The idea of the transmoral has roots, however, already in Kant's *Critique of Judgment*.[11] In artistic creation, Kant says, there is an act that unites the universal and the particular, an act that depends upon no general criterion from outside. Artistic creation, though carried by Reason, is spontaneous, as if it were simply an act of nature. Genius is the natural talent that gives art its rule. [12] Under the impact of the personality of Goethe, Romantic philosophy extended this idea. The creative genius is beyond the law because he posits the law at the same time he creates according to his inborn instinct of genius.[13]

Hegel's early development was deeply influenced by the problem of the alienation of the self from the moral law. This, he thought, was epitomized in Judaism, in which the law stands outside of the self and condemns it.[14] His later philosophy and its idea of mediation arose out of an attempt to reconcile moral law and natural impulse. [15] In his mature thought, the subjection of the subjective disposition of the individual to the common consciousness he calls "morality." A deeper level of morality (*Sittlichkeit*) arises from the concrete spirit, not from abstract rules, and is realized in the common consciousness of the state, which is the realization of the ethical idea.[16] So politics, too, must not construe political life in terms of abstract requirements. It must discover its source in the development of the national spirit, which likewise stands above abstract law, being the expression of the spirit of the time.

Friedrich Schelling is a direct source of the idea of the transmoral in contemporary theology, having had a profound influence on the development of Paul Tillich. Every autonomous act of finite freedom, and thus every act of will, is separated from its ground and is ambiguous. Johann Gottlieb Fichte had already introduced the notion of a primal act (*Urakt*) which preceded all finite acts and which qualified them as finite.[17] Schelling interprets the primal act as a fall, which antedates all finite acts. Every particular act of will is thus a fallen act. The ambiguity of willing and consequently of morality is found therefore to have both its origin and its resolution beyond will and beyond morality. [18]

The idea of the transmoral appears at the heart of Kierkegaard's philosophy of history and of religion. The ethical stage on life's way, [19] which is dominated by the generality, the mass, is superseded by the religious stage, more particularly that of "Religion B," the paradoxical religion of Christianity. In his book *Fear and Trembling* Kierkegaard expressed this distinction, in what has now become a famous illustration, in terms of the biblical story of Abraham.[20] When he went to Mt. Moriah to sacrifice his son Isaac, Abraham could neither explain nor justify what he was doing in any (general) ethical categories. From the standpoint of the generality, the mass, what he was about to commit was murder. But this very command, which could in general only be condemned as an infraction of ethical standards, he held to be the voice of God.[21] Nor was there any hope of extenuating this predicament by the knowledge of a possible way of escape. Just as there was no possible justification of the act, there was no possible (general) explanation of the redemption, when Abraham received Isaac back again, in a "repetition" understood only by faith.

It is predominantly by way of Kierkegaard that the idea of the transmoral has passed on to contemporary philosophy and theology.

Theologically the idea of the transmoral has had important consequences. Idealistic philosophy after Kant tried to cut the jugular vein of the individualistic, rationalistic philosophy of human willing. It distinguished between a more superficial morality of will and a deeper morality of the idea. In connection with the latter it is possible to speak of grace. With the subsequent fall of idealism, the overall pattern of the conflict of the personality ideal with the science ideal was not abandoned. Within this framework, however, the idea in its totality was depressed to the level of nature. Now every idea was declared to have a subjective origin, being objectified for human and willing in the interests of satisfying human needs. Moreover, it was no longer possible to think of the acting subject as unambiguously striving toward goals that it could unambiguously set for itself.[22] Both the idea and the act of will that intends it become ambiguous. As a consequence there must be a reinterpretation of the notions of transcendence and of grace. The origin of human need is discovered in a transcendent act which precedes all acts in time. All history is fallen history. Since every finite act is ambiguous, human salvation cannot depend upon the act of the individual, in which he sets for himself a goal and then seeks to bring it to realization. If a reconciliation is to be found, it must be from a transcendent source in the existing situation, by grace. But the ideas of transcendence and of grace have been re-interpreted. Because every individual act falls under the horizon of the transcendent fall, having as its ineluctable destiny to be ambiguous, there is no possibility of a transition within history from a primitive innocence to guilt nor for a transition within history from wrath to grace.

The idea of a transcendent fall is that of an event which is not an individual event distinct from the inner life of man but which is supposed to be prior to any of his own individual acts. It opens up the idea of a history that is transcendent to the course of history regarded as a series of individual events in time. Anyone who is thoroughly familiar with the contemporary theology that stands in the line of Kierkegaard, will discern in the treatment of the idea of transmorality the configurations of the contemporary theological view of history. It is to this that we now turn.

Historicness (*Geschichtlichkeit*)

The movements we have been discussing arose within the Humanistic tradition of Western philosophy at the time of the Restoration, in reaction to the prevailing rationalism of the Enlightenment. This newer thinking had a definite historical orientation.

Thought that is completely historically oriented will surrender everything to the historical stream. It will conceive everything as a phenomenon of history, as having its origin and its end within history and as being subject, even at its very center, to the dynamics of historical change. Historical thinking places one radically within the historical situation and denies him the right to step out of it into a supposed realm of timeless truth.

In this sense Hegel's philosophy was historistic. Everything was a phenomenon of history, having its meaning only in its particular historical situation. Supposedly non-historical criteria were regarded to be abstract. Ultimate truth of the absolute spirit was present in the most individual fact, which from the standpoint of the abstract ideal was meaningless but which reflected nevertheless the absolute spirit from its own perspective.[23]

It is only because Hegel still regarded the positive historical situation to be the expression of absolute spirit that he was delivered from a complete historical relativization of the idea of truth. When this idea of absolute spirit fell away, as it did with the breakdown of the idealistic synthesis, truth became altogether relative to the stream of history.

Contemporary philosophy and theology have been concerned in the most intimate fashion with the problems of time and history. For existentialistic thought the solution does not lie, any more than it did for Hegel, in attempting to step out of history and time but in discovering ultimate meaning in the most individual historical event.[24] What, conceived from the standpoint of an abstract standard, can have only negative significance, as an exception, is the locus of absolute meaning. This moment in which ultimate meaning is found is not regarded to be on the level of history, however, as it is open to the neutral historical investigator, but on the level of the historic (*Geschichte*).[25] How does one arrive at the meaning of this important term?

The meaning of the historic in existential thought can be approached only by distinguishing it carefully both from the supratemporal idea and from the temporal positive historical fact as it is open to the historical investigator. What is in principle open to historical investigation is called by contemporary theology "history" (*Historie*). It is the level of ordinary historical event that is as such open to the methods of historical research, e.g., genetic explanation and the tracing of historical analogies. The historic (*Geschichte*), on the contrary, is supposed in a subtle fashion to transcend this level.

In explaining this distinction, appeal often is made to the usage in the German language. *Historie*, it is said, refers to the historical event considered from the abstract point of view of the historian; *Geschichte* refers to the historical event in its full concreteness. Indeed, this distinction occurs in the German language, while it is altogether lacking in English. We can also admit that the current theological usage corresponds more or less with that of the German language. We must not, however, allow a facile appeal to a linguistic distinction to blind us to the complexities of the distinction in dialectical thought.

The complexity of the interrelatedness of *Historie* and *Geschichte* in dialectical thought does not allow us to be satisfied with the distinction in the above oversimplified form. Insofar as the dialectical thinker is aware of the implications of his own dialecticism, he does not intend these words to refer to two distinct realms of event or to two separate aspects

of the same event, nor does he employ them to distinguish two separate avenues of approach, e.g., a neutral, scientific attitude in contrast
to faith. In more technical language, the distinction between *Geschichte*
and *Historie* does not have in mind two separate areas of being (*Seins-
gebiete*) nor two separate epistemological or methodological avenues of
approach (*Denkmethoden*). In a fashion that will become clearer only later
on, the dialectical position seeks to overcome this distinction.

The "level" of the historic is supposed to transcend the level where
one thing can be set over against another thing, i.e., one domain over
against another domain, one method over against another method, or a
knowing subject over against a known object. In existentialist thought
the "level" of the historic opens up only in what is called an existential
involvement or encounter, in which there is cognition only in the act of
existing and existing only in a peculiar cognitive awareness. There is no
longer a clear distinction between an observing subject and an observed
object. The distinction between subject and object is supposed to have
been overcome.

We have now arrived at the point at which we can open up the broadest and most formal meaning of the term "historicness." Distinctions like
those of subject and object, supratemporal ideals and positive historical
facts, metaphysical interpretation and positivistic historical explanation,
are thought to have a common root. The very distinctions themselves are
supposed to have arisen out of a deeper source, a fundamental objectifying attitude, which views things in general instead of encountering
them existentially. Thus we arrive at the formal definition of the historic. *It is not general.*[26] What is historic cannot be grasped (in general)
as an instance of a general rule nor understood (in general) in terms of
some genetic explanation. It is disclosed only by transcending the fundamental objectifying attitude. It describes a supposedly deeper, more
concrete "level" of human existing.[27]

Other facets of the idea of historicness will appear if we approach
it from a slightly different point of view. As we have discovered, historicization involves the dissolution of all supposedly supra-temporal
metaphysical truth in the historical stream. Every position is thought to
have its origin and its end within history and is regarded as being subject at its very center to the dynamics of historical change. Using the
insights we have marshalled, we can say that, within the framework of
the ideal of science, all facts have been given a positive historical base.
They have been reduced to historical phenomena. The result is a com-

plete historical subjectivism and relativism. From the exalted heights of objective truth with ultimate significance, there is a plunge into the abyss of sceptical and even nihilistic groundlessness.

In its more mature forms, existentialist thought has concentrated its attention upon the philosophical or theological interpretation and conquest of this nihilism. As we have suggested before, its characteristic response has not been to sidestep the nothingness that has arisen from historical relativism. Its stratagem has been to encounter it, and, in a sense, to pass through it. Existentialist thought has aptly been called an encounter with nothingness.[28]

The philosophy of Martin Heidegger is in large measure characteristic of this response. In the face of the dissolution of meaning in historicism, Heidegger asked again the question of the being of beings (*das Sein des Seienden*), i.e., the question of a concentration point that could provide unity and meaning to our experience of beings.[29]

If he was to discover this concentration point, Heidegger had to find a proper entrance way. Not wishing to impose an ideal construct on the facticity of being, he had to limit himself to discovering an entrance way to being by way of that facticity itself.[30] This he discovered in the being that as a matter of fact is always engaged in asking the question about its own being. This being *is* not. It is always transcending itself, and is therefore always ahead of itself. It *is* only in an interpretation (hermeneutic) of itself and its world. It is this that characterizes the being of man as being-there (*Dasein*) in contrast to all other beings.[31]

That being-there (*Dasein*) has its being only in its interpretation of itself and its world, means for Heidegger that it cannot be considered except abstractly in separation from the world. The fundamental structure of human existence is being-in-the-world.[32] That is, the subject may not be considered first in isolation, as a being that has certain qualities, and then considered in relationship to the world. Its being is fundamentally being-in-the-world. It is at any moment actively engaged in a process of constituting its world in terms of an on-going hermeneutical understanding of that world. It is itself always being constituted by its understanding of itself and its world. Simultaneously, in its hermeneutical understanding of itself and its world it is, at any moment, already embarked. In its own self-creation it is given to itself, in a particular hermeneutical understanding. In the most intimate fashion, being-there (*Dasein*) is in situation.

That the self is in situation does not mean primarily for Heidegger that it is in a situation that in some fashion can be pinpointed and therefore distinguished from the self. That indeed is true. Heidegger's very problem arose from his admission that human existence is completely relative to the historical situation. Thus human existence can be understood genetically in terms of its historical, social, psychological, etc., connections. But this is to understand it only in general.

What Heidegger has had in mind is that being-there (*Dasein*) is in situation in a deeper sense than it is possible for anything else to be in situation. Its being is not given in general, either in terms of a superhistorical ideal or a particular explanation. It is historic. But this is at the same time to say that it is free; for if its being is not given in general, it depends upon its own self-constituting of itself. Nevertheless, in its free pro-ject it is at the same time given to itself by a source that is not at its disposal. Its freedom is a finite freedom.[33]

For the early Heidegger, the Heidegger of *Being and Time*,[34] this finiteness was brought to its highest pitch as being-there (Dasein) – individualized in an active confrontation with death.[35] Again it was not the case, Heidegger thought, that being-there had its being, which was then related to death. Its being was a being-unto-death, a steady wresting of meaning from the abyss of meaninglessness.

It is this image of existentialism that has most fully captured the popular imagination. It was epitomized in the early Sartre, who portrayed the titanic struggle of the isolated and alienated individual to create himself in the face of a foreign and threatening world, a situation from which there was, to use his own expression, no exit.

Heidegger maintains that it was never his intention to remain at this point. The subject that of itself creates itself, he says, is an isolated subject, i.e., an objectified subject, and is therefore subjective. According to Heidegger, the early Sartre did not get past the point of the subject in its isolation. The result was a complete subjectivism and even nihilism.

Heidegger's proposed solution of the problem fits into the pattern we have been discussing. The subjective (nothingness) arises from the justified negation of any and every supposedly objective ground of ultimate truth. All of them have been shown to be subjective in origin. However, if the subjective itself is now regarded to be the result of a deeper, more fundamental objectification, which embraces both it and the supposedly objective truth, then the subjective has been upended, rendered incapable of being isolated. One must then look beyond both subject and object in their mutual interrelatedness to a more original "level," which is "prior" to the primary objectification that gives rise to the subject-object distinction.

Heidegger believes that he has thereby relativized the entire scheme of subject and object. Even though they must remain in tension, they are deprived of their stark opposition. The isolation of either one can be referred back to a more fundamental source, the objectification which Heidegger calls "the forgetfulness of being."[36] This forgetfulness, he thinks, is the hallmark of metaphysics.

From the vantage point he thinks he has won, Heidegger interprets the slogan of the early Sartre, "existence precedes essence," to be itself a metaphysical slogan. What it means, he says, is that the being and meaning of human existence is a creation of the existing self. Such a position, however, isolates the self and falls into a complete subjectivism and nihilism. [37] From Heidegger's point of view, such self-creation, considered alone, can be thought of only as an external act of will, a subjective creation of values, that obscures the true source of meaning instead of revealing it. [38] Both the simple affirmation that there is objective ultimate truth and the simple denial of it are on the same level. They are both metaphysical and are the result of the forgetfulness of being.

If that is the case, nothingness (*the nihil*) takes on a new significance. It cannot have a simply negative meaning. What from one point of view, the viewpoint of metaphysics, is purely negative takes on a positive meaning as well, thereby becoming ambiguous.

What is from one point of view simply negative, the destruction of metaphysics, assumes a positive meaning as the only avenue by which the deeper source of meaning can be brought to appear. Indeed, Heidegger says that this negating is carried by that deeper, more original ground itself. Being is "prior"; it is more concrete. In a fashion, it embraces the negation, employing it as the instrument of its own disclosure.[39]

If it is possible to discern the deeper ground of being and meaning only through the negation, and if the negation itself is said to be carried by being as its more original and concrete source, it is clear that it is impossible to separate the two (ontically), as if they were two separates provinces of being. It is for Heidegger impossible to consider being, as if it were a separate domain, as distinct from the history of the destruction of metaphysics, which is the history of the forgetfulness of being. In fact, this history itself is regarded by Heidegger as arising from the initiative of being. It is what he calls a *Schickung*[40] of being. Being is now considered as acting, as setting or posting situations. Human existence must be seen, not only as acting but as being acted upon, as being in situations that depend upon a more fundamental history in being itself (*Seinsgeschichte*).[41]

The development of thought we have just sketched, what in Heidegger's thought is called the "reversal" (*Kehre*), is not peculiar to Heidegger. It has taken place in all of the major existentialists as they have passed from a more antithetical phase of their thinking – where there is a sheer negation of the world and of all given content and where human existence is viewed as a self-constituting of oneself in the face of nothingness – to a synthetical phase – where there is a supposed joining of the self with a situation that is "posted" by a transcendent origin. Indeed, this reversal is not at all recent in existentialistic thinking. It has always been present in the thought of the philosopher Karl Jaspers and the thought of the philosopher-theologian Paul Tillich. It is possible to speak of a change of mood or a reorientation in Heidegger's philosophy; but he himself insists that there was a preparation for his reversal even in his early major work of 1927, *Being and Time*.[42] It is Jean-Paul Sartre who of all the major existentialists has made the most startling about-face from a purely antithetic to a more synthetic point of view.

Sartre now claims that Marxism has to offer the all-embracing anthropology of our time, the only anthropology that views man concretely in the fullness of his socio-economic being. This anthropology cannot be opposed or set aside, except at the expense of becoming reactionary. Setting it aside would be an external, artificial act of will. If the Marxist anthropology is to be overcome, it will occur only dialectically, from within, and that only when the times themselves have changed.[43]

In the two best-known phenomenological existentialists, Martin Heidegger and Jean-Paul Sartre, there is, therefore, a turn in the direction of a radical historicism, in this sense, that the decisions of the self are now thought to depend upon the situations brought into being by a history which arches over and conditions the self in its own historicness.

The convincingness of Heidegger's position depends upon whether he has truly reached a concrete level of being. It depends upon whether being is truly prior and whether the antithesis of subject and object has successfully been relativized by considering it as the "result" of a primal objectification, a forgetfulness, what some thinkers call a "fall." There are reasons, we believe, to think that Heidegger has not really stepped back into an area of concrete reality that is original and all-embracing.

It is clear that this concrete level of being cannot be regarded to be a separate and distinct sphere, as a being distinct from other beings. To think of it in this way would be to commit what Heidegger regards to be the fundamental error of metaphysics, i.e., to forget the ontological difference, to forget that being is not on the order of beings. No more than the object can be separated from the subject can being be separated from the dialectical interplay of subject and object in their mutual tension. Being must in some fashion take up into itself the history of the forgetfulness of being, in which there is the metaphysical attempt to establish an objective ground of being and where there is the inevitable reaction and the genesis of nihilism. Apart from this dynamic element, being would petrify into something, an object, a supposed metaphysical ground. As we have seen, Heidegger himself maintains that the forgetfulness of the truth of being, with its history, is itself a mittence (Schickung) of being. Metaphysical thought arises because of a peculiar set of circumstances which are themselves posted by being and which arise therefore by way of an inner necessity. Apparently there is in Heidegger's thought a strict correlation between being and the dialectical movement that is required if being is to be disclosed.

Further, the level of being as Heidegger conceives it is not truly original. Far from being a natural, unspoiled, unobjectified area of being, it itself is dependent upon the dialectical movement by which it is approached.[44] If the experiencing of being is to take place, the entire natural experiencing of man must be upended. Our natural way of experiencing is ordinary, average, and conventional. It remains caught within the forgetfulness of being. We can open up the experiencing of being only by penetrating beyond this level. That approach is by way of a method, indeed, which is supposed to transform from an abstract thinking-about-being to a concrete thinking-being. That does not take away the fact, however, that the approach to being must be prepared for by way of a generally valid thinking, a general method in terms of which certain universally negative judgments are made. It obscures the true state of affairs to say that these negations are themselves the instrument of being. Instead, they are a result of an autonomous theoretical thinking.

This distinction between history and historicness as it is made by dialectical thought involves such critical negations, which are actually constitutive of the level of the historic. In making the distinction it becomes clear that historicness cannot be subject to the boundaries and limitations that pertain to history. The historic event is supposed to be the once-for-all event in which there is the presence of ultimate meaning. Yet the singularity of this event cannot be rigidly defined nor can it be limited to the mathematically single event.[45] The historic act may not be confined to a single, finished act, for that would be to limit it to the objectifying, spatializing thought that pertains to nature. As soon as any definite limits are set, they must again be broken through dialectically. Paradoxically, the historic event is once-for-all (*einmalig*) and yet is essentially repeatable. Nevertheless, the historic event cannot be thought of as a congeries of repeated events, which as such would lack an inner unity and coherence.

The truth of the historic event, therefore, must lie beyond the level of mathematic unity and diversity or that of logical definition or confusion. It cannot, however, be approached directly, as if it were a separate order of being. It can be approached only dialectically, by way of the movement of setting and breaking boundaries, a movement that is supposed to be a pointer to the deeper ground by which it is carried.

These observations must lead us into a more extensive discussion of the idea of truth in dialectical thinking.

Truth as Event

The complexities of the dialectical position we have been examining bear also on the question of truth. Existential philosophy and theology have discussed the problem of truth within the framework of a historically oriented dialecticism.

Truth is, consequently, understood in terms of encounter, an encounter that takes place before any standpoint has been taken. The other must be approached as a thou, without any preestablished valuing, which would define boundaries and would set off one person from the other. Truth is not a particular content of truth, nor is the communication of truth the communication of content from one person to the other. Truth is, on the contrary, on the order of an event. It is not something given; it is a process, a going-on, which cannot be fixed in rigid categories and concepts. Truth is more a path or way than an established preserve.

If one criticizes a view of truth as dynamic process, however, he ought to be fully aware what kind of dynamism and what kind of process he is attacking. Process might mean an ongoing development or progress on the analogy of the growth of the biological organism. It might refer to a stream outside of the self into which the self can be taken up. Although either of these may serve as analogies of the existential dia-lectical position, neither one does it strict justice. Its idea of process is of the historical-dialectical type that we have examined.

If one criticizes the dialectical position for having an idea of truth as process, as act, as event, he must also be careful not to reject these terms indiscriminately, employing terms in opposition that might imply that he advocates a completely static conception of truth. To plead abstractly for an idea of unchanging truth in contrast to process might leave one with a staticism that is just as untenable and out of keeping with truly biblical thinking.

Contemporary theology does not stray because it opposes a simple intellectualism, or moralism, or legalism; it errs because it is built upon a modern dimensional view of reality, stemming from the humanistic tradition, which bifurcates reality into a sphere of nature and a sphere of freedom. In the contemporary form of this dialectical scheme it is diffi-cult to account at all for the place of the intellect, morality, and law with reference to the revelation of God. They are, first of all, identified with nature and are reduced to general truths which are construable by posi-tivistically oriented science. Freedom is, first of all, freedom from nature.[46] If concepts of nature, e.g., logical distinction, moral will, cause, are brought back on the level of freedom, it is only with a difference, one that answers to the demands of a neutral, autonomous ideal of freedom. [47]

Again the philosophy of Heidegger can serve us as a paradigm of the development of contemporary theological thought. That is not to say that Heidegger is a theologian. He is not. Nevertheless, within his thought the implications of the contemporary dialectical view of reality have been working themselves out with remarkable clarity and consistency.

According to the later Heidegger, truth is rooted in the "mittence of being" (*Geschick des Seins*) and is itself historic. It roots in the history within the mystery of being, it is communicated in a lighting process of revelation, and it is received in an encounter or dialogue of man with being. There cannot be, therefore, any deposit of ultimate truth. Truth is an event. Nevertheless, truth is not simply the process of apprehend-ing this event. It is beyond both, where the truth and its apprehension in thought are finally one.

Heidegger's more recent philosophy has been characterized as thought about thought. Setting our discussion with this context, we must discuss briefly the relationship between logic and a supposedly deeper thought that is revelatory of being.

Metaphysics, and its uneasy oscillation between position and negation, is the consequence, Heidegger believes, of the dominance of logic. Critical thought must destroy metaphysics. It negates. But critical negation as simple negating is yet under the dominance of logic. It results in nothingness. Nothingness, viewed only from the standpoint of this negating, i.e., the simple negating of metaphysics, results in a complete subjectivism. This entire opposition, of position and negation, is still caught within the limits of metaphysics in the broader sense of the term, the objectifying thinking that is the forgetfulness of being.

Thought under the dominance of logic is forgetfulness of being. When nothingness is interpreted only as a negating, i.e., simply antithetically, it cannot ask the question of being. As we have seen before, Heidegger does not attempt to circumvent this negation. He does not try simply to set it aside. A simple rejection would be forced, being a violent act of will. Instead, he seeks to disqualify it by upending the subjective, critical thought that brings it into being. Again his approach is to view logic as being rooted in a more original, more fundamental level of being, which gives it its legitimation and establishes its possibility.

Unwilling to allow that there is an avenue of approach to being apart from thought, Heidegger has developed the idea of a thought which transcends the level of logic and which is nevertheless a stricter kind of thinking than that which takes place under the domination of logic. Much of his later writing deals with this thought and with the kind of speech in which it is expressed.

This thought is not ordinary thought, the kind of thought that characterizes both metaphysics and positive science. Both of them talk about being(s). There is, Heidegger says, a more original thought, which is a thought of being. In this expression Heidegger intends to use the genitive "of" in both an objective and a subjective sense. Thought is thought of being in the sense that it is directed to being. It is thought of being also in the sense that it is thought that is posted by being. True and original thinking does not live by its own power. It is the mittence (*Geschick*) of being and is itself historic (*geschichtlich*).

Thought in its most original sense is, therefore, not simply thought about events. It is itself an event, an occurrence. It cannot be directed toward a static object, nor can it communicate established truth. It is encounter.

The dynamic character of this view of thought and of the corresponding idea of truth accounts for the fact that Heidegger so often employs the analogy of the way or the path to describe it. Thought is not static. It does not stand by the side of the way, contemplating it. It itself is on the way. It is underway. It is the going-on of thought, its thought-ful questioning, that is its being-on-the-way. In the process of its questioning it constructs its own path. That does not mean, however, that thought has therefore become arbitrary. Thought may not build its own way in a willful fashion. It must be attentive to the way. That is to say, that thought is in the mittence (*Geschick*) of being and that its truth consists only in giving heed to the situation as it is posted by being.

Thought in the deeper sense of the word is therefore supposed to have broken the tyranny of logic and to have stepped back into the mittence (*Geschick*) of being, which is the very transcendental presupposition of logic, that which accounts for its very possibility.

At this point, however, we unearth deeper and more religious roots of Heidegger's thinking. His philosophy, more than others, is supposed to circle around thought. It is thought which must provide the avenue for the approach to being and which must be the receptacle for the reception of the revelation of being. Heidegger's trust in thought is manifested by his having it participate in the concentration point. Thought, he says, creates its way as it goes along. At the same time, he is exceedingly jealous that this constructive activity not be called "subjectivistic." Even though the way is not laid out objectively, i.e., in general, Heidegger insists that thought must be attentive to the way. That is to say, at the same time that it constructs its own path, it must do so within the broader lines that have been staked out by being.

This might appear to be a confession of modesty with regard to thought. If thought is posted by being, it can no longer be regarded, Heidegger thinks, as being independent, as having the disposition over its own activity. We should observe, however, that Heidegger's view identifies thought in its mittence (*Geschick*) with the ultimate concentration point of meaning. It is no more possible for him than it is for the later Sartre to hold that thought as posted by being can be criticized from an outside source. Thought has been thought most consistently into a completely historistic context. Its mittence (*Geschick*) has in effect been equated with the voice of being, which in Heidegger's parlance signifies what others call the voice of the divine. Heidegger's historicism becomes thereby a stronghold for human autonomy.

The pattern that we discerned in Heidegger's view of historicness recurs in his view of thought and of truth. Thought cannot be thought apart from the critical thought that is caught in the domination of logic. Inauthentic thinking is in the mittence (*Geschick*) of being. Thus Heidegger can make the startling claim that to the lighting of being there belongs also the path of error.[48] As a consequence, truth is consigned to the borderline. It needs error. Truth is only in the active overcoming of error. Since the only mode of expression is that which is under the domination of logic, it follows that the revelation process of being must be hidden at the same time that it is revealed. True thought, Heidegger maintains, respects the mystery of being and preserves it. The mystery of being, as it is being revealed, is also hidden. Likewise, the speech in which its revelation is revealed both reveals and conceals at the same time. Their unity lies beyond the opposition of revealedness and hiddenness.[49]

Thus inauthentic thought, the thought that we have equated with the science ideal, is still allowed its autonomous critical activity. This is the case in spite of the fact that it is supposed to have been relativized by being called the result of the forgetfulness of being. By its negating it excludes the idea that there is any delimitation of truth whose bounds need not immediately be broken through dialectically. And such a denial is possible only if autonomous thought is not only carried by the deeper ground of being and truth but is somehow constitutive of it.

In spite of all his exertions, Heidegger has not truly discovered the concentration point in which thought and truth obtain their meaning. His idea of truth, like his idea of event, remains ambiguous, its meaning dispersed in a fundamental antinomy.

⚜ ⚜ ⚜

The pattern of dialectical thinking that we have discussed above, with its ideas of the transmoral, of the historic, and of truth as event, is what has prepared the soil for contemporary theology. It is this soil in which the theologies have grown which have dominated the theological scene in recent years and which dominate it still.

Contemporary dialecticism has no real place for one who wishes to confess with the Scriptures that God revealed himself in Jesus Christ in a circumscribable event at an ascertainable time in the past, that his salvation depends upon a work of Christ performed once and for all as a full satisfaction for sin, and that the gospel of reconciliation has been given to the church with the command to proclaim it to a world that lies outside of its pale, a world that must repent and accept the gospel if it is to be saved. Contemporary dialecticism would insist, instead, that man in his error is already embraced by the truth, and that the light of truth must hold to its bosom the shadow of untruth. For contemporary dialecticism the real culprit is likely the one who maintains that there is a gospel that has once and for all been given to the saints, and who frames his program in terms of proclamation of that gospel instead of continually laying his road as he goes along the way of dialogal encounter.

REFERENCES

1. For a more detailed analysis of this development see Herman Dooyeweerd, "The Secularization of Science," *The International Reformed Bulletin*, No. 26 (July, 1966), 2-17 (original French, "La sécularisation de la science," *La Revue Réformée*, 5 (1954), 138-155) and *A New Critique of Theoretical Thought*, I (Philadelphia, 1953).

2. Herman Dooyeweerd, "The Secularization of Science," 15; *A New Critique*, I, 403ff.

3. Friedrich Schleiermacher, *Der christliche Glaube*, 6th ed. (Berlin, 1884), I, 7.

4. Compare Paul Tillich's early evaluation of Schleiermacher in his *Religiöse Verwirklichung* (Berlin, 1930), 128, where he calls his approach "subjective" and his later evaluation in his Systematic Theology (Chicago, 1951), I, 15, where he says that Schleiermacher's approach is not subjective.

5. In its transcendental (*übergreifend*) nature, this feeling must be stripped of the qualities that characterize a purely psychological feeling. It cannot be "represented" or, in contemporary parlance, "objectified." It is no longer within the confines of nature, as conceived since Kant, where subjective feeling is directed toward an objective goal for a certain purpose or end. (Cf. Dooyeweerd, *A New Critique*, I, 388). This, for Schleiermacher, is the terrain of thought and of will. Anything that can be objectified, i.e., anything that is for thought or for will, is part of nature.

6. One discerns the personality ideal in contrast to the science ideal in Schleiermacher's twofold idea of freedom. The activity of the self (*Selbsttätigkeit*), he says, is the feeling of freedom, as domination over finite reality. He continues, however, that this feeling of freedom can hardly be thought to represent the deeper sense of freedom, the feeling of absolute dependence, for the latter is beyond both simple domination and the simple limitation of it. Schleiermacher, op. cit., 16.

7. Cf. Albrecht Ritschl, *Die christliche Lehre von der Rechtfertigung und Versöhnung,* 2nd ed. (Bonn, 1883), III, 4-5.

8. Ibid. 9-10.

9. Ibid. 3.

10. This is the crux, e.g., of Bultmann's criticism of the older liberalism. Cf. Rudolf Bultmann, "Neues Testament und Mythologie," *Kerygma und Mythos* (Hamburg-Volksdorf, 1954), I, 25. Interestingly, much the same criticism has been lodged against Bultmann himself from the standpoint of the New Hermeneutic. Cf. James M. Robinson and John B. Cobb, eds., *The New Hermeneutic* (New York, 1964), 38, et passim.

11. Cf. pars. 44-50.

12. Immanuel Kant, "Kritik der aesthetischen Urteilskraft," *Immanuel Kant's Werke* (Leipzig, 1921), VI, 99, 176, 180, 181.

13. Cf. Friedrich Ueberweg, *Geschichte der Philosophie* (Berlin, n.d.), IV, par. 10.

14. G. W. F. Hegel, *Early Theological Writings,* trans. T. M. Knox, with an introduction, and fragments trans. Richard Kroner (Chicago, 1948), 9-10; cf. 20f.

15. Ibid., 11-12.

16. Ueberweg, op. cit., par. 7.

17. Dooyeweerd, *A New Critique,* I, 414, 416, 432.

18. Manfred Schröter, ed., Schellings *Werke* (Munich, 1958), IV, 280ff.

19. There is a double use of the term "ethical" in Kierkegaard's thought. On the one hand, he employs it in the sense that it has in idealistic philosophy to designate the autonomous freedom of man, the human act as inward self-determination. On the other hand, he uses it to designate the level of the external, conventional valuing of the generality of mankind, the mass. The latter usage also has roots in German idealism and prepares the way for the later existentialistic views concerning mass man and the impersonal one (*das Man*). The context of the latter usage is fully discussed in the treatment of Kierkegaard by Karl Löwith, *From Hegel to Nietzsche* (New York, 1964), 151, 158ff., et passim.

20. Søren Kierkegaard, *Fear and Trembling* (Princeton, 1941), 9ff.

21. Kierkegaard's Abraham in *Fear and Trembling* meticulously avoids presenting to his son Isaac the image of a demonic God by pretending that it is he who hates him and not God. Thus he hopes to spare his son the need of hating God. It is, however, only a step from Kierkegaard's position to the thought that there is an irrational, demonic dimension within God himself, the God in terms of whose command, without any apparent or hidden reason, this act is to be performed.

22. This is the pattern of the criticism of Fichte by Schelling in his philosophy of freedom. He rejected Fichte's moralistic position that the finite subject strives endlessly toward the ethical idea. To Schelling it makes no difference that the goal is infinitely removed. The finite act, he thinks, may not be regarded simply in negative terms as falling short of an ideal that is transcendent to it. The criticism involves the very possibility of

establishing unambiguous goals and of representing the subject as striving unambiguously toward them. Both the ideas and the finite subject have become ambiguous. The individual act takes on the positive significance of being an active resistance to the ideal. Cf. Schelling, "Philosophische Untersuchungen über das Wesen der menschlichen Freiheit," *Schellings Werke*, IV, (Munchen, 1958), 243ff. This idea recurs in Kierkegaard's *Philosophical Fragments* (Princeton, 1946), where in his famous experiment of thought he declares that the individual must be regarded as in active opposition to God if the moment is to have significance.

23. Interpreting Hegel's logic within the framework of the idealistic reaction to the ideal of science, Dooyeweerd calls it "antirationalistic." It is, he says, "nothing but an antirationalist, universalistic logic of historical development." The truth of the absolute spirit wells up out of the irrational historical situation (*A New Critique*, I, 472).

24. We believe, together with Richard Kroner, that Kierkegaard's idea of the Moment was clearly prepared for in the philosophy of Hegel. Kroner goes so far as to say that it was not Kierkegaard, but his great master, Hegel, who was the inaugurator of existential philosophy. Cf. Hegel, *Early Theological Writings*, 46.

25. Even though we recognize that the ideal of personality has undergone a crisis in existentialism, we see the existentialistic notion of the historic as yet another attempt to discover a concentration point within the framework of the ideal of personality in its opposition to the ideal of science. Thus, within an existentialistic instead of an idealistic context, many of the same patterns recur.

26. That the method of definition proceeds from the formal to the contentful itself poses a problem. Historicness is contrasted with generality, in the extended meaning given to it in existentialism. The meaning of historicness depends upon this exclusion. Nevertheless, in some fashion, historicness must be thought to be prior to this negation. Here appears the problem of the dialectic between generalizing thought and being, which will dominate the latter portion of our discussion.

27. The above method of approach does not make it necessary to deny that the existentialistic idea of historicness is foreshadowed in idealism. It is prepared for in the idealistic contrast of the concrete idea to the general, rational categories of nature. It is virtually present when the concrete idea is linked to a historical figure, as we have observed in the thought of Albrecht Ritschl. The existentialist believes, however, that the idealistic view of historicness can still be understood in general. Existentialism has radicalized the idea of historicness.

28. Helmut Kuhn, *Encounter with Nothingness* (London, 1951), xiii-xvi.

29. Martin Heidegger, *Sein und Zeit*, 6th ed. (Tübingen, 1949), Introduction.

30. This is brought out forcefully in the approach of William J. Richardson, *Heidegger: Through Phenomenology to Thought* (The Hague, 1963), 64f.

31. Heidegger, op. cit. 7, 12.

32. Ibid. 52ff.

33. When one describes the idea of historicness (*Geschichte*), he should not ignore either of these perspectives. It is common to say that the existentialistic idea of historicness means that the self is in situation. That is true; but as a bare statement it ignores the fact that it is only *Dasein*, whose being is not given in general, that can be tied to its situation in this most intimate sense.

34. *Sein und Zeit* first appeared in 1927.

35. Martin Heidegger, op. cit. 235ff., 250, 258f., 266.

36. Martin Heidegger, *Über den Humanismus* (Frankfurt, 1947), 17, 26; cf. 21. The place that the idea of the forgetfulness of being occupies in Heidegger's philosophy corresponds to the place of the transcendent fall in the thought of Schelling, Tillich, Nicolas Berdyaev, etc., and to the place of the primal objectification in the thought of Karl Jaspers which is the source of the subject-object distinction.

37. Ibid. 17ff.

38. It is a mistake to think that existentialism is a revival of a philosophy of valuing. Values, for Heidegger, are only subjective, being a product of subjective human willing. In agreement with the existentialistic consignment of the idea to the level of nature, Heidegger regards idealism to be a philosophy of willing, the expression of the will to will. Ibid. 34-35, 44.

39. Ibid. 23ff., 27, 32ff., 43f.

40. To translate this difficult word Richardson coins a neologism, "mittence." By this he means an event in which being is disclosed, when the event is conceived as proceeding from the initiative of being. William J. Richardson, op. cit. 435.

41. The criticism of metaphysics results in nothingness. But the metaphysical distinction of subject and object is relativized by being also referred back to a more primarily forgetfulness of being.

Therefore nothingness is not simply a negating; it has a positive content and points beyond to being. That being encloses nothingness thus accounts for its positive significance. The entire situation depicts the history of being, which is a mittence (*Geschick*) of being itself.

42. Martin Heidegger, op. cit. 17.

43. Jean-Paul Sartre, *Critique de la raison dialectique*, I (Paris, 1960), 21, 9, 29.

44. A similar line of argumentation is found in Johannes van der Hoeven, *Critische ondervraging van de fenomenologische rede*, I (Amsterdam, 1963), 142, 144ff., 153, 237, 258, 350f.

45. Heidegger's phenomenological method, Heinrich Ott says, must penetrate beyond the outer husk to the thing itself. Speaking of Heidegger's notion of being-in-the-world, he says that he is not interested in the external delimitation but the inner structuration. It is a meaning form in contrast to spatial form. Heinrich Ott, *Denken und Sein* (Zollikon, 1959), 52f.

46. Cf. Herman Dooyeweerd, *A New Critique*, I, 53.

47. For example, the Swiss philosopher Karl Jaspers declares on the one

hand that true selfhood is historic (*geschichtlich*) in contrast to the generality of nature; on the other hand, he must reintroduce generality on the level of the transcendent. The transcendent, he says, is *das Einzigallgemeine,* the uneasy synthesis of unity and multiplicity. This generality, however, is supposed to rise above all heteronomy. Karl Jaspers, *Philosophie,* 2nd ed. (Berlin, 1948), 694.

48. Heinrich Ott, op. cit. 126.

49. Ibid. 177.

PART TWO

DISCUSSIONS ABOUT
THEOLOGY AND APOLOGETICS

ANALYSIS OF THEOLOGICAL CONCEPTS: A METHODOLOGICAL SKETCH [1]

What was God doing before he created the world? asks the skeptic. Calvin calls very shrewd the answer of the man who replied "that he had been making hell for over-curious men."[2] Augustine is more reserved, saying, "I answer not, as a certain person is reported to have done facetiously (avoiding the pressure of the question) 'He was preparing hell', said he, 'for those who pry into mysteries.' For more willingly would I have answered, 'I know not what I know not ...'."[3] Both answers assume, however, that there are some questions one may not ask, some questions that are out of bounds, that transgress the limits of what is meaningful.

One might object that it is wrong to suppress any questions, that to do so is to impose an alien authority on the human mind, that this is both illegitimate and unproductive -- illegitimate because it is destructive of man's humanity, of which his rational powers are constitutive, and unproductive because the questions, though suppressed, will return and will undermine any dogmatic standpoint one has adopted.

It can be shown, however, that even those who argue that human questioning may not be limited do so on the basis of presuppositions. The claim to human autonomy implied in the above objection is meaningful only within a framework of presuppositions that cannot be derived from the idea of autonomy itself. In fact, it can be asserted that every position involved has presuppositions, which, furthermore, are at bottom religious, involving an unquestioning allegiance to an ultimate commitment. One's presuppositions will determine whether he will remain within the limits within which questioning is meaningful, or whether, transgressing them, he will lapse into meaninglessness.

To object across the board, therefore, to limiting the scope of questioning is to fail to take into account the limitations imposed by one's own starting point. At issue, then, is not whether there will be a limit to questioning: it will be as to where this limitation falls. This, in turn, will be guided by the presuppositional framework within which one moves.

⚜ ⚜ ⚜

We sketch the framework within which thinking is meaningful, that is, within which, centered in the Christian transcendence standpoint, it can come to its rights.

To be meaningful, thought must operate within the bounds of created reality. Here it has certain limits. Both it and its contents are revelational of the Creator God. Revelation sets a boundary to thought. That is to say, thought cannot transcend what is given by revelation, in order to grasp hold of God, the Revealer, as he is in himself. To ignore this limit is to fall, as Calvin knew, into vain speculation. There are, furthermore, horizons connected with revelation, to which all revelation conforms. The first of these is the incomprehensibility of God. God has revealed and is revealing himself; nevertheless, he is incomprehensible in his revelation. It is impossible to exhaust the revelation of God or to gather into a rationally tight system what he has revealed. God's incomprehensibility in his revelation, furthermore, does not diminish as that revelation increases. The more God reveals himself the more it becomes apparent that he is incomprehensible. Incomprehensibility, therefore, is a constant horizon of the revelation of God. All revelation is characterized by the fact that it displays God's incomprehensibility. Closely related is the accommodation by God in his revelation to the finite condition of man. As Calvin recognized, we do not see God in his revelation as he is in himself but as he presents himself to us conformable to our ability to understand. That does not mean that we should thereupon seek to establish how it is that God has accommodated himself, in what respects our knowledge of him differs from what it would have been if he had not accommodated himself to us. In every act of revelation God comes to us in a way conformable to human capacity. This is a constant horizon of revelation. It holds for all revelation, that God accommodates himself in it to the limitations of human capacity. Again, very closely connected with this is another horizon, namely, the anthropomorphic character of divine revelation. If God reveals himself according to human capacity, it is in a way that is conformable to human experience and expression, so that revelation is a human-like manner of expression, in talking about God.

Again, too, it is improper to ask what God is apart from this manner of speaking. It should simply be understood that all revelation is anthropomorphic. Its human-like character is a constant horizon of revelation.

Another characteristic of revelation is that, even as it prevenes, bearing in upon man, he is responding, either positively or negatively, to God's communication of himself in his revelation. Even though one may indeed speak in terms of man's responding to God as he imparts himself in his revelation, he should not think of this revelation as simply existing "out there" somewhere, inertly, and of man's response as somehow following upon it, as if he were, "subjectively," to strike upon and apprehend it. On the contrary, God in his revelatory impartation actively confronts man, and as this revelation impinges upon man's awareness he is already responding, either for or against its author. Again, as Calvin recognized, for man in his estate of rectitude, responding to God in a positive manner was as natural as breathing the air. This was his true state of nature, and in this state of nature he both served God and was truly himself. If he does not so apprehend and embrace the revelation, it is not because it is inertly, as some say "objectively," out there somewhere, still waiting to be apprehended, but because, by reason of sin, he is blind and is actively resisting it.

Again, one is confronted with a horizon of revelation. All revelation is focused on man, who, in the concrete revelational situation, is responding either for or against God. If the term is understood properly, this might be called the "existential" horizon of revelation, although the manner in which we have expounded our thoughts is incompatible with any form of existentialism. It might, nevertheless, be called "existential," because revelation does not have its meaning apart from address to man and response on his part. It may be said just as well that revelation confronts man and calls for decision. It is, however, always productive of decision. There is no neutrality with respect to God, to his person in his self-confrontation with man. One is in his being either for or against God, and is truly himself only in his free and joyful acceptance of God in his self-impartation in his revelation.

What we have just elaborated is, in point of fact, simply an interpretation of biblical teaching concerning the Creator-creature relationship, as it bears upon knowledge. This relationship forms the proscenium within which the entire drama of human thought and life is played out.

What is the idea of creation? It is, as the Scriptures teach, that God brought all things into being out of nothing by the word of his power. "In the beginning God created the heavens and the earth" (Genesis 1:1). The Bible teaches us that what is was not made out of what appears (Hebrews 11:3). We may distinguish God's creating (*bará*) from all "making" (*asá*). We can say that we "make" something out of something that already is, as we fashion an earthen pot from clay. In contrast, we teach that God created "out of nothing" or "into nothing," without using any pre-existent material, not even an unformed matter or chaos. Otherwise, we understand, he would be a demiurge and not the Creator.

Yet, the limits of our thought are disclosed in that we are able to form an idea of what creation is only in terms of what itself is created. We must think of God's creating in a "moment" of time, for instance; but is not time itself part of the creation?

It is impossible for us, bound as we are to the horizon of created reality, to conceive in our own power what creation out of nothing (*creatio ex nihilo*) is. We can only approach it, without being able to grasp it in a concept. For every concept that we can employ has its meaning within the confines of created reality.

Everything is created, all of reality and, within reality, all of our thoughts concerning it. As Augustine and Calvin knew, we can only respond in worshipful praise to the God who has brought all of this forth, whose love accompanies our every moment, whose providence embraces our entire lives, and who as Creator is nearer to us than any father or mother, brother or sister, husband or wife.

ↄ ↄ ↄ

If what we say of creation is true, the same holds for God himself. We confess, in faith, that he is the Creator, who is above all things. Nevertheless, as we have said, we know him only as he has condescended to us in his revelation, speaking in a manner conformable to our understanding, in a way that is human-like.

Shall we seek to understand God in his relation to the world? How shall I understand, as Augustine asked, how God can be "before" all things, when temporal relations have their meaning within the created cosmos? Did not God, as Augustine taught, create time along with the creation?[4] Is it not, therefore, vain speculation to attempt, by the power of human understanding, to advance beyond the limits of creation and to inquire as to what God was doing "before" he created the world? What do we know of this, except what God has revealed to us, understanding all the while that what he has disclosed veils a mystery before which we can only bow ourselves in adoration?

Shall we think of God with regard to space? How shall we bend to our understandings that this God who, as the Creator, is far exalted above all things, is also, as the Creator, the one who is not separated from us, even as our closest earthly companion is, by a space, but, even as Paul commends some ancient poets for sensing, is the one in whom we live and move and have our being (Acts 17:28)?

Nevertheless, as we pose questions and problems about God and his creation, we must acknowledge that these have their meaning only in terms of what God has revealed to us concerning himself and his creation, so that in facing the problems and in forming our concepts, we have a notion of the limitations, of the inadequacies, of this understanding.

Thus, we may come to understand, that all of our thought must be carried by and must reflect back on the creation and its Creator, and our relationship to him as his creatures, upon whom he has fixed his love.

⏚ ⏚ ⏚

The viewpoint we have presented throws into question a nearly universally held opinion concerning theology, that its terrain is constituted by the relation to God, possibly to what is regarded to be ultimate reality. Theology is widely held to deal with the relationship to the ultimate or with the ultimate relationship. This view is represented, for instance, by the current inquiry into the meaning of "God-talk." It also lurks in such a question as the following: "What is the theological meaning or the theological interpretation of this or that?," if what is referred to is its meaning in relationship to God and to his revelation.

On our view, relating to God and to his revelation is not on the order of relating within the cosmos. It is relating as a creature to the Creator. According to this teaching, everything in the cosmos is created, is subject to God, and is revelatory of him.

Furthermore, this relationship to God is not, first of all, a problem, as if one, for instance, were confronted from the outset with the problem of the meaningfulness of "God-talk." Prior to all theoretical questioning, to all facing up to theoretical problematics, is the presence of the revelation of God, in which God is actively communicating himself, and the active responding by man as he is faced with that revelation. Our understanding of Scripture leads us to assert that there is a knowledge of God prior to all questioning about him and his world.

No questioning is possible except in the medium of the revelation of God. Questioning in an "existential" sense, in the sense of doubting what God has said, is apostasy. Far from itself serving as a locus of unconditional concern and thus as a portal to the unconditional, "existential" doubt is disobedience to what God has revealed and to what the Scriptures teach is clearly revealed in man. Questioning, in the sense of putting theoretical questions, is possible, furthermore, only on the background of a framework of presuppositions, which themselves are not of the nature of theoretical thought, but which, indeed, are at bottom religious.

Theology shares with all theoretical thinking the fact that it is bound to the created order of reality, that it is subject to God in his revelation, required to live out of and to reflect back on that revelation.

◢ ◢ ◢

In the language of everyday thought, we make distinctions: God/man; Creator/creature; man/world; soul/body; etc. These are simple analytical distinctions. We understand them, in a deepened awareness, as we respond to God and his revelation in the day-to-day life of faith. Our thought turns, for example, in a spiral fashion, back upon God as the Creator, who has brought all things into being. We know, as we respond to the teaching of Scripture, that God cannot be on the same level as what he has created. He may not be identified with something of wood, of stone, or metal, or even something more ethereal, like "spiritual substance." As witnesses to this truth we have the remarkably simple but devastating assaults of Isaiah and Jeremiah on idolatry. A man makes a log and of the one end fashions for himself a god and of the other end makes kindling wood with which to warm himself. How foolish (Isaiah 40:19; 44:15-17)! And we may not forget the divine commandment, "Thou shalt not make unto thee any graven image" (Exodus 20:4).

In the language of everyday discourse, furthermore, the Bible uses the words "God" and "man" in various relationships. Sometimes it is in a simple antithesis: We are not to be men-pleasers but pleasers of God

(Ephesians 6:6). We are not to fear what men can do to us (Psalm 56:4). Christ himself placed the concerns of his kingdom into sharp contrast to what are even important concerns of life. If a man does not hate his father and mother, he says, he is not worthy to enter the kingdom of God (Luke 14:26). We also remember the saying, "Let the dead bury their dead" (Matthew 8:22). We can understand what these uncompromising statements mean, that serving God and doing his will must take precedence over everything else, and in case of conflict the concerns of the kingdom must prevail. We can also understand the warning implicit in Paul's statement, that one who is married seeks to please his wife, while one who is not married seeks to please the Lord (1 Corinthians 7:32-33). We should know better than to make of such statements a simple exercise in logic, falling, for instance, into an unbiblical world-flight, misanthropy, or misogyny.

Reasoning in its concrete fashion, the Bible also relates God and man in other ways. It argues, for example, for the superiority, for the superior steadfastness, of the covenant of God. Even if it is a human covenant, it reasons, no man abrogates it; how much more established is the covenant of God (Galatians 3:15)! Here there is no antithesis between God and man, between the divine and the human. There is, on the contrary, an implicit sanctioning of human arrangements.

Living in a world ravaged by sin, we might not expect to find much thought in the Bible of harmony between God and man. We should not forget, however, that in the beginning God declared the creation good. Further, as Augustine also understood, sin is parasitical; it must depend for its existence on the created order of things, upon which it feeds and which it distorts. Sin indeed distorts; it does not, however, destroy. In every sinful act and in every sinful situation, the created order of reality shines through.

That we employ verbal distinction in ordinary speech, even placing one term over against the other, does not mean that we assume that there is a basic dualism. That we associate terms closely, like Creator/creature, does not mean that there is a basic unity. We must understand the meaning of the words we use in ordinary discourse, in terms of biblical teaching, as we interact with it in our life of faith.

As soon as we have begun to think theoretically, however, using theoretical concepts, we indeed cannot do without our pre-theoretical understanding; nevertheless, we must give an account conceptually of what confronts us as a theoretical problem.

In scientific theology, one is obliged, therefore, to give an account of why it is impossible to attain to a theoretical concept of creation or of the relation between the Creator and the creature. At the same time, however, he must render an account of the fact that all of our theoretical conceptualization is led by an idea of what is the boundary between God and the cosmos, his creation.

It has been argued that the created character of the cosmos is manifest in its complete lack of self-sufficiency with respect to its Origin, the Creator God. This would entail that theoretical thought, being itself part of the cosmos, would have no self-sufficiency in forming theoretical concepts. Theoretical concept-formation, even in theology, is led by pre-theoretical presuppositions. It has its meaning within a presuppositional framework, which is of a religious character.

Far from being a more or less accurate expression of a God-relationship, theoretical theological concepts will be developed as they reflect a pre-theoretical commitment either for or against God. Theological concepts, therefore, will have to be analyzed, even as all theoretical concepts, in their depth.

For theology this is important. There is a tendency to think of theological concepts as if they were "counters," able to be moved about like terms of a mathematical equation. Theological concepts, however, are formed within a context, where in a theoretical attitude of thought one is faced with theological problems. These problems, furthermore, appear within a field of inquiry, which itself is qualified in a certain fashion. Theology functions, as a science, just like the other sciences, within a created context of meaning, of which it should be aware and of which it should give a theoretical account. Neither theology nor its concepts escapes the need to reflect. There must be a critical, methodological awareness of what transpires in theological concept-formation. Theology, therefore, is not in the position of giving us the "ultimate perspective" on things. It itself depends upon more ultimate considerations.

It is necessary to locate theological reasoning and the concepts employed in it within the context within which they have their meaning.

⚒ ⚒ ⚒

How then might we seek to delineate the area of study comprising the field of theology? What we have said about the God-relation leads us to reject the idea that it constitutes the terrain of theology. Theology as a science must be qualified by something that is able to constitute it as one field of investigation in contrast to others, for example, sociology, psychology, or law. There is in things, however, nothing that is not related to God. It is impossible, therefore, to accept a viewpoint such as the widespread one we have described, that it is things in their ultimate meaning that are related to God and his revelation, and that this relation constitutes the terrain of theology. Things themselves, even in their tritest dimensions, are related to God and his revelation. They are, per se, created beings, subject to God and revelatory of his almighty Creator will.

It has been suggested that it might be "faith" that provides the differentia of the field of theology. On this view, theology would deal with the revelation of the Covenant God, in its structure and development, as man responds to it in faith. We do not explore this view further here, except to point out certain characteristics of faith, as illustrations of theological concept-formation.

By faith we understand the quality of the response of man to God, as he is confronted with God in his revelation and accepts God and his Word in ultimate assurance. In its deficient mode, it is expressed in man's turning away from the true God and seeking the ultimate ground of his assurance elsewhere, in an idol. A faith can result in confession, articles of faith, a community of the faithful, cultic practice, etc., though not necessarily all of them at once. In our Christian faith, we understand that all of these are subject to the Word of God, more particularly, the Scriptures, which provide the key to all faith and life. The institutional Christian church is a community of the faithful, gathering in obedience to the Word of God to engage in worship, to hear the preaching of the Word, to administer the sacraments, and to exercise discipline in the name of Jesus Christ. It is a confessing community, joined in the corporate expression of its faith.

In the above there comes to view the position, first developed by Abraham Kuyper, that faith is a function. That is to say, everyone manifests faith, either in the true or in a false direction. Everyone will have something in which he vests his ultimate assurance, even though it be an autonomous reason which appears to do away with all faith. Everyone will have something in which he trusts ultimately. As we have suggested, a Christian vests his faith in God in Christ, as he is revealed in the Scriptures.

That faith is a function comports with the position we have set forth. Just as everyone is motivated religiously, so everyone will place his trust in a source of ultimate assurance, directing it to the true God or to an idol. That faith, however, is not something that is, as it were, added on, as an attitude that has to be superimposed on one's "natural" endowments.

One of the major questions facing modern theology, in the wake of the successes of rational criticism, was whether there was still room for theology. It appeared that there was no more place for relating God to the course of nature and history. Since theology was associated with the God-relation, that meant that theology was gradually deprived of a place among the academic disciplines. The history of liberal theology, as it responded to the rationalistic challenge, was that of one attempt after the other to retain, on the one hand, the rational, critical attitude, and, on the other hand, to discover room for theology, interpreted as the discipline having as its terrain the relation to the absolute, to God, as it appears within or at the boundaries of human experience.

From the Kuyperian point of view, however, there must be a challenging of this pretended autonomy of thought itself. The gauntlet must be thrown down to every position that allows a place to a supposedly neutral rational criticism, even though it subsequently seeks to establish a relation to the absolute, to God. The truth must be established that everything has its being in its relationship to God, who has revealed himself in Christ. Nature and history themselves are subject to God. The sciences must not seek to usher God out of his creation; instead, they must realize that they as disciplines are dependent upon the revelation of God, which alone is in a position to direct them to the successful execution of their tasks. On Kuyper's view, furthermore, there is a place for theology as a science. As one truly receives God, being encountered and encountering him in his revelation, he takes him in his revelation as the ground of his assurance. The side from which theology can approach things, in contrast to such sciences as psychology, sociology, and law, is that of faith.

⚓ ⚓ ⚓

We can illustrate theological concept-formation by taking an example as it relates to faith. Before we begin to think theologically, we already know something about faith. God has revealed truths about it. A believer, having exercised faith, is familiar with it and its contours. Nevertheless, there arise strictly theoretical questions concerning faith, which involve strictly theoretical problematics. The answers to such questions, we have said, cannot be neutral. This is ruled out by the nature of thought itself. Even theology, we have claimed, must reflect on its foundations and must acknowledge that it is dependent upon considerations that are themselves not scientific.

A theological concept such as "faith" is developed as a concept in confrontation with a theoretical *problem*, a problem that is theologically *qualified*, i.e., a problem that appears within this particular *field* of investigation. Furthermore, the problem is put by one or more theological investigators, who have assumed a theoretical attitude of thought.

One can ask the following question, not only practically, but also theoretically: "What is true faith?" In answering this and other theoretical questions, one must form theoretical concepts, and this will of necessity involve method. This scientific activity, furthermore, will lead to reflection, for example, on the method one is using and on the field of inquiry to which the method pertains. One is induced to give an account of what he is doing in his scientific activity. In theology, too, one's attention will be drawn to the need for prolegomena.

This scientific approach, employing as it does method, is, however, not the beginning-point. Even before he puts a theological question, one already knows, be it pre-scientifically, something about both the questions and the answers. One knows from Scripture, and from his own experience in the light of Scripture, that faith without works is dead, being alone. He also knows that to be justified one must believe, even as Abraham believed. It is quite legitimate to ask questions on this level. Yet, putting them thus is neither to put a theoretical question, faced with a theoretical problem, nor to delineate a theoretical answer. Questions such as "What is true faith?" can also be put in a theoretical fashion, which will require a theoretical answer involving the formation of theoretical concepts.

In order to illustrate this point further, let us examine somewhat more closely the idea of faith.

Faith is often understood theoretically, as the *act* of believing, as a *concrete, subjective* act of appropriating what is the *object* of faith. What we apprehend in faith, furthermore, is often regarded to be supplementary to what we can grasp "naturally." In traditional Reformed theology, we find supernatural faith, in relation to its object, analyzed into *notitia* (the intellectual apprehension of the content of faith), *assensus* (the assent of the will to the content of faith), and *fiducia* (the believing adherence to the content of faith).

One can ask theoretical questions about such a formulation, however. Does not true apprehension in faith depend upon spiritual understanding, which, in turn, is unthinkable apart from our heart's having been opened up by the Spirit of God, so that we both assent to and embrace the truth? Our previous analysis of the revelation situation fairly requires this. There we established that it was the natural estate of man to respond freely to God manifesting himself in his revelation.

If, furthermore, one considers faith to be in essence a supernatural apprehension of the object of faith, he understands it as something one obtains, as an attitude one assumes, who in his natural estate does not have faith. Such a view does not grasp the idea that one always has a faith, whether it is turned in the true or in a false direction. Likewise, this position does not encourage examining the concept "faith" in depth. "Faith" has become a designation for something, like a thing one has obtained, a substantial whole. There is no suggestion that one must look in depth into the concept, to discern the religious dynamics at work in it, as faith is turned either in the true or in a false direction. On the contrary, viewing faith as a modally established qualification of human activity requires that one reflect on the activity of the one who "has faith" and on the context indicated by the modal qualification, namely, on the relation of the act of faith to acts qualified in other ways. These are but two directions in which the concept "faith" will have to be explored.

If one considers faith to be the concrete act of apprehending the content of faith and then inquires as to what faith is, he may be inclined to reduce "faith" to its lowest common denominator. He may inquire what is common to faith in all of its manifestations, and then seek out the specific characteristics which, like branches, must be added onto the trunk in order to arrive at a concept like "true faith." True faith might then be regarded as faith mixed with love, as faith paired with works, etc. Following such a procedure, one starts out by taking the concept "faith" nominally, one might say, "at face value," without any sense of need to analyze the concept in depth.

Within this tradition, a distinction has indeed been made between *fides informis* and *fides formata*, that is to say, between a faith that has not and a faith that has been mixed with love. Thus the Roman Catholics have said that it is not faith alone that justifies, but faith mixed with love. One might acknowledge that there is here some "opening up" of the concept of faith. At best, however, it is only in a teleological fashion. Faith is seen to anticipate love, as its end; love is seen to complete faith, as its goal. Faith, however, is still considered in lowest-common-denominator terms.

For such thinking the attitude is prevalent that concepts are like counters, like things that can be moved about like terms in an algebraic equation.

In our view, faith is an aspect of human experiencing, at work in every human act. One cannot avoid, therefore, believing; he can only observe his faith changed in its direction, for example, as his eyes are opened to the truth of the Gospel. "Losing one's faith," on this view, cannot simply mean losing something, as one might lose his pocket-knife. It might mean that one had lost the true directedness of his faith, losing hold on the Gospel. It might mean that there was a change of direction of one's faith, so that it became vested in something else. In any case, it could not mean that, having lost his faith, one landed up faith-wise with a tabula rasa. On this view, also, a "faithful act" would be an act of faith in the true direction. Or it might refer to a faithfulness of one to the direction he has chosen. It would not mean, however, that somehow, in addition to his natural powers, he enjoyed the exercise of a supernatural endowment, the ability to apprehend a content of faith.

As we have said, faith will qualify an act of adherence to what one takes as the source of his ultimate assurance. From the Scriptures we understand that this faith, in its true direction, will be an opening up to receive the Word of God, with that assurance which is the quality of faith.

It is possible to introduce a lowest-common-denominator kind of thinking into the interpretation of a passage like James 2. "You say you believe in God," James writes, "you do well." And with a noticeable edge of sarcasm, he continues: "Even the devils believe and tremble." In understanding the meaning of "faith" here, do we abstract from its positive manifestations and consider faith to embrace what is characteristic of the true believer and of the devils? In such a case, we should take "faith" nominally. To this faith, which is common to believer and unbeliever alike, we should then have to add traits like love, obedience, and works, if it is to be understood as true faith. One must grant that in our ordinary language we speak in such terms, as we shall observe more in detail later on; but here we are not involved, as James is himself, in speaking in every-day terms, but in an examination of theological concept-formation.

An alternative point of view, from which the meaning of faith can be understood, stands in conscious opposition to a nominalist position. It takes the "nominal" or "historical" faith exercised by the demons here as a distortion of faith, a deformation of what faith is pure and simple, that is, as to its idea, in its original meaning. "Historical faith" or "nominal faith" is a deformation of the idea of faith; in this manner, an idealistic approach might set itself up in opposition to a nominalistic one.

We shall not enter into this controversy. We refer to it only to illustrate the kind of problem one is confronted with as soon as he passes from the level of naïve thought, with its concrete concepts, to the level of theoretical thought, with its scientific concepts and with its need to give an account methodologically of what is going on as one forms them.

One need not interpret the James passage, however, as a scientific theological discourse. He can see it for what it is, a practically directed diatribe against those who *say* that they have faith, but whose words are *empty*, just as empty as the words of someone who says "be warmed and filled" and who gives one in need nothing for his back and nothing for his stomach. Indeed, James speaks in such a way as to assert that one must not only have faith but also works. One must not take "faith" here, then, as a theoretical concept, which would almost force him to think of faith nominally, reducing it to a term expressing what is had in common by believer and devil. Is then true faith this kind of faith, plus something else? The passage itself does not support this kind of interpretation. It is not at all necessary to understand it as employing theoretical concepts. In our everyday speech, we use expressions such as we find here. "Don't just say you love me," says a neglected wife, "do something about it. Otherwise, your love is empty!" Florist ads intone "Say it with flowers!" That is not to imply that marital bliss is nominal love plus a bouquet of roses now and then! A study of the passage should show up the untenability of thinking of faith nominally, because what Abraham is said to have done, namely, offer up Isaac, is identified with what the Scriptures refer to when they say, "Abraham believed God and it was counted to him for righteousness." Exploring the passage conceptually, one must account for the fact that faith is not only set side-by-side with work but is also said to stand behind and embrace it. The "work" of Abraham was an expression of faith. It was faith doing something. What the passage teaches is itself non-theoretical; it is, however, what any biblically inspired theoretical theologizing will have to take into account and also give an account of.

When we put a question theoretically, such as "What is faith?," we must clearly delineate the concepts involved and render an account of what we are doing. That we are brought to give a theoretical account of what we are doing is a clear indication that we are involved in doing scientific theology.

$$\text{\it ﻬ ﻬ ﻬ}$$

Analysis of concepts within the field of theology, be it an exacting task, is imperative if we are to know what we are about in our theologizing. It is also necessary if we are to provide a foundation for comparing theological systems in a meaningful way. Theological terms do not have the same meaning in all theological systems. One cannot get at the meaning of the terms, however, by taking them nominally, at their "face value," and then combining and re-combining them. Theological concepts must be analyzed in depth. There is more inclination to do this on the part of the idealists, we have observed, than on the part of the nominalists. We ourselves must go further. We must lay bare the framework within which the concepts of a theological system have their meaning, a meaning that will depend upon religious directives, which have to do with one's response to God in his revelation as it centers in Jesus Christ.

REFERENCES

1. This article is based on a paper delivered at the annual meeting of the Evangelical Theological Society, meeting at Simpson College, San Francisco, December 26-28, 1977.

2. Calvin, *Institutes*, I, xiv, 1 (Allen trans.); cf. Calvin, *Commentary on Genesis, Argument.*

3. Augustine, *Confessions*, XI, xii, ed. Whitney J. Oates, *Basic Writings of Saint Augustine*, I (New York: Random House, 1948), 190.

4. Ibid., xiii.

MAY WE USE THE TERM "THEONOMY". . . ?

For "the law was given through Moses; grace and truth came through Jesus Christ" (Jn 1:17). It was with this bold contrast that the writer of the fourth gospel announced the coming of the new age. The age introduced by the giving of the law at Sinai was coming to an end; a new age was at hand.

The life and message of John the Baptist also expressed this contrast. They reflected his own position in the history of redemption. Standing on the threshold of the new age, John looked back on what had gone before and anticipated what was to come. When he was asked who he was, he "confessed freely, 'I am not the Christ' " (Jn 1:20). He said, "Among you stands one you do not know. He is the one who comes after me, the thongs of whose sandals I am not worthy to untie" (vv. 26-27). John's message was couched in terms of this sharp contrast. He himself stood at the end of an age that was passing away; he announced an age that was coming. This new age began with the appearance of the Messiah, Jesus Christ. When John saw Jesus, he said, "Look, the Lamb of God, who takes away the sin of the world! This is the one I meant when I said, 'A man who comes after me has surpassed me because he was before me' " (vv. 29-30).

The New Testament clearly sets the new over against the old, and it presents the new as superior in every respect. If God spoke before through the prophets, "in these last days he has spoken to us by his Son" (Heb. 1:2). The priesthood in the old order was temporal, but the priesthood of Christ is eternal. This is not a priesthood of mortal men; it is a priesthood founded "on the basis of the power of an indestructible life" (7:16). Perfection could not be attained through the Levitical priesthood, on the basis of which the law was given; it came through Christ, who is "a priest forever, in the order of Melchizedek" (vs. 17). Christ is not a priest of the first covenant, with which there was something wrong (Heb. 8:7), but of the new covenant, which is "founded on better promises" (vs. 6). According to this New Testament teaching, the law was "imperfect," the gospel is "perfect"; the law was "shadow," the gospel is "reality"; the law was "old," the gospel is "new." "By calling this covenant 'new,' he has made the first one obsolete; and what is obsolete and aging will soon disappear" (vs. 13).

Anyone who wants to be true to the biblical message of salvation must give full weight to this sharp distinction. It was in terms of this dichotomy that the apostle John characterized the difference between the old and the new dispensations. This theme recurs again and again in the New Testament. The law had to give way to the gospel.

It would be a great mistake, however, to interpret this distinction, important and even indispensable as it is, apart from its full context. It is indeed a recurrent theme in Scripture: there is a marked contrast between the law and the gospel. Nevertheless, the New Testament and the Old Testament are closely tied together. In relation to the new age the old is expectation. It is on the order of the chrysalis of a butterfly, which must be cast aside when the butterfly emerges; nevertheless, like a chrysalis, the old bears the new. It is also true that the new relates to the old. The New Testament message of salvation stands in unbreakable connection with what has gone before and is even founded on it.

In view of the teaching of the Scriptures themselves, it is clear that the contrast between the law and the gospel cannot be understood out of context. The Scriptures will not allow for the idea that the gospel appeared only after the law had been removed. There is a broad stream of gospel truth that courses through the entire Old Testament. Neither will the Scriptures allow for the idea that the entrance of the gospel meant the abolition of law in every respect. Christ said, "I tell you the truth, until heaven and earth disappear, not the smallest letter, not the least stroke of a pen, will by any means disappear from the Law until everything is accomplished" (Mt. 5:18; cf. Lk. 16:17). The Scriptures indeed teach that Christ is the "end" of the law; Christ is also the "end" of the law in the sense of being the completion, the fulfillment, of the law. He is not only *finis* but also *telos*. He said that he had not come to destroy the law or the prophets: "I have not come to abolish them but to fulfill them" (Mt. 5:17). With the Advent an era, the dispensation of "the law," came to an end; but in Christ the law came to its fulfillment. "Christ is the end of the law so that there may be righteousness for everyone who believes" (Rom. 10:4).

The relation of law and grace, of sin and salvation, is seen more clearly if we view it in the light of the teaching of the apostle Paul in his letter to the Galatians. There he writes that the promise of grace was given already to Abraham (Gal. 3:8b). It was properly established by God himself (v. 17). The promise, Paul continues, antedated the law; therefore, the law did not and could not annul the promise, which was given through faith: "The law, introduced 430 years later, does not set aside the covenant previously established by God and thus do away with the promise" (v. 17). The promise continued on, anticipating the preaching in the New Testament of God's gracious salvation. It served as a foundation for this preaching and even for the dispensation of the law itself.

From this passage we learn that "the law," in the sense I have been speaking of it above, was superimposed on the line of promise. As it were, the law encapsulated the promise; but it by no means annulled it. In fact, it depended on it. It could not be understood apart from it.

If then "the law" stood in this relationship to the line of promise, which was finally the promise of the free grace that appeared in Christ Jesus, how can the New Testament so often speak of the law and the gospel antithetically? Does not Paul himself say that "the law" is not "opposed to the promises of God" (Gal. 3:21)? We can answer this question if we arrive at a more precise understanding of what is meant here by "the law."

In the above passages, as well as many others in Scripture, "the law" refers to a particular arrangement or dispensation. It refers to the Mosaic economy, considered as a whole. God gave the law to Moses, to whom he spoke in the cloud and in the fire (Dt. 5:22). Various observances and ceremonies were typical of this economy. The New Testament very often sets this old dispensation in sharp contrast to the new one, which appeared with the coming of Christ.

In view of Paul's teaching, we can understand that "the law" was a temporary arrangement of a unique kind. It was superimposed on the line of promise, in the interests of this promise itself, which was given to Abraham and fulfilled in Jesus Christ. Seen from the standpoint of the new covenant, this law was "shadow" in contrast to "reality"; but it also had a function. As Paul says, "The law was put in charge to lead us to Christ" (Gal. 3:24). We might think of it as corralling people, so that they could be moved in the right direction. The law had the purpose of showing people their sin and of leading them to Christ (vv. 19, 23). The law also prefigured the salvation that was to come in Christ. Given through Moses, the law was a temporary arrangement; it had a divinely given purpose, but when this purpose had been accomplished, it was set aside. Again, as Paul says, "Now that faith has come, we are no longer under the supervision of the law" (vs. 25).

To understand what was set aside when grace and truth came in Jesus Christ, one must see how the dispensation of the law was characterized. What was unique about it?

Taken as a whole, the old covenant, "the law," had a legal cachet. This covenant was entered through circumcision, the cutting off of the foreskin of the Israelite males, an act by which the people of God were sanctified, i.e., set apart to God (Gen. 17:10-13; Dt. 10:15-16). The meaning of circumcision ran deeper than this physical cutting, but it was clear legally that any male who was to belong to the covenant community had to be circumcised and that any male who was not circumcised could not, for this very reason, belong to this community (Gen. 17:14; Ex. 4:24-26). The law made it clear what was required of the people. Simply speaking, they were to obey Moses (Num. 12). They were to observe certain practices, and they were to avoid others. Some transgressions led directly to expulsion from the community of God's people. Others indeed were punished by death. One who despised Moses' law died (Heb. 10:28). If one was delinquent in obeying the ordinances, he became ceremonially unclean. He then had to become ceremonially clean if he was to remain among the covenant people. The people were required to bring their sacrifices to the priests at appointed times and according to strictly delineated rules. The Israelite belonged to the community of God's people, which was required to conform to the Mosaic ordinances. These were spelled out for him in great detail. Having complied with these commandments, one remained part of the covenant community. One remained within the camp.

That the old covenant, considered as a whole, had a legal cachet does not mean, however, that everything that was taken up in it was legally qualified. To see this, one need only look at the context within which it was given.

In the preamble to the law God announced himself as the one who had brought the children of Israel out of Egypt. He is the covenant God, who has been faithful to his promises. He has called forth his people from the house of bondage. His covenant promises are not expressed in legal terms; it is only the outworking of God's covenant purpose that is expressed in this way. Further, on the heels of God's statement of his covenant faithfulness there is the proclamation of the "first and great commandment," the commandment of love: "Hear, O Israel: The Lord our God, the Lord is one. Love the Lord your God with all your heart and with all your soul and with all your strength" (Dt. 6:4-5). This great commandment flows directly from God's declaration of his oneness and his covenant faithfulness. It is not couched in legal terms. One may also refer to the Ten Commandments. These are indeed commandments, but they are not formulated in legal terms. It is not stipulated exactly what would constitute keeping them or transgressing them, or exactly what the rewards and punishments might be.

In the very giving of the law to the people there was a witness to the limitations of its legal form. It is clear that the meaning of the covenant was that God would be a God to them and that they would be his people. Further, it was always possible to conform to the legal expression of the law and yet not answer to its deeper meaning.

The restrictedness of the legal form of the old covenant is observed in the sacrificial system itself. After God gave the Ten Commandments and certain specific laws, he instructed Israel how he had provided for the atonement of their sins. He presented an entire sacrificial system. This was indeed set forth in detail and legal form -- one knew exactly what he was to bring to the priest in order to atone for his sins and exactly what the consequences would be of any failure to obey -- but this sacrificial system revealed in its very form the limitations of keeping the law. No matter how punctual one was in observing the commandments, the fact that he had to bring his sacrifices instructed him that his obedience was imperfect. His sins had to be atoned for. The limitations are very clear as one looks at the provision for taking the sins of the people and placing them outside the camp. At an appointed time the hands of the priest were laid on the head of a goat, symbolically transferring to it the sin and the guilt of the people. Then the goat was banished. It was driven into the wilderness (Lev. 16:20-22). This act signified that the sins of the people had no place within the camp. They had to be removed if the people were to enjoy the presence of God, which had been promised to them through Abraham. Their sins were thereby also removed from before the Lord, who would not tolerate them in his presence. This provision of sacrifices showed that the obedience to the law that was required if the people were to remain within the camp fell short. The deeper reason that the people could remain inside was not that they themselves had fulfilled the law but that their sins had been removed vicariously and placed outside.

The New Testament tells us clearly that the old covenant, "the law," was imperfect. I have said that this imperfection did not arise simply from the fact that in the old covenant the law had received a legal expression; nevertheless, the fact that it as a whole had a legal tone made it possible for one to keep its provisions in a manner characteristic of it and yet offend its deeper meaning. One could observe merely the "letter" of the law, failing to express its "spirit," and yet remain within the covenant community. The old covenant indeed foreshadowed the new, but it fell short of the new. It was shadow, in contrast to the reality that was to come.

Thus "the law," which was legally qualified and which encapsulated everything within its legal chrysalis, always witnessed to its own inadequacy. It was superimposed on the line of promise, but it never abolished it; it gave the commandments a particular form, but it could never exhaust their deeper meaning; loving God meant observing the legally qualified prescriptions that he himself had established, but these were nothing apart from the love that was the proper response to the one God who has revealed himself in his covenant faithfulness.

In view of the above characterization of "the law," we can understand that it could not be conceived properly as resting in itself. Even though it had a legal quality, the law constantly acted so as to break through its own constraints. Within the old dispensation there were strands that were not legally qualified, and these acted so as to break through the legal form. Throughout, the old covenant offered glimpses of what lay beyond it and on what it depended.

I have implied that "the law" was a legal expression of law in a deeper sense. To be sure, there is a difference between law and any legal expression of law. It must be said here that there is a difference between God's law and any legal expression of it such as that which characterized the old dispensation. The latter depended on the former: "the law" depended on the commandments, which, in turn, depended on the great commandment.

The people of Israel should have discerned what lay beyond the legal form of the law. They should have seen that satisfying the conditions for remaining among the covenant people did not itself mean that they were responding properly to the covenant God. They should have been able to look past the legal form of the law, but in this they often failed.

Many times they "obeyed" but not from the heart. As the law was misunderstood in this way, it was externalized. This externalization did
not arise, however, simply because the law had been given a legal cast.
It arose because of an ignoring of the deeper meaning of the law and a
misunderstanding of its intent.

Thus the prophets had to call Israel again and again to "true obedience." As Samuel said to Saul as he was returning from the conquest
of the kings: "Does the Lord delight in burnt offerings and sacrifices as
much as in obeying the voice of the Lord? To obey is better than sacrifice, and to heed is better than the fat of rams" (1 Sam. 15:22). Christ
condemned the teachers of the law and the Pharisees for their external
obedience to the law: "You give a tenth of your spices – mint, dill and
cummin. But you have neglected the more important matters of the law"
(Mt. 23:23). Christ also spoke of the "inner meaning" of the law: "You
have heard that it was said, 'Do not commit adultery.' But I tell you that
anyone who looks at a woman lustfully has already committed adultery with her in his heart" (Mt. 5:27-28). The ministry of John the Baptist
began with a call to repentance: "The ax is already at the root of the trees,
and every tree that does not produce good fruit will be cut down and
thrown into the fire" (Mt. 3:10; cf. Lk. 3:9). John proclaimed a new age.
The people had to understand that what was needed in their lives was
not surface change, but a new life. Pushed to the extreme, the prophetic
utterances could draw a sharp line between the legal provisions of the
law and the matters of the heart: " 'The multitude of your sacrifices –
what are they to me?' says the LORD. I have more than enough of burnt
offerings, of rams and the fat of fattened animals. I have no pleasure in
the blood of bulls and lambs and goats" (Isa. 1:11).

Such hypocrisy, of course, was not limited to ancient Israel. It is often
present in the New Testament period as well. But external obedience
was more typical of the Old Testament. Formal obedience was all that
was necessary to remain within the camp.

If one "did the works of the law" in this external sense, then, was he
truly doing the works of the law? The answer must be no. The answer
is clear from the prophetic rejection of such external obedience. Christ
objected strenuously to the practices of the Pharisees, who fulfilled all
the demands of "the law" outwardly but inwardly were like foul-smell-
ing tombs. External obedience to "the law" was no true obedience at all.
"The law" was an expression of something deeper, apart from which it
could not be understood.

This depth is seen in Christ's interpretation, his "spiritual" interpretation, of the commandments. Now, was this spiritual interpretation rigorous? Did he take the commandments and, as it were, stretch them out to their limit? If so, many would ask whether this was warranted. Should not one content himself with a normal, a moderate, interpretation of the law? If it was interpreted in such a rigorous fashion, how could anyone keep it? When Jesus told the young man who said that he had kept the commandments that he must sell all his possessions and give to the poor, even the disciples were astonished and asked, "Who then can be saved?" (Mt. 19:25).

Christ did not overextend the meaning of the commandments when he gave them their spiritual interpretation. He was simply expressing their inner, that is, their true meaning. This meaning should have been clear to the Israelites in view of their own history.

That they understood the law as a system through which to attain righteousness meant that they had misunderstood it. They transformed this arrangement, which God himself had established for a special purpose, into something God had not intended at all, a system of works-righteousness. This was, on the one hand, to overestimate the place of the law. They could do this only because they had wrenched the law out of context. It was, on the other hand, to overestimate what they themselves could accomplish. They thought that by keeping the "letter" [KJV] of the law, the "written code" [NIV], they could satisfy the righteous demands of God, whereas, in fact, they could not even obey the written code fully. Scripture tells us clearly that this distortion issues from the "fleshly mind" [KJV], "the sinful nature" [NIV], which attempts to establish its own righteousness instead of accepting the righteousness offered by God himself (Rom. 10:3; 1 Cor. 2:14).

That people understood the law to be a way of attaining righteousness before God means, I repeat, that they had misunderstood it. Indeed, God had intended the law, as the expression of his will, to be a way of life (Rom. 7:10), and insofar as people obey God's will they are blessed (Ps. 119; Jas 1:25); but because of sin the law became an instrument of death (Rom. 7:10, 11, 13). Therefore, the apostle Paul could write, "If a law had been given that could impart life, then righteousness would certainly have come by the law" (Gal. 3:21). But, given the presence of sin, there was no such law! The dispensation of the law, then, was given for a specific purpose. It was not opposed to the promise, Paul said, because it was intended to corral people and lead them to Christ, in whom the promise is fulfilled; however, having been misunderstood and having been taken as a system of works-righteousness, the law stood diametrically opposed of the gospel of free grace in Christ Jesus.

At this point we can appreciate the full force of the statement of the apostle John that the law was given through Moses but grace and truth came through Jesus Christ. We see "the law" as a legally qualified system that had been externalized and that furthermore had become a system of works-righteousness. This is what had come to stand diametrically opposed to the promise. When the apostle Paul contrasted the free grace that is in Christ with the law, he was setting grace up in antithesis to a monolith, an entire, externalized system by which it was thought that one could attain righteousness before God. This accounts for the sharpness of the contrast.

When, therefore, the Scriptures contrast law and grace, as Paul does consistently in Galatians, this goes deeper than simply relating one dispensation, considered as a divine arrangement, to another. Dispensations are related thus, e.g., when the dispensation of the law is regarded as a possible way of salvation (by way of obedience to the law) in contrast to salvation by grace. Some classical dispensationalists spoke as if the "dispensation of the law" was established to test whether Israel could attain righteousness by satisfying the demands of the law. But such a possibility had already been cut off because of sin. Thus, the relation must be viewed otherwise. The old dispensation indeed had a specific purpose, but not to ascertain whether one could attain salvation by his works. It was intended to hold us prisoner, "locked up" until the coming of Christ, and to presage that coming (Gal. 3:22-25). It was the fleshly mind that transformed this arrangement into a system of works-righteousness. It was this system that stood diametrically opposed to the promise. The law had to give way to the gospel!

One can see that throughout Israel's history the Old Testament dispensation, which was imperfect, was indeed like a chrysalis that was showing signs of bursting and of disclosing the new, which it contained in itself. Provision was made in the old covenant for the people through the daily sacrifices. But all this was consummated in the great Passover, the commemoration of the Exodus, when the people had been covered by the blood sprinkled on the lintels and doorposts of their houses and had thus been protected against the visitation of the angel of death, who took all of the firstborn sons of Egypt. This salvation was much more than a legal satisfaction for the individual sins of the people; it was the great redemption, the paradigm of the final redemption that was to be realized in Jesus Christ. As the people were leaving Egypt, they were baptized into Moses in the cloud and in the sea (1 Cor. 10:2). This baptism spoke of a death and a resurrection, of a total commitment. It foreshadowed the New Testament believer's dying and rising with Christ. Within the old covenant itself there was ample testimony to the fact that what is required by God is not external obedience, a formal, legalistic observance of the law, but a heart commitment, a commitment of the entire person to the covenant God, who is faithful to his promise. That the old dispensation was "shadow" made one look forward to the reality of salvation in Christ.

Now, what changes took place when the new arrived, when "the law" gave way to "grace and truth" in Jesus Christ? Against the above background, the picture can be brought into focus. The chrysalis, the expression of the law in legal form that characterized the dispensation of the law, fell away, allowing what was inside to come to free expression.

If the old age, taken as a whole, was the age of the law, the new age is the age of the Spirit. Now, the line of promise, which was present before but was encapsulated in the dispensation of the law, has been set free. Abraham had been promised a seed; his descendants would be more than one could number. The Scriptures tell us that this "seed" was Christ. Further, the words of God that are called the Ten Commandments were also set free. Now their "deeper" meaning, i.e., their true meaning, stands at the forefront. Further still, the shadows have given way to reality. The ancient sacrificial system has been dismantled. Now Christ has been offered once and for all for the sins of his people. He himself bore our sins on the cross, himself having been set outside the city gate (Heb. 13:12).

The new age, the age of the Spirit, is set sharply over against the dispensation of the law. The apostle Paul writes, "... circumcision is circumcision of the heart, by the Spirit, not by the written code" (Rom. 2:29). Again, Paul writes, "We have been released from the law so that we serve in the new way of the Spirit, and not in the old way of the written code" (Rom. 7:6). Another reference is especially telling: "He has made us competent as ministers of a new covenant – not of the letter but of the Spirit; for the letter kills, but the Spirit gives life" (2 Cor. 3:6). In this dichotomy, the "letter" is identified with the old covenant, the "Spirit" with the new. The old is bondage; the new is freedom in Christ.

This dichotomy runs through the teaching of the New Testament. Paul likens the old dispensation to Hagar, who was the bondwoman, and the New Testament dispensation to Sarah, who was the freewoman (Gal. 4:22-23). In this allegory, the apostle Paul expresses the difference between the two covenants. The one is a covenant of bondage, the other is a covenant of freedom. When the apostles and elders were faced with the question whether believers had to be circumcised and obey the law of Moses in order to be saved, Peter said, "Why do you try to test God by putting on the necks of the disciples a yoke that neither we nor our fathers have been able to bear?" (Ac 15:10). After Paul explained the allegory of Hagar and Sarah, he wrote, "It is for freedom that Christ has set us free. Stand firm, then, and do not let yourselves be burdened again by a yoke of slavery" (Gal. 5:1).

But if the age of the law encapsulated things that did not have a legal cachet, the age of the Spirit is not opposed to law in any and every sense. The Old Testament prophets do not characterize the age of the Spirit as one of lawlessness. Some, like the so-called "enthusiasts," have misunderstood at this point and fallen into antinomianism. To the contrary, the prophets characterize the age of the Spirit as a time when the law of God will be written on people's hearts, when the true meaning of the law and of obedience to the law will come to expression.

In this regard, the teaching of the Scriptures differs sharply from that of modern humanism. According to the latter, law has its source, its ultimate origin, in autonomous human personality.

According to the Bible, on the contrary, the human personality is subject to God's will, which is expressed in his law. The issue, then, is whether the law has been "internalized," in the sense that obedience to it is a matter of the heart and its inclinations. If the law is fully "internalized," obedience to it is as natural as breathing air. Here the law is not "external," in the sense of impinging from outside on the "thoughts and intents of the heart"; it comes spontaneously to expression, because the "thoughts and intents of the heart" are in harmony with it.

If one speaks of internalization here, however, he must take care. The prevailing view is that law is per se external, or even foreign, to human life and that it must be "internalized" if it is to square with autonomous human personality. According to the Scriptures, God's law as such is not external. In its original intent, it is not foreign to man and to his life. The Scriptures teach that love, as the service of God with one's whole heart, is what characterized man in his original, sinless estate. It was internal; it was man's natural attitude.

Looking ahead, as they were faced with the outright sinfulness or external obedience of the people, the prophets discerned a time when the people of God would no longer be disobedient and when obedience would be more than outward conformity to the requirements of the law. As Jeremiah writes, "No longer will a man teach his neighbor, or a man his brother, saying, 'Know the Lord,' because they will all know me, from the least of them to the greatest" (Jer. 31:34). This passage is reflected in the Book of Hebrews, where the writer says that God declared that he would establish a new covenant with the house of Israel: "I will put my laws in their minds and write them on their hearts. I will be their God, and they will be my people" (Heb. 8:10). This is the way in which freedom is understood in the new covenant. In the new covenant arrangement, it is characteristic that obedience comes from the heart. Obedience is of the Spirit, and not of "the written code."

The biblical idea of freedom is clearly expressed in the illustration of the servant and the son (Gal. 4:1-7). The servant or slave stood at the periphery of the family. He was dependent for his actions on what others said. He took orders as to what he was supposed to do and not to do. In contrast, the son stood at the center of the family. He had free access to its affairs; he stood in a relation of intimacy to its head, the father. Significantly, he did not take orders from someone else; he himself was the guide of his own actions. In this sense, he was autonomous. But this illustration cannot be used to support a humanistic view of freedom, as if the human spirit were the source, the origin, of law. It can only mean that one who is a son guides his own life, according to the law, which is not external but is written on his heart.

The New Testament teaches that Christian believers are sons and not servants (Gal. 4:6-7; cf. Heb. 3:5-6). They have the law written on their hearts, not just on tables of stone. They do of themselves, of their own inclination, what is required by the law. And the love of the heart is not contrary to law. Christ himself said, "If you love me, you will obey what I command" (Jn. 14:15).

To obtain a further appreciation of this biblical teaching, let us again look at the meaning of the law. In the discussion, I have used the term in various way, according to the teaching of Scripture. I have spoken of the dispensation of "the law," which was a special arrangement introduced by God with a pedagogical purpose. I have also spoken of the

Ten Commandments, of which I have said that they themselves are not expressed in legal terms; they were encapsulated in the dispensation of the law, which was not entirely legal but which had a legal cast. Finally, I have spoken of "the first and great commandment," the commandment of love, which followed upon God's announcing himself as the one God, the faithful covenant God, who had brought the children of Israel out of Egypt. He said through Moses, his servant: "Hear, O Israel: The LORD our God, the LORD is one. Love the LORD your God with all your heart and with all your soul and with all your strength" (Dr. 6:4-5). This "summary" of the commandments, which is better thought of as their heart and soul, was reiterated by Jesus Christ, who called it "the first and greatest commandment" (Mt. 22:38). One may also use the term to refer to the order that God has placed in the cosmos, through which he speaks in his general revelation. It is through this general revelation that we can understand that there is a distinction between the law and the legal.

We often speak of the "law of love" as the "summary" of the Ten Commandments. This is acceptable. This commandment, as we find it in Deuteronomy and as it was quoted by Jesus Christ, indeed summarizes what is contained in these commandments. We might interpret the word *summary* in such a way, however, as to obscure the relationship that the "law of love" has to the Ten Commandments. The latter should not be thought of as a set of individual statements or rules, each standing by itself, which were then given general expression in the law of love (a typical nominalist error); instead, one should think of the law of love as the heart and soul of the commandments. If one truly loves, in the biblical meaning of the word *love*, he has kept all the commandments. If, on the contrary, he has "kept" all the commandments without love, he has kept them only externally. In a sense, as we have seen, he has not kept them at all. The commandments are of a piece. They hang together. In fact, in their deeper meaning, they are one. They are all expressions of love for God and for one's neighbor. Looking at them from another direction, we see that they come to a focus in this love and do not have their meaning apart from it. Thus the apostle Paul could show the Corinthian Christians "the most excellent way": "And now these three remain faith, hope and love. But the greatest of these is love" (1 Cor. 13:13).

In the light of what has been said above, one can understand the oft-criticized statement of the church father Augustine, "Love God and do what you will." Many people object to this statement. The Ten Commandments, they argue, are the content of the law of love; therefore, how can one know what love is apart from the commandments? To say "Love God and do what you will" is inadequate. There is some truth to this criticism. In our age, as in many others, the word love has been so emptied of its meaning that it is difficult to understand what is intended by a statement such as that of Augustine.

If one understands love in its full scriptural connotation, however, one can make much more sense of the Augustinian saying. In this light, love must be understood in terms of the total response of the whole person to God, as he has been revealed in Christ. This is the God who brought his people Israel, body and soul, out of Egypt. Were not the people of God baptized into Moses by their passage through the Red Sea (1 Cor. 10:2)? Are not all believers baptized into Christ, dying with him and being raised with him into a new life? We are to love God in Christ wholly. As the Scriptures say, "We were ... buried with him through baptism into death in order that, just as Christ was raised from the dead through the glory of the Father, we too may live a new life" (Rom. 6:4). If we look at the catalog of virtues that spring from love (1 Cor. 13:4-7), we can understand more fully how one can say, "Love God and do what you will."

It is easy to show that love for God and for one's neighbor issues in the commandments. No one who loves God will want to serve any other god. No one who loves God will set anything within the creation in his place. No one who loves God will desire to empty his name of meaning by using it carelessly or inappropriately. No one who loves God will deprive him of the worship that is rightly his. Furthermore, no one who loves God will despise his fellow man, taking his life unlawfully from him, or desiring to take his possessions. He will not lose himself in a misplaced desire, a jealousy, for what his neighbor possesses. As the apostle Paul says, "He who loves his fellow man has fulfilled the law" (Rom. 13:8; cf. Gal. 5:14). The commandments flow from love in its full scriptural sense, and they depend on it.

In the age of the Spirit, the commandments are still in force. In fact, it is commanded that one love God and his neighbor. A true love will not ignore these commandments. Further, in the age of the Spirit, there are legal arrangements. But the focus has shifted. The age of the Spirit does not have a legal cast; the legal arrangements are no longer "up front." Instead, the New Testament believer, as a son or daughter and not a servant, will serve God in Christ as one who has died and is risen with

Christ, so that he or she may live a new life. In the age of the Spirit, the focus is on serving God freely, from the heart.

In various connections, we observe how we are to serve God – in obedience to his will as expressed in his law but not in a way that is legally qualified. I will refer here to the family, to marriage, and to the church.

The well-regulated family will establish firm rules, some of them with a legal cast. Children need such rules. Rules provide a structure within which children can grow. In the loving environment of the home, on a simple scale, the child must know exactly what is required of him and what the consequences will be if he breaks the rules. As a child matures, however, he will need fewer and fewer rules of a legal kind. Maturity will not bring with it an abandonment of the principles that make a good home; but, as the child matures, he will follow them by reason of personal understanding and conviction. Thus there is an analogy also within the modern family to the passage from the Old Testament to the New Testament economy. The Old Testament believer was like a child, who needed to be under the guidance of tutors and governors; but when children are older, they should have the maturity and understanding to do what is right of their own volition. In the grown family, there is indeed some place for legally qualified rules; but these will have a place only because they are useful: when they are no longer useful, they will be put aside.

A marriage relationship should be nurtured according to sound biblical principles. These will not have a legal cast, however. Of course, there is always a legal side to the relationship of husband and wife – think, for example, of the legal consequences of their marriage vows – but in a healthy marriage relationship the legal will not be "up front." Any marriage in which the legal is "up front" is already in serious trouble.

In the church, the elders must give careful attention to what makes the church the church: the sound preaching of the Word, the proper administration of the sacraments, and the faithful exercise of discipline. But none of these is legally qualified, not even church discipline. Discipline in the church is, first of all, a matter of applying sound biblical principles. Good discipline manifests itself in how well the commands of Christ are presented and followed, in the power of the Holy Spirit. At times, e.g., when there is controversy or when discipline cases cannot be resolved by simple admonition, the legal is very much in evidence; but such times are difficult for the church, no matter how necessary it is to go through them, and it is good when they are left behind and the church can return to its normal life.

In the New Testament age the legal is still present. As some have argued, there is a legal side to all human relationships. There is a legal side to the family, to marriage, and to the church. But in the New Testament period the legal is not "up front"; rather, it comes to the fore only when that is needful.

It is interesting that the exemplary case of discipline in the New Testament, the judging and punishing of Ananias and Sapphira, did not take place within a legally qualified situation, such as we find in the Old Testament dispensation. When the disciples brought their possessions to the common treasury, there was no stipulation as to how much they should bring. Ananias and Sapphira were judged, not because they did not bring a set amount, but because they purposefully misrepresented what they had done. They were judged for hypocrisy. Having sold their land, they were completely free to decide how large a gift they would bring; but they agreed between themselves that they would pretend that their sacrifice was greater than it actually was. Faced with this dissimulation, Peter said, "Ananias, how is it that Satan has so filled your heart that you have lied to the Holy Spirit and have kept for yourself some of the money you received for the land? Didn't it belong to you before it was sold? And after it was sold, wasn't the money at your disposal? What made you think of doing such a thing? You have not lied to men but to God" (Ac. 5:3-4). It is also interesting that the punishment of Ananias and Sapphira, though a just retribution, was not part of a legally established scheme. This judgment was intended to serve as a warning to the church, not to set a pattern for church discipline.

In all their relationships New Testament believers do not have less responsibility than their Old Testament counterparts for obeying God's will as expressed in his law; in fact, they have greater personal responsibility, because it is not legally stipulated exactly what they should and should not do. The New Testament constantly assumes that believers are not servants but sons and daughters, with both the privileges and the responsibilities of those who are children in a loving household.

Now I must pose the main question of this chapter: "May we use the term *theonomy?*" In view of the above, the answer must be yes. The word theonomy is simply a combination of the Greek words for God and law, *theos* and *nomos*. It refers, in the context of this book, to the rule of God through his law. As we have seen, the Scriptures teach that Christians are to obey the will of God and that this will is expressed in his law. Christ himself joined love for himself with keeping his commands. This is important to remember as we observe modern theologians refusing to say that love can be commanded or insisting that there is at best a tensionful, dialectical relationship between love and law. The life of man as a whole is subject to an order, a lawful order, which holds for him and for his relationships. If this is true, then the use of the term *theonomy*, or a synonym for it, is not only allowed but is necessary.

If one uses the term *theonomy*, however, he should be clear as to what he means, more particularly, what he means by God's law. We have seen that law, as understood in the Scriptures, has several levels: 1) the central commandment of love toward God and one's neighbor; 2) the explication of what this love means, as we find this in the Ten Commandments; and 3) the legally qualified prescriptions, which were elaborated in order to regulate the life of the people and to lead them to Christ. As we have seen, we may also speak of God's law in the sense of 4) the order that God has placed in the cosmos. If one uses the term *theonomy* to refer to the rule of God through his law, he must indicate what kind of law he has in mind, so that he can make it clear what he means by the rule of God in any particular context.

It is only when we have distinguished the various meanings of "law" and understood how law functions in various ways in God's dealings with people that we can answer the question as to what laws apply in the church today. If we do not do this, we are likely to repeat errors of the past, falling, e.g., into antinomianism or legalism.

As we have distinguished various kinds of law, we have observed that there is continuity as well as discontinuity between the old and new dispensations. We cannot discover an adequate criterion, however, if we think only in terms of continuity and discontinuity. We cannot, for instance, anchor continuity in the nature of God, saying that God's law is an expression of his will and is unchanging, just as God is unchanging. This statement is true, taken by itself; but it is true of God's law only in its central meaning. In view of the teachings of the Bible, it is inconceivable that the commandment of love will ever be abrogated. It is also inconceivable that there will be any changes in the meaning of God's law as expressed in the Ten Commandments. But this does not at all apply to the manner in which these commandments have been worked out (some would say "positivized") in the various arrangements that God himself has established. As we have seen, the legally qualified form that the law took in the old dispensation was not at all unchanging; it had a purpose, and when that purpose was fulfilled, it was set aside. In seeking an answer to the question as to what laws are valid today, we should avoid what, for this purpose, are abstract criteria. We can understand the continuity and discontinuity between the two ages only as we have distinguished the various meanings of law and have understood how law has various functions in God's dealings with human beings.

Thus, we may not assume that every law in the Old Testament age without exception continues to apply until it has been revoked. The sharp disjunction between the old and the new ages will not allow us to assume this. The legally qualified provisions we find in the old dispensation cannot be dealt with on the above basis. The dispensation of the law, which I have likened to a chrysalis, has been set aside; the new age has come. Any specific, legally qualified provision of the Old Testament may be applied in this new age only if it fits. The criterion for its usefulness will be a New Testament one.

In answering the question as to what laws apply today, one must take into full consideration the teaching of the Scriptures themselves as to the nature of law and its relation to the Old Testament and New Testament economies. Remember in this regard that New Testament believers are sons and daughters, not servants, and the church should be zealous to preserve the freedom that its members have in Christ. Attention must be focused on instilling in them a deep love for the One who loved them and gave himself for them and a consuming desire to serve him according to what he has commanded. And, as he said, his commandments are not burdensome.

The authority of Christ is preeminent in the church; it is unlimited. But the church itself, as an institution, has limited authority, even over the lives of those who are its communicant members. It may not seek to have authority over the life of the Christian in every respect. It should not overregulate. It should faithfully perform the task that Christ has given to it. Within its sphere, it has the glorious opportunity of exercising spiritual persuasion, seeking to bring men and women to a knowledge of Christ and to the service of Christ with their entire selves. In doing this, the church will call men and women to obey Christ's commands. But if the church falls into legalism, it will constrict rather than expand the lives of its members in their service of Christ. It should seek to inculcate a deep respect for law in the various forms it has taken in redemptive history; but in guiding its members it should have a firm grasp of what it means that the law was given through Moses, but that grace and truth came through Jesus Christ.

THE TRANSCENDENTAL PERSPECTIVE OF WESTMINSTER'S APOLOGETIC [1]

Westminster Theological Seminary has a full-scale department of apologetics. This makes it stand out among major theological seminaries. In most of the main line seminaries apologetics waned in proportion to the growth of liberal theology. In liberal seminaries, apologetics suffered because of theological liberalism's understanding of the Christian faith, and it finally disappeared.

Theological liberalism focused on spiritual life, as it understood it. Especially in its Ritschlian form, it placed at the center an overwhelming spiritual experience of the person of Jesus. For the faith of the church, it said, Jesus has the value of God. But both this faith and the Christ it confesses lie beyond the pale of doctrinal formulation. Of itself doctrine was regarded as rigid and dogmatic, an ossified expression of the dynamics of the spirit. Doctrine was given second place, as a symbolic expression of the life found in Jesus Christ. The tactic then was to penetrate beyond doctrinal formulations, with their particularity and rigidity, to the dynamics of the life of spirit. Within this climate of thought, apologetics, as a defense of a doctrinal formulation of Christian faith, was downgraded and finally eliminated. It was replaced by comparative religion, the philosophy of religion, the psychology of religion, and now even by the phenomenology of religion.

In response, the founder of Westminster Seminary, Dr. J. Gresham Machen, said that Christianity is not first a life but a doctrine. If one is to give himself to Jesus Christ, Machen said, he must know the one to whom he is committing himself. One cannot have faith unless he possesses the assurance that the object of his faith is worthy of his confidence. If one wishes to know what Christianity is, furthermore, he should not refer to a modern idea of spiritual life but to what Christianity meant as it was established by Christ himself. On its part, Machen said, liberalism has departed from historic Christianity and is no true Christianity at all. True Christianity is historic Christianity. Historic Christianity is such that it confesses truths to which it must hold and which it must defend when attacked. Thus, in view of Machen's adherence to historic Christianity, it is not surprising that Westminster Seminary retained apologetics as an independent discipline within its curriculum. It agreed with Machen that historic Christianity is capable of rational defense. As you know, Machen himself used historical proofs in the service of the gospel. Cornelius Van Til differed from Machen in that he insisted that one must examine closely the foundations of proof; but he agreed with Machen that Christianity is capable of rational proof. He accepted Machen's invitation to become the first professor of apologetics at the Seminary.

It may surprise one that apologetics was also downgraded among Reformed thinkers. Apologetics seemed to require a defense posture. Its history could be interpreted as a series of retreats. Always on the defensive, it appeared condemned to abandon one redoubt after the other to the forces of unbelief. For one who wanted a positive strategy this kind of apologetics had lost its allure.

With such an idea of apologetics in mind, the great Dutch theologian and journalist Abraham Kuyper tried to avoid a strategy of retreat. He opted for a powerful thrust forward. Rejecting defensive apologetics, he highlighted the power of the Christian world-and-life view, especially as it had been understood in its unity and integrality by the Reformed faith. Kuyper found the strength of the Reformed community in its isolation, free from the taint of compromise of its basic principles. Its world view was to be jealously guarded in its purity and vigorously applied in its implications for all thought and life. Accordingly, Kuyper was very much opposed to obscuring boundaries (*de verflauwing der grenzen*), especially the boundary between belief and unbelief. He rejected the ill-advised attempts to effect syntheses between Christian and non-Christian principles. On Kuyper's view the Dutch word for principle, *beginsel*, has a richer meaning than its English equivalent. It stands closer to the German word *Prinzip*, which may suggest a force that drives one along, or the Greek word *arche*, in the sense of a "first principle." For Kuyper a principle is something that impels and molds. Christian principles are major forces that direct and form the life of the Christian community. Driven by Christian principles, the Christian community should not assume a defensive stance; it should busy itself with bringing to fruition the meaning of its principles in every sphere of life – in the church, the state, the family, the school, the business establishment, etc. Since he identified apologetics by and large with defensiveness, Kuyper had little place for it, and he became a major source of whatever distrust of apologetics there is within the Reformed community.

Within Kuyperian circles, Christian apologetics has been replaced, in great measure, by Christian philosophy. There has been a vigorous, positive effort to construct a philosophy based on the Scriptures, a philosophy that is truly philosophy and not covert theology. This tendency came to clear expression, as you know, in the systems of Professors D. H. Th. Vollenhoven and Herman Dooyeweerd of the Free University of Amsterdam. Advocates of this philosophy sometimes wonder out loud whether there is still any room for Christian apologetics. They do not include it in their curricula, and they sometimes look askance at the makeup of a department of apologetics as we have it here at Westminster.

Christian philosophy is very important. I myself am very interested in it. Apologetics, I shall say, needs a Christian philosophy. I must insist, however, that there is still an important place for Christian apologetics. As long as the gospel is being preached, as long as there is missionary activity in the church, as long as the church maintains contact with the cultural situation around it, the proclamation of the gospel will be met by challenges that call forth the reasoned defense of the faith that is called apologetics and the reflection on that reasoned defense that is the science of apologetics. Indeed, apologetics can benefit from Christian philosophy. It will also inevitably relate to problems that are the province of Christian philosophy. Nevertheless, apologetics is not simply Christian philosophy, and it will never truly be replaced by Christian philosophy.

Now, do we not find among contemporary theologians an interest in apologetics? Do we not come across a distinction among contemporary theologians between kerygmatic and apologetic theology?

Indeed, we find such a distinction here. Contemporary theologians do indeed speak of apologetic theology. We must be careful, however. What is often meant is quite different from what I have in mind. In contemporary parlance, apologetic theology is theology that holds that the message of the gospel does not come down from above, like a plumbline, without any relation to culture or without having any anticipations within culture. Apologetic theology relates to culture. There are anticipations of the gospel, it is said, within the cultural milieu. Possibly culture is said to ask the questions and theology give the answers.

Apologetic theology of this kind has taken radical forms. It is suggested that the question concerning the gospel arises even from the deepest denial of the gospel witness, that an affirmation of God and his grace arises even from the most profound denial of him and the most solid repudiation of his grace. This line of thought intends to break the back of any position that holds to a doctrinal Christianity that comes to us with divine authority. It claims, furthermore, that no relation to God is authentic unless it has been tested in the fires of unbelief. This viewpoint has been expressed in the formula: atheism in the religious act. "Atheism" has been a major theme in contemporary theology. Such an apologetic theology has arisen out of a desire to demonstrate solidarity with modern man in his unbelief and even despair. In Hegelian fashion, it has sought the positive in the negative; but in no way has it sought to offer a foundation for our confidence in the truth of the gospel once and for all delivered to the saints. It does not offer a proof of doctrinal Christianity. Quite the contrary!

As I proceed, I shall accept as apologetic that which offers itself as proof of the Christian faith. An apologetical stance will have to assume that Christianity can be rationally defended. Furthermore, I shall not accept any end-run around doctrine. A Christianity that is rationally defensible cannot be a doctrineless one, where Christ is understood not to have made any claims for himself. Even as they hold to such a position, some persons may still want to speak of doctrine. But I shall refuse to call "doctrine" that which has arisen, phoenix-like, from the ashes of the destruction of doctrine. The Christ whom we preach is the Christ who witnessed to himself and who was witnessed to by God, who said, "This is my beloved Son...." An apologetic must respect God's witness to Christ and Christ's witness to himself. Considering who Christ is, these are at bottom one and the same. We must take our stance, as Kuyper, solidly within the framework of the Christian world-and-life view, but at the same time offer a rational defense of Christianity. In doing so, we shall even have to distance ourselves from those who say that there must be a criterion for faith but who refuse to accept any simple, normative criterion for what that faith is.

Under the leadership of Dr. Cornelius Van Til, Westminster Seminary has developed a presuppositional apologetic. This means, on the face of it, that one cannot defend the Christian faith without presuppositions derived from that faith. It also means that one must challenge the presuppositions of unbelief. Christian apologetics must challenge that which lies at the foundation of man's rebellion from God and his Word. There is now a wide spectrum of presuppositional apologetic, within which there are considerable differences as to what is meant by presupposition and how presuppositions are related to faith.

To understand the Westminster presuppositional apologetic, one must see it in its radicality. It was radical in its beginnings. It is radical in its systematic formulation. For it presuppositions are not simply intellectually formulated principles, on the order, let us say, of theoretical axioms. Nor are they simply postulates, which may be drawn from theology as a scientific discipline. As Van Til sought already as a graduate student to challenge unbelief, he came with a radical Christian world view, in the spirit of Abraham Kuyper, and with the purpose of challenging unbelieving thought at its root. His thought was essentially this: Given anything that is meaningful – indeed, given anything at all – one can provide an account of the fact that it is possible only on the foundation of God's revelation in Jesus Christ, as witnessed by the Scriptures. What is (namely, being) is possible only on the presupposition of a full-orbed Christian theism. Any other starting point is inadequate; it will be unable to offer us a standpoint from which we can understand the world in its unity and diversity.

Thus Van Til's thought moved in a direction he rightly called "transcendental." He inquired as to what lies at the foundation of the possibility of what is (being) and of meaning. A transcendental argument moves from what is to the conditions underlying its possibility.

Van Til would not have been able to take this stance if he had not steeped himself in the Reformed tradition, especially as that was represented by Abraham Kuyper. Van Til's position hung from the biblical teaching of the absolute sovereignty of God, the Creator. It was molded by the scriptural teaching that God imparts himself in his revelation and that this revelation is unitary, extending to everything created. Thus Van Til emphasized the organic unity of general and special revelation. His position turned on the idea that man is a covenant being, whose entire existence is dependent upon and focused on God, in his revelation, so that man comes to himself in covenant obedience. Thus, given any thing, one need not look away from it in order to refer to God and his revelation and/or to human response to that revelation. The sovereign God who has revealed himself in Jesus Christ is already present everywhere in his revelation, and man, who was given the position of God's vicegerent, is already responding to him either for the good or for the bad. As Van Til understood it, God's revelation extends not only to what is outside of man but also to the human response to this, impelled by the power of the Holy Spirit.

It was with this spiritual and intellectual equipment that Van Til sought to challenge the humanistic philosophies of his day, notably idealism and pragmatism. In this his attention focused on idealism. It is indeed the case that Van Til's purpose was not simply to refute idealism. That would have been an exercise worthy of a paper on Christian philosophy. In idealism, however, one had a most refined attempt to reflect on man in a radical way. Furthermore, idealists were claiming that their efforts expressed Christian truth in a manner that was defensible to the modern mind. Finally, the idealists themselves were criticizing pragmatism for having failed to attain to a comprehensive position. Now, if the idealist position itself was found wanting on this same score, pragmatism would fall with it. In his doctoral dissertation, "God and the Absolute,"[2] Van Til argued that idealism, in spite of its pretensions, still fell short. For the sovereign Creator-God of the Scriptures it had substituted the Absolute. This Absolute, however, was unable to comprehend all of the facts; there was always something left over. Thus idealism was doomed to take the position that it itself had sought to overcome. It inevitably fell into pragmatism, with its idea of an open universe. It is only as the mind focuses on the sovereign Creator-God of Scripture, who has revealed himself in Jesus Christ, Van Til argued, that it can reach a standpoint deep and broad enough to see God, the self, and the world in proper perspective.

Van Til developed this argument in the interests of the proclamation of the gospel. But it itself was not simply proclamation or, if you will, preaching. The Westminster apologetic is argument. It is argument, indeed, that completely depends on the revelation of God, but it is argument still. It is argument of a special kind, which Van Til himself called transcendental.

Of course, Christian apologetics arises within the context of the proclamation of the gospel. It must live from the truths of the gospel; it may serve as an important adjunct, as a reassuring support, to preaching.

But it itself is not simply preaching. Van Til himself pointed out its focus when he described it as the reasoned defense of an integral Christian theism against the attacks of unbelief. The systematic character of apologetics is determined by this focus. Thus, there is much preaching that is unaccompanied by apologetics, and no apologetics is simply preaching. Furthermore, the proclamation of the gospel is not dependent on apologetics. Its compulsion is finally that of the witness of the Holy Spirit to the Word.

It is as the gospel is preached, in obedience to the evangelical mandate, and as it confronts human culture that the situations take shape that call forth apologetics. Christian apologetics arises in an attempt to answer the challenges to the faith that emerge as the faith is proclaimed and has effective contact with its cultural milieu. Thus apologetics certainly has in mind the promulgation of the gospel, in answer to the great commission, and it may indeed serve as an important adjunct to missions, as it does to preaching; nevertheless, it is not missions. Apologetics must focus on constructing reasoned argument. Its systematic focus is reasoned defense. If it takes for itself a goal like that of rhetoric, namely to convince, and if it is satisfied when it had been convincing to some people, it may well lose its systematic focus and in the long run undermine itself. It is important to keep this systematic focus in view and to distinguish apologetics from missions in the interests of preserving missions itself. The impact of the gospel is not dependent on reasoned argument, no matter how scriptually founded it may be. As with preaching, the power of missions is finally that of the witness of the Holy Spirit to the Word.

Argument, whether that of Christian philosophy or apologetics, must be carried out on the foundation of the truth of the gospel, from which it must live and upon which it must reflect, and it must depend on the power of the Spirit. Apologetics will discover its focus in responding in a reasoned way to the challenge of the culture within which the gospel is proclaimed, in fulfillment of the missionary calling of the church, and it will criticize this culture as to its foundations; but the gospel and its power are deeper than any cultural phenomenon. The gospel must be allowed free play. Apologetics should also reflect on the religious roots of the culture in which the gospel is being proclaimed; thus it will have to reflect on the depth of the cultural encounter that brought it forth. In reflecting on its cultural milieu, apologetics will of necessity reflect on itself, on its own religious presuppositions.

Westminster's radical apologetics responds to attacks of unbelief in a fashion that is based radically on the message of the Scriptures. As I have suggested, it does so in a radical reflection on the ground of the being and meaning of the cosmos. This reflection is possible, I say, only in obedient response to the radical message of the Scriptures, as incorporated in a radically founded Christian world-and-life view.

Westminster's apologetics subjects cultural phenomena to a radical critique. It seeks out their religious foundations and at the same time reflects on its own. Van Til, along with his Reformed colleagues, has done much culture critique, as we observe in his analyses of Greek culture. We must take careful note, however, of how this critique explores culture in depth. It does not simply examine a culture to see how it bears or impinges on theology. It does not simply examine the theological presuppositions of statements that issue from non-Christian milieu, or, for that matter, even from Christian milieu. If one takes the radicality of Van Til's transcendental method into consideration, he can only conclude that Christian apologetics must examine and criticize the religious impulses already at work in any given culture. The transcendental thrust of Dr. Van Til's thinking at its very outset entails, I believe, the need of transcendental critique of culture and of cultural phenomena. Arising within a cultural context, Christian apologetics must reflect on that culture as to the religious impulses that impel it, and in so doing Christian apologetics will of necessity reflect on itself and its own foundations.

Transcendental critique, in the sense I have been describing it, is a very important ingredient of Reformed philosophy and apologetics. It is required by a radical point of departure, such as that Dr. Van Til took as his own in entering upon his apologetical effort. The only question, to my mind, is how this transcendental critique can best be carried out.

⚓ ⚓ ⚓

Presuppositional apologetics is often criticized for being fideistic. This criticism must have in mind more than the fact that presuppositional apologetics claims that argument for Christianity must be built on faith. To label an apologetic "fideistic" must imply that it stands in the way of true argument for Christianity. As I understand it, fideism holds that Christianity is not in need of defense, or that defending Christianity means introducing arguments that distort it, that is to say, that there is an incommensurability between rational argument and Christian faith. Westminster's apologetics has always rejected fideism, understood in this way. It has always stressed that Christianity is capable of rational defense. In fact, Dr. Van Til has insisted that we must be able to "prove" things to the opponent of Christianity. I should say that any position that admits the propriety of rational defense of Christianity is not fideistic. The issue between presuppositional apologetics and its critics on this score will revolve around what kind of argumentation is used.

A more advanced criticism against presuppositional apologetics is that it cannot enter seriously into a rational defense of Christianity, because it has already presupposed, or assumed, the truth of its own position. The presuppositional argument is guilty of reasoning in a circle, of committing the fallacy of *petitio principii*, of assuming what must first be proved. Any rational argument, such critics maintain, must not do this. It must leave the conclusion open, if only for the sake of argument. One need not abandon his personal convictions, but they may not be allowed to influence the course of the argument. Certainly, they may not prejudge the conclusion of the argument.

This point leads to yet another related criticism of presuppositional apologetics. The presuppositional argument, it is said, having failed to place itself on a basis, a common basis, that would make true argument possible, is thereby consigned to a dogmatic affirmation of the Christian faith over against its critics. The result is dogmatic head-butting, without true communication and without the possibility of coming to a fruitful solution of the problems.

Certainly, a presuppositional apologetic may not settle for a dogmatic head-butting – an uncommunicative setting of one set of presuppositions over against another. Its claim that all argument is controlled by presuppositions might suggest this. And the manner in which some interpret the presuppositional apologetic has indeed led to this conclusion. But this, I wager, is the result of a misunderstanding.

We are aided in grasping what apologetical confrontation means, if we understand that the presuppositions involved are not simply personal. We are not talking about a situation where one set of personal presuppositions are simply set up over against another set of personal presuppositions. We are talking, as I suggested before, about a situation where we are attempting to show that Christian presuppositions are necessary if one is to give an account of his life and thought. The issue revolves around the presuppositions that offer the transcendental ground of our experience. What must be presupposed if our experience and its meaning is to be properly accounted for? Put negatively, we claim that if the opponent of Christianity is faithful to his own assumptions he will be unable to give an account of his experience. Lose hold of the proper point of departure and you will be unable to avoid landing up in difficulties, which will not go away simply because you reason more accurately but only because you begin to occupy the true starting point.

We are helped to understand the situation, furthermore, if we understand that the difficulties appear on the scene, not because of what we ourselves conclude, but by a process that resides in the nature of things. That is, abandon the true starting point and you will be led into these difficulties, in spite of your best efforts to avoid them.

As I point out to the students in my required course, The Encounter of Christianity with Secular Science, this form of reasoning was present in the apologetic of the Scotsman James Orr. Lose your grip on the true point of transcendence, he said, which is found in the God-man Jesus Christ, and you will be bound over inextricably to a set of circumstances, which will lead you into despair. The pattern of Orr's apologetic appeared clearly in his argument from history. As there was a departure from the God-man Jesus Christ, there was an inevitable descent, as we may observe, from a choice between Christianity and humanism, between Christianity and scepticism, and finally, as this process hit bottom, between Christianity and despair. It is as we observe the necessary outcome of the abandonment of the true starting point, Jesus Christ, that we obtain a proof, be it indirect, of its validity and necessity.

Now, our department of apologetics has pointed out to several generations of students the inadequacies in James Orr's position. But the basic form of the argument remains, the same fundamental argument that we use and that offers us an indirect proof of the truth of the Christian starting point. As I have said, the argument is negative, indirect, transcendental. Lose hold of the true point of transcendence and you will be unable to attain to a unitary, coherent understanding of your own self and your world.

This inability will be an indirect argument for the validity of the true starting point, which must be assumed if the difficulties are to be overcome.

This transcendental argument is not dependent on personal considerations alone. It depends on what it has discerned to be a structural state of affairs within the creation. This state of affairs is able to be discerned only in the light of God's revelation and will not be understood adequately except in terms of obedient response to that revelation; but it is there, and it can be pointed out to those who would be critics of the Christian faith. No argument, even this one, is able to coerce the opponent to believe; nevertheless, the opponent may again and again be cornered and confronted with what are the inevitable consequences of his having assumed a false starting point. Possibly, by the grace of God and the witness of the Holy Spirit, he may be induced to abandon his false point of departure and embrace the true one in Jesus Christ.

Whatever else one may point out in the apologetics of Dr. Cornelius Van Til, it is undeniable that he used this kind of argument. A case in point, as I suggested, is his dissertation, "God and the Absolute," where he argues that if we abandon the true, transcendent starting point in the God of the Bible and place our trust, immanently, in the Absolute of the idealists, we are unable to account for the unity and coherence of our experience. He himself calls this form of argument indirect and transcendental. Another case in point is his argument in his *Christian-Theistic Evidences*, where he argues that if we abandon the true starting point we are bound to transgress and even obliterate boundaries, leading us into irrationalism. Thus, he argues, in the history of psychology we observe a false rationalistic beginning and a consequent descent into irrationalism. Again, the negative outcome of having abandoned the true starting point is regarded as a confirmation of the validity of the true starting point. Here too the argument is indirect and transcendental.

The Christian apologist does not simply hold to his own presuppositions and butt with them against his opponent's presuppositions. He attempts to show his opponent what are the inevitable consequences of holding to his own false starting point, his own false presuppositions. He can do this because of the structural state of affairs that pertains, to which he is able to direct his opponent's attention. He does not admit that the truth of the Christian faith may be held in abeyance or that his opponent may be allowed to assume that God and his revelation can be put on hold, awaiting the outcome of the argument. His argument assumes all along the truth of the Christian position.

Van Til's critics, as we saw, often accuse him of setting up a head-to-head dogmatic confrontation between opposing positions. Some critics also accuse him of having suppressed the use of evidence.

Whatever partial justification there may be for such criticism, it does not follow from Van Til's use of transcendental method. A transcendental apologetic does not tone down or eliminate what is given and its meaning; it only argues that the unbeliever is unable to account for the possibility of what is given. He must fail to grasp the ground of the possibility of everything that is.

In regard to this transcendental orientation, one may remember Van Til's illustration about the unbeliever's use of borrowed capital. The unbeliever uses the good gifts of God, which are spread abroad in the creation and on which he depends in his thought and life, without giving God the glory. He is able to do what he does because he is using borrowed capital. The transcendental thrust of Van Til's position is also incorporated in his well-worn illustration of the little girl who is able to reach up and strike her father only because she is sitting on his lap.

In one or another writing, Van Til says that he never wished to downgrade historical argumentation of the kind used by Dr. Machen; he only wished to assure that scientific investigation be carried on with proper attention to the presuppositions involved. Van Til's view of common grace also conforms to this pattern. It allows for the fact that even those who deny God and his grace are capable of great accomplishments; but it also requires one to explore in depth the religious presuppositions of these unbelievers and observe how their accomplishments would not have been possible at all if their unbelieving assumptions had been carried through consistently.

The place of evidence in Van Til's position was discussed recently by Thom Notaro, in his book *Van Til and the Use of Evidence*.[3] That Van Til has always had a place for the use of evidence has not been lost on the careful reader of his works; nevertheless, it is good that this point has received careful, systematic treatment.

In spite of the truth of the points I have just made, however, another line of thought in Van Til has indeed militated against what is given and the meaning of what is given. This line of thought stands in the way of his use of evidence. Van Til suggests that to dwell on what is given presupposes that it is neutral and lands one in contingency. In order to avoid contingency, one must *look away* from what is given to its ground. One must *relate*, he says, to God, who is the ground of all being and meaning. Because of this strain in his thinking, Van Til has had difficulty with the twin ideas of a created order and of a structure of creation. Professor Hendrik Stoker, of South Africa, pointed to this difficulty in Van

Til's thinking in his chapter in the Van Til volume, *Jerusalem and Athens*.[4] Stoker says that Van Til has focused on the *vertical* and has given too little attention to the *horizontal*. Indeed, if we use this somewhat unfortunate distinction between vertical and horizontal, we may say that Van Til has insisted that we must relate the horizontal to the vertical, if we are not to fall into contingency and destroy the possibility of obtaining a proper view of the unity and diversity of the cosmos. Following this line of thought, he must insist that one *look away* from the idea of an order and structure within the creation. Along this route, "generality" becomes identified with "neutrality" and the way is blocked to exploring in depth what is given and its structure. As I pointed out, the latter way is that which is followed in transcendental argument. Transcendental argument does not *look away* from what is given; it explores it in its depth, discerning that which lies behind or underneath it and establishes the ground of its very possibility. In view of what I have said, Van Til's suppression of the given and of evidence, to the degree that it actually takes place in his thought, must be attributed to a failure to come fully to grips with the implications of his transcendental method.

$$\mathcal{L} \quad \mathcal{L} \quad \mathcal{L}$$

The issues to which I am referring were brought out, though not fully enough, in the volume published in honor of Van Til, *Jerusalem and Athens*. As we look to the future, we should keep in mind the need to carry on the discussions that were begun there. We should continue them in order to come to a clearer and more consistent expression of the radical, reformational apologetic instituted by Van Til himself.

As we look to the future, we should be mindful of the resources within the Christian philosophy that has grown up in Kuyperian soil. That is especially the case since Van Til himself has spoken highly of it and has acquainted his students with it for many years. If this philosophy is understood in its transcendental signification – which, unfortunately, is often ignored – it is clear that it refers to transcendental presuppositions in a way that dovetails with the main thrust of the Westminster apologetic. If one analyzes what is given, it says, he will observe that his experience is structured and that it can be viewed from the point of view of various aspects or modes. This modal order comprises one of the "horizons" of our experience, as Dooyeweerd calls them, which underlie and help to account for the possibility of our experience. This philosophy has also given much attention to the self, as it stands *coram deo*, before the face of God, in covenant obedience or disobedience. This self is transcendent; nevertheless, reflection on it is transcendental. It is a reflection, not as in idealism of the spirit on spirit, but of the self on itself as it also had much to say about the structure of human experience, a structure which itself is completely dependent on God and witnesses to him in its every part. The self accompanies every human activity, and this activity cannot be accounted for except in reflection on the self and its attitude toward God, other selves, and the world.[5]

The Calvinistic philosophy has also explored the driving forces that stand behind human life and thought. An important part of the Calvinistic philosophy is transcendental reflection on the religious motives underlying life and thought. It is quite in line with the transcendental thrust of his own position that Van Til has also spoken of religious motives when he, for instance, has undertaken a critique of Greek culture. Indeed, he has insisted that all of the so-called religious motives can be understood within the framework of the one that dominated Greek thought, namely, the motive of form and matter. In this, I believe, he is mistaken. But this is no place to argue the point. The important thing to observe here is that Van Til has been willing to speak of religious motives as he has engaged in culture critique. Should that surprise one, when he considers the fact that Abraham Kuyper gave such an important place to principles, in the sense of motivating forces? According to the Calvinistic philosophy, the religious motives accompany one in all his thought and action. They color how one will respond to God, either in covenant obedience or disobedience. These religious motives are not found by looking away from what is given in experience and its structure; they are discovered only by exploring experience and its structure in depth.

As I said, Christian apologetics is not Christian philosophy. Nevertheless, in its defense of the faith, it will bear on issues and use resources that are the domain of Christian philosophy. Our Westminster apologetic has benefited greatly from the philosophical insights that have come to us from our Reformed community. As we look to the future, we should explore these relationships even more carefully in an attempt to make our apologetics even more solid and effective for Christ.

As we look to the future, we should continue to work on our apologetics. We should seek to purify it of elements that do not properly fit in with its radical, transcendental orientation. Apart from this radical orientation, it cannot offer a sufficient challenge to unbelief. This radical orientation is necessary if it is to reflect, as an apologetic, the radical demands that the gospel brings to bear on our life and thought. It is incumbent on the Christian community to develop the means to serve Christ in the radical way that his person demands. Our Westminster apologetic has been given to us by God as one instrument with which our Christian community can serve him as he has revealed himself in Jesus Christ.

As Christians, we rejoice in the fact that we have Christ in our hearts. To have Christ there is of supreme importance. We are united with him in his death and resurrection. In him we have the hope of eternal life, both now and at his second coming. But we may not forget that this same Christ who lives in our hearts, as we live in him, is the cosmic Christ. According to Scripture doctrine, he is one with the Father; he was with the Father at the creation; he now sits at the right hand of the Father, to intercede for us as an eternal high priest, of the sort that Melchizedek was; he is the one who will come again to redeem his purchased possession so that we may be with him where he is, in a new heavens and a new earth. Our Christian lives, centered in our hearts, important as they are, do not stand alone. They are taken up in the great cosmic drama of redemption, which our apologetic is calculated to serve. All rulerships and powers are being placed under Christ's feet; there will come a time when he will give all things to the Father, that the Father may be all in all. Even so, come, Lord Jesus! Maranatha!

REFERENCES

1. Slightly revised version of an address delivered by the author on the occasion of his inauguration as Professor of Apologetics at Westminster Theological Seminary, 4 March 1986.

2. Van Til followed this with an article, having the same title, in *Evangelical Quarterly*, vol. II (1930). This article is reprinted in Cornelius Van Til, *Christianity and Idealism* (Philadelphia: Presbyterian and Reformed Publishing Co., 1955), 7-35.

3. Thom Notaro, *Van Til and the Use of Evidence* (Phillipsburg, NJ: Presbyterian and Reformed, 1980).

4. *Jerusalem and Athens: Critical Discussions on the Theology and Apologetics of Cornelius Van Til* (ed. E. K. Geehan; Nutley, NJ: Presbyterian and Reformed, 1971), 27, 31, 46, 48, 57ff, and passim.

5. Cf. Herman Dooyeweerd, *A New Critique of Theoretical Thought*, I (Philadelphia: Presbyterian and Reformed, 1953-58), 34ff.

PROGRESSIVE AND REGRESSIVE TENDENCIES IN CHRISTIAN APOLOGETICS

The year 1928 marked an important turning point for Christian apologetics. In that year Cornelius Van Til left his pastorate in the Christian Reformed Church of Spring Lake, Michigan, and took the position of Instructor of Apologetics at the Princeton Theological Seminary. The following year the reorganization of that seminary precipitated a break with it on the part of the majority of those who wanted to carry on the witness for the Reformed faith that characterized the Old Princeton. Van Til was one of those who left Princeton to found the Westminster Theological Seminary, Philadelphia. It was then at Westminster, and not at Princeton, that the new method which he was developing began to take root.

In a broad segment of the Christian church apologetics had fallen into almost complete disrepute. That was for the most part the result of the attacks of humanism and of liberal theology. They dismissed apologetics as a case of special pleading, or as the vain attempt to defend an outworn theological position by means of bad arguments. Apologetics was indeed carried on by evangelicals, largely in America and in Britain; but it depended for its insights and its methods almost exclusively on the older apologetic positions, which were widely considered to be outdated.

Even among Reformed thinkers apologetics had received hard blows. The powerful Dutch Reformed tradition had virtually abandoned apologetics under the influence of the penetrating criticism of Abraham Kuyper. To his mind apologetics meant taking a defensive position against the attacks of unbelief. This was too weak, too passive. To support his attitude he could appeal to the history of apologetics itself, which showed the miserable spectacle of the retreat of the defenders of the faith from one rampart to another, including less and less within the radius of that which it was thought necessary or even possible to defend.

The defenders of historic Christianity often satisfied themselves with salvaging various fundamentals, which, even though they were certainly basic to the Christian faith, nevertheless did not represent that faith in its fullness and power. The defenders of the faith appeared to be exchanging the grand structure of classical theology for a hovel, from which, after having abandoned the citadel, they might at least carry on guerilla warfare against the interlopers.

That dreary history arose, Van Til thought, not simply because the defenders took a defensive position instead of going over to the attack. It was, first of all, because the defenders of the Christian faith had allowed the attackers to occupy some ground in their own right. To give them some right to territory, to allow that they in their own right could attain to truth, a truth which they could master without any reference to the Christian faith at all, was to allow them within the Christian perimeter, to concede to them an advantage which it was thereafter impossible to stop them from exploiting.

If, on the other hand, the invader could be denied all right to truth, he would be denied a foothold altogether. The entire terrain could be claimed for Christ, and the invader challenged as to his right to be there at all.

Thus Van Til sought to reinstate apologetics, but on a new basis. He admitted the force of Kuyper's criticism of apologetics as it was carried on traditionally. He saw the need for abandoning a passive and defensive attitude and for resuming the offensive. Nevertheless, he recognized that even a good offense demanded that the enemy be denied any foothold behind the defensive lines. Otherwise even the best offense would become stalled because of the confusion the enemy would be sowing in the rear.

⚓ ⚓ ⚓

The major trend in modern Christian apologetics had not sought to work on a consistently Christian foundation. It drew from the empiricism which flourished in the soil prepared by modern scientific discovery. Under this influence it was thought impossible to prove Christianity. One could not compel another on rational grounds to accept the Christian faith. Such a proof could be valid only on the foundation of a strict rationalism. That is to say, it would require an argument that proceeded from indubitable premises and drew necessary conclusions on the basis of strict logical deduction. But the idea that any such argument could refer to real states of affairs had long been abandoned. Instead, apologetics declared itself to be satisfied with a lesser goal. It attempted to establish a presumption in favor of the Christian faith, which in the absence of any compelling reason to the contrary, would be enough to establish a practical certainty, i.e., an assurance that was sufficient to act upon. Thus one was supposed to be able to establish a practical certainty which, if acted upon, would not prove contrary to what would be expected of a rational man, i.e., a man of sound judgment in practical affairs.

If it was impossible to set forth the reasonableness of every doctrine of Christianity with the same force, it was at least possible to establish enough to make the acceptance of the rest that much easier.

An illustration of this kind of reasoning is the famed argument for life after death presented by Bishop Butler. In his argument Butler capitalized on the faith in the regularity of nature which had been cultivated by the success of the classical physics. Although it is impossible to construe nature according to an airtight rationalistic scheme, he thought, its regularity is such that we daily exercise a practical faith in it. We assume that in its constitution and course it will continue the same, unless there is a compelling and sufficient reason to think otherwise. We observe life in man with all its vicissitudes; nevertheless, we also observe that none of these is sufficient to destroy the continuity of his life. Since reason does not demand it and since we have never experienced this discontinuity, there is no compelling reason to think that it would. Unless death is of a quite different order, we may rationally assume that it will not totally obliterate personal identity. Since there is no sufficient reason to think otherwise, it is rational to place one's practical faith on the probability that there is a life after death.

There are many basic similarities in the argument of William Paley, who is famous for his arguments from design. He also seeks to establish a presumption for the Christian faith and leans heavily on the idea of sufficient reason. If one walks along and his foot strikes a stone, he says, there is no sufficient reason to suppose that it has not lain there from eternity; but if one strikes against a watch, which shows marks of design, the situation is different. There is sufficient reason to think that a watch has not lain inert from eternity but that it is the product of design. If our experience is that things evidencing design are the work of a designer, then by analogy we can argue that the universe, which also shows the marks of design, is the work of a great designer, who has fashioned everything for the benefit of the sensible creation.

Further, he argued for the specific truths of the Christian faith on the basis that there is no sufficient reason to reject the force of the testimony of the original witnesses, a testimony that was able to stand up against persecution. A presumption for Christianity is established which, in the absence of sufficient reason to the contrary, is able to commend itself to the faith of rational man.

* * *

Between Bishop Butler and William Paley came the acute Scotsman David Hume. He brought to bear on Butler's arguments the type of criticism that is current even today in naturalistic circles. The argument of Butler had sought to appeal to experience to establish the probability of things that lay beyond the scope of experience. Hume answered that the only basis for throwing over a bridge between what was within experience to what was beyond experience was by means of the cause-effect relationship. But this relationship had meaning only within the bounds of experience itself. It could not serve to build a bridge over to that which was beyond experience. Butler had opted for an empirical method. Let him then remain with it! Furthermore, Butler had appealed to what was beyond our experience to serve as an explanation of what was within experience. But if one has to cut off the process of explanation somewhere by an arbitrary act, why begin it at all? Could one not just as well assume that the universe is its own explanation as to seek grounds of explanation beyond it?

Just as significant, or more significant, than any rational argument that he set forth was the fundamental shift that took place in Hume's thinking, towards a functional, psychological basis of understanding. He sought to understand the unity of the world and of the self in terms of the tendency of the mind to think in terms of a continuum, filling in the gaps where necessary. Thus, if Butler appealed to the classical physics with its idea of inertia – that there is established a presumption in favor of the Christian faith which in the absence of a sufficient reason to the contrary can merit the practical faith of the rational man – Hume transferred this notion of inertia to the inner life. The ideas of the unity of the world and the self, and also the notions of miracle and the supernatural, are ascribable to the tendency of the mind to proceed beyond what is available to experience. Miracle stories are understandable as the fabrication of the untutored, primitive mind, to which the stories of the miraculous and the wonderful are agreeable.

Reformed apologetics acknowledges that there is an element of validity in Hume's criticism of the traditional apologetical stance. The latter had come to accept much of the same trust in nature and in reason which animated the major thinkers of the time. That attitude was fundamentally deistic. Reason and nature were accorded an independency from God. He created them indeed, as a master watchmaker fashions a wonderful precision watch. But God was thought to have the position of one who could be established by reason instead of being the one without whom reason would lose its foundation and meaning. In the history of deism this independent reason first became the arbiter and later even the substitute for God and for his revelation. Even evangelical thought, which differed from deism by retaining the idea of revelation, nevertheless allowed reason an independent status, only insisting that it be supported and supplemented by faith. Even among the evangelicals the idea took hold that the life of reason was possible to everyone who exercised sound judgment. God would not ask more. More than what was expected of a man of sound judgment, who was capable of regulating his own affairs, would not be required by God. God was thought to be universally available to man by way of his rational powers. Then it was necessary to supplement this natural awareness with truths which were specific to Christianity and which were necessary to salvation. These could be supported by the arguments from miracle and from prophecy.

The result was that a large segment of human life was disengaged from direct contact with the self-revealing God. Man was surrounded in great measure with an impersonal universe in which he would not be confronted with the demands of the Christian faith. The result of this deistic influence upon evangelicalism was to make it vulnerable to the attacks of more radical deists, who sought to depend solely upon reason and to jettison faith. It also laid it bare to the attacks of Hume. The latter simply carried the empirical position, placed in the setting of a neutral reason, to its consistent expression. If one started within experience, an experience which to all intents and purposes was declared to be neutral, was there indeed any sufficient reason to look to a ground of explanation beyond experience -- particularly so, if all such attempts were easily explainable in terms of the tendencies to excess of the undisciplined mind? Thus the experience of the man of sound judgment was declared to be sufficient to itself, without the need of anything from outside to interrupt its serene course.

Van Til recognized the validity within limits of Hume's criticism. If one assumes the position of neutrality, there is no reason he can subsequently bring to bear that will be sufficient to deflect him from his path. The law of parsimony will demand that he seek to explain his experience in the simplest available terms, those which are closest to him, which are within his experience itself. And were he to attempt to rise to an explanation which is beyond his experience, the greatest explanation he could attain would still be a finite one. According to the law of parsimony, one cannot reason to a cause which is greater than what is adequate to explain its effect. Since the effect is obviously finite and imperfect, the only god to whom one can reason will himself have to be finite and imperfect.

⚓ ⚓ ⚓

Recognizing that the method of Hume undermined not only the traditional arguments for Christianity but also the foundations of the unity of the world and the self, the idealists looked for a more adequate approach. Relief was sought in a transcendental direction. This meant a more radical departure. The mind was to be guided back to its own most ultimate presuppositions.

This approach was supposed to be concrete, in the sense that from the outset all the factors involved were to be taken into consideration. In its activity the mind is supposed to be reflecting back on what it is, not only as a goal to be attained but also in its own deepest impulse.

The apologist who sought to capitalize on the idealistic legacy of Kant and Hegel, as they were interpreted and modified by Thomas Hill Green, was the Scotsman, James Orr. Orr's method allowed him to begin with a confession of the Christian faith and to insist that it was the full Christian faith, not some preliminary religion of nature, that he was defending. It is, Orr claimed, the Christian faith that offers the presuppositions (postulates) which present us with the possibility of understanding our experience. The Christian faith thus becomes for James Orr the transcendental ground of our experience, that which provides it with its foundation and legitimation.

Orr maintained that without these presuppositions experience would degenerate into chaos.[1] There would no longer be any way to establish the ground of the possibility of experience. The only foundation for the order and the uniformity of nature is not something derived from our experience itself but is the absolute system within the mind of God. To strip away this presupposition and to seek within experience itself for a foundation is to fall into chaos. Similarly, the presupposition for the interpretation of history is the person of Jesus Christ. If one does not presuppose him as the source of meaning, the interpretation of history proceeds by an inner necessity of its own down the road to irrationalism.

Presuppositional apologetics has capitalized upon elements of the method which emerged from the transcendental idealistic movement as were used by James Orr.[2] It has adopted a concrete approach, taking into consideration from the outset the full commitment of the Christian thinker. It has more or less taken over the transcendental method, seeking to establish it more purely. It has also benefited from the dialectical thrust of the argument. Only on the basis of a correct starting point is it possible to provide a transcendental foundation for the possibility of experience. Starting from a false point leads thought inexorably to turn into its opposite and to destroy itself.

Indeed, James Orr's position meant a definite advance along several fronts. He helped to break the hold that the Newtonian world machine idea and the classical physical notion of inertia had obtained on Christian apologetics. No longer was it thought that a presumption could be established for the Christian faith which in the absence of a compelling reason to the contrary would be sufficient to warrant the practical faith of the rational man. Instead, the Christian position became the ground of the very possibility of experience. The world of nature was not thought of so much as an independent world-order from which it could be reasoned to the Christian faith but a world-order whose very foundation was now to be reflected upon and established.

Nevertheless idealistic and rationalistic elements in Orr's position intruded upon and affected his argument. The truths of the unity, simplicity, etc., of God are regarded to be taught by the Hebrew-Christian tradition; they are the truths after which human reason has ever been seeking without ever finally attaining. Orr emphasizes throughout, however, the affinity between the divine rational spirit and the human rational spirit. This affinity makes it possible to understand and to appreciate the necessity of the incarnation. Orr retains the notion that, once having understood such central ideas and thus having gained a foothold in the supernatural, one can that much more easily proceed in accepting additional teachings of Christianity. Orr's idealistic faith in the power of the idea of human reason leads him to views that are reminiscent of deism. Christianity becomes too much a re-publication of what is essentially open to universal human reason, the reflection on the human level of the universal divine reason.

⚓ ⚓ ⚓

Orr's apologetics stressed to advantage the importance of presuppositions and of one's starting point. This attitude is reflected even more in the position of Van Til. The latter does not wish to allow for any starting point that does not take into account from the outset man's concrete situation as it is revealed in the Scriptures. That is to say, any starting point will have to take into account that man is the creature of God, surrounded on all sides by the revelation of God, a revelation that addresses him and that confronts him at all times with the responsibility to serve God with his whole heart; that man has been corrupted in his entire being by the fall into sin, so that he is of himself unable, apart from the principle of regeneration, to come to a true interpretation and expression of this revelation of God; and that in Christ is God's final revelation, the hub of interpretation both of the inner meaning of the creation and also of the redemption that God has provided for the salvation of lost mankind.

Thus in his important pamphlet, "Why I Believe in God," Van Til does not consider his early Christian training and his Christian commitment to be accidental matters, in essence irrelevant to his intellectual stance; instead, these represent the framework within which thought and experience have their true foundation and apart from which they fall away into meaninglessness.

This has then been paramount in establishing Van Til's polemical, apologetical stance. If one fails to assume a starting point that presupposes the Christian faith, he has no foundation for making intelligible judgments at all. Unbelieving man must be challenged with this claim. And over against his claims must be set the claim of Jesus Christ, which alone is adequate to make experience meaningful.

Thus it was Van Til who conceived of a progressive apologetics, which sought to entrench itself solidly behind the strong walls of historic Christianity, using the weapons forged by the richest stream of theological thought, and challenging the opponent, not only to wrest the initiative away from him but even to deny him a solid position from which to launch an attack at all. Paradoxically this apologetical method build upon the foundation which was laid by Kuyper himself; it sought to avoid that which in Kuyper's eyes stigmatized all previous apologetical method.

Van Til's apologetics pointed in two directions at once. It tried to show that it is only on the foundation of Christian presuppositions that meaningful discourse is possible. It also tried to show that the failure on the part of non-Christian thinking to attain the true starting point of thought means that it is impaled on the horns of a dilemma. Its attempt to interpret everything according to a criterion acceptable to the autonomous man means that it is driven inexorably to the opposite, namely, to an irrationalism in which meaningful discourse has become impossible. No matter what the difficulties may be, considered in detail, there is the possibility of a meaningful approach to thought and to life only when one is entrenched solidly behind the walls of a full-orbed expression of the Christian theistic position.

The method is, then, not to reason to the full theistic position from a standpoint outside of it, but to stand within the Christian theistic position itself. To fail to stand within this position, and to recognize that God's being is that of the Creator and that man's is that of the creature, is perforce to take a principle of unity that embraces both God and man and that thereby excludes the Creator-creature relationship. Van Til is ready, for the sake of argument, to take the position of the opponent, the one who has rejected the Creator-creature distinction and is therefore bound to set up his own standard as to the unity and the diversity which is in the cosmos. Every possible starting point the autonomous man can assume is not embracive enough, not inclusive enough to interpret all of the facts. One is always confronted with facts that at least possibly will not fit into his scheme of interpretation. His interpretation of the universe along lines that he himself thinks in terms of his self-sufficient reason (his abstract rationalism) strikes up against the irreducible brute facts which he must fail to incorporate in his system (his irrationalism). That one starts out with an autonomous rationality means inevitably that he will land up with an irrationalism. This should be pointed out concerning every possible non-theistic starting point (of which there is really basically only one) in order that the autonomous man may be shown the inherent hopelessness of his position and be challenged to accept the Christian theistic world view, only in terms of which is there the possibility of predication.

☙ ☙ ☙

The forces at work in Reformed thought have produced a number of apologists who may be called "presuppositionalist" and who in some measure at least have sought to erect an apologetics on a different foundation from that of the classical evangelical position. Van Til, of course, belongs to this number; but so do Gordon H. Clark and Edward John Carnell. All of these are opposed by a number of thinkers who have never felt that the older apologetics has been severely challenged or by men who are fully aware of the method of the new apologetics but have chosen consciously to oppose it.

Prominent among the presuppositionalists has been Gordon H. Clark of Butler University. Clark has maintained that it is impossible to reach a complete, rational foundation for one's world view. A world view must be opted, by the Christian and by the non-Christian alike. The set of presuppositions must be chosen which is able to introduce the maximum amount of coherence into one's position. Clark has consistently argued that it is the central axioms which can be derived from the Christian faith that can bring the maximum amount of consistency into the interpretation of one's experience. Although for the finite mind this consistency cannot be perfect, nevertheless the difference is so great that the choice for the Christian faith is clearly preferable. Thus Clark's apologetical method has entailed showing the internal inconsistencies of the alternatives to the Christian faith and commending Christianity as the option that is most able to produce rational interpretation.

Insofar as Clark maintains that a coherent explanation of experience depends upon the choice of a set of axioms, he can be called a "presuppositionalist." The criterion of adequacy, that of logical consistency, gives Clark's position a rationalistic cast.[3]

In his writings Clark extols reason far more than the majority of secular philosophers do. There is an acid rebuttal of anyone who would ascribe to the idea of truth anything but an analytical sense. According to Clark, truth can be expressed only in propositions. It is only propositions that can be true or false. Furthermore, true propositions are regarded to be true unqualifiedly. Any deviation from this point of view, he thinks, must be unmasked as at best an incipient irrationalism.

As to its method, Carnell's early book, *An Introduction to Christian Apologetics*, follows Clark's position closely. In his early apologetical stance Carnell seemed to be clearly a disciple of Gordon Clark. Later, however, a clear difference emerged between them. The rift can be accounted for in part by a decided shift in emphasis on Clark's part. It also involves, however, a change in Carnell's position. In his later writings he gives a much broader interpretation of the basis of his apologetical method.

Clark has now taken the position that the predicates "true" and "knowledge" can be ascribed only to what is contained in the Scriptures of the Old and New Testaments, as the infallible word of God, and what may be deduced therefrom by good and necessary inference. Whatever is derived from other sources – e.g., from experience – may indeed be helpful and convenient; but it cannot lay claim to being truth and knowledge.

Thus Clark now chooses as his central axiom the statement, "The Bible is the Word of God." Having opted thereby for what is to be the source of true statements, he then proceeds to deduce by strict logical inference the truths, the knowledge which can be derived from this axiom system.

This development in the statement of Clark's position is discussed at some length by Dr. Ronald Nash in the volume, *The Philosophy of Gordon H. Clark*.[4] To Nash's mind the new statement involves a major shift, an unfortunate departure, from Clark's earlier viewpoint. Nash leaves the impression that he wants to follow the lead of Carnell. He rejects Clark's new position and stresses the criterion of systematic consistency.

It must be questioned, however, how much Clark's present statement is a real departure from his earlier view. Was it included by implication, or at least as one of the possible consequences, of his earlier viewpoint? Does the present statement simply involve the development in a particular direction of the tendencies within his thought?

If Clark always insisted that one must decide for a system of axioms, and if these axioms were propositions which were unqualifiedly true, the question would naturally arise as to the source of these preferred statements. Clark always discovered the source of these fundamental axioms in the Christian faith. Their origin is in the intellect of the sovereign God, who knows all things and is therefore able to know all things correctly. It would follow that it is only by divine revelation that these propositions would be available. Since the Scriptures are the revelation of God, the repository of the divine truths, they easily become the exclusive source for what, in Clark's eyes, has the only claim to being truth and knowledge. So it becomes understandable that he accepts as his central axiom, "The Bible is the Word of God." By this means he establishes the truth and knowledge status of all the statements in the Scriptures. These then serve as subsidiary axioms, universal propositions from which one can deduce additional knowledge.

Clark's position is that of a metaphysical theism in which truth and knowledge are restricted to theoretically founded statements. The source of knowledge is the complete theoretical intuition in the divine mind and whatever portion of that knowledge God has chosen to reveal. Knowledge is possible only because of God's theoretical intuition and only because he has revealed part of that truth in an infallible book.

Carnell, as we have observed, learned much from Clark. In his early thought he was presuppositional and rationalistic. Yet, it appears to me that even in his early thought he did not stress as much as Clark did the metaphysical founding of the principle of formal consistency. Carnell insisted that knowledge depended upon choosing fundamental axioms; but his emphasis lay on testing these axioms by applying the principle of logical consistency. The test of an option is its capability of introducing a superior measure of consistency. The rational man, Carnell said, would accept the system that is attended by the fewest difficulties.

Although he was a pupil of Clark and was long regarded to be an advocate of a Christian rationalism, Carnell's works after his *Apologetics* demand a broader basis of interpretation. Carnell's later development took him well out of the sphere of Gordon Clark, and even requires a re-interpretation of the *Apologetics* itself.

As we have remarked, Carnell did not stress as did Clark the founding of the principle of formal consistency in a metaphysic. He does not escape the problem of content, however. He only approaches it in a different way. The problem appears in his search for a point of contact in "culture" for the Christian faith. His thought then moves in various directions, along functional lines, as he thinks he can find such a point of contact first in one and then in another place.

This insight, it seems to me, is the only means of conceiving as a unity the methodology of his diverse writings. In his early *Apologetics* he seeks his point of contact in the human rational faculty; in *A Philosophy of the Christian Religion* he appeals to values; in *Christian Commitment* it is the judicial sentiment which he exploits; and in his later *The Kingdom of Love and the Pride of Life* he seeks to make contact with the unspoiled consciousness of the happy child.[5] In each case he supposes that he has discovered a fulcrum about which an argument for Christianity can turn. If one can bring the unbeliever to recognize the deeper implications of what he himself is saying, he can lead him gradually into an acceptance of the Christian position.

It is probably Ronald Nash who stands closest to Carnell's early position. He shows, on the one hand, a disinclination to go along with Clark in the outworking of his metaphysical grounding of the principle of logical consistency. On the other hand, there is no indication that Nash is committed to Carnell's later attempt to throw a bridge over between Christianity and culture, by discovering various points of contact between them. Nash appears to want to settle for the law of contradiction, without giving any essential place to a metaphysical foundation for it. In this respect he appears to stand close to the early position of Carnell.

The above positions all claim in some fashion to be presuppositionalist; yet, they all suffer from the disability of not challenging fundamentally enough the neutrality of thought. Clark's position reserves the predicates "knowledge" and "truth" for what is in the Scriptures and to what may be deduced from them. In contrast, what we learn from experience can have only a certain usefulness. Thus he is content to accept an operational interpretation of scientific concepts. Scientific theories are useful in controlling nature; but they have no claim to truth. Thus it is impossible that science should ever be able to challenge the truth content of the Scriptures. Yet, the position on the foundation of which Clark makes this claim also involves that the truth of Scripture does not possess any intrinsic relevancy to scientific investigation. It simply towers over it, as truth towering over that which is useful but not truth. In its own domain, so long as it is content to remain with its claim to operational significance, science goes its own way.

The identification of knowledge with what is absolutely adequate theoretically, and thus with what emanates by revelation from the divine archetypal intellect, paired with the assertion that the content of the Scriptures, as the revelation of God, has exclusive claim to the status of truth, brings with it some interesting consequences. The exalted status of adequately grounded theoretical knowledge is thus accorded to the request of Paul concerning the cloak he left at Troas, while the intimate awareness which exists between husband and wife is denied the status of knowledge altogether, because it is not revealed in Scripture. To be more exact, it might be said to be knowledge that there is a relationship between husband and wife which is called "knowing"; because the Scriptures teach that there is. But on Clark's testimony it is impossible for one to say that he "knows" that such a one is his wife.

The method of the later Carnell is one that expressly seeks a common ground between the Christian and the non-Christian positions. His method is to seek a common ground between the believer and the unbeliever. The kingdom of love, which is the point of contact he seeks in his book, *The Kingdom of Love and the Pride of Life*, is a purely natural love and not an evangelical one. It is the kingdom which is intuited by one who is acting as a happy child would act, according to the dictates of the heart, one who has not yet been duped into the self-assertiveness of the will to power. Carnell's method is to establish a common ground in what "happy children" or "all good men" intuitively feel, and then seek to throw a bridge over to what is specifically Christian, "for the kingdom of heaven is the eternal phase of the kingdom of love." [6] The clash, or at least the uneasy juxtaposition of these two elements (generally religious and specifically Christian) is all too apparent. That is evident, for example, in Carnell's discussion of death. The heart, we are informed, acquaints us with the proper etiquette for attending a funeral. "Since the bereaved have united their hearts with the departed, they cannot believe that death has spoken the last word. They know that if the dead do not count, then the living do not count, for the living and the dead form one unbroken fellowship. Thus, a good person will do his best to assure the bereaved that death has not dissolved the kingdom of love, and that in the kingdom of heaven there will be a renewal of lost fellowship. This means that whenever a person communicates assurances of hope to the bereaved, he is really saying that the soul is immortal and that God will overrule the verdict of death."[7] From such a sentiment, which Carnell appears to ascribe to everyone who intuits like a child, the transition to the more specifically Christian idea of a double resurrection, both of the just and the unjust, appears to be possible only by a sleight of hand.[8]

Methodologically, Carnell announces that his approach is unified. His method is to erect a bridge, by whatever means, between Christianity and culture. However, the term "culture" is used in a popular but very undefined sense to include whatever falls within the human realm, outside of the gospel. Thus a bridge is to be thrown between the human and the divine, between the temporal and the eternal. This clearly does not provide a basis for avoiding the danger of method dispersing in all kinds of directions. Appeal is made at one time to the law of contradiction (the analytical function), at another time to the judicial sentiment (an analogy within the juridical sphere), at another time to the law of love (considered as the sentiment of the healthy child, thus possibly as a sense of harmonious life). What then is to tie these together? Does not the idea of truth dissipate in all directions? Further, if the conception of truth is not controlled from the outset by the Christian commitment, will not the transition from any supposed point of contact in "culture" to the specifics of the Christian faith always take place by an illegitimate infusion of the new wine of Christian meaning into the old skins of unbelieving thought? At least in the above volume the transition appears to be a violent one.

Another apologist who lays claim to being a presuppositionalist and who has been attracting attention recently is Dr. Francis Schaeffer of L'Abri, Switzerland. He has become especially popular for his critique of culture from a Christian point of view. He has been particularly concerned to trace in modern thought and culture a trend towards irrationalism and despair, which is the result of the failure to start with the supposition of the Christian faith.

In his method Schaeffer lays special stress, like Clark and Carnell, on the law of contradiction, especially on the law of excluded middle. One of his most frequent complaints is that thinkers have laid aside the analytical distinction between truth and falsehood. Instead of holding that there is an either-or, they assert that there is a both-and. Thus instead of analytical distinction there is a fateful synthetic attitude, which blurs boundaries. There is a point, he maintains, in the history of thought, somewhere in the period between Kant and Hegel, that the line was crossed irremediably from an analytic to a synthetic point of view. This line he calls the "line of despair."

There is, it must be admitted, a real element of truth in Schaeffer's contention that something happened about this time to the idea of truth. There came into being a dialectical logic, which sanctioned the antinomy. This logic is certainly present in Hegel. Further, even though it is difficult to see why Schaeffer is so nonchalant about setting Kierkegaard on one line with Hegel, when the former set his either-or sharply over against Hegel's both-and; nevertheless, a deeper acquaintance with Kierkegaard reveals that he, too, in his idea of truth had little respect for the ordinary canons of logic and that for him existential truth is paradoxical. From these nineteenth-century thinkers it is not difficult to trace a line of irrationalism down into the present and to illustrate this irrationalism in all kinds of movements within contemporary culture.

One thing among others that Schaeffer leaves unexplained, however, is why the apostate philosophy was that much better before it learned to employ dialectical logic. Is a philosophy *per se* better which is willing to employ simple analytical distinctions, distinguishing, for example, formally between truth and untruth? The answer might lie, as far as Schaeffer is concerned, within his method itself. His critique of the loss of the will to distinguish is propaedeutic. To one to whom the very distinction between truth and falsehood has become blurred, one cannot even speak intelligibly of the gospel. Thus there is the necessity of re-establishing the possibility of communication before one actually proceeds to present the gospel or an apologetic in the narrower sense of the term.

Schaeffer does not ask, however, whether the same apostate motives that are at work in philosophies where there is a rejection of the law of excluded middle and an adoption of a dialectical method are also at work in philosophies where there is a clear distinction between what is true and what is false. He simply tries to reinstate the making of distinctions. Among many who call themselves "presuppositionalists," it is the custom to defend the law of contradiction on the grounds that it is the only possible foundation for intelligible discourse whatsoever, even of the discourse that might go into its own denials. Possibly Schaeffer would be content with such a defense of the law of contradiction and its companion, the law of excluded middle. At least, I have not seen him discuss the question whether there are inherent limits to logic. Even if we grant, however, that all intelligible discourse involves making distinctions, it does not follow that the analytical function is its own foundation, or that it is without limits, or even that all of the law-structures in the creation must be approachable simply by way of analytical distinction.

⚒ ⚒ ⚒

A full discussion of progressive and regressive tendencies in Christian apologetics would have to deal also with those positions which do not see any inherent difficulties with the classical apologetical approaches. A notable case is the view being set forth by John Warwick Montgomery, which he admits is an attempt to revive the type of method advocated by Bishop Butler. Such a discussion is beyond the scope of what can be included here. We must be satisfied with bringing out some of the tendencies of those systems which call themselves "presuppositional," both those which are consistently so and those which allow some element of neutrality in their method.

It is characteristic of Van Til that he has sought to be consistently presuppositional, and his criticism of other positions always centers in the fact that in some way they have fallen short and have introduced an element of neutrality and of autonomy. They have fallen prey to a regressive tendency in apologetical method. Van Til, on the contrary, wants to be truly progressive.

Van Til has asserted again and again, therefore, that one cannot prove Christianity directly. That is an impossible undertaking, because it is impossible to assume a stance outside of Christianity in a meaningful way from which such a proof could proceed. Thus, as we have said, Van Til must entrench himself within the walls of the Christian faith, and he must argue from the impossibility of the contrary. This method seeks to establish an indirect proof of the faith. An outstanding characteristic of Van Til's method is that it is concrete – that it takes into consideration in an intimate way from the outset the full involvement of the committed Christian believer, with his entire background and training. Moreover, it takes into consideration that this believer is one who is responding to God in his revelation, through which the believer knows himself to have been created by God, to have fallen into sin, and to be redeemed in Christ. We have observed that this concreteness is characteristic of a transcendental approach. It involves that there is in all one's activities a reflection back on oneself in the fullness of his selfhood. In this sense, a carefully guarded one, the method might also be called "existential." In this spirit Van Til has continually stressed that man must be seen as a covenant being, one who is continually responding at the very center of his existence, where all his activities come to a focus, to the self-revelation of God through Christ.

With this method we are in fundamental and hearty agreement. Carrying on in the transcendental line, while purifying it of elements foreign to a truly Christian approach, belongs today, we think, to a progressive apologetical stance. It is in this spirit of fundamental agreement and in the same spirit of desiring to further discussion in the interests of stimulating a more progressive attitude in apologetics that we are constrained to pose certain questions concerning this very important movement.

↙ ↙ ↙

How do certain elements of Van Til's thought square with his often-asserted stress on the central focusing of man in all of his functions in a unity on God in his self-revelation in Christ?

Van Til maintains that there are only two basic starting points, the believing one and the unbelieving one. The believer will recognize that he is a creature of God and that God is his Creator. In everything he will recognize that he is dependent upon God. The unbeliever will set himself up in the place of God, denying in effect the Creator-creature distinction. Christian thought is consistent only when it takes the Creator-creature distinction fully into consideration. It is important to note the exact meaning that attaches to the recognition of creatureliness. It means, indeed, that the creature recognizes himself to be dependent altogether on God, who is sufficient to himself – "self-contained," as Van Til would say. This self-sufficiency involves also that God knows all things, because all things are comprised in his creative will. The recognition of creatureliness involves for Van Til, therefore, the recognition that there is a prior and completely adequate theoretical knowledge of a creative character (analysis) in God, both of himself and of his creation, and that all human activity in knowing must be viewed on the background of this original knowing, all limited comprehension on the background of the complete comprehension in the divine mind. Thus the creature must think analogically, thinking the thoughts of God after him.

The denial of creatureliness in this respect Van Til associates with a claim to have complete comprehension on the human side. That cannot mean simply that the unbeliever asserts that he has complete comprehension of everything. That is nowadays generally denied, and Van Til is aware that most thinkers reject the notion that it is possible for man to have complete knowledge. In Van Til's thought the term "comprehensive knowledge" has in this connection a technical meaning. It is any claim to knowledge which does not acknowledge that there is a prior (archetypal) theoretical comprehension on the part of God and which does not acknowledge that the human mind is dependent in its own interpretation, as it tries to fit together the web of its experience, upon that prior interpretation. Thus, whether the unbeliever claims to know all things or not, he in effect asserts that he knows all things if he sets up his own judgment as the standard. Even if he does nothing else, he makes in effect the universal negative judgment that there is no archetypal intellect to whose thoughts he must submit.

It is indeed of the utmost importance to claim, as Van Til does, that there is an analogical relationship between man and God, and between God's activity and man's activity, in the sense that they never should be thought to be set over against each other. Man's thought and activity must always be related to God's. Man lives *coram deo*. As Van Til himself puts it, man must be aware that he is living in a totally personal environment and that in all parts of his self and his activity he is responsible and responding to God in his self-disclosure. Precisely how should that analogical relationship between God and man be conceived, however? At what point does man's life come to a focus in its relationship to God? Van Til would undoubtedly reply, as he has done many times, that the focal point is at the very heart of man's existence, as Kuyper put it, where the rays of his life come together.

There is, however, an element in Van Til's approach that leads us to broach questions, and to compare his position with that of the philosophy he himself has ardently recommended for many years, the philosophy of the cosmonomic idea of Vollenhoven and Dooyeweerd.

For Van Til the model for the divine intellect seems to be the analytical judgment. Van Til describes God's knowledge as analytical. That is to say, whatever content is comprised in it is there from the very outset. God is completely open to himself. There is nothing new for God either in himself or in his creation. On the contrary, man's knowledge is synthetic, in the sense that there must always be the weaving of new experiences into the fabric of what is already known. Thus Van Til can say that the synthetic activity of the human mind is possible on the background of the prior analysis of the divine mind.

Such a view brings up immediately the question of the foundation of theoretical thought. Van Til does indeed claim that human theoretical thought is in need of a foundation. This foundation is discovered, however, not in something beyond theoretical thought but in the archetypal theoretical intuition of the divine intellect. For this reason it cannot be said that Van Til dismisses *per se* the ideal of comprehensive theoretical knowledge. In order to know anything, it is necessary to know everything theoretically – i.e., at least on one level. It is not necessary on the human level to know everything in order to know anything truly, because there is already comprehensive knowledge on the divine level, and God can convey truth to us. To infer that one can have comprehensive knowledge on the human level is, as we have seen, to deny in effect the Creator-creature relationship. To retain the Creator-creature distinction one must accept the limitedness of his own theoretical knowledge and confess his dependence on the prior analysis in the mind of God.

The place that Van Til gives to the theoretical-logical is being emphasized by his current criticism of the distinction between the pre-theoretical and the theoretical. He is asserting that if there is to be intelligibility all discourse must be at least incipiently theoretical. This position, it would appear, makes theoretical thought the locus of intelligibility, the ground of meaning. However such a position might possibly clash with other thoughts in Van Til's philosophy, it certainly dovetails with the status he gives to theoretical analysis in the archetypal intellect.

Our discussion has brought into focus a disagreement between Van Til's position and that of the cosmonomic idea philosophy which demands careful scrutiny. One of the beginning insights of the philosophy of Vollenhoven and Dooyeweerd was that the logical (analytical)[9] is an aspect of the cosmos, dependent for its meaning upon a created structure of reality which is itself not analytical in character. Thus in his early writing, *Logos en ratio*, Vollenhoven struck out against the logos doctrine, which had had such a history in both Christian and non-Christian thought. Logical distinction was itself possible because of the divinely created order in which the logical aspect was embedded. Furthermore, even though the making of a logical judgment was an act which was logically qualified, it could not be thought that man's act-life as such was so qualified. The logical was only one aspect among many of man's total act. Thus analytical distinction takes place in every human act; but man's act life as such cannot be properly conceived as itself being logically qualified. This insight was to have considerable implications for the entire scheme of concept-formation as it was developed in this philosophy.

Thus, for the cosmonomic idea philosophy, meaning and intelligibility do not have their foundation even in the logical – much less in the theoretical-logical, which is a deepening of the logical (analytical) distinguishing which accompanies all our activities.

Thus, too, as one is brought to reflect upon the unity of his selfhood, in the concentrating of his entire life on God in Christ, he cannot think of this concentrating as having a theoretical-logical focus.

For Van Til also the focus of man's life in its wholeness should be deeper than the theoretical-logical. Van Til has constantly asserted that no function of man (his intellect, his will, or his emotions) should have the primacy. He has battled against the prevalent notion of the primacy of the intellect. Nevertheless, it must be asked whether Van Til's metaphysical notion of the archetypal intellect does not clash with the more central notion that man in the center of his being is constantly in the act of responding to God in his self-revelation in Christ. A clearer resolution of this problem is a pressing need.

✒ ✒ ✒

Without entering into a full discussion, we shall simply sketch at this point a number of the issues that arise if one holds that the concentration point of intelligibility and truth lies in theoretical thought, e.g., in a divine archetypal intellect. These points will be phrased largely in question form, to stimulate the discussion that must arise concerning these crucial problem areas.

1. A particular aspect of Van Til's presentation bears mention first, which concerns his appeal to the analytical judgment. The analytical judgment is one in which there is nothing in the predicate which is not contained already in the subject. In the synthetic judgment, on the contrary, the predicate adds something that is not contained in the subject. It appears that Van Til's approach, even if inadvertently, draws heavily on this distinction. It plays a role in describing the difference between divine archetypal thought (analytical) and human ectypal thought (synthetical). Even if one should grant that it was never the intention to say that the divine intellect is an analytical judgment (which, we admit, would have a strange sound), and if one should grant the possibility that the analytical judgment provides only a philosophical expression for the divine creative sovereignty; nevertheless, the use of this model influences the discussion in an interesting fashion.

Prominent in the definition of the analytical judgment is the question of logical extension. What is included in the subject? Is anything included in the predicate that is not already in the subject? Characteristic of the synthetic judgment is that something new is added to the subject. There is the need of synthesizing the new with what is present already. The question then arises, whether the prominence given to the idea of logical extension will lead to certain emphases, e.g., upon prediction, to the exclusion of others.

No one who truly confesses the Christian doctrines of God's sovereignty and creation will admit that anything falls outside the scope of God's sovereign disposition. He will not admit that there is any counter-force to God, something that is past, present, or future which falls outside his knowledge and his plan. Putting this confession in the context of the pattern of the analytic judgment, however, may well account for peculiarities in the discussion. If on the philosophical level the problem is understood as to whether there is or there is not anything new, as to whether there are any new facts to be incorporated in one's system, and if the crux is discovered in relating one's own finite situation, in which there are new facts, to God, for whom there are no new facts; then the question may have been put in such a way as to eliminate important perspectives. It keeps the discussion on the concrete (plastic) level of individual things (one speaks of "facts" and "events," etc.). It may well obscure the structural question of the law-order of the creation, for this law-order is one which is an overarching framework which makes "facts" and "events," etc., possible. Further, if what the cosmonomic idea philosophy says is true, this framework cannot be described in logical terms; for logic is but one aspect among others of the order, and each one of the meaning aspects of the order is transcendental in character and is not of the nature of a logical category.

2. Our discussion leads us then naturally into another question, whether if we take the theoretical-logical as the concentration point we can do justice to the problem of the formation of theoretical concepts. Taking such a position would appear to entail that the order of the cosmos is itself understood ultimately in terms of theoretical-logical distinctions. Is this the case?

Characteristic of the approach of the cosmonomic idea philosophy is the idea that one cannot understand the basic structure of things in terms of more general and more specific concepts (genera and species). Taking the idea that meaning must be understood in theoretical-logical terms must hide from view the transcendental character of the meaning of the various sides of reality, must eliminate the possibility of understanding the structures of individual things (which do not subject themselves to being understood in terms of genus and species, whole and part), and must obscure the transcendental direction to the point where the rays of life come together, a "point" which is not one aspect or part of the cosmos in distinction from any other part, but that in which all of the rays of the cosmos find their focus or concentration.

To our mind, it also cuts one off from exploring a fruitful avenue to understanding the meaning of the central biblical commandment of love. The latter may not be understood as a particular virtue among others. It is that in which all of the powers of man, in all of their fullness, are oriented to God, responding to him in his self-disclosure in his revelation.

3. The question of concept-formation leads us directly into yet another. If the ground of intelligibility and meaning is found in the theoretical-logical, are we not faced with a problem? If we admit then that something is not theoretical-logical, we say in effect that it falls outside of the locus of meaning. In that case we must account for the respect in which this non-theoretical element falls short. One of the most common ways of accounting for this, of course, has been by distinguishing between the theoretical-logical and sensation. We have encountered a position, that of Gordon Clark, in which the theoretical-logical is said to coincide with knowledge, but is then distinguished and set over against the terrain of what has operational usefulness.

One can identify this respect in which something falls outside of the locus of meaning, it would seem, only by setting it up *over against* the source of meaning. This is, however, to give up the possibility philosophically of accounting for the coherence and unity of the cosmos. We can render such an account only if we discover a totality of meaning in which all the rays of the cosmos have their focus. It is possible only if the ultimate perspective of thought is seen in a religious concentration on a unity which transcends all of the diversity of the cosmos and thus transcends the possibility of setting up one thing over against another.

Is it not better to lay aside the notion that the locus of meaning resides in the theoretical-logical, and to see the theoretical-logical as a human activity which is taken up in the law-order of God's creation, an activity which must depend upon this law-order for its possibility and whose final service must be a constant transcendental reflection back on the point transcending itself out of which it lives and in terms of which it has its impulse and direction?

4. If the above question is to be answered in the affirmative, and if theoretical-logical thought is to be considered as being transcendental, are we not required to enter into a critique of thought as such, to lay bare its ultimate driving motives and to see that it becomes aware of its ultimate-

ly transcendental character? Indeed, in the present stage of discussion in Reformed circles, this is a question that cannot be ignored and is one that is of the utmost concern for a progressive apologetical stance.

If one considers the source of meaning to be in the theoretical-logical, and if he sanctions this idea by seeing the fullness of theoretical knowledge in the divine archetypal intellect, is he not restricted to setting finite theoretical apprehension on the background of ultimate theoretical apprehension? This indeed might be classed as an attempt to found finite understanding transcendentally in the complete theoretical intuition of the divine intellect; nevertheless, it would appear to exclude the very possibility of entering into a critical, transcendental discussion of the roots of theoretical thinking *per se*.

In the interests of the conceptual clarification of the problems confronting Reformed thinking today, it is of real concern that questions such as the above be faced. They have been set forth here in the interests of furthering the discussion of that progressive apologetics that Van Til has introduced into the Reformed arsenal.

REFERENCES

1. This is the pendant in Orr of the idealistic claim that taking any abstract point of view leads thought inevitably into its opposite. To seek the ground of meaning is to involve oneself inevitably in meaninglessness.

2. In his syllabus, *Evidences*, Van Til commends James Orr for his transcendental method. He offers some corrective ideas; but in general he sides with the elements of the method which we are highlighting.

3. Even though Clark's position may be called "presuppositionalist," it is questionable in what sense it is transcendental. Clark does not bring one to reflect on what is the fundamental driving motive of his thought.

4. Ronald H. Nash, ed., *The Philosophy of Gordon Clark* (Philadelphia: Presbyterian and Reformed Publishing Co., 1968).

5. Edward John Carnell, *The Kingdom of Love and the Pride of Life* (Grand Rapids: Eerdmans, 1960), 6.

6. Ibid. 19.

7. Ibid. 21.

8. Ibid. 97.

9. We have used the term "analytical" in the sense it has in the expression "analytical judgment" and also in the sense pertaining to the analytic aspect of logical distinguishing. We use it here in the latter sense.

CROSSCURRENTS

The collection of essays presented to Dr. C. Van Til and the responses he has made to them in the dedicatory volume celebrating his 75th birthday[1] have touched issues of such fundamental importance that a continuation of the discussion is highly desirable. In fact, for anyone who wishes to labor in the spirit of Van Til's reformational apologetics a firm grasp of certain of these problems has become a necessity. It is in the interests of furthering this discussion and of bringing it into a greater degree of understanding concerning my own contribution that I write what follows.

In the latter part of my essay[2] there is a pointed summarization of certain lines of thought in Van Til followed by four questions that arise if someone takes his point of departure within the theoretical attitude of thought. It is important to understand this section of my essays in terms of what has preceded. The intent and force of the questioning can be understood only in terms of my previous description and interpretation of Van Til's position as an illustration of transcendental apologetical method. This I presented as the most advanced and progressive effort today in the age-old attempt to relate the message of the Scriptures to those whom Schleiermacher called its cultured despisers. This earlier section comprises the body of the essay. The latter section was intended to pose the question, in effect, whether certain indicated lines of thought in Van Til really belong within the transcendental apologetical framework that had just been sketched. These questions were not intended at all to muffle the positive note that had been sounded before[3]; they were intended to accomplish precisely what was described in the closing sentence of the essay: "They [the questions] have been set forth here in the interests of furthering the discussion of that progressive apologetics that Van Til has introduced into the Reformed arsenal."[4]

It must be understood, therefore, that the line of questioning at the conclusion of my essay does not intend to pinpoint what I believe are the fundamental, controlling elements of Van Til's thought. That is especially true of the four numbered questions at the very end. It is likely a tactical blunder that Van Til's name is mentioned at all in this very last section. The thrust of the discussion here is described in the first full paragraph of page 295, where I say, "... we shall simply sketch at this point a number of the issues that arise if one holds that the concentration point of intelligibility and truth lies in theoretical thought...." The content of the discussion is, therefore, general. It would indeed be foolish to claim that these questions were not intended to refer at all to Van Til's thought. They do; but the reference is at most oblique.

Understanding the structure of my essay has a bearing on its interpretation. When I ask, for example, whether one can understand the central idea of love in the Scriptures if he has started within the theoretical attitude of thought, I do not mean to suggest that Van Til himself has fundamentally misunderstood the Scriptural view of love. The point I am making is simply that whoever begins within the theoretical attitude of thought will be hindered from giving an adequate account of the central idea of love. This distinction, it seems to me, is blurred when Van Til claims that I aver, "By my adherence to the notion of the archetypal intellect I am cut off from a fruitful understanding of the 'meaning of the central biblical commandment of love'."[5] Again, when I stated that in Van Til's thought the analytical judgment had become the model for the divine intellect – the assertion that has apparently drawn Van Til's attention the most – I did not mean to say that Van Til first formulated an idea of the analytical judgment and then proceeded to construct his idea of God. In both instances, indeed in every instance, the critical summarization and questioning were carried out against the background of an appreciation for the profoundly scriptural and reformational orientation of Van Til's thought. After having described this position, I simply asked whether there might be elements within his thinking that get in the way.[6]

It might well be objected that what I have made the butt of questioning, far from being something that might be jettisoned, is the heart of Van Til's method. I am fully aware that the line of interpretation I have offered cuts across the grain of much other interpretation. My own interpretation, however, which I have held since my student days and which was suggested strongly by Van Til's own teaching, has the advantage of placing his thought squarely within the circle of the reformational viewpoint he himself has so vigorously advocated and which I myself follow. Thus I emphasized Van Til's understanding of man as a covenant being who is always responding either positively or negatively to God's own self-impartation in his revelation, a point concerning which Van Til has taken appropriate notice in his reply.[7]

Other developing lines of interpretation, on the contrary, place at the center precisely what I have put in question. As a consequence there is an almost complete suppression of the reformational side of Van Til's thought. This paradoxical state of affairs has, I believe, an adequate explanation, but one that I shall not attempt to explore here. The justice of the observation made above, however, may well become evident in the course of events themselves as these interpretations are better understood as to their implications.

In the meanwhile, I stand by the interpretation I have presented in my essay. My purpose now will be to introduce greater clarity into my part in the discussion in the interests of furthering the discussion as a whole.

⚓ ⚓ ⚓

That my essay intended to present a viable interpretation of Van Til and to pose relevant questions for discussion does not remove the fact that Van Til's response is largely negative. There is even the suggestion that I have misunderstood his position.

I should not want to minimize the importance of the issues as far as the construction of a truly Christian methodology is concerned. My own questioning, however, proceeded against the background of a fundamental appreciation of the main thrust of Van Til's position. My interests are basically the same as his. The issues between us, it seems to me, revolve around the question as to how this orientation is to find proper philosophical expression. It is within this context of basic agreement that the discussion of the issues should proceed.

In his reply to my contribution, Van Til denies categorically that he has ever made the theoretical-logical the locus of meaning.[8] He also makes what appears on the surface to be an irrelevant comment, that if he had really made the analytical judgment the model for his view of the divine intellect he would have been thinking along the lines of unbelief.[9] On closer inspection, however, these statements appear to be tied together within Van Til's position, in terms of his understanding of the relation of the Creator and the creation. The issue is referred to the difference between the attitude of the apostate mind, which must think "in general," in terms of something that is supposed to embrace both God and man, and the attitude of the believing mind, which always prefaces its thought with the distinction between the being of God and the being of man. One may not speak "in general"; from the outset the Creator-creature relationship must have constitutive significance. One may not, therefore, legitimately use such terms as "being" or "thought" without taking into consideration whether it is the being or the thought of the Creator or of the creature that is in mind.

Since Van Til identifies the "theoretical-logical" with the attempt of man to construe logically the facts of experience, the suggestion that he might have made the theoretical-logical the locus of meaning is for him tantamount to saying that he has sanctioned the very thinking "in general" that his entire position has been calculated to avoid. It would be to engage in the thought of apostate man, who must absolutize both his being and his knowledge.[10]

On this background it is understandable that my questioning was met with some consternation. It would seem that I have accused him of making thought "in general" constitutive and that I myself have fallen into the same trap by asking for a critique of thought "in general." Within the framework of Van Til's position both would be an expression of the apostate and not of the regenerate mind.[11]

When I spoke of things "in general" I did not mean, however, to affirm what Van Til rightly denies, that one can properly deal with being apart from the Creator-creature relationship and that there is a being that embraces both God and the creation. My references to this and that "in general" certainly do not encourage the use of human thought apart from divine revelation and apart from the awareness of its own limitations in the face of that revelation; they are only in the interests of what Van Til himself has encouraged as long as I can remember, namely, a structural analysis of God's creation.[12] It is my view also that there is such a created structure, including a structure of theoretical-logical thought, one that is capable of being laid open by careful analysis. In my opinion, therefore, to speak of things "in general" is not necessarily to speak of these as "neutral," as constructs of apostate thinking.

For the construction of a Christian philosophy and apologetics the issue concerning the meaning of "generality" is more important than might appear on the surface. The position I have represented holds that there is a created order of reality in common to the believer and the unbeliever alike, but turned, as D. H. Th. Vollenhoven puts it, either to the "right" or the "left" according to the religious attitude of the heart as it responds either in obedience or in disobedience to God's disclosure of himself in his revelation. As I point out in my essay, Van Til also emphasizes this heart response to God's revelation. He understands the Creator-creature relationship, however, as that of two kinds of being,[13] with the requirement of defining both the beings and the relationship between them. "Generality" is interpreted to mean the expression of the apostate mind that, ignoring the Creator-creature relationship, takes something to embrace both the being of God and the being of man. If one should thoroughly examine this question of generality, he would most likely have uncovered the central problem at issue.

My own questioning also focused on this problem, which is at bottom the problem of transcendence. In my essay I expressed my agreement with Van Til's teaching that man is a covenant being, surrounded with the completely personal environment of God's revelation.[14] I affirmed the importance of holding that there is an analogical relationship between God and man. My question was, "Precisely how should that analogical relationship between God and man be conceived, however?"[15]

This, and not that of the analytical judgment, is the central question I asked. In continuing the discussion I first associated Van Til's view with that of Abraham Kuyper, that the focus of man's existence is in the heart, where the rays of his life come together. Then, however, I went on to ask whether in his definition of God and his relationship to the creation Van Til has not imported certain notions that distort his basically correct understanding of man's heart relationship to God. It is at this point that my question belongs concerning Van Til's use of the analytical judgment. What I claim is that the use of the distinction of analytic and synthetic structures his point of view, screening out certain perspectives.

Before one objects to my line of questioning, he ought to take note of the fact that Van Til readily admits that he took over the analytic-synthetic distinction from idealistic philosophy. This was in line with his practice of employing concepts from the philosophy contemporary with him at the beginning of his career to express theological truths. This he did for the sake of communication.[16] In his reply to me Van Til explains why he used the term "analytical,"[17] to express that "God does not need to look beyond himself for additions to his knowledge,"[18] an explanation that tallies with my own discussion.[19] Furthermore, with respect to the notion of the divine archetypal intellect, he refers to it in so many words.[20] Again and again he speaks in terms that imply that in God there is the metaphysical unity of elements, e.g., subject and object, that must remain discrete on the creaturely level.[21]

I myself am ready to admit that in making my point about the use of the analytical judgment, I did not allow clearly enough for an aspect of Van Til's thought. There is reason to hold that such terms as "analytical" are not intended by Van Til to hold for the deity in other than a provisional way. Philosophical terms are used to express theological truths. In addition, Van Til says in his reply, as well as elsewhere, "Our knowledge, i.e., our conceptual formations and judgments, are always limiting concepts."[22] This viewpoint is taken into account when I say, "... if one should grant the possibility that the analytical judgment provides only a philosophical expression for the divine creative sovereignty; nevertheless, the use of this model influences the discussion in an interesting fashion."[23] This statement of mine, however, is far enough removed from my original assertion that Van Til has used the analytical judgment as a model that the connection may not be sufficiently clear.

My question is, in effect, whether by his use of such notions as the analytical judgment Van Til does not so structure the discussion as to screen out perspectives. If this is the case, there is sufficient warrrant for calling the analytical judgment a "model." That Van Til can find little sense in my question hangs on his identification of the analytical with the concrete human act of forming concepts and of judging and his correct observation that he has always insisted that this human activity is finite, limited to what God has revealed. If this is the case, how is it possible for one to ask about his use of *the* analytical judgment (in general) as if he thought it could be applied univocally both to God and to man? This line of thought might also be the explanation for the curious assertion that the analytical judgment is an invention of apostate thought.[24] This then would be a judgment considered in and of itself, in general. However, by construing it within the framework of his own thinking, Van Til misses, it seems to me, the force of my questioning. He does not ask himself seriously enough whether there might be some point to my asking him whether in taking upon himself the task of defining God and the Creator-creature relationship he has not elevated some aspect of the created cosmos, using it, however provisionally, as a model, thus screening out perspectives and doing injustice to his proper notion that the center of man's existence is in his heart, where the rays of his life come together. My essay purposefully limited itself to questioning, in order to indicate its own provisional character. It intended to probe, not to pulverize. Nevertheless, my questioning was serious. Indeed, further questioning will be necessary in the interests of clarifying the issues, a clarification that has become necessary if real progress is to be made.

Allowing for the fact that Van Til wants to delimit human theoretical thought and that he insists that human concepts have only the provisional character of limiting concepts, the question is nevertheless inescapable as to precisely how this thought is to be delimited. This question was foremost in my mind when I asked about the foundation of theoretical thought.[25] My answer was that Van Til delimited human theoretical thought by means of the divine archetypal intellect.[26] Does this claim manifest a basic misunderstanding of his position? One must certainly proceed cautiously, taking into consideration what I have just pointed out, that Van Til holds that human concepts have only a limiting character. However, he speaks in such a fashion of the boundary between God and man that my questioning is seen to be relevant.

In defining the divine being Van Til stresses its absoluteness and self-sufficiency, paired with its comprehensive knowledge. In God there is the unity of subject and object, the universal and the particular, and the one and the many. Van Til thinks of God as the concrete universal, the eternal principle of interpretation. For him God is our ultimate constitutive concept. God is described in terms that, if taken at their face value, can only mean that in God there is the metaphysical unity of our experience.[27]

The idea of the divine being, however, is also understood to have a critical function. Van Til understands the boundary between God and man in terms of a critical limitation, that one not suppose that he can attain to the unity that there is in the divine being and knowledge. In fact, one may not take this unity as an ideal to be striven for.[28] As we have said, one absolutizes himself if he supposes that God does not exist as an absolute being to whom he must subject his being and his knowing.[29]

We observe that the boundary between God and man is defined in terms of this critical function, in terms of not bringing to unity elements of experience. That one is a creature means that it is impossible for him to bring to a unity factors that are united in God; it is even reprehensible for him to attempt it.[30] For example, the knowledge situation is described in terms of the problem of the relationship of subject and object. The problem of knowledge has a solution because subject and object are united in the divine mind. Yet to seek for this solution other than on the "eternal level," i.e., within the mind of God, is to violate, even to abrogate, the Creator-creature relationship.

We have asked whether Van Til's understanding of the Creator-creature relationship does not screen out certain perspectives. Here is a case in point. Does not the view just described at once sanction the run-of-the-mill understanding of the subject-object relationship? Does it not lock one into this particular understanding? Does it not forbid him to seek another interpretation, upon pain of absolutizing his own intellect and of destroying the relationship of the Creator to the creature?[31] These are questions that bring this side of Van Til's thinking into confrontation with the attempt of Vollenhoven and Dooyeweerd to embark on a reformation of philosophy, which includes a reinterpretation of the subject-object relationship.

I shall mention one more illustration of this screening process. In his reply Van Til again commends Vollenhoven, [32] in whose work he found support for his "idea that a biblical, covenantal framework of thought includes a Christian view of the place and the function of logic."[33] With Vollenhoven he wishes to speak of the "logical function" and of the "logical aspect." Close inspection reveals, however, that Van Til has a very different notion of what this logical aspect is. In fact, it is questionable whether in terms of his position, as he has reiterated it in his reply, he can come to the kind of insight Vollenhoven has concerning the logical as an aspect.

When Van Til speaks of the logical aspect, he refers to what human logic can embrace, what Vollenhoven would likely call the "analyzable." Human thought, which Van Til identifies with the forming of concepts and judgments,[34] has a certain range. For Van Til, therefore, "aspect" has the sense of "part," namely, that part of things that is within the scope of human logic. The question is, therefore, what is open to man in his formation of concepts and making of judgments. For Vollenhoven and the cosmonomic idea philosophy in general, on the contrary, judgments and acts of judging in their scope are not themselves the logical aspect. They are concrete and individual, possessing a logical aspect. This aspect itself is not a concrete thing; instead, it is a particular "mode" (a "how") in which things exist, one among others in an order of aspects. Concrete, individual things participate in some fashion in every aspect of reality. Thus to understand theoretically the logical judgment and the act of judging logically, one must understand the place of the logical aspect in the order of all the aspects of reality. In this order it has its established place, apart from which it is meaningless. To come to the idea of "aspect" as held by Vollenhoven one must have passed from the concrete (plastic) horizon to the modal horizon of reality. In my essay I asked whether Van Til's line of approach did not restrict him to the concrete level of things.[35]

It is clear that the kind of analysis engaged in above could degenerate into an aimless and theoretically sterile "nitpicking." I should hope therefore that it might be left behind as quickly as possible in favor of a more constructive approach. The examples given above can serve, however, to illustrate the need for further clarification, which will be best accomplished in an atmosphere of free and open discussion on the background of the common interest of constructing a truly Reformed philosophy and apologetics.

⚓ ⚓ ⚓

I readily admit that much of my line of questioning has derived from my interest in confronting Van Til's position with that of the cosmonomic -idea philosophy. That interest has not arisen from a slavish devotion to this philosophy, nor from a desire to be nettlesome. I have been confronted with questions such as those I have asked for a considerable time, and I have long attempted to bring them to discussion. In this I have been prompted by a single overriding consideration. The unity that has long been presumed to exist among the major representatives of the so-called Calvinistic philosophy is no longer so assured as it once seemed. That is not to say that there is no unity. There is as much unity as there is in many another school of philosophy. My own interpretation of Van Til's position, as I have said, places him squarely within the camp of those who hold to this general philosophical position. There is a broad unity of the major proponents of this school, namely, Herman Dooyeweerd, D. H. Th. Vollenhoven, C. Van Til, and Hendrik Stoker, in their attempt to erect a philosophy on the foundation of a Reformed world-and-life-view. But that does not take away the fact that from the outset this broad unity of purpose has covered up a wide divergence of philosophical approaches and solutions. Is that particularly unusual in the history of philosophy? Over the last decade especially there has been a growing sensitivity, perhaps even a hypersensitivity, to these differences. By itself this might and indeed should be brushed aside as inconsequential to the real work of theoretical reflection. More important for the long term is the fact that there is a growing number of dedicated younger men, each of whom must find his own way, if he is to be true to his calling. Each, on the foundation of his basic commitment, must make his decisions in a philosophically responsible fashion. In this situation problems such as those I have raised will have to be formulated and discussed as profoundly and clearly as possible.

My desire, which is reflected in the very structure of my essay, has been to emphasize the unity among the adherents of the reformational philosophical standpoint, while at the same time putting the questions as well as I can both to myself and to others. Thus I myself have put currents into motion, while being sensitive to those which come from other directions. In the crossing and re-crossing of these currents there can be a stimulus to deeper reflection on what it means to think on the foundation of the Word of God.

REFERENCES

1. Ed. Robert Geehan, *Jerusalem and Athens: Critical Discussions on the Theology and Apologetics of Cornelius Van Til* (Philadelphia: Presbyterian and Reformed Publishing Co., 1971). (Hereafter cited as JA.)

2. "Progressive and Regressive Tendencies in Christian Apologetics," JA, 275-298.

3. The attitude taken in my essay, reflected even in its organization, makes it difficult to understand the concluding paragraph of Van Til's summarization of the problems I raised. JA, 299 (second paragraph from the bottom of the page).

4. JA, 298.

5. JA, 299.

6. A gentle reference by Van Til to my query concerning the analytical judgment may be found in his pamphlet Toward a Reformed Apologetics (no place, publisher, or date indicated), 25, where he concedes that as to his use of this notion he may have failed to get his true intentions across. There may still be a misconception of my intent, however, when he states that some have asked whether he is speculative first and scriptural afterward. Whatever others may have thought or written, it was not my intention to place matters in such a simplistic framework.

7. JA, 298.

8. JA, 299.

9. JA, 300.

10. JA, 300.

11. The line of thought described above has been followed through by Douglas Vickers in his review of *Jerusalem and Athens (Westminster Theological Journal*, XXXIV [1971-1972], 174-179), where he engages in vigorous denunciations of my discussion of things "in general." His remarks climax in a sweeping statement that reflects well the fundamental point that Van Til himself is attempting to make in his own reply: "To argue, as Knudsen does, for a 'critique of thought as such ... and ... its ultimately transcendental character' (297) is to expose apologetics to betrayal by empty questions which bypass a Reformed philosophy completely. It fails to confront what Van Til has called ... 'the basic point of the matter ... that *nothing*, no fact or law, can be seen as it truly is except in the light of the revelation of God in Christ through Scripture' (p. 305" (WTJ, XXXIV, p. 177). Vickers's reply itself reflects, however, a fundamental misunderstanding of what I meant by "general."

12. This is encouraged even in Van Til's reply to my essay, "My position is that man should by the logical gifts he has from his Creator discover the 'law-structures' of the universe" (JA, 300).

13. This point is clearly made in one of Van Til's major syllabi, "God has one kind of being ... the universe has another sort of being ..." (*Apologetics*, 1951), 8.

14. JA, 291, 292-293.

15. JA, 293.

16. Van Til, *The Defense of the Faith* (2nd ed., Philadelphia: Presbyterian and Reformed Publishing Co., 1955), 23. (Hereafter cited as DF2).

17. JA, 300-301.

18. JA, 301.

19. JA, 293, 295.

20. In the context of a discussion of the analytical character of God's knowledge – God's "knowledge of himself is ... entirely analytical" – Van Til says that God "knows himself by one simple eternal act of vision." DF2, 37.

21. This is clear in DF2 and in his *Survey of Christian Epistemology* (copyright, Den Dulk Christian Foundation, 1969). (Hereafter cited as SCE.)

22. JA, 302.

23. JA, 295; cf. JA, 296.

24. JA, 299.

25. JA, 293.

26. JA, 293.

27. E.g., SCE, 72, 96, 144.

28. SCE, 47, 59.

29. JA, 292.

30. If one desires to contest my interpretation he might well lay himself open to the query, whether the metaphysical unity in God might just as well

be the guarantee of the possibility of solving the one-and-many problem on the creaturely level. Does not the absolute personality of God provide the guarantee that our creaturely existence is surrounded by a completely personal environment?

31. SCE, 59-60.

32. "I was especially delighted with Vollenhoven's work on the necessity of a Christian methodology." JA, 303.

33. JA, 303.

34. JA, 302.

35. JA, 296.

PART THREE

ANALYSES OF MODERN THEOLOGIANS

SYMBOL AND REALITY IN NICOLAS BERDYAEV

According to Nicolas Berdyaev, a symbol is an external sign that objectivates an inner reality.[1]

A most basic use of symbol is in communication. In this sense a symbol is an intermediate sign, the objectification of an idea.[2] A formal sign communicates a subjective meaning to someone. Thus there is the use of signs, e.g., in conversation, sign language, or even in art. In this function a symbol unites the communicating parties; but in uniting them it presupposes that they were separated and were in need of being united.[3]

Berdyaev uses the word "symbol" also in a broader sense. The human spirit objectivates itself, e.g., in its artifacts and institutions. These external vehicles reflect the spirit which they objectivate. Nevertheless, no deposit of spirit can contain the fullness of the spirit. It can be only symbolical, not fully representing but only indicating the reality it objectivates.[4]

For Berdyaev a certain sense of inadequacy attaches therefore to the term "symbolical." The symbol is needed for communication in a world of separation, where spirit is isolated from spirit and where union is sought by means of conventional signs[5] In this sense the symbol is a function of society, serving to hold it together.[6] That is true not only of the linguistic symbol but of all human laws and institutions. Indeed, it characterizes the rational function of man in general. Reason is the faculty in man, says Berdyaev, in terms of which he adjusts to the world-process. [7] Even the universal validity which reason seeks is itself social, being a means of universal communication.[8] In all its manifestations it can overcome the separation in the world only in terms of external generalities.[9] Reason and its concepts are adequate to the objectivated world of separation; they are inadequate to express the spiritual realities which this world objectivates.[10]

In further describing the world Berdyaev closely approaches the analyses of certain existentialists, notably Martin Heidegger and Gabriel Marcel. The world is the terrain of the outward, the ordinary, the impersonal, the general.[11] The externalizations or deposits of spirit, the symbols, are at hand, readily available to anyone who desires them. Being conventional, they can be appropriated or *had*, without any corresponding inner transformation of being. [12]

In large measure Berdyaev's thought took form in rebellion from what he regarded to be the unreal and therefore only symbolical nature of human society. He regarded the position and power that accompany social function and the possession of material goods as being only symbolical, because they do not necessarily correspond with any real qualities in the person.[13] Berdyaev anathematized social forms, usages, and politeness.[14] He characteristically resented the family and family life as pertaining to the genus and as suppressive of the person.[15] Especially the social role, like that of the mayor or the clergyman, was regarded by Berdyaev as being merely symbolical.[16] Merely symbolical is everything that is objectively accessible, externally accessible to someone apart from any inner transformation.[17]

What is in this fashion external, is for Berdyaev a symbol, a shadow, an appearance of the real. At the extreme limit Berdyaev uses the term "symbol" in a way that makes it almost identical with deception.[18]

The external, merely symbolical world corresponds to what the existentialist calls the "inauthentic." The symbolical world is for Berdyaev the fallen world. He thinks of the world as being alienated or as having fallen from God and from man's inner life.[19]

That Berdyaev speaks of the world as "fallen" means for him that there is no static boundary between it and the reality from which it has fallen.[20] Instead of speaking in rational, conceptual terms, which he believes would only indicate a hard and fast boundary to the world and would imply that the world is sufficient to itself, Berdyaev employs what he thinks of as the dynamic, "mythical" language of event to express the source of the merely symbolic nature of the world. He says that nature is fallen; but he intends to express thereby the idea that the confines of nature can be breached.[21] It is possible to pass from the sphere of the merely symbolical to that of the real.[22] For Berdyaev the problem is how to pass from symbols to reality.[23]

As Berdyaev's thought takes this turn, we encounter a different use of the word "symbol." It is possible for one to avoid confusing the symbolic with the real, to avoid thinking that there is a hard and fast boundary to the world, as if the world were sufficient to itself. It is possible for one to discern that the world is only symbolical, that no deposit of spirit is ever adequate to the spiritual reality it externalizes, but that these symbols provide a link with a world beyond.[24]

Berdyaev holds that the events in the objective world of nature and of history are symbolical of events in the depths of the primal spiritual life of man and of God.[25] He does not seek the real therefore in the external world but in the depths of spirit. This transcendent domain cannot be grasped by the reason; it can only be symbolized. This symbolization is "mythical."[26] It is a symbolization in terms of imagination of that which is beyond the possibility of conceptual expression.[27] It is only as the world is seen to be symbolic of the divine that it obtains meaning and significance.

Though he calls them "mythical" Berdyaev does not mean that the symbols are accidental, artificial, or wrong. He believes that they are reasonable and inevitable since it is only by symbolization that the real, the transcendent, can be expressed.[28]

Throughout his philosophy, in his social ethics as well as in his metaphysics, Berdyaev describes this ascent to reality in similar terms. It is the negation of the negation.[29] If there has been a fall from an original life into the generalities imposed in the attempt to adjust to the "realities" of the finite world, there must in turn be a negation of this externalization and a return to primal reality if selfhood and meaning are to be regained. This is not a fall and a return simply regarded; instead, the passage through the external world of separation is thought of dialectically as a phase or a moment in the development of the human spirit. At the outset limit Berdyaev sees the world as meaningful, transfigured by the spiritual activity of man.[30]

From our previous discussion we can see that there is an ambiguity in Berdyaev's use of the word "symbol."[31] On the one hand, we have seen that Berdyaev identifies the symbolic with the external, objectivated world. What is symbolic is the result of a fall from the spiritual. What is most symbolical, e.g., the state,[32] is therefore that which is furthest away from the real, that which is most opaque to the spiritual. Using symbol in this negative sense, Berdyaev speaks, for instance, of symbolic ethics in contrast to realistic ethics,[33] and he claims that there is a conflict between symbolism and realism.[34] Elsewhere, however, Berdyaev contrasts nature as opaque to the real with nature as symbolic of the real. Nature is opaque if, as in classical art,[35] it is mistakenly identified with the real and is thought to have its meaning in itself. It is symbolic if it is seen to be open to a reality beyond itself.[36] The ambiguity can be expressed in terms of a contradiction. Berdyaev says, on the one hand, that all the objective is symbolical; on the other hand, he says in effect that some of the objective is not symbolical.

The ambiguity appears also when Berdyaev distinguishes between conventional and realistic symbolism.[37] Conventional symbolism refers to the apotheosis of the external world, with its conventionalities, and the confusion of it with the real. Realistic symbolism sees the real beyond everything external, finite, and relative. It sees the incommensurability between the supposed realities of the world and the true reality of the spiritual, and it will not allow any final imprisonment of spirit in the rationalized, hardened forms of nature.

The fact that Berdyaev qualifies the term "symbol" indicates that deeper distinctions underlie that of symbol and reality and give them their meaning. The key to these deeper distinctions is found in his idea of objectification. Along with many other contemporary theologians, in particular those who have been influenced by existentialistic thinking, Berdyaev links the Fall with objectification.[38] In turn, the way of salvation is the realization of the primal, spiritual life, where objectification is overcome.[39]

For Berdyaev objectification is virtually identical with symbolization in the negative sense,[40] and the objective has all the characteristics that we have associated with the symbolical, with its generalities and conventionalities. The objective realm is that which is amenable to the intellectual faculty, the understanding and its concepts. In terms of its conventional concepts the understanding establishes hard and fast boundaries between man and his world, between man and man, and between man and God, first isolating them and only then uniting them in a mechanical fashion.[41] In this connection Berdyaev rejects the traditional view of theism and the primacy of the Creator-creature distinction as being the result of a rationalization and objectification of the divine.[42]

Like Martin Buber, Berdyaev would distinguish this objectified realm from that of the I-thou relationship. When an "I" meets a "thou," he says, the objective world disappears and the world of existence reveals itself to us.[43] In the I-thou relationship one attains to the level where he no longer thinks of others as things with attributes.[44] He does not even see God as the *ens realissimum*, a being with attributes, rigidly distinguished from man.

At the center of Berdyaev's thought is not the idea of the self-containedness and independence of God. Instead, he speaks of a dynamic, theogonic process in the divine life. Speaking "mythically" and not literally, God is always being born out of the primal abyss (*Ungrund*) of freedom.[45] There is an existential dialectic between the divine and the human. As the mystics have said, when man is born, God is born, and when God is born, man is born.[46] Between God and man there is, first of all, not communication but an inner affinity and communion. To express the labile relationship between the divine and the human Berdyaev, following Solovyev, places at the center the idea of the God-man, of deified humanity.[47]

The final sense of objectification is discovered, however, only when the objectified is seen to be the realm of necessity. Berdyaev considers the conventionalities and generalities of the world, created in the need for communication, as a principle of compulsion.[48] Those who fill social roles – a pope, a mayor, a father, etc. – in the very nature of the case have something inauthentic enter their lives. At bottom this inauthenticity arises not because of a dishonest use of function, wealth, possessions; it arises because of the very fact that the functionary must fulfill social requirements. He is determined by the outward demands of his function, and he cannot be himself. These demands impair one's spontaneity and freedom because they come from the outside as necessity and law.[49]

As we have intimated before, Berdyaev does not think of objectification as being ultimate. It is on a second plane, being the result of a rationalization. Objectification is the result of a fall, the issue of a transcendent choice of freedom. For this reason, Berdyaev says that the Fall itself is a testimony to the grandeur of man, and objectification points to a transcendent freedom, through which it can also be overcome. Human freedom and personality can be realized, however, only in a negation of the objectivated world of necessity.

For Berdyaev spirit, both human and divine, is freedom, personality, and creativity. As we have seen, he believes that it is possible to transcend the objective in the I-thou relationship, where one is no longer considered in terms of his attributes, in terms of his qualities in a certain connection or function, but where he is experienced in and for himself, in the full worth of his free personality. For Berdyaev this takes the form of a communion, not a communication, of freely associating persons (*sobornost*).[50] This inner I-thou relationship must be seen in terms of a creative freedom, in opposition to all normative structure, which can belong only to the objective realm of I-it relationships.

Berdyaev thinks of creativity on the order of the freely creating artistic imagination before it takes into consideration the necessities imposed by its medium of expression.[51] Berdyaev himself gives a colorful personal illustration of what he means. He says that he composed his writings quickly, even in a state of dizziness, not disturbing the cascade of his thought even by the consultation of books. He says, "Only in the white heat of creative ecstasy, when none of the divisions into subject and object had yet arisen, did I experience moments of fulfilment and joy."[52]

Creativity is rooted in freedom.[53] Creative freedom is conditioned by nothing at all, neither in the natural nor in the historical or social worlds. It is rooted in meonic freedom, out of which both God and man proceed.[54] Only in free creative activity is man really himself, a personality with true dignity and worth.[55]

Berdyaev calls creative freedom "primal life" or "first life."[56] It is the real, in contrast to all appearance.[57] Though it can only be symbolized on the level of the objective world, it is nevertheless able to be grasped immediately by primal consciousness, by an active, creative intuition.[58] Unlike many, Berdyaev holds that there can be an immediate contact with reality, where one is plunged into first life.[59] Primal consciousness can do without symbolism. Spirituality, Berdyaev says, should be realized and not symbolized.[60]

Berdyaev allows to everyone the possibility of an immediate realization of freedom, creativity, and personality. This realization is in opposition to objectification and symbolization. Nevertheless Berdyaev insists that creative spirits be involved in the active transformation or transfiguration of the world.

Even human creativity and transfiguration, however, are ambiguous. Berdyaev contrasts symbolic creativity with realistic creativity and symbolic transfiguration with realistic transfiguration of the world.[61] Symbolic creativity and transfiguration seek to change the world, but they do not give a true place to freedom and personality. Man and God are still conceived on the order of the object. Realistic creativity and transfiguration, on the contrary, give human freedom its rightful place.

In realistic transfiguration nature would be taken up in spirit and would become meaningful. There would be the elimination of the generality, conventionality, and external compulsion that Berdyaev usually associates with objectification. Here symbolization would gain its positive sense.[62] It is in this sense that Berdyaev uses the word "symbol" when he says that symbolic thinking contrasts with rationalization, overcomes hard and fast boundaries, indicates the awakening of spirit,[63] means a freeing of the human spirit from the world,[64] and involves a transcendence of the opposition of subject and object.[65]

Transfiguration of the world, though a goal, is nevertheless eschatological. The realization of a transfigured world can come only at the "end" of the world.[66] The free flight of the human spirit is inevitably brought to earth. The creative imagination is bound to consider the necessities imposed by its medium and to become conventional. There is therefore always a tragic disproportion between the inner fires of creativity and their outward realization.[67]

The stubborn ambiguity in Berdyaev's use of the word "symbol" is not without some parallel in the idea of objectification itself.[68] We have been using the term "objectification" solely in a negative sense; however, our discussion has intimated that Berdyaev does not employ it without some positive significance. We have said that Berdyaev sees a testimony to spirit in the fact that externality, conventionality, and compulsion in the world are the result of a process of objectification or a "fall." Even though he relegates communication to a lower level than communion, Berdyaev sees in objectification a witness to the attempt of spirit to establish ties and communications in the fallen world.[69] Objectification has a positive connotation when it, with its accompanying exteriorization, is seen as a dialectical moment in the development of the spirit.[70] These illustrations, which could be multiplied, indicate in one way or another that Berdyaev gives the primacy to freedom over external compulsion. Nevertheless, the outer is not the inner. Nature in its externality and necessity still remains in polar tension with freedom. Throughout Berdyaev's thought spirit is in an antinomic relationship to the world – for instance, when it sees in history a reflection of itself but yet sees history as being foreign to itself.[71]

There is reason to believe that the ambiguity in the use of symbol and reality and the underlying ambiguity in objectification cannot be reconciled within the framework of Berdyaev's thinking.[72] Instead, it arises from the basic unreconciled tension between nature, with its connotation of external necessity, and human freedom and personality.

In this study we have set a limited goal. We have analyzed Berdyaev's distinction of symbol and reality, to show that its meaning is dependent upon deeper motives in his thinking. We have found these deeper motives in his idea of objectification, viewed on the background of an unreconciled tension between nature and freedom.

REFERENCES

1. Nicolas Berdyaev, *Cinq meditations zur l'existence* (referred to herefter as *CME*) (Paris: Aubier, 1936), 115.
2. Idem. Cf. Nicolas Berdyaev, *Freedom and the Spirit* (referred to hereafter as *FS*) (London: Geoffrey Bles, 1935), 52. Spirit and Reality (referred to hereafter as SR) (London: Geoffrey Bles, 1939), 171.
3. *CME* 115f., 190f.; cf. SR 56.
4. *FS* 59; SR 52, 57, et passim.
5. *CME* 115, 191f.
6. *SR* 63; *CME* 117, 198.
7. *FS* 53; *SR* 121.
8. *CME* 72; cf. Roman Rössler, *Das Weltbild Nicolai Berdjajews* (Gottingen: Vandenhoeck und Ruprecht, 1956), 17.
9. Rössler, op. cit., 88.
10. *FS* 66.
11. *CME* 177ff., 183f., 191; *SR* chap. III. Berdyaev's view resembles closely Heidegger's analysis of the impersonal world of the One (*das Man*). Cf. Nicolas Berdyaev, *The Destiny of Man* (referred to hereafter as *DM*) (London: Geoffrey Bles, 1937), 20, 91ff.
12. *SR* 154, 173; *DM* 149; *CME* 116, 128.
13. *DM* 82.
14. *CME* 116.
15. Nicolas Berdyaev, *Dream and Reality* (referred to hereafter as *DR*) (London: Geoffrey Bles, 1950), 50, 71f. Cf. *CME* 184.
16. *DR* 115; *DM* 81, 93.
17. *SR*, 62, 154. Cf. Eugène Porret, *La philosophie chrétienne en Russie: Nicolas*

Berdiaeff (Neuchâtel: Éditions de la Baconnière, 1944), 109.

18. *DM*, 18; Nicolas Berdyaev, *The Meaning of History* (referred to hereafter as *MH*) (New York: Scribner's, 1936), 202; *SR* 59, 62.

19. *DM*, 18, 36. Berdyaev's view of alienation resembles Karl Marx's idea of "abstraction". *SR* 161.

20. Cf. *CME* 69, 74; Rössler, op. cit., 129, 131.

21. *FS* 52.

22. *SR* 55.

23. *DM* 18.

24. *FS* 59.

25. Nicolas Berdyaev, *Dialectique existentielle du divin et de l'humain* (referred to hereafter as *DEDH*) (Paris: Janin, 1947), 31; *DM* 151; *FS* 33f., 70f.

26. *DM* 24.

27. *MH* 21; *FS* 70.

28. *DM* 18; *FS* 17, 70.

29. Cf. *DM* 13; *DEDH* 26.

30. *SR* 64.

31. Roman Rössler points out this ambiguity in the following terms: "Es muss ... darauf hingewiesen werden, dass der Symbolismus im Ganzen des Berdjajewschen Werks keine eindeutige Position einnimmt, dass der teils positiv, teils negativ wertend vorgetragen wird und von einer inneren Widerspruchlichkeit erfullt ist ..." (op. cit., 121). See also my *Symbol and Myth in Contemporary Theology* (Unpublished dissertation for the Union Theological Seminary, New York, 1952), 33ff.

32. *CME* 188.

33. Porret, op. cit., 129. Cf. *DM* 139.

34. *SR* 170, 61ff.

35. *SR* 57.

36. *FS* 62.

37. Cf. *SR* 52, 169, 60f.; *FS* 54f.; *DM* 18. The same ambiguity appears with reference to the word "real," in the distinction between naive realism and true realism. *SR* 170. Cf. *MH* 202.

38. *DM* 35ff.; *SR* 64. Rössler says, "Die Objektivation ist ... das Wesen des Sundenfalls" (op. cit., 129).

39. *CME* 38, 65ff., 69f., 88, 112, 185.

40. *FS* 56. Cf. Rössler, op. cit., 132.

41. *CME* 52f.; *DM* 151.

42. *FS* 196, 62.

43. *CME* 112.

44. *Cf.* SR 56.

45. *DM* 29.

46. *SR* 121f.; *MH* 202.

47. *SR* 133f.; Porret, op. cit., 76ff.

48. Cf. Rössler, op. cit., 88.

49. *CME* 183ff.

50. "Sobernost" is the Russian translation of *katholikos*. Berdyaev uses the term to express his idea of primal communion, which transcends the artificial and conventional relationships in the objective world. Cf. SR 60; *CME* 190f. Cf. Rössler, op. cit., 146f.

51. *DM* 129.

52. *DR* 220.

53. *DM* 126f.

54. *DR* 213.

55. *CME* 150.

56. *DM* 149.

57. *SR* 173.

58. *SR* 171; *DM* 296.

59. *SR* 168; *DM* 18.

60. *SR* 56, 171, 177.

61. *DR* 214f.

62. Cf. *SR* 64.

63. *SR* 64, 104, 119, 130; *CME* 70.

64. *CME* 70.

65. *FS* 55.

66. *DR* 214.

67. *DR* 214; *DM* 129.

68. Cf. *SR* 52.

69. *SR* 52.

70. *SR* 44f.; *DM* 38f.

71. *SR* 45.

72. Cf. Rössler, op. cit., p. 129.

THE AMBIGUITY OF HUMAN AUTONOMY AND FREEDOM IN THE THOUGHT OF PAUL TILLICH

The recent death of Paul Tillich has not brought with it a diminution of interest in his thought. He is recognized as a leading figure in contemporary theology. It has been predicted that the influence of his thinking will increase rather than diminish. The current publication of his collected works in the German language[1] is making many of his writings available that were formerly difficult to obtain. This in itself will stimulate scholarly interest, making it much easier to study his thought in depth and to give careful attention to the meaning of his concepts.

One of Tillich's major philosophical concepts is that of autonomy. It is fundamental to his idea of freedom. It furnishes, we believe, one of the major axes about which his thought revolves.

1. THE EMERGENCE OF THE IDEA OF AUTONOMY

Like other existentialists Paul Tillich acquired his passion for freedom and autonomy in reaction to what he regarded to be an overweening authority. In his autobiographical sketches[2] he presents a vivid portrayal of the influences with which he broke. Born in the medieval town of Starzeddel, Tillich moved at the age of four to a somewhat larger town, Schönfliess-Neumark, which was also built on the medieval pattern. Existence in a small town, he says, gave to a child with some imaginative power the feeling of narrowness and restrictedness. Of this the surrounding town wall was a symbol. The town gave the impression of being a small, protected, self-contained world. This circumscribed existence in Schönfliess was interrupted from the time Tillich was eight years old by a yearly trip during the summer vacation to the Baltic Sea.

This excursion was the great event of the year for him, an escape from the restricted horizon of the life of the townspeople. Another escape was afforded by several trips he made to the city of Berlin.[3]

A still deeper influence was the authoritarian structure of Prussian society. Officials, Tillich writes, were strictly subservient to their superiors and authoritarian towards their subordinates. This hierarchy centered in a remote and inaccessible officialdom in Berlin and finally in the Emperor. Permeating everything was the influence of the army, which inculcated its ideology into the people from their early childhood.[4]

Most penetrating and lasting, he says, was the impact of the authoritarian system on his personal life, especially on its religious and intellectual side. Both his father and his mother were strong personalities. He pictures his father as a kindly but stern and authoritarian personality, strong in his orthodox Lutheran convictions to the point that he would become irritated with those who differed with him. His mother came from the more democratic Rheinland, but she was deeply influenced by the rigid morals of Western Reformed Protestantism. Tillich felt that both of them exerted a restrictive pressure on him, both in his thought and in his action.[5]

Partly because of his father's connection with the church as a minister, Tillich identified the authority of his parents with the will of God.[6] For this reason it was profoundly difficult for him to break with it. The attempt filled him with a deep sense of guilt.[7]

It was his father, Tillich says, who unwittingly provided him with the means of breaking with these restraints. In the tradition of classical orthodoxy his father loved philosophy and used it extensively. He could do this because he was convinced that there could be no conflict between a true philosophy and revealed truth. He entered with his son into long philosophical discussions. These, Tillich writes, belonged to the most happy moments in his positive relationship with his father. Nevertheless, it was through these discussions that Tillich's breakthrough to autonomy took place. "From an independent philosophical position a state of independence spread out into all directions, theoretically first, practically later."[8]

From the ages of fourteen to sixteen Tillich attended the humanistic gymnasium in Köningsburg-Neumark. When his family moved to Berlin in 1900, he completed his studies at a humanistic gymnasium there. Education in the humanistic tradition stimulated in him a great enthusiasm for the language and literature of the Greeks.[9] His liking for the Greek language was a vehicle, in turn, for his love of Greek culture and especially the early Greek philosophy. At the gymnasium he experienced the tension between humanistic education and the religious tradition which he encountered everywhere in history, art, and literature. He writes, "... in Europe the religious and humanistic traditions (of which the scientific world view is only a part) have been, ever since the Renaissance, in continuous tension. The German humanistic *Gymnasium* was one of the places in which this tension was most manifest."[10]

It was, therefore, from these two sources, the love of philosophical discussion and intimate contact with classical humanistic culture, that Tillich received a strong impulse to autonomy in opposition to external authority (heteronomy).

From this time Tillich never abandoned the ideal of autonomy. Especially his break with the authority of his parents left an indelible mark upon him. As he writes, "It is this difficult and painful breakthrough to autonomy which has made me immune against any system of thought or life which demands the surrender of this autonomy."[11]

As it worked itself out in his thinking this breakthrough was to result in Tillich's rejection of the possibility of discovering the ultimate source of the meaning of reality in anything that transcended the actual, real situation. It resulted in the rejection of all supernaturalism and eventually of idealism, which for Tillich was a kind of supernaturalism.

Tillich's experiences as an army chaplain during the first World War helped to shatter his idealistic commitment. The real transformation came, he says, during a night attack in the Battle of Champagne in 1915. All that night he tended the wounded and the dying, many of them his close personal friends. As he walked among the dying men, he says, much of his German classical philosophy broke down. This experience shattered his belief that man could master in a cognitive way the essence of being.[12] The final blow at heteronomy was struck by Nietzsche. During the war Tillich enthusiastically read Nietzsche's *Thus Spake Zarathustra*. It was then that the last vestiges of heteronomy fell away.[13]

As we have already suggested, however, Tillich's breakthrough to autonomy was in some fashion a hesitating one. Although he keenly felt the restrictedness of the life in Schönfliess-Neumark, of the authoritarianism of Prussian society, and of the influence of his home life, he broke with them only with the greatest difficulty. This break, when it came, was accompanied by a profound sense of guilt. This was especially true when he tried to free himself from the authority of his parents. "Every attempt to break through was prevented by the unavoidable guilt consciousness produced by the identification of the parental with divine authority."[14] Elsewhere he writes, "I was able to reach intellectual and moral autonomy only after a severe struggle. My father's authority, which was both personal and intellectual and which, because of his position in the church, I identified with the religious authority of revelation, made every attempt at autonomous thinking an act of religious daring and connected criticism of authority with a sense of guilt."[15]

For Tillich, therefore, breaking through to autonomy meant trespassing a religious boundary. Later he writes with approval of the conception that autonomy means breaking a taboo accompanied by a sense of guilt. "The age-old experience of mankind, that new knowledge can be won only by breaking a taboo and that all autonomous thinking is accompanied by a consciousness of guilt, is a fundamental experience of my own life."[16]

As we shall see, this attitude is reflected later in Tillich's idea that the actualization of freedom, i.e., the actual expression of the free act here and now, involves a break with what is the ground and the source of content of that freedom. The actualization of freedom is inevitably connected with a sense of guilt.

On the one hand, therefore, Tillich broke decisively with external authority. On the other hand, this break occurred only at the expense of overcoming a religious resistance and was united with a consciousness of the inadequacy of human autonomy when it is left to its own devices. He had little trust in the creative power of purely autonomous thought. Free-wheeling intelligence was suspect to him. "In this spirit," he writes, "I delivered a series of university lectures dealing specifically with the catastrophic failures, past and present, of autonomous thought, e.g., the development of Greek philosophy from the emergence of rational autonomy and its decline into skepticism and probablism to the return to the 'new archaism' of late antiquity. It constituted for me conclusive historical evidence of the inability of autonomous reason to create by itself a world with real content."[17]

That one criticizes the self-sufficiency of autonomy does not of itself mean, however, that he abandons it. For Tillich the direct abandonment of autonomy could only have meant a return to heteronomy. This he rejected. "Once a man has broken with the taboos of the most sacred authorities, he cannot subject himself to another heteronomy, whether religious or political."[18] "Submission to divine or secular authorities, i.e., heteronomy, was precisely what I had rejected. I neither can nor want to return to it."[19]

This ambivalent attitude towards human autonomy became characteristic of Tillich's thought. While he held tenaciously to the principle of human autonomy, he recognized that autonomy by itself was empty. His solution was not to abandon human autonomy but to discern in it, as it comes to its own boundary, a depth in terms of which it is deprived of its self-sufficiency even while it is being preserved. Noting the inability of autonomous reason to create by itself a world with real content, Tillich called for "... a theonomy, that is, an autonomy informed by a religious substance."[20] It is this dialectical position that we must explore.

2. THE SENSE OF HUMAN AUTONOMY

The idea of autonomy remained a keystone of Tillich's thought. To the end he continued to press the claims of rational autonomy over against heteronomy and myth. That is to say, nothing was allowed to have an ultimate claim on man that was not identical with the inner demands of Reason. Nothing was admitted as literal truth that did not square with the demands of enlightened criticism. Ultimately it was autonomous man who had to establish the law of his own activity. Anything that would qualify as part of the essential structure of being would have to pass the test of autonomous critical rationality.

According to the idea of autonomy, man himself must establish the law of his own activity. No law may impinge on him from outside, that is, from a source that is not identical with the inner structure of his own being. [21] In this sense autonomy is necessary to the idea of humanity. Any ultimate law coming to man heteronomously acts like a foreign body in the human organism. It destroys the structures of Reason and thus annihilates man as man.[22]

Autonomy expresses itself in autonomous human willing and in the autonomous cultural form. Here, in the actualization of the idea of autonomy, another sense of autonomy comes to expression.

Autonomous culture arose, Tillich says, by way of breaking the mythico-religious view of the world. Autonomous rationality broke the myth and substituted for it the *logos*. Thus arose the conception of the world as being sufficient in its own rational structure.[23]

The establishment of autonomous culture, however, is subject to the same dialectic we have observed before. Cultural creation, Tillich says, is the activity of spirit. The fundamental category of the spiritual is the creative.[24] Creativity is original, concrete, and individual; nevertheless, it is characteristic of spiritual creativity that it cannot will the individual in opposition to the general. In its intention it must always be oriented to the general.[25] Nevertheless, spiritual creativity is always actualized in the particular form. The unity of the intention to the general and realization in the particular, Tillich says, is the hallmark of creativity and spirit.[26] In direct proportion to the degree of autonomy it attains, however, the cultural form loses contact with its creative ground and becomes void of meaning. Under the influence of autonomous rationality the cultural form, deprived of its creative depth, is set up as something in itself, as a self-sufficient finite form. Concurrently the spirit itself pretends to be self-sufficient. It becomes isolated from the world. Everything outside of it comes to stand over against it as the terrain of its domination.[27]

In his book *Die religiöse Lage der Gegenwart*[28] Tillich subjected this pattern of autonomous culture to an extensive analysis. It was characteristic, he said, of the rational-technical view of the world. It was epitomized in capitalism, which Tillich viewed as an extreme expression of self-sufficient finitude in its alienation and emptiness.[29]

No cultural form, however, no matter how secularized it has become, altogether loses its contact with its creative ground. The creative ground of being continually breaks into form.

During his summer interludes at the sea Tillich experienced what was to become a symbol for him of the encroachment of the infinite ground of being on finite form. He was struck by the broad expanse of the sea pressing in against the finite limits of the land.[30] Later he thought he discerned in expressionistic art how the infinite breaks into finite form.[31]

Tillich maintained that it was impossible to isolate the finite form and to insulate it from this encroachment. At the depth of form is the infinite. No finite form can contain the infinite ground of all things. No form can ultimately be sufficient to itself.

Tillich's language most naturally brings to mind the image of an unbounded fullness which cannot be contained in any form. This image indeed sets forth a fundamental aspect of Tillich's thought. It does not suffice, however, to express his thought in its complexity. The image of a fullness of content which spills over the edges of an inert container is not adequate. Tillich's view can be understood only in terms of the idea that there is ambiguity in the autonomous spiritual form itself. The self-transcendence of form is what denies to it any possibility of resting completely within the confines of its finitude.

Thus we have discerned in Tillich's thought a double meaning of autonomy. On the one hand, there is the idea of autonomy. On the other hand, there is the actualization of this idea in autonomous form, which in its isolation becomes void of meaning. In its emptiness human autonomy betrays that it has become separated from its own ground, the source of its meaning. We must point out, however, what is an important key to understanding Tillich's position. It is only in the autonomous act that the content of human autonomy and freedom can be realized.

The idea of autonomy, therefore, is a major axis upon which Tillich's thought turns. To abandon human autonomy is to fall into some kind of heteronomy. Tillich must hold that it is in the ambiguity of human autonomy itself that a dimension of depth opens up.

3. THE INFLUENCE OF FRIEDRICH SCHELLING

At the time he completed his studies for the doctorate Tillich already had an articulate position with respect to the ambiguity of human autonomy. This can be attributed to his elaborate and profound study of the philosophy of Friedrich Schelling, which provided him with material for dissertations both for his doctorate in philosophy and for his licentiate in theology.

Schelling's philosophy was to have a profound influence upon Tillich. This he himself humorously ascribes to the fact that he made a bargain purchase of Schelling's works, which he read through several times with enthusiasm. More seriously, he accounts for this influence on the basis of the inner affinity between Schelling's thought and his own.[32]

In the Spring of the year 1909, after passing his first theological examination, Tillich began to study Schelling's *Philosophy of Religion* with the purpose of writing a paper to submit for his licentiate in theology. This plan of study was abandoned when he received a stipend from the city of Berlin to study for the doctorate in philosophy. Tillich decided to use the materials he had gathered in his study of Schelling in order to fulfill the requirements of this grant. Under its provisions he completed his doctoral dissertation, *Die religionsgeschichtliche Konstruktion in Schellings positiver Philosophie, ihre Voraussetzungen und Prinzipien.*[33] This he defended in 1910. Later he summarized the results of this study in another dissertation, *Mystik und Schuldbewusstsein in Schellings philoso-phischer Entwicklung*,[34] which he submitted in 1912 for the licentiate in theology.

The earliest and most immediate impact that Schelling had upon Tillich came as a result of the affinity between Schelling's philoso-phy of nature and the feeling for nature that Tillich developed as a child because of the proximity to nature of his home in Schøønfliess-Neumark and because of his summer excursions with his family to the sea.[35]

In his second period, immediately after his initial defense of the Fichtean philosophy, Schelling took the position that nature itself had its own potency. Instead of being simply the inert material for the domination of spirit, it was individual and creative, having the same power of self-determination (*Selbstsetzung*) that Fichte had ascribed to the creative ego. Schelling became an opponent instead of a defender of Fichtean philosophy. Fichte, he said, had regarded nature to be only the material for the dominating activity of free personality. In this fashion he depotentized nature, depriving it of any content in itself.[36]

A more subtle influence on Tillich came from Schelling's philoso-phy of freedom. There are close ties between this and his philosophy of nature. Tillich, however, places Schelling's distinctly nature-philo-sophical period within what he calls more broadly his "first period," the period of his identity philosophy. Schelling's philosophy of free-dom characterizes what Tillich calls his "second period," which commences just prior to the writing of his *Freiheitslehre* (1809).[37]

It is the position that Schelling took in his second major period that particularly molded Tillich's thought, especially with regard to the idea of the ambiguity of human autonomy and freedom. The influ-ence of Schelling at this point was most important. A grasp of these ideas is very helpful for understanding Tillich's own personal devel-opment and for understanding the structure of his thought.

As we have already observed, Tillich divided Schelling's develop-ment into two major periods. In the first Schelling rings the changes on identity philosophy. From an original advocacy of Fichte's phi-losophy of freedom Schelling moves to a philosophy of nature, in which he advocates an organo-logical view that nature possesses its own self-activity and content (*Gehalt*). Passing through an aesthet-ic idealism he emerges with a mysticism of intellectual contemplation.

The characteristic trait of this first major period, Tillich says, is that Schelling had not yet effected a synthesis between mysticism and the consciousness of guilt, between immediate contact with the absolute and the awareness of being separated from the absolute. There is yet no synthesis between identity and difference. Schelling's second major period is characterized, he continues, by such a synthesis.[38]

With the establishment of this link a pattern emerges in Schelling's thought that has had the most profound influence on Tillich. We can see this pattern in Tillich's later views concerning the relationship of essence and existence, the idea of a trans-historical fall, the idea of the transmoral, the demonic, the ambiguity of history, the doctrine of divine grace, etc.

The key to understanding Schelling's development, Tillich says, is his reflection on the principle of identity and its relationship to the moral categories.[39] Where there is a profound understanding of the moral law, it discloses the anti-divinity of willing, the animosity of the subject to God.[40]

What has occurred in Schelling in his second period is that he has drawn into the center the notion that the human spirit is ambiguous. Human autonomous willing, which is the inescapable expression of human freedom, had already become problematical for Schelling. Actual freedom and autonomy come only as the result of a fall from the ground of freedom. In every actual expression of autonomy and freedom, in every act of will, there is arbitrariness. In every arbitrary act there is the threat of contentlessness. Schelling's second period begins when this ambiguity of human autonomy and freedom is drawn into the orbit of the realization of meaning itself. The transition comes when there is a synthesis of the apprehension of meaning and the sense of alienation from the divine ground.

If every expression of will is ambiguous, it is clear that the will cannot be used to explain the origin of the ambiguity itself. Nor can the solution of the ambiguity be a result of an unambiguous willing of an unambiguous goal that stands outside of it. Both the origin and the solution of the ambiguity come to stand outside of the province of human willing. According to accepted terminology, they become "transmoral."

4. THE IDEA OF THE TRANSMORAL

The idea of the transmoral roots in the soil prepared by Rousseau's distinction between a level of conventionality and a deeper level of nature beyond human conventionality. The distinction of conventional willing and a transcendent depth reoccurs in Immanuel Kant's *Kritik der aesthetischen Urteilskraft*. In artistic creation, Kant says, there is an act which unites the universal and the particular, an act which depends upon no general criterion from outside. Artistic creation, although it is carried by Reason, is spontaneous, as if it were simply an act of nature. Genius is the natural talent which gives art its rule.

Romanticism set a morality of genius over against the conventionalities of society, which are the fabrication of human willing. Strongly under the influence of the personality of Goethe, it advanced the idea that the creative genius is beyond the law because he posits the law at the same time he creates according to his inborn instinct of genius.

Thus the notion arises that the source of meaning lies beyond the level of human domination by the conscious act of will. It lies in an irrational dimension beyond the distinction of nature and freedom.

The tendency to unite freedom and necessity characterizes, Dooyeweerd says, the second phase of the development of idealism. It was embodied in the historical thinking which arose at the time of the Restoration.[41] In contrast to the rationalistic, individualistic philosophy of the Enlightenment, this movement did not give a central place to the human will. Its idealistic phase discovered its concentration point in the super-individual, concrete spirit, which transcends rational law and the human will which is directed to it. The individual subject and its willing is overarched by a spiritual force which is free in the sense that it is not a mere natural necessity but which is necessary in the sense that it lies beyond the reach of human arbitration.[42] Individuals were thought, for instance, to participate in a national spirit. Although they might alter abstractly rational elements within the spirit, they were nevertheless subject to it as to a transcendent necessity.

This second phase of idealism was strongly influenced by Schelling. The pattern we have observed in the later Schelling, however, involves some changes. Here the existentialistic elements in Schelling's thought come to sharper expression. This means that the spirit can no longer be thought of as that which unambiguously transcends the level of human willing. As we have pointed out, the spirit becomes ambiguous. The concentration point must now be sought beyond the idea. The concentration point is still found in the historic, but in the more radical sense of *Geschichtlichkeit* (historicness) as it is understood by existentialism. This notion carries through and radicalizes the idea of the transmoral as it appears already in the context of idealism.

Schelling states his position in his philosophy of freedom in the context of a critique of Fichte. He rejects Fichte's moralistic view that the finite subject strives endlessly towards the ethical idea which is an indefinitely removed goal. Fichte placed this goal indefinitely in the future in the interests of the freedom of spirit. Were it not indefinitely removed, it would at some point be simply given and would thus become a part of nature. For Schelling, however, it is of no consequence that Fichte holds that this goal is infinitely remote. The finite act, he thinks, may not be regarded altogether in negative terms as falling short of an ideal that is transcendent to it. It must itself have a positive significance. It itself must have content.[43] In the line of Franz Baader, Schelling says that the individual act of will takes on positive significance since it is an active resistance to the ideal.[44]

Schelling praises Kant for his notion that the act of finite freedom is arbitrary.[45] He criticizes Fichte, on the contrary, for holding that finite freedom is simply the unambiguous expression of the idea of freedom. For Schelling the actualization of freedom means a fall from the ground of freedom.[46] Every act of freedom is inevitably an arbitrary act. Every act of will, i.e., every actual expression of human autonomy, is guilty. Under the influence of Jacob Böhme, Schelling holds that the ideas are restless and fall towards existence.[47]

The synthesis which characterized Schelling's second major period took place, Tillich believed, when Schelling came to the position that it was precisely in this act, which was separated from its ground and was inevitably guilty, that there was the realization of meaning. Meaning could be realized, he concluded, only in the act which from an abstract point of view, i.e., from the viewpoint of the ideal, was altogether negative.

Schelling's criticism of Fichte calls into question the very possibility of establishing unambiguous goals and of representing the finite subject as striving unambiguously towards them. Both the ideas and the finite subject have become ambiguous. The exclusive locus of meaning is in the act that is inevitably guilty. Yet, one must go even further. The moment which from the standpoint of the ideal is negative must in some fashion be productive of meaning.[48]

This pattern was introduced without any essential alterations into Tillich's thought. For him the finite act of will, the actualization of human autonomy, is inevitably arbitrary. By reason of an overarching destiny the act of finite freedom is a fallen act, separated from its own ground and therefore threatened with meaninglessness. It is impossible to think that this existential predicament can be overcome by a simple return to the ground of freedom or by setting the finite subject on a path that extends indefinitely into the future towards an ideal of unambiguous freedom. Any such pattern was rejected by Tillich. It involved, he said, a static view of transcendence. As we have already observed, the source of meaning must in some fashion be identified paradoxically with the existential moment.

5. THE IRRATIONAL

If the finite act of freedom itself is to have significance, the source of meaning may not be separate from it. This means that the existential situation must be tied up integrally with the origin of meaning.

As we have observed, Tillich said that spirit must always intend the general. Nevertheless, the actualization of meaning is always in the individual moment. It is here, in the situation which from the standpoint of the general must appear as a limitation, that meaning appears. In the moment there is an intrusion of the creative ground of being.

In its actualization spirit seeks to realize form. Spirit is the forming capacity of man that issues in his cultural creations. An outstanding trait of the creative ground, however, is that it breaks through form. Tillich held that the infinite ground of being was destructive as well as creative. It is the creative-destructive (*schöpferisch-zerstörerisch*) ground. Tillich called it divine-demonic.[49]

Tillich associated the demonic closely with the breaking of form. From the standpoint of the cultural form the demonic is completely negative in its form-breaking role. Tillich, however, does not simply contrast the demonic with spirit. Form-creation and form-destruction are not only antitheses.

It is just where spirit is at its maximum intensity, in an individual of superabundant personal power or the cultural creation of extraordinary breadth and influence, that the demonic appears.[50]

Tillich spoke often, for example, of the demonry of capitalism, not because he thought of it as an insignificant force but just because he recognized it to be a spiritual movement of great power and influence.[51] In such spiritual realizations the demonic appears as that which exceeds the bounds of form, as represented for example by the classical ideal of form, measure, and harmony. As an illustration Tillich refers to the demonic as it is manifested in primitive art, in primitive masks and rites.[52] The demonic is irrational. In contrast to the rational it is a purely negative quantity. Nevertheless, it also has a positive sense. It appears as an overarching power[53] which grasps and overwhelms one.[54] It transcends the bounds of that which can be brought under the domination of the subject taken in isolation from the object of its domination.[55]

As an overarching power the demonic is not simply the absence of form. The axis of meaning does not lie completely on the side of rational form. What lies outside of form is not simply an inert matter waiting to receive a form. Agreeable to the position of Schelling, Tillich sees the negation not only as a negative quantity but also as a positive force. The demonic is in active opposition to form. It is, in addition, something that itself takes on form and thus exerts a positive creative influence. It is therefore ambiguous.[56] It is the creative-destructive force which underlies and is the creative source of meaning of everything that is.

The idea of the demonic displays the transcendental direction in Tillich's thought. It has an overarching (*übergreifende*) character which is manifest in the fact that it is supposed to embrace both form and the negation of form. In Tillich's thought this transcendental direction takes an irrational turn. The demonic is an overarching force that transcends the powers of man's rational calculation and domination.

This creative ground does not appear directly, however. The demonic manifests itself as a fixation of a finite form, endowing it with unconditioned meaning. This is the aspect of the demonic that was most often emphasized by Tillich in his later writings.[57] Here he most often makes the point that the demonic is something conditioned which lays claims to being unconditioned. It is true nevertheless that in the demonic claim to unconditioned status Tillich always discerned a testimony to the fact that all culture has a religious foundation and depth, a relation to the unconditioned ground of meaning. Demonic distortion is the presence of religion in its deficient mode. It is indirectly a testimony to the creative ground.[58] In dialectical fashion this religious depth is not seen directly as a matter of fact but only indirectly in the conquest of demonic distortions.

Whether Schelling elaborated a view of the demonic I am not yet able to say. It is certain, however, that the pattern that Tillich discovers in Schelling's second major period dominates his own view of the demonic.[59] Tillich says that the demonic is that which is contrary to form and that which is at the same time something positive. It is a form of antiform. The demonic is not less positive; it is a positive contrariety. [60]

6. THE DOUBLE SENSE OF AUTONOMY

We have pointed out that Tillich maintained, together with Schelling, that every actual manifestation of human autonomy and freedom is arbitrary and is empty when it is taken by itself. The actualization of freedom involves a break with the ground of freedom. This is the character of finite freedom, of freedom, as Tillich put it, under the conditions of existence.

Yet, Tillich points out that Schelling did not think of this break as a simple one. The boundary is not closed. If finite freedom has fallen from its ground, it is nevertheless connected with it. It is still the idea of autonomy and freedom which must establish the essential meaning of freedom.

As we have pointed out, Tillich did not believe that this idea could be realized in point of fact, or that it could even be considered as an unambiguous goal. It is an abstract possibility which hovers above the real and which can never be realized unambiguously in it. It has a function in Tillich's thought nevertheless.

This idea embodies the fullness of meaning of the humanistic faith in human autonomy. It acts also as a guarantor of that autonomy. Essence is the locus and the guarantee of the infinite value of personality.[61]

If the main thrust of Tillich's thought went "beyond morality," he was concerned nevertheless with the moral. Its concentration of meaning was found in essence. The imperative that stems from essence is not that of an external, heteronomous law. It is identical with the idea of autonomy itself. The law of the moral is, Be what you are potentially. The moral imperative is the demand to become actually what one is essentially and therefore potentially, namely, a centered personality in a community of personalities.[62] Anything that contributes towards demoralizing the center of personality, in turn, is anti-moral.[63] In this sense Tillich's ethics are completely inward. Obeying the will of God is obeying the inner imperative of one's autonomous nature.[64] This and not any external imperative is the ground of moral action.

On this background it is not difficult to see why essence is the guarantor of human autonomy. It provides the abstract ground for rejecting anything that comes to us with a demand that is not simply identical with the inner structure of our being. What is opposed to the inner structure of our essential nature we rightly oppose.[65]

If the idea of autonomy gives us the abstract right to ward off all heteronomy, the autonomous rationality which is the expression of that idea will as a matter of fact demolish every heteronomy that seeks to establish itself. Heteronomy is dissolved within history in the acids of criticism.

Thus autonomy has two faces, the idea of rational autonomy and the autonomy of the rational, critical faculty, which when left to its own devices issues in the abyss of nothingness.

Tillich never relieved the tension of essence and existence on the level of philosophy. He defined freedom, in Schelling's line, as the possibility of the transition from essence to existence.[66] This transition is always a leap, of such a nature that existence cannot even meaningfully establish essence as an unambiguous goal. To make this attempt is the error of moralism, which is helpless to deal with the exigencies of the human predicament.

As we have already suggested, the thought of Schelling and Tillich thrusts them towards the view that the tension of essence and existence can be "overcome" only in the identification in some fashion of the source of meaning with the bruteness of the existential situation. As we shall see, Tillich will discover this point in the paradoxical intrusion of essential manhood into history under the conditions of existence.

Because existence is not a simple break with essence it is possible for the question concerning this paradox to be asked. Because existence is aware that it is fallen from its ground it asks this question as a matter of fact.

REFERENCES

1. Paul Tillich, *Gesammelte Werke* (Stuttgart: Evangelisches Verlagswerk, 1959). (Hereafter referred to as *GW*).

2. Autobiographical sketches are found in Paul Tillich, *The Interpretation of History* (New York: Charles Scribner's Sons, 1936), 3-73; *The Protestant Era* (Chicago: University of Chicago Press, 1948), ix-xix; and Charles W. Kegley and Robert W. Bretall, eds., *The Theology of Paul Tillich* (New York: The Macmillan Co., 1952), 3-21. Most recently a revision of the sketch in the *Interpretation of History* has appeared with the title *On the Boundary* (New York: Charles Scribner's Sons, 1966).

3. Kegley and Bretall, *The Theology of Paul Tillich*, 6.

4. Ibid. 7.

5. Ibid. 8.

6. Ibid. Paul Tillich, *On the Boundary*, 36-37.

7. Kegley and Bretall, *The Theology of Paul Tillich*, 8.

8. Ibid.

9. Paul Tillich, *On the Boundary*, 30.

10. Kegley and Bretall, *The Theology of Paul Tillich*, 9.

11. Ibid. 8.

12. *Time* (March 16, 1959), 47.

13. Ibid.

14. Kegley and Bretall, *The Theology of Paul Tillich*, 8.

15. Paul Tillich, *On the Boundary*, 36-37.

16. Ibid. 37.

17. Ibid. 37-38.

18. Ibid., p. 38.

19. Ibid. In his discussion of Karl Barth, "Kritisches und positives Paradox," Tillich maintains that one ought not to resist autonomy as such but only demonically distorted autonomy. "Das Gesetz aber, dem die Autonomie gehorcht, ist gut, ist Wahrheit und Gerechtigkeit." Jurgen Moltmann, ed., *Anfange der dialektischen Theologie*, I (München: Chr. Kaiser Verlag, 1962), 170.

20. Paul Tillich, *On the Boundary*, 38.

21. Paul Tillich, *Systematic Theology*, I (Chicago: University of Chicago Press, 1951), 84.

22. "The denial of Reason in the classical sense is antihuman because it is antidivine." Ibid. 72.

23. Ibid. 80; *GW* V, 203-205.

24. *GW* I, 211.

25. *GW* I, 213-214.

26. *GW* I, 214.

27. According to Tillich's usage, the elevation of spirit above nature as the terrain of its domination is the pattern of the personality ideal. It epitomizes

the structure of self-sufficient finitude.

28. Berlin: Ullstein, 1926.

29. Paul Tillich, *Die religiöse Lage der Gegenwart*, 72.

30. Paul Tillich, *On the Boundary*, 18.

31. Paul Tillich, *Die religiöse Lage der Gegenwart*, 49ff.

32. Paul Tillich, *On the Boundary*, 47.

33. Inaugural Dissertation. Breslau: Fleischmann, 1910.

34. *Beitrage zur Forderung christlicher Theologie*, XVI, 1. Gutersloh: Bertelsmann, 1912. Published also in *GW* I, 11-108.

35. Paul Tillich, *On the Boundary*, 17.

36. Schelling's attack on Fichte for depotentizing nature is paralleled by Tillich's attack on Immanuel Kant as a supreme example of the personality ideal, as he interprets it. Cf. *Die religiöse Lage der Gegenwart*, 39.

37. *GW* I, 15; *GW* IV, 136.

38. *GW* I, 16, 77; cf. 40, note.

39. *GW* I, 14; cf. 13.

40. *GW* I, 17.

41. Cf. the discussion by Herman Dooyeweerd, *Encyclopaedia der rechtswetenschap*, I (unpublished syllabus), 243ff. Dooyeweerd's comments on the historical school are made in the context of a discussion of this standpoint in jurisprudence, particularly as represented by Friedrich Carl von Savigny.

42. Ibid. 247.

43. Manfred Schröter, ed. *Schellings Werke* (München; C. H. Beck'sche Verlagsbuchhandlung, 1958) IV, 243ff.

44. Ibid. 258.

45. *GW* IV, 137.

46. *GW* IV, 137.

47. *GW* IV, 46, 66ff.

48. This point, though obscure and difficult, appears to be demanded by the logic of the situation. Apparently Søren Kierkegaard also though so, for he writes, "Now if things are to be otherwise, the Moment in time must have a decisive significance, so that I will never be able to forget it either in time or eternity; because the Eternal, which hitherto did not exist, came into existence in this moment." Søren Kierkegaard, *Philosophical Fragments* (2nd ed., Princeton: Princeton University Press, 1962), 16.

49. Paul Tillich, *Das Dämonische: Ein Beitrag zur Sinndeutung der Geschichte* (Tübingen: J. C. B. Mohr, 1926), 32, 11, 8, 9.

50. Ibid. 17-18.

51. Ibid. 42.

52. Ibid. 5f.; cf. 8.

53. Ibid. 8.

54. Ibid. 13f.

55. Thus the demonic breaks through the pattern of what Tillich calls the personality ideal. Cf. Ibid. 14.

56. "Die Tiefe des Dämonischen ist gerade die, dass das Sinnhafte und Sinnwidrige in ihm unlöslich verbunden sind." Ibid. 42.

57. Cf. Paul Tillich, *On the Boundary*, 40.

58. In Die religiöse Lage der Gegenwart Tillich writes, "Wo aber das Dömonische auftaucht, da kann die Frage nach seinem Korrelat, dem Göttlichen, nicht ausbleiben." Cf. Paul Tillich, *Das Dämonische*, 14, 39.

59. James Luther Adams points out that Tillich's view of the demonic is influenced by Jacob Böhme and Friedrich Schelling. *Paul Tillich's Philosophy of Culture, Science, and Religion* (New York: Harper and Row, 1965), 52. Tillich himself says that Schelling pointed to the demonic background of all existence. GW IV, 136-137. "In der Beschreibung der ersten seiner Potenzen (universale Seinsmächte) besceibt er den shöpferisch-zerstörischen Untergrund alles Lebendigen ..." GW IV, 137.

60. The pattern comes to expression clearly in the following passages: "Es gibt ein positives Formwidriges, das in eine köstlerische Form einzugehen imstande ist. Es gibt nicht nur einen Form-Mangel, sondern auch eine Form der Form-Widrigkeit, *es gibt nicht nur ein Minder-Positiven, sondern auch ein Gegen-Positives*." Paul Tillich, Das Dämonische, 6. "*Die übergreifende Form, die ein gestaltendes und gestaltzerstörendes Element in sich vereinigt, und damit ein Gegen-Positives, eine positive, d.h. formschaffende Formwidrigkeit.*" Ibid. 8. Cf. Adams, op. cit. 49.

61. Paul Tillich, *Morality and Beyond* (New York: Harper and Row, 1963), 24-25.

62. Ibid. 19-20.

63. Ibid. 20.

64. Ibid. 24.

65. Ibid. 24, 50.

66. GW IV, 137.

THE AMBIGUITY OF HUMAN AUTONOMY AND FREEDOM IN THE THOUGHT OF PAUL TILLICH

II

The question is frequently asked whether Tillich's thought may be called "existentialistic" or whether it is mingled with idealistic elements. Walter Leibrecht, for example, calls Tillich an existentialist.[1] He adds the qualification, however, that Tillich was never satisfied with mere existential analysis. Leibrecht believes that Tillich drives beyond the existential analysis, e.g., of separation and estrangement, to the point of identity where the infinite reveals itself in the finite.[2] In Tillich's thought, he says, there is a passionate search for the "... lost identity in the ultimate union of the separated...."[3] "... Tillich knows that there is no union without reconciliation of estranged existence to its essence."[4] Because of this element in Tillich's thought, Leibrecht calls him an "idealist." Yet, with his idea of estrangement, Leibrecht thinks, Tillich clearly goes beyond idealism. The break, however, is not a definite one. "This emphasis on man's estrangement from the divine does not lead to a real break with idealism ... It is Tillich's 'idealist' passion for identity, in fact, which has made him especially sensitive to the very element of man's separation. His radical search for unity inevitably leads him to stress the reality of man's fall ... and his radical understanding of sin and despair as estrangement from essence drives him to the acknowledgement of the final union of the ultimate with that from which it is estranged."[5]

We ourselves have already observed that Tillich had a place for essence as well as for existence. Man is not entirely given over to his situation; there is still the recollection of the essential state from which in his finite freedom he is fallen. Tillich retained in his thought the *idea* of human autonomy, which was indispensable to his ethical theory. It could be argued, therefore, that Tillich's thought was not purely existentialistic.

No matter how important such a discussion might be in itself, however, the debate whether Tillich's thought is existentialistic or whether it combines existentialist and idealist insights is unfruitful so long as the inner structure of his thinking has not been laid bare so that it is possible to obtain a clear notion regarding the status of the idea of human autonomy as essence in its relationship to existence. If it does not disclose the ambiguity of the idea such a discussion can be more confusing than helpful.

To say that Tillich does not altogether break with the idea of essence is not to say that his thinking is inconsistently existential as if he were guilty of a simple lapse. It does not mean that he has failed to carry his critique of essentialism to its conclusion. That Tillich's retention of the idea of essence is not a simple inconsistency is manifest when the status of essence in its relationship to existence has been understood.

1. The Ambiguous Status of Essence

We have already pointed out that Tillich followed the lead of Jakob Böhme and Friedrich Schelling in teaching that the idea is ambiguous. The idea expresses the inner meaning of autonomy and freedom. It is impossible, however, for the idea to be realized unambiguously. As we observed, that is not because the real cannot simply contain the fullness of the idea nor because the real in its negativity falls short of the idea. Finite form must be self-transcending. By the same token the idea cannot be thought to transcend the real unambiguously as a quiescent eternity hovering over the real or even as a more or less distantly removed unambiguous goal, a limiting concept.[6] The idea itself is ambiguous, falling towards existence.

We shall have to explore this ambiguous status of the idea further as we proceed. Here we must be content simply to point out how the idea is dialectically related to the real.

The idea cannot rest in itself, isolated over against the subject. Any such view, whether the idea was considered to be an eternity hovering over existence or a quiescent goal, Tillich called an idealism, a kind of super-naturalism which doubled the world, creating a second world beside the real world. Any view in short which did not acknowledge the ambiguity of the idea was guilty of doubling the world.[7]

The only world therefore is the real world. Tillich was fond of saying that the only world is the real world, this is the only world that is. Thus the idea could not have an independent status unambiguously. Indeed, in a fashion that we can discuss adequately only in the sequel, the idea must in some fashion be a projection of the real.[8] Tillich knew and accepted the criticism of the idea by the "realistic" philosophers, who viewed the idea to be the ideological projection of the real situation, or as Karl Marx called it, the "material conditions" of life. Seen from the side of the real world, the idea is an abstract ideal, a production of imagination which cannot unambiguously be the norm of human action.

Nevertheless, Tillich could not think of the idea as being a simple projection of the real situation. In some sense it retained an independent status. Even though the idea could not be constitutive for any act it retained a critical function. Every real act is transcended by the idea as an abstract possibility which judges it and which establishes its inner sense and limitation.

Viewed from the side of the idea, there is ambiguity in the idea itself. It is always tensionful. It tensionfully anticipates the real.

If this peculiar, tensionful status of the idea is to be maintained there can be no relaxation of the dialectic, no isolation of one pole over against the other. The idea cannot be explainable in terms of the real situation. Nor can the real situation be thought of as being subsumable under the idea as a particular instance of a general rule. The idea and the real are related dialectically, in a tensionful unity, a unity which is supposed to be rooted in a depth, an original synthetic level in contrast to the level of separation.

Nevertheless, this unity can never be given as a matter of fact. The "level" of depth cannot be thought of as being one level in contrast to other levels. Otherwise there is again a doubling of the world. The depth can be discerned only in the tensionful unity of the idea and the real, which is always present under the conditions of existence. The depth is supposed to appear through this tension as the transcendental ground of meaning.

Like that of many existentialists, Tillich's dialectical position took shape in an effort to overcome the crisis of thought of our Western civilization, largely the crisis of historicism. According to his analysis this crisis sprang out of the crisis of human autonomy and freedom. Historicism, he thought, arose out of the isolation of the historical subject over against the trans-historical, rational ideal. In his attempt to overcome the crisis of historicism he stands in the line of the Romantic-idealistic philosophers but with the modifications introduced by his encounter with existentialism. It is in the interests of solving this crisis that Tillich presses the notion of ambiguity and it was in this encounter that he developed his distinctive philosophy of history. It is to the analysis of this crisis that we now turn.

2. The Crisis of Historicism

A moderate historical thinking arose already in the eighteenth century. The Italian philosopher Vico was the first to develop a historical method of science in contradistinction to the mathematical science ideal of Descartes.[9] The historical method of science, however, did not make gains until the time of the Restoration after the French Revolution. There arose an idealistically oriented historical thinking which rejected any mathematically conceived eternal law standing above the stream of history to which the individual in history must adjust his actions and which began to think of meaning as arising by an inner dialectical necessity out of the historical group in its actual historical development. For Hegel the meaning of the absolute was expressed in the sum total of its factual historical unfolding. This meant a historicization of reality. The spirit is identical with its historical development. Its sole arbiter and justification lies in history and not beyond it. This historicization was accompanied, however, by the faith that this historical development was the embodiment of the idea of Reason. History, even when it was completely real, i.e., when it was not subsumed under an abstract, trans-historical ideal, was nevertheless completely rational.

Historicism began to reveal its radical consequences when the idealism which had spawned it broke down.[10] Then the faith was shattered that the course of history was the expression of the absolute idea. The ideas themselves were declared to be products of the historical stream. This meant a radicalization of the historistic position. As Dooyeweerd writes, "This transition started as soon as the idealistic foundation of the historical mode of thought was itself submitted to an historical explanation. The French thinker, August Comte, ... was the first to subject both the Christian belief and the Humanistic belief in the so-called eternal ideas of human reason to the historicistic view. With him the idealistic philosophical position was replaced by a positivistic one."[11] The ideas themselves were declared to be speculative or even to be ideological projections of real historical situations. Thus historicism began to reveal itself consistently in its relativistic and nihilistic implications.

With the breakdown of idealism the historical science ideal was locked into a position where it could deal only with the discrete, positive facts of history in their causal interrelationships without any hope of appealing to a trans-historical standpoint in terms of which the unity and the meaning of history could be established.

Indeed, when everything is viewed in terms of an historical common denominator, there is a unity of perspective of a sort. A consistent historicism holds that everything is a phenomenon of history, arising out of the stream of history and descending into it again. Nevertheless, even though there is a unity of perspective, there is a *crisis of meaning*. Every historical moment is completely immersed in the historical nexus of cause and effect. Within this historical connection no one moment deserves to be elevated to a position which might serve as the center and as the standard for other moments. There is therefore no standpoint from which the historical might be seen as a meaningful unity in the diversity of its moments. Even because everything is viewed from an historical point of view the *meaning* of history is dispersed. One becomes lost in the diversity of historical moments without any hope of escape.

Tillich's thought resembles that of the major existentialists in general in that he accepted the challenge of the crisis of historicism, which in its extreme outworkings suspended thought over the abyss of historical relativism. Tillich accepted this crisis and made it into a moment of his thinking. In this respect his thinking can be called "realistic," because it does not want to take refuge from the crisis of historicism in a "mystical" elevation above the real but to remain within the real historical situation. In this desire Tillich is not really different from Hegel. His attitude, however, reflects the more radical position of Nietzsche, who did not wish to blunt the edge of the situation by appealing to any trans-historical idea. For Tillich himself any such appeal to a trans-historical ideal is heteronomous if it is allowed to mitigate the starkness of the real historical situation. The situation in all of its radicality must be taken up in one's starting point.[12]

Tillich's thought, like that of the major existentialists, involves therefore a hermeneutic of irrationalism and nihilism. As we have already pointed out, Tillich viewed this crisis to be an effect of autonomous reason as it had become separated from its ground. As a consequence of this separation, the subject becomes isolated from the object, an absolutization and formalization which leads to a loss of content. The historical is isolated from the historical subject, which stands outside of it and gives it meaning by manipulating it for its own ends. On the other hand, the historical subject must now consider even itself to be a product of history. As Wilhelm Dilthey pointed out, the subject can only glide above the diversity of historical situations, an epiphenomenon of the real forces of history which mold its existence.[13]

It is not difficult to see why Tillich, faced with the problem of historicism, was very concerned with the problem of content (*Gehalt*). This problem faced him from the first, but it stood particularly in relation to the crisis of historicism as he was entering upon his university career. Then he struck out along a path that would also be followed by others, when he concluded that the historical subject in relation to which the moments of history become relativized is itself not the ultimate subject but is the result of a fall, an objectification of a more original level of being.

3. The Solution of Ernst Troeltsch

Formative in Tillich's development was his rejection of the solution of the crisis of historicism proffered by Ernst Troeltsch. Troeltsch keenly analyzed the consequences of the idea of the autonomy and the neutrality of history. The situation in which he lived in Germany after the first World War, he complained, was completely saturated with historicistic positivism. There was an endless reflection on the factual material of history without obtaining a clue to its deeper meaning. This resulted in a complete anarchy of viewpoints which threatened to plunge into a complete nihilism. Troeltsch sought the answer to this crisis in a compromise as effected by the historical leader between the idea of human autonomy and the historical situation.

In his work *Der Historismus und seine Uberwindung*[14] Troeltsch sets forth the idea of human autonomy, of human self-determination, as the content of the morality of conscience. The ethical idea, which is at the foundation of ethics and morality, is distinguished from the ethics of culture, which is related to real areas of culture.[15] In contact with the real situations of history the idea cannot be fully realized. It strikes and must give way to the stubborn realities of life.[16] Thus the morality of conscience must be tempered by giving attention to cultural values. Troeltsch discovers the key to relating them in the creative compromises which are effected by leading personalities in history as they seek to relate the transcendent ideal to the demands of the historical situation. [17] Even though these creative compromises themselves arise out of the particularity of the historical situation, Troeltsch is convinced that they are able to form a community of spirit which has enough universality to be generally valid.[18] They are universal enough to be considered more than the product simply of the individual in history. If one is not satisfied with this strategem of compromise, he is forced to think of the ethical norm as a limiting concept without any content at all, an empty projection beyond the confines of history, unrealizable except in human imagination.[19]

Thus Troeltsch allowed for the idea of autonomy; nevertheless he set limits to it. The idea must always be adjusted to the real situation. The result is an uneasy compromise position. One must rely upon the ability of the historical former to compromise if he is to avoid having his idealism evaporate into an empty utopianism.

Without doubt Tillich was much stimulated by the attempt of Troeltsch to meet and to solve the problem of historicism. Nevertheless he rejected the attempt.[20] That is not to deny that various elements of Troeltsch's attempt reappear in Tillich's thought. Tillich retains the idea of autonomy. He also acknowledges that this idea comes up against an impenetrable barrier in the brute facts of history. Nevertheless Tillich is not convinced that the compromise solution of Troeltsch goes far enough in linking the idea and the situation in a dialectical fashion.

In contrast to Troeltsch, Tillich does not opt for an idealistic solution even though it be a compromise one. He accuses Troeltsch of absolutizing the ideal, with the consequence that the real offers resistance.[21] Indeed, Tillich does not then give up the idea of autonomy, but he seeks to bring it into a thoroughly dialectical relationship with the real. This means that the claims of the real situation must be given their due.

We have already suggested again and again the direction that Tillich's thought took. He allowed the negative implications of autonomous rationality to come to their full expression. This is tantamount to accepting the historical situation in all of its starkness, without any mitigating appeal to a trans-historical source of meaning. As we have observed, if Tillich was to seek an origin of meaning at all, it had to coincide with the positive historical situation, which from the standpoint of the abstract ideal is completely negative. This approach Tillich regarded to be imperative. Friedrich Nietzsche, he said, once and for all opened up the abyss of nothingness.[22] It could be closed again only at the expense of dishonesty. Schelling, too, had seen this abyss. Tillich's approach is obviously dependent on the pattern he discerned in the later Schelling. He criticized Schelling, however, for having opened up the abyss and then having closed it again.[23] For Tillich this meant a covert return to heteronomy. The critical tendencies of autonomous rationality must be allowed to have their full effect.

4. The Limiting Situation of Doubt

In contrast to an idealistic position, Tillich's thought took a direction that was suggested by the teaching of his theological professor at the University of Halle, Martin Kähler. In his teaching Kähler emphasized the doctrine of justification by faith. Paul Tillich and a number of other theologians took this doctrine and extended it to apply to the cognitive as well as to the ethical realm.[24] One is justified by faith not only while he is yet a sinner but also while he is yet doubting.[25] In this fashion Tillich wanted to open the way to accept doubt, the child of autonomous rationality, in its most radical consequences.

A stimulus to Tillich's reflections on doubt at the outset of his university career was the lecture delivered by Ernst Troeltsch in which he maintained that the Christian faith would not be affected if it should become historically improbable that Jesus ever existed.[26] Tillich responded to this paper with a lecture of his own. In it he sought to break through the idealistic framework which underlay Troeltsch's assertion; he did not, however, challenge the threat of historical doubt to the image of the historical Jesus.[27] As such the historical elements in the picture of Jesus are theologically irrelevant.[28]

Tillich allows the negative implications of autonomous rationality to press to their limit and takes upon himself the burden of historicism in its most extreme nihilistic consequences. This should be enough effectively to refute the claim that he did not carry through his criticism of idealism to the end. It then became imperative, however, to account for this doubt all along the line. If the problem of nihilism was to be met, it was necessary that any ultimate starting point be able to contain this radical limiting situation of doubt. What from the standpoint of an abstract idea of cognitive truth would be completely negative would have to be contained in the concentration point of meaning.

The important question might yet be asked, however, as to the grounds Tillich had for extending the idea of doubt to its limit. Certainly very few people, if any, experience doubt in the acute form demanded of a limiting situation. It would also be difficult to maintain that Tillich thought that everyone would as a matter of fact have to pass through an extreme experience of doubt before coming to faith. The more reasonable position is that such psychological questions are more or less beside the point. The extension of doubt to its limit has a methodological, or, more exactly, an ontological significance.[29] What this significance is will have to be one of the key questions of our subsequent discussion. At this point it is possible to say, however, that the extension of doubt to its limit is supposed to open up the way for the revelation of a deeper level of being, a level which will not be able to appear directly but will always have to be in tension with the limiting situation of doubt itself.

The importance for Tillich's thinking of this orientation can scarcely be overestimated. Christoph Rhein is correct when he points out its importance in his able introduction to Tillich's thought, *Paul Tillich: Philosoph und Theologe*.[30] Rhein correctly emphasizes the importance of Tillich's application of the idea of justification by faith for his position as a whole.

The limiting situation of doubt which is embraced in Tillich's notion of justification by faith involves the radical negation that anything which is for the isolated subject, i.e., anything that is within the confines of the subject-object relationship,[31] can function as the Archimedean point of meaning. The negation involved in the limiting situation of doubt is necessary therefore to establish the transcendental direction of Tillich's thought. Tillich regards the isolated subject, e.g., the historical subject, itself to be the result of a prior objectification, thus placing it on a secondary plane. The subject-object relation itself arises by way of a "fall" from a deeper level, which is supposed to underlie and give substance to the level of subject and object. And this deeper "level" on which the isolation of the subject is supposed to be overcome is that of the historic (*Geschichte*). Thus Tillich's earlier wrestlings with the question of the ambiguity of the autonomous rational subject are incorporated in the outlines of his emerging philosophy of history.

Together with the existentialists Tillich supposes that he has carried this negation farther than idealism, life-philosophy, neo-Kantianism, and rational phenomenology did. The implication is that these movements have not been able to attain to a transcendence standpoint of radical enough depth.[32] In some fashion they employ as an Archimedean point something that is a possible object for the isolated subject. Idealism has sought the concentration of meaning in the idea. This was challenged when it was shown that the ideas were projections of real or "material" situations. Life philosophy has set up an avenue of intuition in contrast to the cognitive as the way of access to the real. This, according to Tillich and others, issues in irrationalism. Neo-Kantianism has sought to find a means of embracing all standpoints in the cognitive judgment, and has set off from each other various realms of value in terms of various transcendental categories. Rational phenomenology moved away from the epistemological level in rejecting the orientation to the theoretical judgment in favor of a direct intuition of essence in the thing viewed in a pure field of phenomena. But it then considered the idea (*eidos*) to be quiescent intelligible essence and bracketed everything which belonged to the existential situation.[33] The existentialist has thought of himself as being more radical in his negation and therefore more able to point to the standpoint from which the world can be viewed in its totality, free from any particular synthetic standpoint. Thus he has accused previous positions of having elevated some particular (*ontic*) area to the status of a concentration point of meaning. He denies that it is possible to discover the locus of meaning, e.g., in a special way of knowing, an intuition beside cognitive knowing, or some special area within the object (*Gegenstand*) itself. He supposes that he has discovered in his notion of the historic a means of avoiding any particular synthetic standpoint and of overcoming the isolation of the subject in a more original, transcendent source of meaning.

If Tillich is to accomplish this, it is obvious that he cannot do so by way of an external, heteronomous limitation of the scope of autonomous rationality. Instead, autonomous rationality must be allowed to extend to its limit. Thought must drive to its own boundary. Only in the self-transcendence of autonomous thought itself will the way be opened to the revelation of the depth of being. Rational form must transcend itself.

We have already seen, however, that the revelation of the depth of being will always appear nevertheless as something which can be pinpointed, which is one thing in distinction from something else. Furthermore, this particularization cannot be regarded as something accidental with reference to the synthesis conceived of as a goal to be obtained. The only way in which one may conceive of the depth of being is through the particular forms, i.e., in their depth. However, the bounds of every form must continually be broken through, so that the depth of the form will be revealed. The form may not be absolutized, made opaque by letting it stand on its own without reference to the divine-demonic ground. It must be shattered in its self-sufficient finitude and become symbolic.

Tillich's thinking leads him at this time in the direction of a theology of culture. That is to say, he moves in the direction of seeking to discern at the heart of every cultural form the direction to the depth of meaning which is revealed even in its most secular expressions. In this he carries out the program of mediation he adopted also from his mentor Martin Kähler of seeking to mediate between the historical situation and an unconditioned criterion of meaning.

5. HISTORICAL REALISM

Short of the dialectical complexity of Tillich's theology of culture there lie many important aspects of his thinking which bear mention before we proceed farther. As we have seen, Tillich was concerned to discover a path that would take him between appealing to a timeless criterion above history and dissolving everything in the relativity of the historical moment for the isolated historical subject. This led Tillich in the direction of laying the foundations of an historical realism.

In our discussion the term "realism" now takes on a somewhat different hue. It now no longer refers to the terrain of that which is for the autonomous subject in its isolation. It is no longer virtually identical with the sense of the situation or the "material condition." In the sense we now have in mind Tillich uses it as indicating where the locus of meaning is to be found. That is to say, without leaving the terrain of history in a "mystical" elevation above history or without reducing history to what is below history (reductionism), Tillich desired to interpret history in terms of itself, to develop an historical approach to the understanding of history.[34] Thus Tillich seeks to steer between subsuming history under a timeless ideal or explaining it in a causal fashion in terms of something other than history. History is to be explained from within history itself.

In order to gain a historical method of interpreting history Tillich turns to the method of the spiritual sciences as developed by Wilhelm Dilthey.[35] He links this method with the idea of *Gestalt* as it was developed especially in the field of psychology. In his *Das System der Wissenschaften nach Gegenstände und Methode* [36] Dilthey applies this concept to the study of history and the other so-called spiritual sciences (*Geisteswissenschaften*).

The *Gestalt* idea originated in biology. Its use was then extended to the study of psychology, history, etc. In this idea of *Gestalt* Tillich thought he had discovered a notion that could escape an empty idealism on the one hand and the reductionism inherent in naturalism on the other hand.[37] The idea of Gestalt offers a means of approaching the philosophy of history in a fashion that will offer a refuge for the idea of human autonomy without losing contact with the real contours of history.[38]

The same motive dominated the association of the Gestalt idea with the spiritual science method of Dilthey. This method was developed by Dilthey in order to avoid interpreting spiritual life in terms of an ideal above it or reducing it to something inferior to it by explaining it in a causal-mechanical fashion. Thus Dilthey developed his method of empathetic understanding, which was supposed to be able to understand the spiritual phenomenon from within. The spiritual science method is supposed to explain spiritual phenomena in terms of other spiritual phenomena. Thus every particular moment of spiritual meaning is supposed to be understood in the context of a spiritual totality.

In Tillich's thought the use of the idea of *Gestalt* and the adoption of the method of the spiritual sciences merges with the older influence of the irrational historical thinking which he inherited from Schelling and from Hegel.[39] The spiritual totality which is a cultural group has a spiritual center. Out of this center arise symbols which give expression to its life. These symbols are not imposed from the outside, i.e., in terms of any general rational criterion outside of the spiritual life of the group. They arise freely, yet with dialectical necessity, from the depths of the cultural totality itself. [40] The truth of a primary symbol, Tillich will say, is its necessity for the symbol creating consciousness. [41] With respect to these symbols Tillich employs a biotic analogy. The primary symbol arises out of the life of the spiritual group, it grows, and it dies. Its dynamic is controlled from within. In its deepest sense, one which we must yet prepare the way to understand, the symbol is religious. The religious symbol has nothing outside of itself to which it refers at all and falls entirely outside of the domination of the rational subject who would subject it to general laws. Thus one discerns in Tillich's notion of the symbol creating spiritual totality the influence of the irrational historical position with its idea of the union of necessity and freedom as it was initiated by the philosophy of Schelling.

6. THE CULTURAL MATRIX

Tillich's idea of historical realism shows the influence of the historical school. As we have observed, this school, under the influence of
Schelling, spoke of an irrational depth beyond the level of nature and
freedom. It is in this idea of the cultural community that Tillich seeks
a provisional answer to the problem of unity in culture. The unity of
form of a cultural community is expressed in central symbols which
arise spontaneously out of the life of the community yet as by an inner
necessity. In this fashion Tillich preserves the autonomy of the cultural community in its symbol creation. In the sense that no other source
can be established, the historical group produces its own content. It
may not be subsumed under a trans-historical idea nor explained in
terms of something outside of it in a causal-mechanical fashion. It must
be understood from within, in terms of the symbols which it produces
autonomously out of its own depth.

The idea of a depth which lies beyond the opposition of freedom and
necessity extends to the symbol itself. The symbol is not impressed on
the cultural unit from outside, i.e., by an act of rational willing; it arises
out of the depth of the cultural community itself by reason of a necessity
that is not mechanical but is nevertheless beyond the scope of all possible human willing and domination. The autonomy of the true symbol,
in contradistinction to the sign, is shown in the fact that it has an inner
connection with what it symbolizes. The sign, on the contrary, is conventional. It stands for something; but it itself has no inner relationship
to what it signifies. The sign is a matter of willing, the conventional use
of a shorthand for communication.

It is only as the center of gravity shifts from the irrational center of
the group to the periphery, from the depth to the rational surface, that
rational considerations can have any effect. Arising by a transcendent
necessity the primary symbol cannot be changed at will according to
some rational (external) criterion. It is, however, possible for symbols to
lose their power for the symbol-creating consciousness. Then they are
able to be criticized and they can fade away.[42]

The influence of the historical school on Tillich's view of the cultural
group is also seen in the position he gives to *ethos*. Within the community it is the *ethos* which is productive of its activity. That is to say,
fundamental to the life of a group is the communal solidarity of feel-

ing which arises spontaneously but as by an inner necessity out of the depth of its life. *Ethos* is then distinguished from the codified laws of the group, which are rationalizations of this more fundamental *ethos* and which occupy a secondary plane. The *ethos* of a group is at the foundation of its jurisprudence.

It is interesting that in this part of his thinking Tillich can distinguish between a center and a periphery of a cultural community, allowing for a gradation, e.g., from a central *ethos* and its rationalization in law. This phase of his thinking is very close to that of the irrational life-philosophy. Tillich's relationship to the historical school brings him to a position regarding culture that is universalistic, which sets him off from the bulk of existentialists, whose thinking, at least superficially considered, is strongly individualistic.

However, Tillich's dialectical position demands that he overlay this pattern with a more basic one. It is not adequate for him to think in terms of a gradation between a center of a spiritual community and its periphery. More fundamentally Tillich does not at all hold that there is a center of a culture in contradistinction to a periphery, as if the center were an original life-experience which is progressively rationalized and externalized as it moves out towards the circumference. That he cannot simply distinguish a center from a periphery sets Tillich apart from the life-philosopher. From his own standpoint he must reject life-philosophy as being insufficiently dialectical and therefore irrationalistic.

As we observed already in our early discussion of Tillich and Schelling, Tillich's philosophy does not allow for a simple distinction between form and content, rational and irrational, depth and surface, etc. We observe now that Tillich's philosophy of culture also benefited from insights he gained from the position of Schelling with its view of the ambiguity of human autonomy and freedom. To realize itself the depth of a culture must express itself as finite form. It is thereby formalized and threatened with contentlessness. One cannot understand Tillich unless he recognizes how fundamental this externalization and this formalization are. As we observed earlier, the depth of a culture cannot appear directly but only indirectly and dialectically in the overcoming of its distortions. The picture, as we observed, is not that of an inert container (form) being unable to contain an infinite content. Instead, the picture is that of the form in its isolation and contentlessness transcending itself and pointing to the depth of content which is beyond the possibility of being pinpointed, either as the pre-rational center or as the rational circumference of a cultural group. There is no indication that Tillich believed that one could actually stand on this boundary as a matter of fact. The limit, which is a formal transcending, is taken to be a guardian standpoint, which serves as a horizon of all our experiencing, making it impossible to discover the source of ultimate meaning in something which is a possible *Gegenstand* for the isolated consciousness. The boundary, which is indicated by the limiting situation of doubt, is necessary. Critical autonomous rationality must be allowed to have its say along the line, only then to discern in its own self-transcendence the presence of a depth of being which is the ultimate source of its content.

A fundamental place is given, therefore, to critical rationality, which sweeps over the entire range of things, e.g., *ethos* as well as jurisprudence, and criticizes them in their formal independence. Unlimited autonomous rationality in Tillich must be seen as the means of criticizing anything that can be the possible *Gegenstand* of isolated consciousness and therefore as a pointer to the depth of everything particular in a transcendent level of being. The problem must then revolve around the relationship between the self-transcending of this autonomous rationality and the depth of meaning which is supposed to reveal itself in this self-transcending. Has Tillich truly found a concrete starting point beyond all particular syntheses? Has his thought truly moved in a transcendental direction? These are major questions we must ask of Tillich as we follow him further in the development of his theology of culture.

References

* The first part of this article appeared in the 32nd volume (1967) of *Philosophia Reformata*, 55 sq.
1. Walter Leibrecht, ed., *Religion and Culture: Essays in Honor of Paul Tillich* (New York: Harper and Bros., 1959), 5, 6.
2. Ibid. 6.
3. Ibid.
4. Ibid.
5. Ibid.
6. Leibrecht's remarks do not make this clear. They can be interpreted to say that Tillich thought of essence as a goal and of salvation as a return to one's essential being. In our opinion misunderstanding along this line makes it

impossible to grasp Tillich's notion of ambiguity.

7. Tillich at one time called such a view "theoretical asceticism." Cf. Paul Tillich, "Kairos und Logos," *Kairos: Zur Geisteslage und Geistenwendung* (Darmstadt: Otto Reichl Verlag, 1926), 30, et passim. It isolated the subject from the ideal norm, to which it had to adjust itself as to an alien source of meaning.

8. That this is the case is shown by the fact that Tillich said freely that the idea of God was a projection. Nevertheless, it was not simply a projection. The issue, he said, is whether the projection hits something.

9. Herman Dooyeweerd, *In the Twilight of Western Thought* (Philadelphia: Presbyterian and Reformed Publishing Co., 1960), 64.

10. Ibid. 78, 79.

11. Ibid. 79.

12. Tillich's starting point will have to be concrete, in the sense that it may not idealize but must include in principle the situation taken to its extreme limit. This is characteristic of the idea of the historic (*Geschichte*).

13. The alienation of the subject has been a major problem for existentialistic thought, e.g., that of Karl Jaspers. Cf. Robert D. Knudsen, *The Idea of Transcendence in the Philosophy of Karl Jaspers* (Kampen: J. H. Kok, 1958), 8ff.

14. Ernst Troeltsch, *Der Historismus und seine Überwindung* (Berlin: Pan Verlag Rolf Heise, 1924).

15. Troeltsch, op. cit. 33.

16. Ibid.

17. Ibid. 47.

18. Ibid. 44-45; cf. 47.

19. Ibid. 60-61.

20. Paul Tillich, "Kairos," *Kairos: Zur Geisteslage und Geisteswendung* (Darmstadt: Otto Reichl Verlag, 1926), 2.

21. Cf. Kurt Herberger, *Historismus und Kairos: Die Überwindung des Historismus bei Ernst Troeltsch und Paul Tillich* (Marburg: Hermann Bauer, 1935), 20. "Tillich points out that when Troeltsch absolutized the idealistic center of human spirit, freeing it from the judgment of the Unconditioned, there was an immediate reaction from the side of nature. He says that Troeltsch should have seen in this reaction a testimony to the Unconditioned." Robert D. Knudsen, *Symbol and Myth in Contemporary Theology* (mimeographed, 1963), 48.

22. Paul Tillich, *The Interpretation of History* (New York: Scribners, 1936), 37.

23. Ibid. 35f.

24. Paul Tillich, *The Protestant Era* (Chicago: University of Chicago Press, 1948), xiv.

25. Ibid. xv. Cf. *The Interpretation of History*, 34. The importance to Tillich of this step is shown by his statement that without it he could not have

remained a theologian.

26. Paul Tillich, *The Interpretation of History*, 33.

27. Ibid. 33-34.

28. This is a well-known standpoint of radical contemporary theology, appearing, e.g., in Rudolf Bultmann. It does not eliminate altogether the notion that certain historical elements in the picture of Jesus are theologically relevant; but if they are relevant, it is not because they are historical but because they are demanded by the dialectical framework of historicness (*Geschichte*).

29. Tillich's position in this respect stands in the line of the contemporary ontological discussions of the irrational phenomenological movement, e.g., Martin Heidegger. Tillich's orientation from the first was congenial to this movement in spite of his difficulties with some of the positions of existentialism. We have already pointed out how his idea of the demonic points in a transcendental direction. Our further discussion will have to point out these interrelationships in more detail and with greater precision.

30. Christoph Rhein, *Paul Tillich: Philosoph und Theologie: Eine Einführung in sein Denken* (Stuttgart: Evangelisches Verlagswerk, 1957).

31. From the standpoint of the cosmonomic idea philosophy one must understand subject and object here in the sense of the antithetical relationship of theoretical thought. This, as we shall see, is involved in Tillich's idea of the isolated subject, and the problematics of the antithetical relation are tied up with his attempt to transcend the subject in its isolation.

32. Tillich says that he developed his philosophical position in reaction to neo-Kantianism, value theory, and phenomenology. *The Interpretation of History*, 36f. By "value theory" he presumably means the Baden school of neo-Kantianism.

33. Ibid. 37. Cf. Paul Tillich, *Gesammelte Werke*, I (Stuttgart: Evangelisches Verlagswerk, 1959), 134. (Hereafter cited as *GW*.)

34. Tillich speaks of the "historical type of interpreting history" (Paul Tillich, *The Protestant Era*, 21). In the historical manner of interpreting history, "History is an independent and, finally, the outstanding category of interpreting reality" (Ibid.26).

35. Skirting the twin dangers of idealism and a causal-explanatory position stems from Dilthey, whose influence has been felt on the irrational phenomenology.

36. Taken up in Paul Tillich, *Gesammelte Werke*, I, 109-293.

37. Cf. *GW* I, 138.

38. Cf. *GW* I, 143.

39. Tillich himself acknowledges his debt to Hegel in his philosophy of culture. In this philosophy, he says, he combines Hegel's idea of the objective spirit with Nietzsche's idea of the creative.

40. Paul Tillich, *Systematic Theology*, I (Chicago: University of Chicago Press, 1951), 11ff., 239ff.
41. *GW* V, 208.
42. *GW* V, 210-211.

THE AMBIGUITY OF HUMAN AUTONOMY AND FREEDOM IN THE THOUGHT OF PAUL TILLICH

III

Interpretation of Paul Tillich's thought that has any hope of being adequate must take into consideration its dialectical structure. If the interpreter does not take this approach, he will be limited to discussing particular elements of Tillich's thinking without grasping what gives it its inner coherence and unity. For it is only in terms of the structure of Tillich's thought that the concepts with which he works obtain their meaning.

Since Tillich was a profound and rigidly systematic thinker, such an approach in depth is possible. Tillich himself relates the various elements of his thought to their systematic center. Thus apparent difficulties must be approached with caution. Before one points out discrepancies and contradictions, he must be certain that he has viewed them against the background of the dialectical structure in which they appear. It is only when this structure has been taken into account that any fruitful confrontation with Paul Tillich can take place.

As we have seen, an examination of the idea of the ambiguity of human autonomy and freedom is a fruitful approach to understanding the dialectical structure of Tillich's thought. Within the idea of freedom, Tillich observes, there is an impulse towards realization, and this realization is by way of a "leap" or a "fall." That is to say, the realization of freedom inevitably involves a contradiction of the *idea* of freedom. As Tillich says, freedom grasps itself as freedom only by setting itself against its own meaning.[1] This realization is quite necessary if there is to be freedom at all; nevertheless, the realization of freedom involves a contradiction of the essential meaning of freedom.

That is the case because the universalism inherent in the idea of freedom is denied. In the actualization of freedom there is inevitably an arbitrariness.[2] There is no sufficient reason why any particular synthesis chosen in the act of freedom should have been singled out rather than any other. A choice is made inevitably, otherwise there would be no realization of freedom at all; nevertheless, the choice is an arbitrary choice of will from among any number of possibilities each of which has equal right.[3] In the act of freedom there is a contradiction of the universality which inheres in the idea of freedom. The individual act must choose between possibilities, each of which essentially has equal right; thus it cannot realize the universality inherent in the idea of freedom.[4]

For this reason guilt attaches inevitably to the historical act. In the face of the universal claim of the idea of freedom, every choice is a limitation, which must set aside a range of possibilities. Thus every free act is a guilty act. And since this free choice is indispensable to the realization of the idea of freedom, one is guilty even before the act.[5]

Even though it stands in contradiction to the idea of freedom, the real act of freedom, Tillich said, bears testimony to the idea of freedom from which it is fallen. It suggests the idea, which hovers over and which judges the real; it suggests its own essential meaning.[6] The real transcends itself.

As we have observed, Tillich refused to be satisfied with the merely "existential" situation of freedom; he retained the idea of autonomy and freedom.[7] We have also seen, however, that Tillich did not think of the idea of freedom as something that existed as an actual condition before the fall, as a goal attainable in the future, or even as an ever-receding ideal limit. These he rejected as a doubling of the world. To regard the idea as being able to be represented unambiguously is to fall into fantasy, i.e., the fantastic projection into the plane of reality of what, be it ever so significant, is the product of imagination.[8] One must stay with the real. As Tillich's slogan reads, "There is only one world." The real may not be transcended "really," as if one could take a step actually outside of it. That would be to assume a transcendent position that would relate heteronomously to the situation. Every supposed transcendent position of this sort, as we have said, falls under the ban of the idea of autonomy and will eventually be dissolved in the stream of time.

One must remain with the finite syntheses in the world. Nevertheless, by reason of the universal demand of the idea of freedom, there must be a continual breaking through the confines of every boundary. Even though it be imperative to realize freedom in the particular act, there must be in the name of the idea of freedom a negation of every particular synthetic standpoint, a constant dialectical breaking through of boundaries, while yet remaining on the level of the real.[9]

1. A Philosophy of Meaning

Tillich's philosophy is a dialectical realism. He himself indicated this by calling it "belief-ful realism," "a realism with depth," "a self-transcending realism." He has also been called an "ecstatic naturalist."[10] Obviously the term "realism" is intended to set his position off from idealism, which he would accuse of ascribing an independent status to an ideal meaning, loosing it from its connection with the actual power situations in the world.

From what we have said before it should be clear already that the contact of meaning with the real situation cannot be that simply of a causal, so-called "genetic," relationship. As we have already observed, Tillich's orientation was towards the philosophy influenced by Wilhelm Dilthey, a philosophy of meaning which tried to skirt both idealism and naturalism. Thus Tillich veers away from a causal-explanatory method, which he dismisses as being naturalistic, and moves in the company of those who give themselves to the analysis of meaning-totalities, the analysis of types, of meaning-structures.

That Tillich ascribed a transcendent status to essence meant already that he could not think of it as simply the product of real forces, as having simply an ideological status. It cannot be explained adequately in terms of a causal-explanatory method, i.e., simply as a projection.

Thus Tillich embraced what he himself called a "meaning philosophy." In this he did not want to lose contact with the real; nevertheless, the contact with the real had to be understood in meaning-terms.

This development made him very congenial to the irrational phenomenological movement, which had learned from Dilthey but which desired to free itself, even more than Dilthey himself had, from dependence upon a causal-explanatory method and to avoid the isolation of any factor that might be used as a key to understanding genetically the human problem. This we have already touched upon in our discussion of Tillich's historical realism.

In this connection, Dilthey himself is criticized by the followers of the irrational phenomenological school for not having altogether escaped isolating the subject, whereby the psychical subject becomes the source for understanding the origin of meaning. Dilthey is praised for his method of empathetic understanding (*Verstehen*) but is nevertheless accused of having stepped outside the bounds of truly hermeneutical philosophy and having fallen into a psychologism.[11] Instead, attention is focused on a closed circle of meaning, of which all of the elements are considered to be perspectives of each other without the possibility of isolating any one of them. No element may stand outside of the circle, where it might have a temporal priority and serve as an explanation of the others. Such a circle of meaning discloses a depth which carries it and which is supposed to provide its source of meaning, a source which cannot be identified with any of the particular elements of meaning but which is their ground.

2. THE AMBIGUITY OF THE SENSE OF CULTURE

Tillich's orientation towards the meaning philosophy influenced by Dilthey accounts for his preoccupation with the question of style. The creative center of a culture manifests itself in a style, which expresses its meaning and which establishes its unity.

According to Tillich, style has its origin in the creative depth of a culture. As such it lies beyond the level of technical domination. It does not have any essential connection with a controlling forming, which Tillich associated only with the isolated subject. By the same token the act of culture creation must be completely taken up within the circle of meaning, without any essential relationship to anything outside of it. However, can an act be completely taken up in a circle of meaning without relating to what is beyond it, e.g., to a structure of law?

As a matter of fact, Tillich conceded both of these points. Connected inevitably with the creative act there is controlling domination, cultural forming. This controlling domination, however, is not allowed to relate essentially to the meaning of culture. It is only accepted as its inevitable accompaniment. Furthermore, one will inevitably consider himself to be related to a standard of meaning outside of himself. But, again, this involves an alienation from oneself, which may indeed pertain inevitably to the free act but which may not be thought of as belonging to the idea of freedom.

Tillich's view sanctions a fundamental antinomy. It is insisted, on the one hand, that the inner sense of culture resides in the creative act of spirit, which is understood in terms of a circle of meaning of which the subject is integrally a part; on the other hand, it is admitted that in the act of culture formation the subject stands inevitably outside of the terrain of its domination.

Indeed, as we shall see more clearly later on, it is imperative that this alienation take place and that the autonomous critical rationality of the isolated subject come into play, if there is to be a preservation of the inner sense of culture.

As we have already suggested, the above antinomy was taken up into the conception of culture itself. Tillich was very much aware that the idea of the controlling domination of material according to a free project[12] belongs to cultural realization. It is impossible to eliminate the notion of controlling domination altogether from the cultural. Tillich, however, did not bring it into direct connection with what he thought was at the heart of culture, namely, the creative cultural act. Controlling dominating remains within the pattern of the isolated and alienated subject, which is the result of a fall from what the subject is in its original sense. The subject within the pattern of the domination motive is isolated and empty, separated from its ground of meaning. The ideas of domination and control belong inevitably to culture, therefore, but stand in antinomic relationship to its inner sense.

The isolated subject is that which has been absolutized and made self-sufficient, in what Tillich called its self-sufficient finitude. It then is regarded to be the source of meaning. It confers meaning on the material of its domination. As an instrument of its domination it employs causal-explanatory method, which analyzes into discrete elements and then builds up again in a synthetic fashion. This explanatory method, however, must inevitably entangle the self within its own web of explanation.

The self, standing outside of its terrain of domination, discovers more and more that it itself is subject to explanation as part of the world over against which it stands. The isolated subject is inevitably entangled in its own web of explanation, and thus becomes instead of a subject an object (*Gegenstand*) of knowledge. In its cultural task, therefore, the self is inevitably alienated from itself.

There is an antinomy involved in Tillich's conception of cultural creation. That he himself would have been ready to admit. The presence of the antinomy is betrayed by the use of the word "inevitably." It serves to relate the domination of the isolated subject to culture creation without allowing it to belong to its inner sense. He thereby retains the idea of domination in relation to culture creation; but at the same time he disqualifies it. The same situation pertains with reference to the relation of the self to causal-explanatory method. The self is inevitably caught up in the web of explanation; but this web is not permitted to ensnare the self in its essence.

Tillich's ambiguous conception of culture creation led him directly into culture critique. Culture is the product of the form-creating spirit; but as spirit expresses itself in its autonomy it becomes isolated from its ground and becomes empty. Tillich became absorbed in tracing out the effects of this alienation in society and setting forth the way in which meaning can be retrieved by rediscovering the depth of the divine-demonic ground. The antinomies are taken up into his developing philosophy of culture, and a solution is sought in terms of theology. Thus Tillich moved forward in the development of his theology of culture.

3. The Cultural Approach to Religion

Tillich used an expression, which came near to being a slogan, to set forth the heart of his theology of culture. Religion, he said, is the substance of culture, and culture is the form of religion. This statement avers, on the one hand, that religion must express itself, if it is to express itself truly, in the context of cultural formation. Without this context religion metamorphoses into something that breaks into culture in an external and destructive fashion. On the other hand, the meaning of cultural form is not discovered simply within this form itself but out of the religious impulse which underlies it and which gives it its meaning.

A number of factors converged to give Tillich's interest in religion a strong cultural slant. We have already pointed out the two-pronged influence which molded Tillich's early life, namely, the strong, conservative Lutheran home environment and the so-called neutral studies of culture in the humanistic gymnasia and in the study of philosophy. Further influences converged on him to turn his interests even more strongly in the direction of the analysis of society and of social action.

Tillich had been born into a good family, one which maintained contacts with the German aristocracy. As a boy, we have observed, he was first sent to a common school; but he was at the same time tutored in Latin so that he might later enter a gymnasium. He was first a student at the humanistic gymnasium in Königsburg-Neumark and then later in Berlin.

Tillich writes that contact with the boys in the common school left him with a sense of social guilt. He strongly felt the discrepancy between their background and his. He began to question his upper class training. He even began to develop sympathies for the commoners, even to the extent of causing tensions with the boys of his own social standing. The guilt that he felt for the condition of the lower classes was responsible in part for his interest while he was a student in a literary and cultural group called *La Boheme* which met in cafes and in other locales in the city of Berlin and occasionally at the seashore.

As Tillich himself describes it, this group was Romantic in its inspiration, distancing itself from the "conventionalities" of bourgeois society. Intellectually it was left-wing, socialistically oriented in its politics, influenced by the thought of Friedrich Nietzsche, and in contact with the international movements of art and literature. Tillich characterized the members of *La Boheme* as being "skeptical, religiously radical and romantic."[13]

Even though he had not broken contact with the nobility, Tillich began to repudiate the bourgeois attitude even with arrogance. He felt an aversion to what he regarded to be the rapacious business attitudes of the middle class. His experiences as an upper class youth and his later experiences in *La Boheme* molded his thinking, giving it a definitely radical, socialistic cachet. During the First World War Tillich was thrown in for the first time with the working classes. This contact further strengthened the influences that he had received before. These influences later bore fruit in his attachment to the religious socialist movement.

Tillich's ever-present feeling of social guilt did not manifest itself immediately, however, in a political will. That came only later, subsequent to the war. It came after the German revolution and after his joining the religious socialist movement. Like that of most of the German intellectuals before the war, he writes, his attitude towards politics had been largely one of indifference. As early as his first political decision, however, Tillich had stood on the side of the political left. The decision was taken a few years before the First World War, after he had reached voting age.

Tillich's experiences in the German revolution of 1918 gave his thinking a new and decisive orientation. He began to form his thinking along the lines of a sociologically oriented and politically formed philosophy of history which had been prepared for, and which was supported by, the philosophy of Ernst Troeltsch. The call to become a religious socialist came to him soon after the revolution. He said that he could not and would not refuse it.

His religious socialist orientation joined forces with his interest in Christian apologetics. Central to his apologetic stance was the idea that Christianity was confronted with a humanism that was itself fundamentally Christian. To provide an outlet for these views Tillich held private discussions on apologetics. It was not until after the war, however, that his ideas on Christian humanism became settled and clear.

Tillich concluded that Christian substance (meaning) was latent in movements among the so-called de-Christianized masses, for example, the worker's movement.[14] His contact with the proletariat after the war had brought him to the conclusion that an apologetics that did not take class distinctions and the class struggle into account was doomed to failure. Successful Christian action would have to be aware of the social situation. In the situation the correct stance would be that of religious socialism.

Tillich's move to religious socialism was bound up with the development of his position as a whole. In his youth he had developed a "nature mysticism," which discerned an independent source of meaning in nature, in contradistinction to the idea that the source of meaning for nature is domination by the sovereign personality. Tillich's attachment to a nature mysticism could be explained in part as a reaction to what he considered to be the alienation involved in the isolation of the subject from nature, which means that nature is conceived as a material to be formed. Nature receives its meaning by way of the controlling domination of the isolated personality. This is, as we have seen, the pattern of what Tillich called the "personality ideal."

For Tillich capitalism became the supreme example of the alienation which had been brought about by the dominancy of the ideal of personality.[15] It had effected a powerful demonization of society, leveling everything and making it material for exploitation. Capitalism meant, for example, an exploitation of nature for the sake of progress.

4. CULTURE CRITIQUE

In his early writings dealing with the critique of culture Tillich reflected the motifs we have been discussing. He is concerned with the expressions on the cultural level of the estrangement of cultural form from its depth of meaning and also for the corresponding manifestations of the isolation of the subject. In his terminology, he was concerned with the effects of self-sufficient finitude.[16]

In the face of these symptoms of estrangement, Tillich was encouraged nevertheless by the emergence of standpoints and of movements which were challenging the self-sufficiency of cultural form. These movements were all characterized by a distrust of self-sufficient finitude and the recognition that it is impossible to think of the self as being in isolation. They all sensed that cultural form had to be broken to disclose a deeper meaning.

The realm of art was for him a most sensitive indicator of the cultural situation.[17] Already during the First World War he had become interested in art, to a great extent as a means of obtaining relief from the oppressive ugliness of war.[18] As a result he spent considerable time observing art productions and in art criticism. It was particularly the close relationship between art and style that made it such a sensitive barometer of the cultural situation. Tillich was of the opinion that the depth of a culture would manifest itself in its style, whose form would express its inner content.[19] The primary task of art is to express significance, which is manifested in its style.[20]

In the realm of art expressionism became for Tillich an indication of dissatisfaction with form that is sufficient to itself. Expressionism broke through form, disclosing a content behind it.

During the nineteenth century, Tillich says, France had the leadership in art. In reaction from idealism and romanticism it developed, as a true reflection of bourgeois society, the naturalistic and impressionistic schools. Their forms are the completed forms of a finitude which rests in itself. Nowhere is there a breakthrough to unconditional content.[21] The expressive element in art was rediscovered about 1900.[22] Expressionism arose with a revolutionary consciousness and revolutionary power.[23] It seized upon older, primitive, and exotic forms, in which the inner power of expression of the real was yet to be found. The discovery of primitive and Asiatic art became a symbol of the departure from the spirit of bourgeois society. Expressionism dissolved the natural forms of things, not in favor of subjective impressions but in order to express metaphysical content.[24] Dissolving the natural form of things expressed the feeling of how inauthentic every organic expression of form is under the dominancy of the bourgeois, rational spirit.[25] It did not seek to express, like traditional religious art, a transcendent world, but an inner transcendence of things above themselves. [26]

It appeared significant to Tillich that where this breaking of form occurred was not in the areas associated with the traditional forms of religion.[27] The mysticism of expressionism stands outside of the religious tradition.[28] It was necessary for the religious consciousness, he thought, to free itself from the symbolism of any particular religious tradition and to express itself in forms wherever they might be found.

If Tillich discovered in expressionism a break with the spirit of bourgeois culture and a challenge to the self-sufficiency of finite form, he thought he discerned in a new brand of artistic realism an even more potent adversary. The new realism, he thought, attacked the bourgeois spirit in its own camp, turning its own best weapons against itself.[29] Unlike expressionism it did not involve simply a breaking of form. Yet, it did not pretty it up, in the manner of an older realism which Tillich regarded to be a sub-standard form of art (*kitsch*).[30] At the outset the new realism expressed itself in a brutal fashion. But when its tendency to caricature had worn off, it brought forms to expression in a fashion, which one could speak of as a belief-ful realism.[31]

In the political realm, the socialistic distaste for capitalism was thought by Tillich to involve a break with the isolated subject, for which everything is simply grist for its domination, without recognizing any intrinsic content in the material to be dominated. For this attitude he discovered a precedent in Karl Marx, who was concerned, even as was Hegel, to liberate mankind from its self-estrangement.

Tillich consistently interpreted Marx in what he called a dialectical fashion. His own realism was strongly influenced by that of Karl Marx. According to Marx, ideas had a real connection in the social matrix. One cannot ignore, Tillich agreed, the connection of ideas with the real, socio-economic situation. But he insisted that for Marx ideals were not simply mechanical projections of this situation. They were indeed projections, but they were more than that. Thus Tillich interprets Marx to be the advocate of a meaning philosophy much like the one he himself embraced.

Like many dialectically oriented theologians, however, Tillich objected to Marx's utopianism.[32] At a critical juncture Marx broke off his dialectic, expecting that there would be a passage into a time of natural harmony in society after the revolution of the proletariat. As he stated in his book, *The Religious Situation*, Tillich felt that the socialist movement had fallen prey to the finite. Abandoning its religious beginnings, in which it held that there was a religious, i.e., dialectical, view of the end, it developed the idea that there would be a temporal end, thus falling into utopianism.[33] Thus Tillich's criticism of socialism is that it is not dialectical enough. In Tillich's language, it came to hold that there could be a direct, unambiguous expression of essence on the level of history.

Because of its failure to recognize fully enough the dialectical character of history, socialism was disappointed in its expectations.[34] Furthermore, for the same reason it was unable to fortify its position against the inroads of realistic socialistic ideas.[35]

Religious socialism suffered disappointments, but through them it lost much of its utopianism. It, more than any other political movement, expressed the concern for what Tillich called belief-ful realism, a position that took with unconditional earnestness the situation of the time and of time in general before the eternal, with a consequent rejection of every kind of romanticism and utopianism, but with the hope of a new situation in society and in economic life in which the spirit of capitalism would be overcome.[36]

5. Contact with the Barthians

For a short while after war Tillich had been the pastor of a church. In 1919 he became a Privat-dozent in theology at the University of Berlin. He retained this post until 1924, when he transferred to Marburg.

During this period Tillich came into contact with the exponents of the Barthian position. He discovered that the students who had studied under Karl Barth had been taught to bypass social problems. They entirely rejected the liberal theologians like Schleiermacher, Harnack, Troeltsch, and Otto. By his encounter with the Barthians Tillich was confirmed in his religious socialist convictions. He turned against Barth's view of the relationship between revelation and culture. He was also confirmed in his opposition to Barth's view of paradox. When he was requested to comment on Barth's position, he contrasted his own view of positive paradox with Barth's view of critical paradox.[37] According to Tillich, Barth was not dialectical enough.[38]

Tillich indeed commended Barth for his insistence on the dialectical character of revelation. Barth, he said, applied a critical principle which denied that the unconditional can appear directly in history. Tillich, however, wanted to penetrate to the positive ground that made this critical dialectic possible. This ground is the transcendent grace and judgment which is present in every relation to the unconditional. Barth excepted one point in history, Tillich complained, from this positive dialectic, namely, the revelation in Christ; therefore, he was not dialectical enough. Tillich did not want to repudiate religion in favor of the revelation in Christ, but to view religion in its ambiguity, in its expression of the divine and demonic forces which are part of all culture.

6. THE RELIGIOUS CENTER OF CULTURE

If it was axiomatic for Tillich to express the religious in cultural terms, he also held fast to the second part of his slogan, saying that religion is the substance of culture. That did not mean for Tillich that he defended any special claim of religion. He distinguished between religion as a special manifestation of culture and religion as it lay at the heart of every cultural creation.

Every particular claim of religion must be subjected to criticism by autonomous rationality. Any special realization of religion, any manifestation of religion beside another, is a projection, an expression of cultural forces. As a particular religion even Christianity is not excepted from this criticism. It has no more claim to being right than any other religion. It cannot assert any superiority because of its supposed historical trustworthiness, superiority of its ethical teachings, its beneficial effects, etc. Viewed from the side of the causal-explanatory method, it can be explained as a projection of partial interests and can be seen to have been detrimental as well as helpful in its effects.

When it is seen from this point of view, considering its universal critical attitude towards all special manifestations of religion, Tillich's position chooses the side of secularism. Tillich supported the secularizing tendencies of autonomous cultural criticism. As we have remarked, Tillich must be able to take into account the extreme limit of cultural alienation from religion.

In the German situation as it developed after the First World War Tillich discerned a split between the conservative forces which were supported by the church, on the one hand, and the proletariat, on the other hand. In his feeling of solidarity with the proletariat, Tillich identified himself with their criticism of the church as a defender of the privileged social position of the upper classes. He maintained that the working class was correct in thinking of the church as a reflection of the power position of the bourgeois class in capitalistic society.

The real force of Tillich's view of the relationship of religion and culture can be understood only if account is taken of the fact that, in his estimation, it is precisely where the process of secularization has come to its fullest expression that religion in the most pregnant sense of the word must be sought. It is precisely here, at the boundary, that religion can be understood as relation to the unconditional.[39] Paradoxically, in spite of the fact that no special claim of religion can have any final validity and in spite of the fact that the most extreme secularism must be validated, every culture has a religious center and root. Not only is culture the form of religion; religion is the substance of culture.

This is the foundational conception of Tillich's theology of culture. It is a *theology* of culture because, following the lead provided by Martin Kähler, Tillich spoke of religious substance as standing in a paradoxical relationship to culture. Here Tillich sought to bring into play what he had learned from Kähler's doctrine of justification by faith.

Here there comes to expression Tillich's use of the term "religion" in its broadest and most pregnant sense, as relationship to the unconditional in every culture. In this sense religion is thought to appear at the heart of every cultural manifestation, and not in a special sphere beside others.

This entailed that there had to be a criticism of everything particular that arrogated for itself the place of the unconditional, that made the pretense of being itself unconditioned. There had to be a criticism of what Tillich called "demonry." It is in terms of a radical transcendence over every cultural realization that the demonic distortions had to be identified as such and to be criticized. This critical attitude, which had to be carried out to its farthest limit, Tillich always associated with the spirit of Protestantism.

In this connection it is interesting to note that the idea of the demonic was supposed to throw over a bridge between culture and religion. The demonic distortions of culture are supposed to indicate in a roundabout fashion that there is a religious impulse present, albeit appearing in its deficient mode. Thus the acknowledgement of the demonic made it possible, Tillich thought, to view socialism apart from religion. Socialism could not be indifferent to religion, as if religion were something accidental, able to be accepted or rejected, as it might if it were only one sphere of culture next to another. It was religious socialism, with its dialectic of belief-ful realism, which was supposed to provide the answer and to overcome the demonry of capitalistic society.

At the time Tillich believed that the situation was ripe for this belief-ful realism. It was a realism, we saw, which took the real conditions into consideration, avoiding the distortions of Romanticism and utopianism. Nevertheless, it was supposed to view the real in terms of its religious depth. The religious, then, would not appear in one realm in contrast to other realms; it would appear in the depth of every real thing. The depth would act as a judgment on everything real; nevertheless, it would also appear as its ground.

It is clear that the negation involved in the critical attitude involves doubt. The religious must be able to include within itself the farthest extreme of doubt and despair. In the context of his view of justification, however, Tillich developed the idea that this necessary criticism, proceeding from the transcendent, was itself awakened and carried by a positive ground. This is in view when Tillich says that the holy embraces both itself and the secular.[40] Every criticism proceeds out of a positive impulse, what Tillich early called a *Gestalt* of grace.[41]

Thus to understand Tillich's position, as it was developing in the context of his social and political thought, it is necessary to understand the place of the religious as he saw it and to take into account the dialectical relationship of autonomous critical rationality and the transcendent ground of meaning.

7. The Question of Dialectic

So confident was Tillich in his dialecticism that in his exchange with Barth he says that no one who repudiates dialecticism may be admitted as a critic of their positions.[42] There can be no "yes" without a "no." That is, more ultimate affirmation must be accompanied by a critical rationality which must be allowed to have its say all along the line.[43]

In evaluating dialectical thinking the place of critical rationality must not be lost to sight. Tillich himself was careful to observe this warning. No matter whether he went on to criticize Barth that his position was not dialectical enough, Tillich commended him for the critical negation that he applied to everything finite.[44] He wanted to do nothing, Tillich said, that would blunt the force of this radical criticism or suggest that it would be appropriate to return to a pre-dialectical view that supposed that ultimate meaning could appear directly in history.[45]

In our estimation, this critical rationality must be brought into connection, as Tillich himself does, with the idea of freedom and its universality. The idea of human autonomy and freedom is retained by Tillich; nevertheless, it is patent that it cannot function for him as the Archimedean point. Its universality has become the empty universality of a critical principle which assumes the standpoint of a guardian, to ward off heteronomy, but which has no content of its own.[46] Tillich speaks of a guardian standpoint which is attained in a formal transcending over history.[47] Failure to take into account the function of critical rationality in Tillich's thinking inevitably results in an interpretation that is not dialectical enough and inevitably means that the unconditional is confused with something that Tillich himself would have denominated finite.

Critical negation has an indispensable place in making the distinction between the unconditional and the finite. Things have meaning, Tillich said, only when they have an unconditioned meaning, depth, and reality.[48] This unconditional meaning must not simply be identified with any one of them. In Tillich's view, it must be set in antithesis to anything that is a possible object for thought (*Gegenstand*). In turning towards the unconditional Tillich's thinking, like that of Kant, takes a transcendental direction. It turns away from every possible *Gegenstand* towards a supposed ground out of which things obtain their meaning.

This turn is easily discerned in aspects of Tillich's thinking we have been discussing. In his discussion with Barth, Tillich spoke of positive paradox as the transcendental ground of the possibility of critical paradox.[49] The two may in no wise be set apart by means of a simple distinction. The transcendental direction is also discerned in Tillich's conception of doubt. What is the criterion to distinguish the superficial, rational kind of doubting from the deeper kind which Tillich said is already justified? There is no simple criterion. The latter is described as a doubting with one's entire self, while he is intently searching for meaning. What then is the self? How is there a reflection back on the self? Tillich would maintain that any doubting within the subject-object relation would be a psychical doubting, a rational doubting, etc., i.e., a doubting that is functional. To turn away from every possible *Gegenstand*, one must turn in the transcendental direction, towards that which is not one *Gegenstand* in distinction from others but which is their ground.

Tillich, and the existentialists with him, have sought to be radical in their negation, thus freeing themselves from the onus of elevating a particular synthesis to the position of the unconditional. In their language, they want radically to overcome the subject-object relationship. This effort is shown in Tillich's attempt to overcome the isolation of the subject. The question remains whether this transcendental reflection has been successful, or whether what is reflected back upon is itself entangled in theoretical synthesis.

Religious socialism foundered, Tillich said, on the question that was most difficult for it, namely, how unconditional meaning could be related to decision in history. Tillich sought his own answer to this problem in the context of his philosophy of history, in his notion of filled time (*kairos*). Here, in the historic (*Geschichte*) the isolation of the subject was supposed to be overcome, and thus the correlative elevation of some part of the world to the position of the unconditional was supposed to be avoided. More precisely, however, it was acknowledged by Tillich that the elevation of a finite standpoint was inevitable. He then sought a point of view which could embrace both the inevitable absolutization and the negation of it. Both the problem and the key to the solution could be expressed most pregnantly in terms of an analysis of the historic.

The historic as understood by Tillich and others can be grasped, however, only by way of negation of one's entire natural way of thought. If at its portal there is such a negation, shall the historic be able to serve as a key to a standpoint in which the relation of all things to the unconditional is disclosed?

REFERENCES

* The first and second part of this article appeared in the 32nd vol. (1967) 55 sq and the 33rd vol. (1968) 32 sq of *Philosophia Reformata*.
1. Paul Tillich, *Gesammelte Werke* (Stuttgart: Evangelisches Verlagwerk), VI, 90. (Hereafter cited as *GW*.)
2. *GW* VI, 89, 90, 91.
3. Tillich does not want any particular synthetic standpoint to be absolutized. He sanctions any actual view that has a claim to originality, i.e., that is *ursprunglichschöpferisch*.

4. Tillich speaks of the universalism of the classical idea of personality. Paul Tillich, *Theology of Culture* (New York: Oxford University Press, 1959), 28.

5. This notion, which appears in Schelling, has passed down through Kierkegaard into contemporary existentialism. Cf. ibid. 102-103.

6. Thus Tillich employs the weapons he can, from Plato to phenomenology, to show that it is impossible to remain with the "existential situation." One must transcend. Cf. Paul Tillich, *Systematic Theology* (Chicago: University of Chicago Press), I, 165, 202f.

7. One might ask whether the idea of autonomy and freedom in Tillich's thought can be anything else than the nostalgic call of an ideal of humanity that he pessimistically no longer considered to be possible of realization. To be sure, in his thinking, as in that of all existentialistically oriented thinkers, there has been a crisis of the ideal of personality.

8. Cf. Paul Tillich, *The Protestant Era* (Chicago: University of Chicago Press, 1948), 68.

9. The transcendence of all boundaries is a presupposition of freedom. Nevertheless, this transcendence is at the same time the expression, as well as the guarantor and protector of the idea of freedom, which is contradicted by every particular synthesis because of its inevitable arbitrariness. Boundaries may be set only dialectically.

10. Walter Leibrecht, ed., *Religion and Culture* (New York: Harper and Bros., 1959), 7.

11. Cf. Hans-Georg Gadamer, *Wahrheit und Methode* (2nd ed., Tübingen: J. C. B. Mohr, 1965), 211.

12. *GW* IX, 149.

13. Paul Tillich, *The Interpretation of History* (New York: Scribner's, 1936), 12.

14. Ibid. 43-44.

15. Cf. the first article of the series, *Philosophia Reformata*, XXXII (1967), note 27; note 36. Cf. *GW* X, 41, 44.

16. *GW* X, 13-30.

17. Paul Tillich, "The World Situation," *The Christian Answer* (ed., Henry P. Van Dusen, New York: Scribner's, 1945), 9, 29, 30.

18. Ibid.

19. *GW* IX, 317. "Stil ist die unmittelbare Einwirkung des Gehaltes auf die Form." Cf. *GW* IX, 318.

20. *GW* X, 33. Paul Tillich, *Theology of Culture*, 69.

21. *GW* X, 33.

22. Paul Tillich, *Theology of Culture*, 74.

23. *GW* X, 34.

24. Ibid.

25. Ibid.

26. Ibid.

27. *GW* X, 36.

28. *GW* X, 35.

29. *GW* X, 35.

30. *GW* IX, 338.

31. *GW* X, 35.

32. The same pattern of appreciation and criticism of Marx is found in the political thought of Reinhold Niebuhr. Niebuhr also learned from Marx's realism but criticized his utopianism.

33. *GW* X, 44.

34. *GW* X, 46.

35. By the term "realistic" here Tillich undoubtedly means an undialectical realism, e.g., a materialism. Such a position would hold that the idea is a simple projection of the situation, understandable in a causal-explanatory fashion.

36. *GW* X, 46.

37. Tillich did this in an article, "Kritisches und Positives Paradox," *Theologische Blätter*, II (1923), 263-269. This article sparked an interchange between the two theologians. The original article and the discussion are reprinted in Jürgen Moltmann, ed., *Anfänge der dialektischen Theologie* (München: Chr. Kaiser, 1962), 165-197. Cf. also *GW* VII, 216-246.

38. Tillich made this claim in his article "What is Wrong with the Dialectical Theology?", *The Journal of Religion*, XV (1935), 127-145. This article appears in German translation, *GW* VII, 247-262. Cf. *GW* VII, 223f.

39. This obviously does not mean that there must be, as a matter of fact, a complete secularization before religion can appear. It is only to say that the meaning of religion, as relation to the unconditional, must be compatible with this complete secularization; that in the most completely secularized situation one must be able to look nevertheless for the manifestation of the unconditional; and that the ultimate religious criterion must include within itself the complete negative judgment on all particular manifestations of religion.

40. Paul Tillich, *The Protestant Era*, p. xv; cf. 213ff.

41. Paul Tillich, *Religiöse Verwirklichung* (Berlin: Furche-Verlag, 1930), 15ff., 46ff. Cf. *GW* VII, 57ff.

42. *GW* VII, 216.

43. *GW* VII, 216-217.

44. *GW* VII, 221, 224.

45. *GW* VII, 216, 217.

46. Tillich's method of transcending would suggest that this idea of autonomy and freedom is able to be discerned by immanent philosophical means. To this end Tillich is ready to employ insights of Plato, the phenomenologists, etc., when they say that we must transcend the actual

states of affairs and give a place to an ideal background. One must ask, however, whether this transcendence is not a reflection of religious faith.

47. Paul Tillich, *Interpretation of History*, 169-170.

48. *GW* X, 12.

49. *GW* VII, 216, 217, 219, 221, 223, 224.

THE AMBIGUITY OF HUMAN AUTONOMY AND FREEDOM IN THE THOUGHT OF PAUL TILLICH*

IV

The religious socialist movement foundered, Tillich said, because it was unable to solve the problem that was most difficult for it, namely, how from the standpoint of the eternal a decision in time is possible.[1]

This movement, for which he had entertained such high expectations, found itself at the time of the rise of Adolf Hitler[2] without political power. Soon its forces were scattered by Nazi persecution, and some of its major proponents, including Tillich himself, were forced into exile. Why had this movement, which for many had appeared to have such potential, been so little able to cope with the developing political situation?

Refusing to take a purely socio-economic and political point of view,[3] Tillich ascribed this inability to fundamental tensions within the religious socialist movement itself, more specifically, as he himself clearly stated, to its failure to solve the basic problem of meaningful action in history.

Religious socialism had set itself off from socialism in general by pointing out a religious depth of things. How then was this depth dimension to be related to the immanent course of history?

The problem involved here leads one to a question that is vital to the view of history underlying contemporary theology: How is it possible to remain within history, not allowing it to evaporate into a simple, non-historical eternity, and yet, at the same time, to arrive at an unconditional in terms of which history can find its center and its meaning?

1. The Dilemma of Socialism

In his own interpretation of socialism, Tillich laid great emphasis on its being a continuation and ripening of a historical process. It can be understood, he said, only as the movement that is the most consistent embodiment of the current of thought running from the Renaissance, through the Reformation,[4] through early capitalism, and culminating in a culture come of age which has rejected the intrusion of any outside powers or authorities.

In his interpretation of this development, therefore, Tillich focused attention on the idea of autonomy. Of it, he said, socialism is the most advanced expression. This trait indeed earned socialism the animosity of the churches, which together with the middle class most often took a conservative stance. This spiritual heritage, however, may not be ignored. It was, Tillich thought, only by accepting the spiritual legacy it embodies that one can truly accept socialism.[5]

At the same time that he observed in it an outworking of the idea of autonomy, Tillich also saw in socialism a reaction to what he considered to be product of that autonomy, the self-sufficient forms of rationalized culture. Modern socialism took shape in opposition to the ideology and the societal structure it attributed to bourgeois, capitalistic society. In all its expressions, socialism advocates a more organic view of human society and societal structures than that of capitalism.[6] Thus it opposes the view that society is built up of a congeries of individuals, each pursuing his own ends, but linked together in a preestablished harmony. Indeed, socialism can defend its own idea of harmony, but not that of a natural harmony of conflicting interests. Socialism has so closely identified the individualistic, atomistic view of society with the so-called bourgeoisie that criticizing it has become tantamount to criticizing the "bourgeois spirit."

Socialism has discovered, on the contrary, in the proletariat, which is the product of bourgeois society, the precipitate, indeed the symbol, of the shortcomings of that society. Thus socialism has identified itself with the lot of the proletariat,[7] finding in its sense of solidarity in opposition to the bourgeoisie leverage for the realization of its own aspirations.

The socialist point of view, as we have presented it so far, leaves important questions undecided.

It leaves unresolved, for instance, the question how it is to view the idea of community over against bourgeois individualism, with its idea of the natural harmony of conflicting interests. Is this community to be thought of as an original, organic unity, one that embodies the idea of universal humanity? Is it enough that the hindrances be removed and that this original, organic community be allowed to come to expression? Or is this community an idea to be attained? Must it be brought to realization, e.g., by applying by means of rational planning an idea of distributive justice? The first option appears to be taken by Marxist socialism. For Tillich nature involves conflict, a conflict that must be transcended.

Undecided also is the question of tactics with regard to the existing structures the new community is supposed to replace. Socialism can involve a fundamental criticism of bourgeois capitalist society that is even revolutionary in its implications; because it holds that it must eliminate the basic structure of capitalist society, replacing it with something entirely new. To compromise is to betray the socialist principle. To adjust to the present realities is artificially to support a decaying societal arrangement that is corrupt at its very center. As a socialist one should attempt to break down this structure, so that another may be allowed to take its place. Nevertheless, in every situation where there is the exercise of historical power, the question arises how to make use of the existing power structures. The socialist, placed in the radical position of seeking to overthrow the existing order, must also attempt to construct a position of power in order to obtain leverage. He will perforce turn his attention to what is possible and will be tempted to exchange his revolutionary program for one of amelioration.

The problem of the relationship of the idea of community to the actual situation is especially acute for socialism because of its historical orientation. It demands that action be truly historical. That demand requires, in turn, that there be an idea of history and a proper criterion for historical action. Where is the meaning of history and the criterion for historical action to be found?

Does the meaning of history reside in the community? If so, will its realization be the expression *par excellence* of the meaning of history? What then is its relationship to empirical history, i.e., history as we know it? Does it stand entirely outside of this history? If this possibility is contemplated, the question arises whether anything can be truly historical that ignores the real historical power situations. Can a criterion of historical action be a real one without taking into consideration the cause and effect relations in history? However, if advocating the overthrow of existing society in the name of an organic idea of community represents choosing a historical criterion of action, in what respect is the societal order which it is to replace to be judged non-historical or to have violated the norms of historical action?

Marxist socialism has attempted to provide a concrete basis for action. It has considered the proletariat to be the class in which the shortcomings of capitalist society have come to expression. As a completely alienated group, the proletariat is supposed to stand altogether outside the structure of capitalist society, being that in which capitalism, as it were, comes to self-awareness. Its very alienation produces the dialectical necessity of change. In its sense of solidarity over against capitalist society there can be discovered, concretely and historically, the real power that may be employed for the revolutionary overthrow of that society. The revolution will mean the eventual realization of the original, organic unity of nature and the expression of the universal idea of humanity.[8] At the point this idea is realized there will be the end of history as we know it and the inception of history in the true sense of the word. True history is that towards which the pre-history of capitalist society is pointing, dialectically, by reason of the increasing alienation it spawns. Thus the group that stands completely outside the present order is the instrument for the realization of the true meaning of history. It is that which in its alienation stands in judgment and which prefigures and presages the new classless society.

Far from being an idea above history to be applied to history by the individual will, the basis for action is supposed to be a real, historical force. It is supposed to be the expression of an overarching historical destiny.[9] Especially with the emergence of Marxist socialism there came a criticism of the idea that the agent of history stands outside of history in a controlling fashion (a notion associated with the "personality ideal") and of the idea that the criterion of history is an ideal lying beyond history (a notion associated with "ethical socialism"). Historical change is not regarded to be the result alone of the willing of the culture. Historical demand is supposed to arise as a dialectical necessity out of history itself. One is obliged to act in agreement with historical necessity. He must read historical destiny, which bears in upon the historical process from its depth. What is required is to act in agreement with historical being.[10]

Marxist socialism maintains, nevertheless, that after the action based on historical necessity of overthrowing the established order has been completed the new, organic community will come as by a natural necessity apart from human contrivance. Thus the meaning of history threatens to be divorced from historical action.

Reading history, identifying the turning points as they are established by historical destiny, involves, by way of contrast, an element of calculation. The attempt can and has been made to support this calculation by means of a historical ideal of science. History is then thought to be ruled by laws that are capable of being mapped out and understood in the interests of predicting the course of historical development. A historical ideal of science has characterized the scientific materialism that has often been identified with socialist-communist viewpoints.

As the recognized leading theoretician of the religious socialist movement, Paul Tillich was steadily occupied with a dialogue with Marxism.[11] He accepted what he conceived to be the prophetic, eschatological view of history of Marxism, its historical realism, its idea of immanence, its dialectical viewpoint, its discovery in the proletariat of the precipitate of the evils of capitalist society, and its demand for a fundamental restructuring of society. In the context of the ecclesiastical situation in Germany, which was strongly under the influence of the Lutheran doctrine of the two kingdoms, Tillich mounted an attack together with the religious socialists on the political stance of the Christian church, which he thought resulted in a traditionalistic sanctioning of the established order. He found his point of contact in the groups that were most alienated from conservative German society, the socialistically oriented intellectuals and the workers. His viewpoint therefore agreed on many important points with that of Marx, from whom he had learned much.

However, in his struggle to express the meaning of socialism, Tillich criticized Marxism in important respects. Basing his effort on an understanding of the "early Marx," Tillich attempted to develop a rounded view of Marx's work, insisting on a "dialectical" interpretation in contrast to the interpretation of Marx that presented him as a scientific materialist. Tillich wrestled with the problem of meaning in history and the relation of history to its goal. As we have observed, Marx introduced into socialism the historically oriented realistic viewpoint which had come from Hegel, in opposition to the position of ethical socialism. *Vernunft* became identified with history. Thus history was elevated to the position of a noumenon. This historical realism, as we have intimated, remained in tension for Marx with the idea that the true beginning of history comes with the emergence of the new, organic community.

Characteristically Tillich attempted to bring the idea of the meaning of history and the real course of history together. Tillich bluntly states that Marx's idea that pre-history ends with the coming of the true history of classless society is false.[12] Our present history, history as we know it, is the only history that exists. Tillich, however, could not be satisfied with the notion that history is, simply speaking, a noumenon. History as we know it has to be transcended.

Here we again come across the dialectical approach we have described before. Tillich did not deny that history is a noumenon in the sense that he claimed that it is something else. He never mounted a criticism of historicism that would eliminate it; history remained for him the frame within which any answer had to be discovered. Thus he was as zealous as Hegel or Marx, in opposition to an "abstract," ethical point of view, to preserve the autonomy of history. It could not be invaded from outside in a fashion that would set aside this autonomy. Yet, as we have seen from the first, Tillich considered autonomy to be ambiguous. To the idea of autonomy he gave the status of essence, of an abstract possibility. Every autonomous realization by itself, however, was destined to issue in emptiness. Tillich's gambit was to accept the autonomy of history in its most extreme outworking, which he discovered in socialism, and without giving it up to subject it to a hermeneutic which would discover in it its religious depth.[13] In this dialectical stance Tillich found a sophisticated rendering of the religious socialist program of offering a religious interpretation of socialism.

In this light it is possible to understand why it is said that Tillich did not think of religious socialism as a kind of socialism distinct from socialism in general. It could be thought of only as an attempt to discover within socialism itself its religious depth. In this light it is also possible to understand the justice of the remark of Heinz-Dietrich Wendland, that to understand Tillich's religious socialism one must always keep in mind the proposition he spoke in his early lecture in Berlin, "Über die Idee einer Theologie der Kultur," that the holy embraces both itself and the secular.[14] Tillich wanted to show that there is no wall between religion and non-religion. In fact, it is precisely at the extreme limit of the secular that the religious appears.

In taking this position Tillich thought he was carrying on the program of religious socialism, to introduce a religious depth into socialist thinking. He understood religious socialism to be a critical purification of socialist faith, as a criticism of utopianism.[15] However, though he himself remained a religious socialist, Tillich pondered the question whether religious socialism itself had not remained enmeshed in the same duality that had plagued socialism, both in its ethical and in its Marxist forms. Had it altogether avoided a romantic utopianism? For Tillich religious socialism still conceived of the "end" as a natural harmony standing, as it were, in the wings, waiting to come on stage once the way had been cleared. The end was still regarded too undialectically as a simple possibility, which could be realized unambiguously once there had been an overthrow of the established order. This "end" had come to stand, therefore next to, i.e., in a simple transcendent relationship to, the present course of history. Religious socialism itself was faced, therefore, with the problem of the relationship of this transcendent "end" to meaningful action in history. It too was locked in the dilemma of placing the criterion of action in a sphere divorced from the real power situations of history or of simply identifying with them. Thus Tillich discovered in religious socialism also the split between a revolutionary-destructive viewpoint and an accommodation to the status quo which appeared to be the sine qua non for meaningful, constructive activity.[16]

Tillich's answer to the religious socialist dilemma was to present a philosophical and theological framework in terms of which he could establish a more intimate correlation between the unconditional and the real. To use his own words, the unconditional had to become judgment and grace in every real situation.[17]

Tillich's criticism of religious socialism and his modifications of it were not innovations for him as a result of his disappointment with its prospects. This is a widely accepted viewpoint, but it does not square with the facts. Credence was given to this view by the article appearing in the *Christian Century* "Beyond Religious Socialism."[18] In this article Tillich indeed points out that he and others were disappointed with the turn of events, particularly in Germany. This worked on Tillich himself; to the point that he lessened his activity in politics. Yet, he ascribes to his religious socialist convictions his resistance to illusions, and he denies outright that he was utopian.[19] It must be held that his criticism of the lingering elements of utopianism in religious socialism agrees with the position that was his from the beginning. The idea of the ambiguity of human autonomy and freedom, which he already entertained at the time of his study of Schelling, would not allow for an unambiguous realization. As we have seen, it did not even allow for an unambiguous idea, whether above history or as a goal of the historical process.[20] For Tillich the realization of essence had become problematic. To express itself, he thought, autonomous freedom must seek realization; but realization in the autonomous act involves a contradiction of the inner sense of freedom. This ambiguity is enshrined in Tillich's definition of freedom as the possibility of the transition from essence to existence.[21]

In the pattern he set forth in his studies of Schelling, there comes to expression, as we have seen, the complex – in its own fashion eschatological – philosophy of history that controls Tillich's interpretation of socialism. Tillich accepted the religious socialist viewpoint, and as to its basic position he never abandoned it. Nevertheless, he sought, by taking what to his way of thinking was a more consistently dialectical stance, to cut off its too simple and utopian expectations.

Without breaking away from socialism and more particularly from the historical realism of Marx, Tillich sought to interpret them within the context of a consistently dialectical view of history. He did not locate meaning in a timeless eternity but in the real course of history as we know it; nevertheless, meaning was not found along the time-line, as a simple realization, but as a transcendent "end," what he paradoxically called the "end beyond the end." This dialectical, eschatological view of history he associated with prophetism, whose spirit he also discovered in Marxism in a secularized form. It was the task of religious socialism, he thought, to point out to socialism its religious orientation by showing it this prophetic strand in its own teaching. This dialectical pattern, which appears to a more or less degree in a considerable number of philosophies of history, comes to exact and detailed expression in Tillich's thought. Its complexity accounts for the difficulty and to some even the impenetrability of his thought. Without insight into this structure, we insist, it is impossible to attain to any true understanding of Tillich's position.[22]

2. Tillich's Answer to the Question of Decision in History

Tillich's own answer to the question of decision in history is presented in the context of his view of *kairos*,[23] of "filled time." His discussion of this idea takes the form, first of all, of an argument for the complete temporalization of reality, which involves, since he conjoins them, the complete historicization of reality.[24] The argument, presented forcefully in his first *kairos* volume,[25] issues in the notion that historicality is an inescapable fate. Everything, including the viewpoint from which one can view the historicality of his existence, is historically conditioned in the most fundamental way.

As we have mentioned, any straight-line rejection of the historiciza-tion of reality is supposed to succumb *de jure* to the idea of autonomy and *de facto* to the dissolving power of time.[26]

Tillich, therefore, assumes a radical stance. There is no exit from time and history, apart from obscuring the true contours of human existence. One may not establish a point outside of time and history, as a point of reference, thereby relativizing time and history in terms of something that is simply transcendent to them. As we have observed, history inter-preted in a historical way must remain the final frame of reference.[27]

We have already described how Tillich's historical orientation involves his acceptance of the theory that history is carried by groups, each of which has its own spirit and style.[28] The various facets of each commu-nity, as symbols, arise freely yet as by a transcendent necessity out of a spiritual center. At this point, we saw, Tillich works with a form-con-tent scheme. There is a continuum of spiritual content at the center and rationalized form at the periphery of the cultural group. This scheme, however, cannot be the final one. One does not solve the problem of the meaning of history within a continuum of form and content; the search for content does not simply reverse the process of rationalization that leads to a progressive externalization and emptying of cultural meaning. Taking his cue from the idea of justification, Tillich thought of content as breaking in at the extreme limit of form.[29] As we have seen, Tillich's dialectical position demands that he take into account the limiting situ-ation of extreme formalization and emptiness, which is for the isolated subject, which is embraced by the divine-demonic ground of reality.

Tillich's insistence bears immediately upon the problem of dialectic and synthesis. Any direct relationship to ultimate content (mysticism) would in effect elevate a particular synthetic standpoint to uncondition-al status. This is a fault, Tillich said, of the sacramental attitude, which has not yet become critical. In the unbroken sacramental attitude one space is set up against others; one content against others, leading to a pluralism of unconditional meanings.[30] The inevitable need to mediate these positions leads to the search for universal form. As the autono-mous forms become disengaged from sacramental content, this, in turn, leads to formalization and emptiness. It is at the extreme limit of this for-malization process that unconditional content breaks in. That is to say, the unconditional is not found, Tillich thought, at either end of the continuum of form and content. This we observed already in our discussion of the demonic. The idea of the demonic illustrates the transcendental direction in Tillich's thought. The demonic is overarching, we said, embracing both form and the negation of form.[31] Unconditional meaning is not encountered directly; it breaks into form, paradoxically.[32] Thus the isolated form is broken in its isolation and in its stark opposition to other forms, and is made symbolic of a ground deeper than even the polar opposition of form and content itself.[33]

Thus we arrive at the pattern of *kairos*, the intrusion paradoxically of unconditional meaning in a "decisive time" or "time of decision." Only in the *kairos* is there a criterion of historical action. What then constitutes a *kairos*? On its "objective" side it is a time that is laden with creative possibilities. On its subjective side it is a time when in a real situation one is compelled to act unconditionally, i.e., with a complete commitment of himself, without the support of any preestablished scheme or system of meaning. This *kairotic* demand, for Tillich, does not arise apart from the necessities of the concrete historical moment; nevertheless, it is supposed to break into the historical moment.[34]

Any exact description of the idea of the historic (*Geschichte*) will have to take note that it is set off from what is non-historical and what is simply historical. How this disjunction is described and how it is supposed to be transcended is a crucial problem for the dialectical views of history.

As we have observed earlier, Tillich's strategem, like that of many others, is to bracket (dis-qualify) this disjunction as a whole, as the result of an objectification and generalization. [35] He then discerns in this disqualification the disclosure of a deeper ground. The ultimate meaning of history appears in the *kairos*, in antithesis to what is non-historical and to what is simply historical.

By way of the *kairos* there is supposed to be the intrusion of unconditional meaning; however, without the critical activity in the foreground the substance in the *kairos* would degenerate into a special content beside other contents, a special sphere beside other spheres.[36] Nevertheless, this critical activity itself, as we have pointed out, is supposed to be carried by a deeper, positive ground, what Tillich early called a "*Gestalt* of grace."[37]

In facing up to the *kairos* philosophy one is confronted with a large number of questions. Among them are certainly the following: 1) How is it possible to identify a *kairotic* situation? 2) How is it possible to decide for a *kairotic* situation? 3) Is the decision for a *kairotic* situation a real act or is it in some fashion a transcendent act?

The question of identifying a *kairotic* situation might be thought to be especially significant because of the painful miscalculation of the situation by Tillich and others after World War I. The question, however, is not only one of practical concern; it is the question of the possibility of a criterion for the *kairos*. It should be clear that within the framework of Tillich's irrational historistic view, no criterion for identifying a *kairos* can be found. To obtain such a criterion one would have to take a position outside of history. That according to Tillich one inevitably comes to stand outside of history we have sought to indicate earlier. This, we saw, was demanded even by the ambiguity residing in his idea of history. [38]

With this we are confronted with our second problem, how it is possible to decide for a *kairos*. Any decision, though impelled by a transcendent necessity, will involve an element of risk. In fact, Tillich maintained that there was arbitrariness in every decision for the *kairos*, demanding a standpoint which could embrace both this arbitrariness and the ultimate content present in the decision.[39]

It follows that the unconditional in the decision cannot be restricted to the empirical level of actual decision for the *kairos*, which would involve deciding for some-thing. It is characteristic of Tillich's transmoral position, as well as that of Kierkegaard, that the empirical decision for the *kairos* takes place and has its meaning on the background of a deeper, transcendent decision. One decides in the medium of a decision that has already been taken. As he is faced with the *kairotic* situation he is already εν κάιρῶ.

What we have said means that for Tillich the unconditional meaning in the *kairos* is not some-thing to be chosen. The *kairos* cannot be something in the future, along the time-line, thus as a particular time in contrast to other times. It is characteristic of such a position as that of Tillich that the *kairos* must be an overarching something in which one is already taken up.[40] If the dialectical, and in its own fashion eschatological, position is not to be destroyed, however, this overarching something may not be allowed to become a timeless eternity.[41]

That there is no rational criterion for the kairos does not mean, however, that the *kairos* idea is unstructured. It is inadequate to designate the idea of the historic (*Geschichte*) as that of simple contingency (unstructuredness) in contrast to necessity (structuredness). Indeed, the negation of structure is an integral part of the idea of the historic; yet, to interpret the idea with simple oppositions like that of necessity and contingency does not bring out either the purpose for which the idea of the historic was developed or the structure of the idea itself. The idea of the historic was developed in an effort, within the context of later idealism and of existentialism, to overcome the effects of historicism. Its intent, brought out clearly in the thought of Tillich, is to overcome this historicism without actually seeking to replace it with something else. It seeks to accomplish this by ascribing historicism to the absolutization of the (objectified) historical subject. The contours of the historic (*Geschichte*) are supposed to emerge in transcending this objectified subject, more broadly, in transcending what is included within the scope of generality. Thus it has been possible for us to observe on occasion that the primary differentiation of the historic is that it is not general.[42]

One can point out certain characteristics of the *kairos*, e.g., that it involves change of a deep-seated kind and that it is the intrusion of something completely new. Tillich associated it with what he called "the shaking of the foundations." Nevertheless, the structure of the idea of the historic and its companion idea of *kairos* is truly laid bare only in the in the kind of structural analysis to which we refer. The idea of *kairos* is obtained only in antithesis to what belongs to the domain of the general, the objectified. Further, the contours of this antithesis are established by the idea of the transmoral, [43] which, as we have seen, had its rise in late German idealism. Thus, in every real act of decision, one will already be involved in a deeper decision against the unconditioned which is, however, embraced and carried by a yet deeper decision for the unconditioned. In Tillich's position there is an ultimate universalism, because even the ambiguities of decision are already embraced in the meaning of *kairos*.[44]

As Tillich's thought developed he set forth the Christ as the answer to the problems of history. In the picture (*das Bild*) of the Christ he found essence appearing under the conditions of existence without losing itself. Indeed, there is a problem of the relationship of this Christ to the actual level of occurrence, to history, because in history there is always the split of essence and existence. However, Tillich maintained, such questions do not touch the heart of the matter, for they themselves are only possible against the background of the power of the new being in Christ. In his probings and even in his doubtings one is already carried by the power of the new being in Christ, a real power present in the church, the community in which this power is manifest centrally. [45]

Again, decision for Christ is ambiguous; nevertheless, even in the committed decision against him there is present the ultimate redeeming power of the new being.

The autonomous critical rationality of which we have spoken does not stop short at the Christ, according to Tillich. Here we must reiterate the point we have attempted to make, that in Tillich's thought there is no simple limitation placed on the scope of critical rationality.[46] Jesus Christ, Tillich said, could be a symbol of the unconditional because he sacrificed everything that was Jesus in him to the Christ. Ambiguous as this statement may be in isolation, it is enough to suggest what for Tillich is actually the case, that criticism and negation are taken up in the picture of Jesus as the Christ itself. Jesus as the Christ was one, Tillich said, who negated himself without losing himself, and who therefore could be the bearer of unconditional meaning. It is in Jesus Christ, interpreted in a dialectical way, that one discerns the *Kairos*, to which all subsidiary *kairoi* point.

3. Summary Statement

It is now time to bring our exposition of Tillich's view of the ambiguity of human autonomy and freedom to a provisional conclusion. We have traced the outworking of this idea through the period Tillich yet resided in Germany, before his emigration to America in 1933. This was the period that culminated in his closest relationship to the religious socialist movement. In this exposition we have sought to indicate how central to Tillich's thought were the twin ideas of the ambiguity of autonomy and the ambiguity of freedom.

In Tillich's thought these ideas largely parallel and coincide with each other. The idea of freedom is filled with the idea of autonomy, of self-determination, i.e., of having power over oneself. Autonomous self-realization, in the centered act, comprises the idea of essential manhood. The idea of freedom, furthermore, embraces the idea of transcending above all particularity. It includes, therefore, the idea of universality. The idea of freedom coincides with the idea of universal humanity. For Tillich, essence, which is a projection but not only a projection of imagination, is the idea of man in his integral power of disposing over his own being. This, as we know, is the substance of the idea of universal humanity as proclaimed by secular humanism. As we observed, Tillich did not see in secular humanism a simple threat to Christianity; instead, he regarded humanism to be filled with Christian substance.

For Tillich freedom is certainly presupposed in essential manhood, which is in the power of imagination. However, to remain unambiguously with the idea of autonomy, to image that there can be a simple realization of completely centered personality, is to give oneself over to necessity. This involves, in turn, that one abandons himself to the primitive powers (*Urkräfte*) of nature. Thus, we see, freedom is not identical with autonomy. Its meaning is to break through essence (necessity). To be free is to stand outside, to transcend, oneself. Thus, as we have seen, Tillich embodies the ambiguity in his definition of freedom as the possibility of the transition from essence to existence.[47]

The ambiguity is also discerned in that the idea of freedom degenerates into a general term. The universality involved in the idea of freedom, in which it is seen to transcend all particularity, diffuses into a general denominator for all of the particular, positive manifestations of freedom. The idea of freedom is expected then to embrace every act that can be called "free." This it obviously cannot do, in any of its realizations, or in any combination of them. Thus in the realization of the free act there is an inevitable transgression of the universalism inherent in the idea of freedom, an inevitable assertion of oneself in one's partiality that is guilty. In the free act there is the expression of a fundamental antimony; to be free one must negate the inner sense of freedom.

As we have observed, the genius of Tillich's position was not simply to express such ambiguities in the ideas of human autonomy and freedom. Others had pointed out these ambiguities before him. Tillich's ploy was to make them an integral part of his philosophical and theological thought. We saw this already in his following the effort of Schelling to effect a synthesis between mysticism and guilt.

From the above we can see that, even though the terms "freedom" and "autonomy" are very closely related and at times even coincide with each other in Tillich's thought, they are by no means synonymous and are not always parallel to each other. In one sense freedom means a break with autonomy, in that freedom is a self-transcending. Within the idea of autonomy, on the other hand, there is the problem of the relationship of the law and the self, and from either side the freedom of man can be threatened.

In the free act autonomy strikes up against a limit in the real and also in destiny. It inevitably strikes against a resistance that is not identical with itself. For the humanistic idea of autonomy this constitutes a crisis. In absolute idealism this crisis was acknowledged; the self was acknowledged to be in a situation that was not simply identical with it. However, the self recollected itself in a deeper sense in the situation, because it could discern in it the manifestation of absolute spirit. This point of view is retained in part by Tillich. In destiny autonomy is supposed to be transcended without being eliminated. In its depth freedom is supposed to have the power of accepting the situation, because it discerns in the situation the element of destiny. It recollects itself in the situation. In its deeper meaning freedom is not contingency in opposition to necessity; freedom is freedom in situation, which is freedom related to destiny. Nevertheless, for Tillich this cannot be the ultimate perspective. This he made clear from the beginning when he said that the way to the solution of the problem of freedom was not simply to retrace one's steps and seek essence, as an unambiguous realization in the past, present, or future. This also comes to expression in his insistence that the solution is not a philosophical-dialectical one but a paradoxical-theological one.

Tillich discerned in the idea itself a tendency to the real. This, he said, was grasped already by Böhme and Schelling. The answer, therefore, must be, will be found, not in an "ideal" recollection of one's essential manhood, but in a real power. It was found, as we saw, in the picture of Jesus as the Christ, in whom essence appeared under the conditions of existence without losing itself. This picture, which considered from the outside, reduces itself to a mass of contradictions, Tillich regarded to represent the power of the new being, in which one is powerfully grasped and which is the power of overcoming the ambiguities of his existence.

In the context of Tillich's paradoxical-theological view, freedom finally takes on the meaning of "redemption." One is ultimately free only by participating in the new being in Christ, which has entered paradoxically into existence. As far as we can see, this redeemed freedom excludes the idea of autonomy, in the sense of transcending it and even of standing over against it. It is, however, not without autonomy, for the new being is that which has taken up the negations stemming from autonomy completely within itself, overcoming them. As we said, for Tillich the picture of the Christ was that of one who denied himself completely without losing himself, thus being able to stand open to the unconditional. There is no manifestation of the new being in Christ, however, that is not subject to the critical activity of autonomous rationality, if it wants to retain its power of being a symbol of the unconditional.

The careful student, as he attempts to think through Tillich's position to its end, will discern there a complex structure that Tillich adopted early and never abandoned. This structure, however, is almost never set forth in its entirety as a basis of discussion or as a framework for criticism.[48] The result is often a lopsided interpretation and a brand of criticism that leaves the deeper student unsatisfied. Difficult though it may be, the disclosing of this systematic framework is a sine qua non for a proper interpretation of Tillich's thought. Thus we present a strongly interpretative brief resume of this scheme.

The given, reduced to the status of the positive (real) and identified with the level of actual occurrence, is transcended in the power of imagination towards an ideal, which if it were reached would be the unity of thought and being. The idea, however, has an ambiguous status. It is explainable in terms of real factors, on the one hand. As an idea, on the other hand, it transcends the real, and is idealistically severed from a real base. It is impossible to discover an ultimate point of reference in the ideal, either by anticipation or by recollection. Thus one is thrown back on the real, but with the difference that he has passed through a trajectory, what Kierkegaard called the "double movement of infinity." For Tillich one must remain with the real; nevertheless, because of the pattern of transcendence, the limits of the real are broken, in a belief-ful way. The entire scheme of real and ideal, in the tensionful relationship of the two poles, is supposed to point to the unconditional ground of being and meaning. The real becomes open or symbolic of the "prior" reality of the unconditional, which intrudes into the real situation, in judgment and in grace.

The essential becomes a critical instance with respect to every realization. In turn, the real is pointed to in every essence. Both the origin of the dichotomy, and the ultimate, paradoxical reconciliation of it, are supposed to be found beyond essence and existence. The origin is in the "fall" and reconciliation is in the new being in Jesus as the Christ.

4. An Analysis of the term "Power of Being"

The contours of Tillich's thought appear in what for him is a most central concept, the "power of being" (Seinsmöchtigkeit). It is said that his ontology is not one of "being" but of the "power of being." In the very ambiguous meaning of this term the lineaments of Tillich's thought can be discerned.

Tillich's concept of the "power of being" was made possible by his acceptance of Schelling's nature mysticism, which discovered in nature the same power of self-determination (potency) that is discovered in the creative ego.[49]

If we now use the term "personality ideal" as it is used in the cosmonomic idea philosophy, and not as Tillich used it to designate the isolated personality in a relationship of domination with respect to nature, we can speak here of an illustration of the inner tendency of the personality ideal to embrace all reality. This tendency came to expression in later idealistic thought, that began to see freedom in nature and nature in freedom. This tendency, as we have observed, is also at work in existentialistic thought, in concepts such as "destiny," "universal guilt," and "amor fati." That Tillich's thought drew from this philosophical tradition made it possible for him to use "power of being" as an embracive term.

An analysis of this concept discloses not only its extremely analogical character but illustrates the structure that underlies Tillich's thought and that gives his concepts their meaning.

Tillich says that being is the power of being. (*Seinsmöchtigkeit*).[50] As he says, it is "the power in everything that has power, be it a universal or an individual, a thing or an experience."[51]

In its barest signification the "power of being" refers to the irrational, arbitrary forces of nature, in contrast to the forms of culture. There are, for instance, the powers of blood and soil. There is the realistic use of power in the political situation. The power of culture formation overcomes the primitive powers of nature; but it tends to become formal and empty. As we saw, Tillich discerned in movements such as Gestalt psychology, in contrast to formal-rational methods, a return to more original contact with the creative ground of all things. Here already there is a deeper sense of "power." In the effort of empathetic-understanding thinkers to avoid the dilemma of naturalism and formal-logical method, Tillich found a reassertion of the power of being to grasp unconditionally. If in culture formation the element of form has gained the upper hand and the subject is regarded to stand in a technical, controlling attitude, e.g., in the manipulation of ideas, there breaks through, as in the idea of *Gestalt*, something that is able to grasp one in an unconditional way. From an early date Tillich was sensitive to the fascinating power of the primitive, especially in art, and its "Dyonysian" distortion of form. In it he discerned, as we saw, the presence of the creative-destructive ground of being.[52] But the formless, destructive element was not only a lack of form; it was itself an active opposition, itself productive of form. Thus Tillich could come forward with the paradoxical statement that it was a form of anti-form.[53] In the demonic, in its transcendental, encompassing character, there was the expression of an ambiguous power that could grasp one unconditionally.

It is characteristic of Tillich's thought that "power" always ties in with the "real." Tillich himself relates it to classical metaphysical "realism" as well to a "realism" of a distinctively modern kind. We shall maintain, however, the position that Tillich's term "power of being" has a meaning that is modern. In their analogical structure "power" and the "real" parallel each other. As we observed, Tillich gave the idea the status of being a projection, but not only a projection, of imagination. It is an abstract possibility that has critical but no constitutive significance. Given constitutive meaning the idea becomes an utopian ideal that is divorced from the real power situations and is empty. The ideal is for the isolated subject. Within the idea, however, there is a tendency towards the real, towards the historical, in Tillich's sense, as the level of occurrence. There is the power of the isolated subject, that stands outside of history in its inner meaning. There is, on the contrary, the experience in the *kairos* of being grasped by a superordinated power (content) that is at the same time an unconditional demand.[54] Tillich's notion of "power" ties in with a historical realism, in which the degree of power is correlate to the degree of historical reality.

Tillich, however, did not carry the latter correlation through altogether. Certain historical realistic positions do indeed carry it through. We find this correlation in an unbroken form in Marxism. For Tillich, however, the correlation is broken, because ultimate power is not manifested in a simple immanent-dialectical way, out of the inner necessity of the situation. Ultimate power is supposed to come in a transcendent-paradoxical way. This state of affairs, which we have mentioned before, is reflected in Tillich's statement that in power there is always an element of powerlessness.[55] Powerlessness is present, he said, because all being must transcend itself.[56]

For Tillich the central power is that of the new being in Jesus as the Christ. It is at this point that the strands of Tillich's antinomic thought focus. From every angle his conception of the Christ is a mass of contradictions; yet, here a principle is supposed to hold that Tillich embraced from the first, that was already manifest in his evaluation of the philosophy of religion of Rudolf Otto. His own position dovetailed with that of Otto, that one does not begin with being (*ontic*) but with meaning. In the new being Tillich thought he had found an origin-al meaning as power. The new being is supposed to have an eschatological priority. As one is engaged in describing the new being, he is already taken up in its power, in which the antitheses involved in his thinking are supposed to have their origin-al reconciliation. The question must inevitably arise, for Tillich as well as for other thinkers who have an irrational phenomenological approach, whether this power is truly original.

It would be worthy of a separate investigation to test Tillich's interpretation of the "power of being" with respect to Greek metaphysics. He applied the term to the religious depth of all metaphysics, including Greek metaphysics, without asking whether the term in its analogical use depended on a structure that is distinctly modern. We assert that Tillich's usage of the term "power of being" depends upon the altogether modern notion of freedom as self-determination.[57]

Our own interpretation hinges on the idea that the structure underlying Tillich's position is a specifically modern one, that stems from late Idealism and existentialism. Thus we ask whether it was proper for Tillich to speak of Greek patterns of thought as if they were compatible with his own. There is in Greek thought the tension between the Apollonian conception of form and the Dyonysian conception of matter; but is there any place for the association of even a religious content of the conception of matter with the self-determination of personality, or for such a complex notion as a form of anti-form? The idea of the breaking of form is discovered in the Dyonysian motive of Greek thought, but there is not the complex dialectic of form and formlessness as it appears in late Idealism, within the context of the dialectic of freedom and nature.

What we have observed concerning Tillich's use of the term "power of being" indicates that one cannot delineate the meaning of this central notion in terms of simple, unambiguous concepts. Instead, the moments of meaning here have their unity only in terms of what, if it is not capable of being described in a logically consistent fashion, is nevertheless a basic structure that underlies the concepts of Tillich's thought and gives them their meaning. Further, this structure embodies ideas concerning the coherence, the deeper unity, and the origin of the cosmos.

5. CONCLUSION

It must be recognized that the idea of autonomy was employed by Tillich critically to thwart de jure and de facto the elevation of any particular synthesis to the position of the origin of meaning. The idea of integrated personality must negate and transcend every actual synthesis, and every absolutized standpoint is subject to the erosion of time. There is, as we have observed, no limit to this critical activity. Nevertheless, Tillich held with equal tenacity to the autonomy of history, in the sense that he refused to allow it to be transcended simply and unambiguously. History, not in the sense that it is for the isolated historical consciousness but in the deeper sense of the historic, must remain the frame of reference. Has then a particular synthesis, in this case a historical one, been elevated to the privileged position Tillich denied to others? We already posed this question in effect when we asked whether Tillich had made history into a noumenon. We claimed that he had, in the sense that he refused to qualify history in terms of a point of reference standing simply outside of it.

The problem we have sketched above would cease to be a problem only if in some fashion the historical itself, in the deeper sense of the historic, either could avoid being a synthesis beside other syntheses and could embrace within itself all possible syntheses, or at least could serve as the frame within which there might appear that which transcends all syntheses and which provides the key to embracing them. That Tillich viewed the matter thus, especially in terms of the second option, is patent. He thought he had discovered on the level of history, in the *Kairos*, a being that reflected in itself this transcendence.

In a *kairos* the key is provided for transcending the absolutization of any synthesis. A synthesis, he thinks, is always for an isolated subject. In a *kairos* the clue is given for transcending the isolation of the subject. Here, on what Tillich regarded to be the level of true occurrence, there appears a being in which are negated all particular absolutizations. It is as a *kairotic* subject that one is taken up into this central event and that one can gain the standpoint from which to discern and criticize the partialities of his existence.

Tillich acknowledged, however, that there would always be as a matter of fact (as he said, "under the conditions of existence") the absolutization of particular syntheses. The truth was supposed to emerge, therefore, within the tension of the existential absolutization of particular synthe-ses and the critical negation of them. This negation was supposed to be deeper than a pure, abstract negation; it was supposed to be carried by a deeper affirmation,[58] which was understandable only in terms of the intrusion of unconditional meaning into the existential situation.

In the statement that the absolutization of any particular synthesis takes place under the conditions of existence, there is the tacit asser-tion that essentially there is no such absolutization. Nevertheless, Tillich gave to essence only the status of abstract possibility, which cannot even be represented without there appearing that ambiguity which drives it towards existence.

This tension points, Tillich thought, to a transcendent being, in which there is the intrusion of essence under the conditions of existence. In Jesus as the Christ one encounters, he said, a being in which there appeared the power of the new being, in overcoming the ambiguities of existence.

In Tillich's idea of essence we discern a pointer to a systatic coherence of meaning, "before" the "fall" of rational freedom and the rise of the antinomy. Nevertheless, this "before" is a mythical expression for what is neither structural nor temporal. It is impossible, Tillich thought, to give a genetic account of the absolutization of particular syntheses and of the antinomies consequent upon it.

It is clear that Tillich took his point of departure within the antithetical relation of theoretical thought. Within this antithetic relation a break is introduced into the coherence of meaning of the cosmos, as the logical aspect of our thought is set up over against a non-logical aspect of reali-ty. As a consequence of this antithesis, there is the isolation of an aspect of reality, disengaging it from the coherence of meaning and setting it over against other aspects of reality. This state of affairs does not at all pertain on the level of pre-theoretical thinking, where the aspects of the cosmos are still related in an unbroken coherence of meaning.

In Tillich's expositions there appear the antitheses characteristic of the-oretical thinking. Of this he himself was very much aware. His method, as we observed, was to retain them, at the same time disqualifying them as belonging to the sphere of what is objectified. In spite of his dis-qualifying them, however, Tillich never made the attempt to eliminate them by way of a reformation of philosophy. On the contrary, Tillich assiduously maintained the antinomies arising from the absolutizing of particular theoretical standpoints – in the interests of the disclosure of unconditional meaning – could appear only through the antinomy, and could appear truly only if the antinomy were kept at its maximum level of tension.

Even though he disqualified the attempt as being impossible to attain, Tillich placed as the initial stage of the movement of transcendence, the "double movement of infinity," the attempt to attain to objectivity, in the sense of a standpoint having universal validity, as the unity of thought and being. Belonging to this metaphysical quest there is an antithesis between the sensory and the logical.[59] The successful completion of this movement of "linear" transcendence would be the attaining of an absolute standpoint, separated from the finite world of sense. Tillich's philosophy certainly does not fall simply within this pattern; it goes far beyond it. It is characteristic of his position, as well as that of other dialectical thinkers, however, that this metaphysical quest and its supposed inevitable self-dissolution are never simply eliminated. The failure to attain to a metaphysical foundation of truth remains as an ineradicable moment in their thought, and antitheses belonging to this quest remain without any attempt being made to eliminate them by way of a reformation of philosophy.

Out of the failure of the metaphysical quest was born a profound distrust in the creative power of human understanding and the conviction that understanding had an exclusively critical function when it came to the question of ultimate truth. From the quest and its supposed inevitable self-destruction arose the set of problems that has brought forth many attempted solutions within the framework of the humanistic personality ideal as it asserted itself in opposition to the science ideal, including the solution proposed by Schelling, to which Tillich attached himself. In this development within late Idealism there was a marked tendency towards the concrete and towards history, interpreted as the sphere of true occurrence; nevertheless, in its deeper interpreters, including Tillich, there has never been the notion that the "historic" can be understood truly in a direct, unambiguous way, but always in an indirect, paradoxical way, in antithesis to, but also in union with the movement of critical rationality. In this acknowledgment is enshrined the insight of Schelling in his attempt to effect a "synthesis" between mysticism and guilt.

Even within the historic, in which Tillich and others have sought to discover the key to transcending the antitheses set up in the metaphysical quest and its failure, there are clear signs that the antithetic relation of theoretical thought has not been transcended. This is manifest, for instance, in the opposition between the ordinary level of event, on which there is supposed to be a dominance of space, and the level of *kairos*, on which there is supposed to be a dominance of time. It is also manifest in the distinction, drawn within Tillich's historicistic thought, between the heart and the periphery of a culture.

In Tillich's view there is, as we saw, an antithesis between the heart of a culture, expressing itself in cultural symbols, and the rationalized periphery of a culture. It is only at this periphery that it is possible for rational discrimination and criticism to have power over the symbol, after the symbol has already lost in vitality and has begun to die, a death to which the power of rational criticism contributes. This antithesis – characteristic in its bare form of life-philosophy (*Lebensphilosophie*) – was overarched in Tillich's thought by a deeper dialectic. Nevertheless, it remained without resolution in his thought. In fact, the dialectical scheme that is supposed to overarch it itself depends upon it. It is only as the process of rationalization and externalization has reached its limit that the question can arise whether here, nevertheless, unconditional meaning can appear.

Tillich's ploy was to keep the antinomies in a state of maximum tension, which is necessary, as we have said, if one pole or the other is not to be isolated and substantialized. This symbolization, in its grasping power, stands over against rational discrimination, willing, and domination. Yet, these are not supposed to stand over against each other as things but in mutual tension.

The antitheses involved, however, set apart what must be seen in their mutual coherence of meaning. Symbolization cannot take place, for instance, except on the foundation of some kind of rational discrimination and control. Symbolization depends upon the cultural base of formative power.[60] Tillich, as we saw, was forced to relate the domination motive to history and to symbolization; but his position allowed him to do it only in an indirect way. He could not allow the idea of controlling forming according to a free project to relate to the inner sense of history.

There is also an indication that the idea of history, in the deeper sense of the historic, itself involves a theoretical synthesis within Tillich's thought. The idea of the symbol-creating group is prominently related to the historical analogy of symbolical power. We have, however, sketched the ambiguity of meaning which attaches in Tillich's thought to the idea of power. Within his thought the way is blocked for the original meaning nucleus of the historical aspect to appear. The moments of meaning of the historical are unable to be related integrally; they come to stand over against each other in a tension that finally proves to be an irreconcilable one. Thus also the way is barred to obtaining a satisfactory criterion for historical action.

As we pointed out, the position of historical realism clearly requires a criterion for the historical. It insists that action, to be truly action, must be truly historical, and that to be truly historical action must be truly progressive. The difficulty arises for this position, however, that as soon as one develops a criterion for history he has come to stand outside of history. That is awkward for a position for which history is identified with the level of true occurrence. To identify historical action is to set it over against other kinds of action. Further, any such criterion of action must be branded "abstract" by historical realism. Thus we face a dilemma. To accomplish what the historically oriented position itself demands one must continually take a stance outside of what it declares to be the embracing source of meaning, or at least the key to it. One must objectify a standpoint outside of the historic, from which history may be dominated.

The same difficulty can be expressed in terms of the problem of transcendence. In the dynamic of history there must be a constant transcending of every actual synthesis. Is this act of transcending a real act or not? If it is not a real act, it is no transcending at all. If it is a real act, then it is possible only by way of an isolated, arbitrary act of freedom, in which the deeper meaning of history is violated. This antinomy Tillich accepted already when he adopted Schelling's idea that the fall of freedom from its ground was the presupposition of the possibility of history.

The alternation between history and apostasy from history involved in his position was very clearly before Tillich's eyes. For him it pointed to the need for a transcendent solution. There was, however, no unambiguous way towards this solution. There was only the abstract negation of every concrete occurrence paired with the abstract affirmation of every concrete occurrence as a possible symbol of the unconditional. Such abstract negation is possible, however, only within the antithetic relation of theoretical thought.

From the above we can see that Tillich was cut off from asking about the genesis of the antithetic relation of theoretical thought; he could

not account for it as introducing a break within a more original systatic order of reality in which the theoretical antithesis has not yet arisen.
He simply began within this antithetic relation.

Indeed, there is in Tillich's thought a reflection of a sort on the genesis
of the antithetic relation, in that the antitheses are declared to pertain
under the conditions of existence. There is, therefore, a reflection back
to a "level" of essence on which the antitheses have not yet arisen. Nevertheless, as we have seen, the level of essence is for Tillich a projection
of imagination. He gives it the status of a possibility that hovers over
every real situation. Having started within the antithetic relation, Tillich
was then obliged to seek the unity of meaning by way of a synthesis of
the aspects distinguished in the theoretical attitude of thought. He took
the way characteristic of the positions beginning with Fichte that rose
up in the context of the personality ideal in its opposition to the ideal of
science, namely, of passing through the antinomy.[61] His quest for synthesis had to root in the antinomy itself.

Tillich's position is not altogether dialectical, if one means by dialectic that one moment of an antinomic relation can be thought to flow as
by a simply "dialectical necessity" from the opposing moment. Thus,
as we have seen, the solution he seeks is not an "immanent-dialectical" but a "transcendent-paradoxical" one. Nevertheless, as we have
also remarked, keeping the poles of the antinomy in a state of maximum tension is of the utmost importance for him. Without this tension
the moments of the antinomy would be isolated and substantialized,
deprived of their dynamic character. There would be what Tillich rejected from the outset, a static idea of transcendence. This would involve
the isolation of a dialectical moment, which would demand in turn that
there be a renewed attempt at synthesis. That Tillich acknowledged that
such isolation and absolutization was inevitable did not mean that he
abandoned the attempt at synthesis. It remained as a moment in the
complex dialectic of making and breaking syntheses that belonged to
his thought from its inception to its end.

Within the context of the personality ideal in its opposition to the
ideal of science there have been repeated attempts of apparently most
disparate character to discover a standpoint from which the totality of
meaning might be understood. From Rousseau's sentimental religion of
nature the path leads to Kant's elevation of the moral ego to the status
of the root of the meaning of the cosmos. Fichte criticized Kant for not
having discovered the truly transcendental starting point, but of having

in effect elevated a general rule to the position of arche, to which the particulars of experience were to be subsumed. In its place he put the creative ego, as the root both of itself and of nature. The idea of the ambiguity of autonomy and freedom, which had been set forth by Kant, soon made its inroads, however, upon notions in ethical idealism. Hegel sought to incorporate fully into his system the idea of the ambiguity of the abstract ego. His obvious intent was to interpret the concrete ego as the absolute source of initiation and return of the meaning of all reality, a source that would embrace all things in their proximate unmeaning as well as their meaning. Hegel has been accused, however, against his obvious intent, of having absolutized and substantialized the ego, of having made it into an idealistically isolated self divorced from the situation of the "existential individual." Thus we have had, in the line of Schelling and Kierkegaard, the existentialistic critique of Idealism. Kierkegaard, for instance, derided the Hegelian system, which was intended to be the description of the odyssey of absolute spirit, but which had to be unmasked as an ideal edifice which was indeed beautiful to contemplate but in which no one could live. Still the criticism proceeds. Existentialism itself has been criticized for isolating the subject, which leads to a "decisionism," in which riskful decision is scarcely distinguishable from subjective, arbitrary adventurism.

Tillich's own philosophy moves within the same problem area. It is occupied, within the climate of thought that arose in late Idealism, with the problem of dialectic and synthesis. He acknowledges the need for a concrete approach, in which there is no isolation of one or another pole of the antinomy, but in which, within the tension of the antinomy itself, there is an indication of something beyond the antinomy and beyond synthesis from which they can be understood.

Like those of the others, Tillich's attempt involves a reflection on the self. Every particular synthesis (object) is for an isolated subject. Through the autonomy of the subject every particular synthesis is transcended.

The entire subject-object relationship, however, is supposed to be relativized by being qualified as objectivized. This fundamental objectification, qualifying the entire subject-object relation, is supposed to qualify all syntheses, e.g., of a social, of an aesthetic, of an ethical kind. In this qualification there is supposed to be a pointer to the historic, which opens up the way to what is above all synthesis. In the historic the self indeed recollects itself; its freedom is paired with a destiny, which is not an external necessity against which the free self would have to rise up in Promethean rebellion. Nevertheless, a point is never reached at which the self, in its autonomy and freedom, can have rest.

Tillich sought, with others, for a concrete starting-point, in which the ego is in-situation. Such a starting-point is supposed by others to rise above all synthesis, as an absolute origin of meaning. We can only conclude, however, that for Tillich it did not provide a true basis for unity. There is always a fall into a situation where arbitrary freedom must set itself up against blind necessity.

For Tillich the philosophic search for a standpoint from which to understand the problem of synthesis must fail. This conviction accounts for his having abandoned the search along purely philosophical lines and having sought for a theological answer.

6. Epilogue

The careful reader will be convinced, along with the author, that in spite of the fact that we have turned over much ground in this series of articles there is much that still lies fallow. Let us hope, however, that a line of approach to Tillich's thinking has been opened up that allows it to be described as to its true contours but also provides a firm basis for criticism. Tillich's thought offers a particularly fruitful field for such analysis and criticism. His own views of history and of decision in history were formed with a profound awareness of the snares involved in the previous attempts to approach these problems. His position is informative precisely because of its wrestling with the profound ambiguities arising within modern thought, as it is dominated by the dialectic of nature and freedom.

That we end our series of articles in concern – that we leave the profound question of dialectic and synthesis as a question – is not inappropriate, considering the fact that Tillich himself regarded the impasses of philosophy to pose the questions that anticipated a theological answer. However, the position of Tillich, just because it is penetrating enough to disclose the *cul de sacs* of immanence philosophy, can be an occasion to pose a deeper question that Tillich's basic allegiances never allowed him to pose, namely, whether the true way is found by accentuating the difficulties inherent in immanence philosophy so that a theological answer will appear relevant and even necessary, or whether a new beginning must be sought by way of a reformation of philosophy, which would provide a new understanding of transcendence and a new approach to the problems of the coherence, deeper unity, and origin of the cosmos. We grant that such a decision cannot be forced upon one. One would be able to continue, as Tillich did, to expound and even to exploit the perplexities of immanence philosophy. But following its turns and twists, he must be challenged to consider the new beginning that a reformational philosophy offers.

When we ask about the possibility of discovering a source of meaning in terms of which our experience can be seen in its coherence, deeper unity, and origin, we do not ask for an altogether coherent theoretical system. Such a system is impossible to attain. We ask, however, for a standpoint in terms of which our thought will cease being driven inexorably in opposing directions, where it will no longer be dominated by a fundamental driving motive, like that of nature and freedom, where there are actually two motives opposing each other in a fundamentally unreconcilable tension. We ask for a transcendence standpoint in terms of which our thought is freed to give an account of the cosmos as it has been created by God – a standpoint that allows for the disclosure of the meaning of the cosmos in its integrality, that allows us to give an account of the unity of that meaning as it comes to a focus in man as the covenant head of creation, and that allows us to discern that this meaning finds its root in God and in his Creator-will, in his plan for man and for the world, which is indeed impenetrable to our finite understandings but which forms the point at which all the strands of our lives comes to a unity.

REFERENCES

* The first, second, and third parts of this work appeared respectively in the 32nd vol. (1967), 55ff., the 33rd vol. (1968), 32ff., and the 34th vol. (1969), 38ff., of *Philosophia Reformata.* These articles cited hereafter as AHAF-TPT.)
I should like to acknowledge the receipt of a grant from the Institute for Advanced Christian Studies, which made possible much of the research that went into the preparation of this final article.
1. Paul Tillich, *Gesammelte Werke* (Stuttgart: Evangelisches Verlagswerk), X, 46. (Hereafter cited as GW.)
2. Tillich had in mind, first of all, the events of 1932, especially those of July

20, when Franz Von Papen deposed the Prussian government and appointed himself Reich Commissioner for Prussia. CF. GW II, 225.

3. Unlike, e.g., Emil Fuchs, who objects vigorously to Tillich's "mysticism" and his failure to discern the true moving forces in history. Note his "Gesellschaftliche Befangenheit im Werke Paul Tillichs," *Zeitschrift der Karl-Marx-Universität Leipzig*, XIII (1964), 83-89. Cf. Tillich, GW II, 134.

4. Tillich's idea that Protestantism is a typical expression of the idea of autonomy (GW II, 25) is connected with his acceptance of ideal type analysis. The element of protest in Protestantism is lifted out of context and is made the leading trait around which the others are grouped.

5. GW II, 21.

6. Heinz-Dietrich Wendland sees, next to socialism, in the German youth movement an expression of the inner unrest of a society that was unsatisfied with itself, so that it sought community (*Gemeinde*) beside the rational structures. "Der religiöse Sozialismus bei Paul Tillich," *Marxismus-studien*, IV (ed. Iring Fetscher; Tübingen: J. C. B. Mohr, 1962), 191.

7. Older religious socialists, e.g., Ragaz, thought of the proletariat as the chosen instrument of God in history. Ibid., 175.

8. Tillich sees here the original contribution of socialism, that the idea of humanity is expressed, not theoretically, but in the sense of solidarity of the proletariat. There is a feeling of solidarity that has at its center the sense of universal humanity (GW II, 24). It is important for interpretation to take into account the relation of the idea of nature to that of universal humanity. A shift at this point is important for Tillich's relation to Marxism. Tillich rejects the idea of nature as an original harmony; it involves the conflict of primal forces. Nevertheless, he does not hold to the automatic harmonization of conflicting interests.

9. Tillich remarks that the "geschichtsobjektive Denkweise" of German idealism penetrated socialism by way of Marx. *Vernunft* was transposed from the sphere of human decision to that of objective necessity (GW II, 23).

10. Cf. Frieda Oberdieck, "Der religiöse Sozialismus des Kreises um Paul Tillich" (Dissertation, Gottingen, 1949), 41.

11. Representative of the continuing dialogue is Tillich's early work *Die sozialistische Entscheidung* (Potsdam: Alfred Porter Verlag, 1933). Since the first edition was confiscated by the Nazis, only a few copies are extant. The work was published in a second edition in 1948 (Offenbach: Bollwerk Verlag Karl Drott) in the series edited by August Rathmann *Schriften zur Zeit*. It has been taken up in GW II, 219-365.

12. GW II, 191.

13. We spoke of this pattern before, when we referred to Tillich's "hermeneutic of irrationalism" in our second article (Knudsen, AHAF-TPT II, 36; cf. ibid., 40). Note the discussion of Tillich's attempt to relate socialism

and religion by way of the "demonic" (AHAF-TPT III, 49).

14. Wendland, op. cit. 169. Cf. our remark about Christoph Rhein (AHAF-TPT II, 39; cf. III, 48).

15. Cf. Wendland, op. cit. 171.

16. Wendland describes the result of socialism's failure to respond to Tillich's criticism thus: "Faktisch hat der Sozialismus diese Kritik Tillichs nicht akzeptiert, sondern ist auseinandergebrochen. Die Einen halten die Utopie der klassenlosen Gesellschaft fest, ohne sie als Symbol einer *alles* Endliche transzendierenden Hoffnung begreifen zu können, die Anderen resignieren, geben also die Utopie, die Zielsetzung preis und wenden sich dem Fortschritt möglicher Reformen zu, was von dem ersteren als Verrat am Sozialismus verachtet wird. Die religiöse Sozialismus dagegen durchschaut die utopische Erwartung und tritt ihr kritischdialektisch gegenüber, d.h., er nimmt am ihr teil und geht öber sie hinaus" (Wendland, op. cit. 171-172). In terms of Tillich's assessment of what religious socialism actually succeeded in doing, Wendland's final statement might well be too sanguine. It correctly represents, however, Tillich's own program of religious socialism.

17. GW II, 191.

18. Vol. 66, no. 24 (June 15, 1949), 732-733.

19. Ibid. 733.

20. AHAF-TPT I, 63-64.

21. GW IV, 137. Cf. AHAF-TPT I, 67.

22. AHAF-TPT II, 33; III, 38.

23. AHAF-TPT III, 51.

24. This historicization is expressed in the identification of history with time. Tillich nevertheless thought of time as in conflict with space, and the contours of history appear in its contrast to generality. These antitheses pose a problem for history considered as an overarching destiny.

25. *Kairos: Zur Geisteslage und Geisteswendung* (ed. Paul Tillich; Darmstadt: Otto Reichl Verlag, 1926).

26. AHAF-TPT I, 67.

27. AHAF-TPT II, 41f.

28. AHAF-TPT II, 42-43; III, 41.

29. AHAF-TPT I, 58, 60, 64; II, 33, 39, 40, 44; III, 48.

30. Cf. GW VI, 20ff., 140ff.

31. AHAF-TPT I, 65.

32. AHAF-TPT III, 48.

33. In the more consistent dialectical thinkers such a transcendental turn is common. It is employed in an effort to solve the problem of synthesis, to avoid the isolation of opposing standpoints. The failure to be dialectical enough is considered to issue in irrationalism. Cf. AHAF-TPT II, 39-40, 44. Thus any simple, external limitation of critical rationality is condemned;

unconditional content must appear at the boundary.

34. That Tillich says that unconditional meaning "breaks in," is supposed to indicate the paradoxical (theological) as opposed to the dialectical (immanent) appearance of unconditional meaning. Thus an element of transcendence is supposed to be injected, and the bounds of Hegelian and Marxist dialectic broken.

35. Cf. AHAF-TPT II, 40.

36. Again we emphasize the fact that for Tillich autonomous critical activity extends all along the line. There is no limit imposed on it. Any such limit would be external and heteronomous. We have shown that, were autonomy thus limited, the foundation of Tillich's attempt to solve the problem of synthesis would be destroyed.

37. AHAF-TPT III, 49.

38. Cf. AHAF-TPT III, 41-42. Tillich wrestles explicitly with the problem of a criterion for the kairos in GW VI, 149-156.

39. Cf. AHAF-TPT III, 51.

40. It is inadequate to claim, as Erich Schwerdtfeger does in his inaugural dissertation *Die politische Theorie in der Theologie Paul Tillichs* (Marburg an der Lahn, 1969), that there is a transition in Tillich's thinking from an earlier view in which it is not yet the case that the *kairos* is a historical consciousness: "... in dem der 'Kairos' nivilliert ist zu einer Möglichkeit innerhalb jeder Zeit, sondern um die Verkündigung der konkreten Krisis im gegenwärtigen geschichtlichen Augenblick" (p. 24). Tillich's position throughout demands that he attempt to steer between a simple given moment and a timeless, non-historical eternity.

41. It is precisely at this point that much criticism of neo-dialectical thinking, like that of Tillich and Bultmann, is currently being made. It is said that the historic becomes historicness, a timeless eternity. It is not correct to suppose that in Tillich's thought, or in that of Bultmann, there is a transition. Nevertheless, the idea of the historic tends to break down in either of the two directions it is intended to avoid. It tends to be identified with a simple given moment or with a timeless eternity.

42. Cf. my *The Idea of Transcendence in the Philosophy of Karl Jaspers* (Kampen: Kok, 1958), 94-97, and "Transcendental Motives in Karl Jaspers' Philosophy," *Philosophia Reformata*, XXXIV (1969), 127.

43. Cf. AHAF-TPT I, 62-64.

44. In Reformed circles it has been particularly Cornelius Van Til who has tirelessly pointed out the universalistic tendencies in dialectical thinking. Indeed, in our opinion, a close analysis of the idea of the transmoral in thinkers such as Kierkegaard and Tillich would confirm this analysis.

45. For a fuller discussion of the position of Tillich concerning the Christ see my *Symbol and Myth in Contemporary Theology* (2nd rev. ed., mimeographed,

1963), 85ff.

46. The point we are making brings into question much current interpretation, particularly from the side of the so-called "secular" theologians, who often claim that theologians like Tillich retain Jesus Christ as a central point of reference because they have not been critical enough and have not yet progressed far enough along the road of secularization. This criticism has been prominent among the so-called "God-is-dead" theologians. Objecting to this interpretation is not mere cavil. The issue concerns basic matters of interpretation, e.g., the problem of synthesis, transcendental method, and the question of supernaturalism.

47. GW IV, 137.

48. The analysis of this scheme lies at the foundation of my own dissertation, *Symbol and Myth in Contemporary Theology,* submitted in 1952 to Union Theological Seminary, New York, and *The Idea of Transcendence in the Philosophy of Karl Jaspers* (Kampen: J. H. Kok, 1958).

49. AHAF-TPT I, 61.

50. GW II, 250.

51. Paul Tillich, *Theology of Culture* (New York: Oxford University Press, 1959), 26.

52. AHAF-TPT I, 65f.; III, 44ff.

53. AHAF-TPT I, 66.

54. GW II, 94

55. GW II, 205.

56. GW II, 205.

57. Freedom is "... Bestimmung durch sich selbst oder Selbstmächtigkeit" (GW IV, 24).

58. Hegel went this far, in his idea of "speculation." Cf. Richard Kroner, *Von Kant bis Hegel,* II (Tubingen: J. C. B. Mohr, 1924, 1924), 155-156.

59. Cf. Herman Dooyeweerd, *A New Critique of Theoretical Thought* (Philadelphia: Presbyterian and Reformed Publishing Co.), I (1953), 158ff., 352; II (1955), 368, 370f., 567f.

60. Ibid. vol. II, 381.

61. Ibid. vol. I, 424.

TRANSCENDENTAL MOTIVES IN KARL JASPERS' PHILOSOPHY

The transcendental element in the philosophy of Karl Jaspers makes it impossible to approach it adequately with the use of simple analytical distinctions. His method is not simply to place one category over against another, e.g., compelling argument over against existential awareness, history over against historicness (*Geschichte*). Instead, his philosophy illustrates to a degree the spiral movement of thought which has been disclosed by the transcendental philosophy, a movement which seeks to penetrate in depth to the origin of meaning of every particular thing, an origin, in turn, which itself is not one thing among others but which is the overarching source which provides all things with their ground and their legitimation. Interpretation of Karl Jaspers ought to take this transcendental orientation into account. If it does not, it will miss what is the central thrust of his entire position.

That Jaspers' philosophy has a transcendental orientation is not at all surprising if one takes into consideration the essay he wrote while yet a student and which he later published as an appendix to his early work, *Psychologie der Weltanschauungen* (1919).[1] It is a penetrating study of the doctrine of ideas of Immanuel Kant.[2] Allowing for the influence of later thinkers like Wilhelm Dilthey, Søren Kierkegaard, and Friedrich Nietzsche on his method, it is nevertheless true that Jaspers' *Psychologie* was influenced heavily by Kant;[3] and it is the student essay appended to it that already set forth the fundamental problematic with which Jaspers was laboring and that indicated the direction of his proposed solution.

It was Jaspers' intent in his *Psychologie der Weltanschauungen* to pass in review the possibilities of the spirit.[4] He did not want to judge the metaphysical truth of a world view; he wanted only to ask about the reality of its spiritual influence. He desired to know what had been spiritually real and what was spiritually possible. As a psychology, his work was supposed only to contemplate understandingly all the possible world views.

For Jaspers, however, a world view did not appear as a ready-made possibility to be opted but as something in which one is already involved as a matter of life. In the *Psychologie* Jaspers' major conception is "spiritual life." It is of the nature of idea, a carrying ground which is supposed to be more than what can be comprised in any rational scheme and which is yet more than the reflection of subjective attitudes. Live participation in the idea was supposed to elevate one beyond the dilemmas of the foreground, most particularly the dilemma of subject and object.

For Jaspers, the dilemma was most acutely that of the opposition of the ultimately definable, dogmatic position, which might be externally appropriated by means of a violent act of will, and the absence of such a position, which might issue in complete disorientation and meaninglessness. In the *Psychologie* it is in terms of the idea that Jaspers seeks the answer. In the foreground one appears to be faced with inescapable alternatives. When one is shaken loose from his shelteredness in a particular rigid world view and is induced to give all other world views equal rights, the only outcome seems to be the nihilistic groundlessness of infinite suspension over the possibilities. The only way of overcoming this groundlessness might appear to be an escape into a new shelter, a new violently appropriated faith. Jaspers, however, considered this alternative to be overcome in the life of the spirit. In terms of the idea of a universal world view, the particular world view might seem to be only a subjective standpoint. Viewed in the light of the variety of possible world views, the universal world view might appear to be only an illusion. But in the life of the spirit one is impelled by a living idea, which is not simply subjective but which is anchored as an idea in the objective. The idea, which appears in the unstable alternation of its subject and object side, is supposed then to provide the overarching ground in which the foreground antinomies are overcome.

Thus Jaspers ascribed to spiritual life a transcendent status. It was supposed to arch over the subject-object relationship. It transcended everything that could be a possible object (*Gegenstand*) of thought (for the subject), and was therefore beyond anything that could be intended (rationally) in an act of will. As spiritual life it flowed over every boundary that might be set. Nevertheless, as transcendent, spiritual life was not supposed to be something alongside of the medium in which it appears. The way of the idea is not the way of mysticism, where there is an attempt to rise above subject and object to an immediate experience of ineffable unity. The way of the idea is a dialectical one, where there is a constant setting of boundaries and breaking through them again.[5] The transcendent idea can be perceived only in the medium of the antinomies of the foreground. Thus the idea is not considered to be one thing among others but the ground which transcendentally provides all things with their meaning.[6]

By the time he published his three-volume *Philosophie* (1932), Jaspers had become convinced that the idea, even in the sense of spiritual life, was not adequate as a concentration point. The philosophy of the idea (idealism) now comes to be, together with positivism, an all-inclusive orientation in the world. It is one of the views which claim in principle to have discovered the means of uniting in a total interpretation the entire range of experience.[7]

The precise reasons for this change, as far as I know, are not set forth in order in Jaspers' writings themselves. The main outline of the reasons, however, is clear from Jaspers' criticism of idealism in his *Philosophie*.[8] Idealism wishes, he said, to develop a final, meaningful interpretation of reality, closing off the idea and ignoring the loose ends that will not fit. The force of the irrational is blunted. It must again be given decisive significance. Thus, in the *Philosophie*, the limiting situations, which are already discussed at some length in the *Psychologie*,[9] are assigned a more central place. The limiting situations are ultimate surds which it is impossible to escape and which mean the shattering of one's possibilities. Their inevitability signs the death warrant for any attempt to round out human knowledge, whether idealistically or positivistically, in a complete system. They bring thought up short at its own boundary, presenting it with a barrier which it cannot of itself overcome.

It is now not the idea but true selfhood (*Existenz*) that comes to stand in opposition to every possible *Gegenstand* of thought. With this, Jaspers has undertaken a more radical reflection. The idea has at least to a degree come within the scope of what is an object (*Gegenstand*) of possible experience and is therefore regarded to be for the subject. This deprives it of its transcendent status. Now, however, thought is supposed truly to have reached its ultimate limits. At the boundary, at precisely the point at which it encounters what is for it an ultimate surd, there is a transformation. In an act of transcending one can perceive that both thought and the limit which it strikes are enclosed in a more ultimate origin, which is true selfhood. In the shipwreck of all human possibilities there is nevertheless the chance of discovering the way to ultimate meaning.[10]

It is in the first volume of what was intended to be a complete work on philosophical logic that Jaspers expounds in fullest detail his developed position.[11] Here he sets forth completely what he first began to do in his Groningen lectures of 1935, *Vernunft und Existenz*,[12] namely, to distinguish various areas which are discernible only in an act of transcending and which serve to establish the meaning and give the legitimation for various kinds of activity. These encompassing horizons (*Umgreifende*) occupy an intermediate position. They are discernable only in an act of transcending. They are not things among other things but are origins in terms of which things gain their meaning and legitimation. Nevertheless, they are not transcendent.

Jaspers distinguishes the immanent encompassing that being itself is (the world), and the immanent encompassings that we ourselves are. The world as an encompassing is that which we are in no way ourselves, the totally other which encounters us and which we encounter.[13] It is the all-embracing origin out of which objects arise for us. The immanent encompassing that we ourselves are breaks down into three modes: empirical existence (Dasein), consciousness in general (*Bewusstsein überhaupt*), and spirit (*Geist*). In this regard, Dasein is the immediacy of my awareness of existing, of being here and now.[14] Consciousness in general is the consciousness in us which is the medium for the attainment of generally valid, objectively compelling knowledge. It is the locus of valid thought.[15] Spirit (*Geist*) has as its characteristic that it is always living and moving in concretely understandable (*verstehbare*) totalities.[16] Though spirit is dependent upon correctness of understanding, it goes beyond. It is the essence of spirit that it sees everything in terms of unities, in which all the moments are experienced as parts of a meaningful whole.[17]

That the totalities of spirit are penetrable only to a degree by consciousness in general indicated to Jaspers that there was in spirit a partial transcending of the split of subject and object. The spiritual whole is itself no an object; it is a power that penetrates everything, bringing together content and substance.[18] Thus spiritual totalities cannot be known simply as objects but only by way of empathetic understanding (*Verstehen*) in which one himself is taken up into the circle of understanding and in the process of understanding others understands and changes himself.[19]

The encompassing of spirit, therefore, has not been altogether demoted from the position that it occupied in the *Psychologie*. It is still somewhat transcendent. However, it displays the pattern of the subject-object relation. Spirit, therefore, has come to occupy an intermediate position between the immanent and the transcendent.

From the time of the *Philosophie* it was *Existenz* that was declared transcendent, being the transcendent encompassing that we can be.[20] In Jaspers' estimation it rose above anything that could be a possible *Gegenstand*. It is clear that for Jaspers *Existenz* was not regarded to be some-*thing* in contrast to other things, i.e., something that could be the *Gegenstand* of an intentional act. It is not a special object, a particular realm of being, or a distinctive aspect of the soul. *Existenz* appears precisely at the point which from every immanent point of view is nothingness.[21] It is at the limit of all possible *Objektsein*. It is, therefore, supposed to be transcendent to the world, conditioning it as a whole. Yet, it is also clear that Jaspers regarded *Existenz* to be more than a limit. He regarded it to be a positive origin, the transcending encompassing that we can be, which is the fulcrum of meaning for everything that is immanent.

That *Existenz* is distinguished as it is from all possible *Gegenstande* and that it appears on the boundary of the world involves that it is discerned in a transcendental reflection. In its transcending to *Existenz*, thought reflects back upon what one is already as a possibility and to what is the hidden motive power behind its own activity. Thought seeks for ultimate being and meaning; but it fails to discover an adequate explanation for this search. That the search for being cannot be sufficiently grounded leads to reflection back on the self. It is possible selfhood (*mögliche Existenz*) that provides the dynamic for the metaphysical quest.[22]

Its transcendent status is supposed to mean that *Existenz* is not something beside thought, or beyond Dasein and spirit. To understand Jaspers' position one must recognize that thought is given the sole right of domain over the entire field of apprehension. There is nothing outside of it which might limit its scope. *Existenz* is discerned at the point where this autonomous consciousness encounters its ultimate limit, in the self-transcending of thought itself. It is discerned at the point which, considered from any general point of view, is nothing. It can be discerned only in a transfiguration of what is immanent. It is a misunderstanding of Jaspers, therefore, if *Existenz* is spoken of as if it were simply distinguishable from empirical existence, thought, or spirit, or from objects in the world. No matter what one may conclude about the success of Jaspers' transcendental approach, the fact that it is such an approach must be taken into consideration in interpretation. To ignore this basic thrust of his position and to speak, for instance, as if Jaspers meant simply by *Existenz* a particular way of apprehending things, a particular mode of action, etc., would be to misconstrue his meaning.[23]

In his elucidation of this origin, Jaspers expresses himself in a fashion that is reminiscent of ethical idealism. *Existenz* (true selfhood) is identical with itself in its self-creation. Its content is not something that can be objectivized and isolated from its realization. The content of *Existenz* is identical with the realization of itself in its free, creative act.[24] In this respect it is transcendent, elevated above everything which is a possible *Gegenstand* for consciousness in general, where, at least to a degree, there is always a split of subject and object, of content and realization.[25]

With the boundary character of *Existenz* in mind, however, Jaspers wanted to make certain that *Existenz* did not come to hover above the world, as it did in the idealistic tradition. He marshalls his strength to show that *Existenz* is only in its relation to the transcendent, from which it senses that it is given to itself; and that it appears only in the medium of what is general, in relation to the world and to the immanent encompassings that we are. There is no completion within *Existenz*; it is only in relation – to the transcendent, to other existences in communication, and to the world.

One can appreciate the interpretation of Jaspers' thought that takes into consideration its transcendental thrust. This understanding raises it far above other interpretations which fail in this important respect. But the question remains whether it is possible for Jaspers to carry out a veritable transcendental approach.

For Jaspers the transcendence to *Existenz* is a reflection back upon the self in contrast to all possible *Gegenstande*. This is the case notwithstanding the assertion that *Existenz* is only on the boundary and that it appears in the medium of what is immanent. The transcendence to true selfhood comes in a trajectory out of the world.[26] Even though Jaspers speaks of a second leg of this transcendence movement, in which there is a return into the world, it remains that after this double movement of transcendence *Existenz* in its union with Dasein is historic (*geschichtlich*). And the fundamental differentiation, the most general designation, of what is historic is that it is not general.[27] It is in opposition to what is in the subject-object relation, which for Jaspers is *per se* general. Thus it is in opposition to all structure which can be a *Gegenstand* of thought, feeling, or will.

Since he introduces in his *Von der Wahrheit* a definite teaching concerning a transcendence to immanent encompassings, it is possible for Jaspers to retain structures that are beyond the possibility of being objectified. These function as transcendental horizons which provide the meaning and legitimation of what falls within their reach. This transcendental orientation makes it possible for Jaspers at least to a degree to avoid a logicizing method. He distinguishes encompassings, each one with its own sense, which are not simply set off from each other in terms of analytical distinctions. It is in terms of these encompassings that concepts such as "communication" and "truth" take on specificity of meaning. There is a mode of communication that answers to every particular encompassing, such as the communication in the medium of spirit and the communication in the medium of generally valid propositions. There is also a variety of truth for each encompassing which has its legitimation in terms of its embracing meaning. Although these are not yet *Existenz*, and although there must be an additional transcendence to the "level" which is transcendent; nevertheless, the level of the immanent encompassings is able to provide a structure which is transcendental in character and which is not simply one objective area over against another.

Nevertheless, the question remains whether the transcendental framework which Jaspers erects in his doctrine of the immanent encompassings is really transcendental. A question can be asked of it, which indeed scarcely has a place within the structure of Jaspers' thinking itself, but which is imperative if there is to be a veritable transcendental critique of philosophical activity. Is the transcendental framework of Jaspers' philosophy truly transcendental or does it already incorporate theoretical-logical elements? This question does not fit the scheme of Jaspers' thought, but failure to ask it means in effect to eliminate the possibility of gaining critical insight into the dependence of theoretical-logical thought upon a structure of reality which itself is not theoretical-logical in character. Such a failure shields theoretical thought in its pretended autonomy *vis-à-vis* the structure of divinely created reality.

This question is germane to the understanding of the immanent encompassings distinguished by Jaspers: the world, empirical existence, consciousness in general, and spirit. That they are supposed to be discerned in an act of transcending does not of itself protect them from the charge of being abstract.

As we have seen, Jaspers describes *Dasein* as the encompassing which we are as we find ourselves immediately in our existence. It provides the foundation for, and is the ground of the legitimation of, immediate, spontaneous, uncalculating activity. It is able to be described as the encompassing of immediate vitality.

In terms of it, Jaspers legitimates, for example, the element of romantic love in marriage.[28] It also legitimates the struggle for existence and the will to power.[29] As *Dasein* one seeks to maintain his place and enlarge his field of power.[30] Within the sphere of *Dasein* there are no inherent limits to this drive. It is essentially boundless. It is indeed true that Jaspers does not allow *Dasein* to stand alone. He insists that it not be absolutized. It must be considered in connection with the rational grounds of consciousness in general and in terms of the unities of spiritual life; nevertheless, in its sense *Dasein* is abstract. It is *per se* unlimited, unbounded. It is also the case that in each expression of immediate vitality there is the presence of possible *Existenz*. Nevertheless, the transcendence to *Existenz* will be a transfiguration of the untrammeled expression of immediate vitality, an expression which is in its sense legitimated by the overarching horizon within which it transpires.

In the encompassing of consciousness in general one has the locus of timeless validity. What Jaspers has in mind is not the making of one or another valid judgment but the timeless sense which inheres in the act of consciousness. Within the sphere of consciousness in general one has the universal applicability of the subject-object relation, which is constitutive for experience in the world.

In consciousness in general the "subject" is set up over against the "object," anything to which one can have an intentional relationship, whether of feeling, an act of will, or thought. It is clear, however, that for Jaspers the subject as one pole of the subject-object relation is not the subject in the more ultimate sense of the term. It is a subject in a derivative sense.[31] In this sense the subject tends in Jaspers' expositions to take on various modal senses. In communication, for example, when one evaluates a situation, a companion, etc., and then enters into communication, it is not as *Existenz* but simply as a social subject.[32] In *Existenz*, on the contrary, there is an identity of the content of communication and the act of communicating, without any prior objectification of that with which one stands in communication.

These observations strongly suggest that the *Gegenstand* relation cannot be discussed even from within the framework of Jaspers' thought without posing at the same time the question of the modal order which underlies the possibility of theoretical activity. That Jaspers proceeds uncritically from within the *Gegenstand* relation, an uncritical attitude that is shielded from criticism by its being related to an encompassing, means that this question does not fit. It forces itself upon one's attention, however, as Jaspers' expositions proceed.

Properly conceived, the subject is *sujet*, i.e., in its entirety subject to the law of God. It is expressed in concrete individuals, as men, animals, inanimate things, etc. The individual participates in all aspects of reality, either in a subjective way (e.g., an animal feels) or in an objective way (e.g., the animal does not make aesthetic judgments but can be judged to be aesthetically pleasing). In the theoretical attitude it is not the subject that is set over against a field of thought, feeling, will; instead, it is the logical aspect of thought that comes to stand over against a non-logical aspect of the cosmic order. There are as many possible theoretical syntheses as there are aspects. The very possibility of these theoretical attitudes, as well as the possibility of understanding them in their deeper unity, is dependent upon the structure of law in which thought is embedded.

Jaspes' starting point excludes the possibility of posing the question explicitly of the relation of the theoretical attitude of thought to the pre-theoretical structure of reality which underlies it and which provides the transcendental foundation of its possibility. This starting point he shares with others who, in an uncritical, dogmatic attitude, assume the autonomy of thought. The prejudice is expressed also in what is, as a matter of fact, his starting point. Jaspers' discussion proceeds from the immanent concerns of orientation in the world, within the so-called subject-object relation, through the elucidation of *Existenz*, to the concerns of a subtly conceived metaphysics. In world orientation the theoretical attitude of thought is assumed to be a datum that may indeed be set forth in its structure but which is not in need of a foundation beyond itself. This, as we have suggested, is confirmed by Jaspers' discussion of consciousness in general as a particular encompassing that we ourselves are.

Indeed, Jaspers does not wish to absolutize the encompassing of consciousness in general any more than he wished to absolutize that of *Dasein*. He says, for example, that consciousness is related to empirical existence, in the sense that it obtains impulse from practical concern.[33]

Jaspers' viewpoint does not allow, however, that *Dasein* affect the inner sense of consciousness in general. The latter stays rooted in its own encompassing, the sense of timeless validity. Jaspers, therefore, would be able to discuss such a concept as "the life of logic"; but he would be able to do so by relating two encompassings that in their inner structure stand apart and even in tension with each other.

In its turn, spirit is the encompassing which realizes wholeness in the movement of understanding and being understood.[34] This understanding is itself understood in the sense of a *Verstehen*, an empathetic insinuation into meaning wholes. Again Jaspers does not wish to dissociate spiritual understanding altogether from consciousness in general. Nevertheless, in its inner meaning, spirit does not embody rational discrimination. Instead, it is irrational. There is no general criterion by which to judge the spiritual totalities; they are judged only in terms of the purity of the expression of their inner sense. As a result, however, there is a dissipation of these life-wholes into equally justified points of view. Jaspers wrote his *Psychologie* with the purpose of passing the various world-view possibilities in review. The *Psychologie* was haunted by the danger of being lost in the multiplicity of the possibilities. The solution, as we have said, was sought in the supposed transcendence of the idea, its elevation above subjectivity and its participation in objectivity, as spiritual life. When Jaspers mitigated this claim to transcendence, the problem of the multiplicity of possible world views became less acute on this level of his thinking. Nevertheless, the question is relevant, whether it is proper at all to speak of meaning totalities as individual meanings having an historical origin, or whether the idea of totality belongs somewhere else altogether. That spiritual wholes occur within the horizon of spirit means that each one of them is sanctioned insofar as it is a pure expression of spirituality. Indeed, they are criticized by rational consciousness, but only by a rational consciousness which stands in an antinomic relation to their inner sense.

Since his *Philosophie*, the problem of the unity of the various standpoints was approached by Jaspers along the lines of the elucidation of *Existenz*. This line of thought was regarded to be more fruitful because it took into account in a more radical fashion the limiting situations. In its quest for meaning under the impulse of possible selfhood reason strikes upon impassable barriers, which, when confronted in a proper fashion, lead to a reflection upon and a realization of one's true selfhood. True selfhood is realized while standing on the boundary within the antinomies of the limiting situations.[35] Within the "sense" of *Existenz* itself this being bound to the situation is taken up. *Existenz* is radically in-situation. It is historic (*geschichtlich*).[36]

If this transcendental reflection back on the self is to be successful it must be a reflection back upon what we are already, in the concentration point of our existence. This is strongly suggested by Jaspers when he says that the impulse for the search for being and meaning is possible selfhood (*mögliche Existenz*). The notion of precedence in a somewhat different sense is involved in the idea of the transcendent status of *Existenz*, as a positive origin (*Ursprung*). The question presses upon one, however, whether *Existenz* is an origin of meaning or whether it is a result of theoretical activity, the endpoint of an odyssey of reason which is finally brought to an ultimate limit, at which limit, in an inscrutable transformation *Existenz* appears. In a dialectical framework the above alternative cannot be regarded as an exclusive one. Both the positive and negative sides must be given their due. *Existenz* must be regarded as a positive origin, which, in effect, embraces one's self in its entirety.[37] Nevertheless, it must be thought to be impossible apart from the steady critical activity of consciousness whereby there is a transcendence towards the boundaries. True selfhood can appear only at the extreme limit of thought. Apart from this constant transcending *Existenz* will be inevitably confused with a *Gegenstand* in the world. It must, however, appear at the boundary of all possible *Gegenständlichkeit*.

In spite of the transcendental thrust of Jaspers' thought, it must be concluded with respect to his position, as well as that of other existentialists, that the notion of the self is possible only *in contrast to* what falls within the scope of generality.[38] Jaspers, like other existentialists, cannot be satisfied with such an antithesis. He must attempt to bridge it. Nevertheless, in spite of his most vigorous attempts, the antithesis remains. And its presence must raise the question whether he has truly entered upon a transcendental reflection upon the self in its integral unity.

From the Christian point of view, reflection upon the self which is manifested in all human activities in all of their diversity is a reflection on the total being of man in his basic choice of position in relation to God. Man can understand himself only in relation to the true God or to a contrived divinity (an idol) of his imagination. This reflection is back on the self as it is already taking a position with respect to God as the sovereign creator, to himself as the point at which there is a concentration of meaning of the cosmos, to its own apostasy in the head of the race (Adam), and to the radical redemption that is provided in Jesus Christ. This framework can provide a basis for understanding man in his unity because it penetrates to the root of human existence. This unity is obtainable only as the life of man is concentrated at its heart upon its true origin.

Apostate thought actively rejects this origin. As a consequence it is forced to take its starting point within the cosmos, which, however, itself does not offer a basis of unity. Thought which ignores the foundation of unity in the concentration of the self on its true origin finds that it is dispersed among the various possible starting points. There are as many possible theoretical syntheses as there are aspects of the cosmos, and no one has more right than any other to be elevated above the others.

Even *de facto*, Jaspers took his starting point within the framework of autonomous theoretical thought. As we have said, this assured that every principle of unity he might choose would show traces of theoretical synthesis. He is never really able to transcend the oppositions within the framework of the *Gegenstand* relation. Thus he is barred from having a truly critical reflection on the presuppositions of thought and fails to gain a standpoint from which he can view the self in its unity.

From the outset one of Jaspers' major problems was the dispersal of thought in the multiplicity of possible theoretical attitudes. Since no one attitude was more justified than any other, thought came to be suspended over the possibilities. The undesired result was the attempt to take position by a violent act of will. For Jaspers both of these spelled nihilism.[39] In the *Psychologie* a solution was hunted for in the idea. In the *Philosophie* there was the attempt to reflect deeper upon the true self. In all his works the theme of breadth and narrowness is a major one. Their reconciliation is one of his major interests. The continual dispersal of thought in the possibilities demands the search for unity; nevertheless, no unity is allowed to stand without being challenged by the openness of the possibilities of existence.

From the time of the *Philosophie* Jaspers located the fulcrum of meaning in *Existenz* in its historicness (*Geschichtlichkeit*) in its relation to transcendence, from which it is given to itself. *Existenz* in its possibility is truly itself only within the narrows of the existential situation, which is no longer seen in its negativity alone but which is transfigured as the voice of the transcendent. The transcendent is discerned where possibility ceases, where freedom and necessity coalesce, and where there is the sense that something must be entered upon if there is not to be the loss of true selfhood.[40] Yet, no position taken before the transcendent is allowed to stand by itself without again being subjected to the challenge of the possibilities of selfhood in the breadth of reason. Jaspers acknowledged that all of the existential relations to the transcendent were antinomic.[41] These antinomies are finally brought together in the conception of the transcendent as the *Einzigallgemeine*, in which unity and diversity are supposed to be reconciled.[42]

Jaspers recognized that the transcendent cannot be conceived of as being simply historic (*geschichtlich*) as is *Existenz*.[43] There must be a generality in it if it is not simply to evaporate into a reflection of the self in its situation. However, this generality is supposed to be a transcendent one, a generality that does not come with a universal claim to truth that can be grasped directly but a generality that transcends such a claim. In his view of the *Einzigallgemeine* Jaspers seeks a generality that is not catholicity,[44] and this can be preserved only if there is a rejection of a revelation having a constitutive claim on philosophy. There must be, after all, an acknowledgment of the autonomy of thought with respect to revelation.

Does Jaspers himself, however, avoid a dogmatism? Does he avoid setting up his own absolute commitment, with its own enlightenment from a source transcending itself, as an ultimate standard? His viewpoint must eliminate in principle accepting the Christian revelation with its world view in any fashion that would make it constitutive for philosophical thought. Nevertheless, Jaspers himself proceeds from a standpoint whose origin cannot be derived from autonomous thought itself. Assuming a starting point that screens thought from giving account of its dependence upon a divinely created order, assuming a starting point that means that the self cannot be viewed except in opposition to nature, assuming a starting point that carries the antinomies even into the relation of the transcendent to *Existenz* cannot be explained by the exigencies of thought alone. They arise from a fundamental commitment, which has taken position against the revelation in the Scriptures – a commitment of which a truly critical, transcendental philosophy must be ready to give account.

264 Robert D. Knudsen – Roots and Branches

References

1. 4th, unchanged edition, Berlin: Springer Verlag, 1954. (Hereafter cited as PW).

2. Leo Gabriel has pointed out rightly the importance to Jaspers of his study of Kant's doctrine of the ideas: "Er widmet der Ideenlehre Kants eine tiefgründige Untersuchung ..., deren sorgföltiges Studium die wesentlichen Ansätze Jasperschen Denken zutage fördert" (Leo Gabriel, *Existenzphilosophie* (Wien: Herold, 1951), 175). In 1956 Gerhard Knauss wrote: "Vorbildlich ist der Ideenbegriff Kants für Jaspers bis heute geblieben ..." (ed., Paul Arthur Schlipp, *Karl Jaspers* (Stuttgart: W. Kohlhammer, 1957), 132). Cf. PW 12.

3. Jaspers himself considered that he was heavily indebted to Kant: "Kant wurde mir zum Philosophen schlechthin, and blieb es mir" (Karl Jaspers, *Rechenschaft und Ausblick* (München: R. Piper, 1951), 339). (Hereafter cited as RA).

4. RA 362. Cf. the discussion in my dissertation, *The Idea of Transcendence in the Philosophy of Karl Jaspers* (Kampen: J. H. Kok, 1958), 8ff. (Hereafter cited as ITPKJ).

5. Cf. Knudsen, ITPKJ 15.

6. Cf. ibid. 16-17. Jaspers' thought even in his *Psychologie* is better approached by analyzing the notion of transcendence than by isolating one or another major term as the central one, even such an important term as communication.

7. Cf. Knudsen, ITPKJ 31.

8. Karl Jaspers, *Philosophie* (2nd ed., Berlin: Springer, 1948), 183. (Hereafter cited as P). Cf. Knudsen, ITPKJ 36ff.

9. PW 229-280.

10. Jaspers' own position was developed in part through his wrestling with the problem of interpreting the life of Max Weber. Weber came for him to epitomize the correct approach to scientific learning. Weber limited himself to particular studies, never making an all-inclusive judgment. Of critical importance, however, was Jaspers' wrestling with the problem of the incompleteness of Weber's personal life. Could this life, which only produced fragments and which shattered in a protracted illness, have meaning? Jaspers answered in the affirmative. It was possible to discern a positive meaning in the total shipwreck of one's aspirations. A major issue became enshrined in Jaspers' slogan, "Im Scheitern das Sein zu erfahren" (P 879).

11. Karl Jaspers, *Von der Wahrheit* (München: R. Piper, 1947). (Hereafter cited as W).

12. Groningen: J. B. Wolters, 1935.

13. W 85ff. Cf. Knudsen, ITPKJ 54-57.

14. "... Unmittelbarkeit des Sichfindens im Sein" (W 54).

15. Jaspers describes consciousness in general as "... der Ort des gültigen Denkens" (W 67). Cf. Knudsen, ITPKJ 58-63.

16. Spirit is the encompassing "... welche in der Bewegung des Verstehens und Verstandenwerdens Ganzheit verwirklichen..." (W 71).

17. "... aus einem Ganzen dem einzelnen Tun und Denken Sinn gibt" (W 72).

18. W 71, 76.

19. "... das im Verstehen des Anderen sich versteht und verstehend sich verwandelt" (W 71).

20. W 77.

21. Knudsen, ITPKJ 77-81.

22. P 17, 229; cf. 326.

23. One of the most consistent interpretations of Jaspers from the transcendental point of view of which I am aware is the work of Ulrich Schmidhauser, *Allgemeine Wahrheit und existentielle Wahrheit bei Karl Jaspers* (mimeographed, Bonn, 1953).

24. Cf. ibid. 193. W 83.

25. W 66-67.

26. Knudsen, ITPKJ 81-85.

27. Ibid. 94-97.

28. Cf. W 993-994, 997-999.

29. P 8, W 54.

30. P 8.

31. This "subject" has variously been called, e.g., the empirical subject, the isolated subject, the objectified subject. It itself is supposed to be the "result" of something prior, let us say, a fundamental act of objectification which is the source of the subject-object distinction.

32. Cf. Schmidhauser, op. cit. 238.

33. W 313.

34. W 71.

35. P 472. Cf. Knudsen, ITPKJ 93f.

36. P 108, 690, 775.

37. Ulrich Schmidhauser has interesting comments to make on this problem. He criticizes Bollnow strongly for thinking that what Jaspers means by *Existenz* is a human heart, presumably a center of human existence in contrast to a periphery. Cf. Schmidhauser, op. cit. 243. As transcendent, *Existenz* must be thought of as the fulcrum of meaning for human existence as a whole, not for one part over against another. As far as I can see, Schmidhauser reflects accurately what must be an important point for Jaspers. We should have to add, however, that this transcendental reflection must be unsuccessful on the background of Jaspers' thought-framework.

38. We must support the claim of Herman Dooyeweerd, expressed in the recent publication in which he confronts existentialism, that the sense of the historicness (*Geschichtlichkeit*) of human existence first takes on the contours given it by existentialism in the theoretical attitude of thought. Herman Dooyeweerd, *Verkenningen in de wijsbegeerte, de sociologie, en de rechtsgeschiedenis* (Amsterdam: Buijten en Schipperheijn, 1962), 19; and the judgment of *A New Critique of Theoretical Thought*, I (Philadelphia: Presbyterian and Reformed Publishing Co., 1953). "Modern humanistic existentialism ... can grasp existence as the free historical exsistere only in its theoretical antithesis to the 'given reality of nature' ...."

39. Cf. Knudsen, ITPKJ 10, 46.

40. Ibid. 118f.

41. Ibid. 145.

42. P 694.

43. P 694.

44. P 694.

RUDOLF BULTMANN

I. Biography [1]

RUDOLF KARL BULTMANN was born on August 20, 1884, in Wiefelstede, in what was then the grand Duchy of Oldenburg. The eldest son of the Evangelical Lutheran minister, Arthur Bultmann, and his wife Helene (née Stern), he came from a family which was close to the Church. On his father's side, his grandfather was a missionary. His grandfather on his mother's side was a pastor in Baden.

Bultmann's early years were spent in the country. From 1892 to 1895 he attended the elementary school in Rastede, the town to which his father had been transferred. From 1895 to 1903 he was a student at the humanistic gymnasium (classical high school) of Oldenburg. There, after 1897, his father was the pastor of the Lamberti church. During his high-school years what especially interested Bultmann, in addition to the study of religion, was the instruction in Greek and the history of German literature. He also eagerly attended the theater and the concerts.

After passing the final examination at the gymnasium in 1903, Bultmann began the study of theology at the University of Tübingen. Upon completing three semesters there, he studied in Berlin for two semesters and finally in Marburg for yet two more. In addition to studying theology, he followed lectures in philosophy and the history of philosophy. In Berlin also he greatly enjoyed the theater, the concerts, and the museums. He himself lists the theological professors to whom he was particularly indebted; at Tübingen, the church historian Karl Müller; at Berlin, the Old Testament scholar Hermann Gunkel and the great historian of Christian dogma Adolf Harnack; at Marburg, the New Testament scholars Adolf Jülicher and Johannes Weiss, and the systematic theologian Wilhelm Herrmann. It was Johannes Weiss who encouraged him to prepare for the doctorate and to qualify as a lecturer in New Testament.

In 1907, however, before entering upon his studies for the doctor's degree, he passed his first theological examination, under the High Consistory in Oldenburg. Here he was a teacher for a year (1906-1907) in the gymnasium. In the summer of 1907 he received a scholarship to Marburg, which made it possible for him to proceed to work toward his degree and his goal of becoming a lecturer in the field of New Testament.

In 1910 Bultmann was awarded the degree of licentiate in theology after writing on a theme proposed by Johannes Weiss, namely, "The Style of Pauline Preaching and the Cynic-Stoic Diatribe." In 1912, upon completion of a research thesis, "The Exegesis of Theodore of Mopsuestia," he qualified as a lecturer in New Testament at Marburg. There he taught as a *Privat-dozent* (roughly the equivalent of an instructor) until the autumn of 1916.

At this time he was called as a *professor extraordinarius* (an assistant professor) to Breslau, where he remained until 1920. Here he was married and had two daughters. Here also he wrote what is probably his most significant work, *The History of the Synoptic Tradition*, which was published in 1921.

In the autumn of 1920 Bultmann was called to Giessen as a full professor, succeeding the famous Wilhelm Bousset. Although he was satisfied with his position, he accepted in 1921 an invitation to return as a full professor to Marburg, the university he regarded as his scientific home. As the successor of his former teacher, Heitmüller, he now received the title of Professor of New Testament and Early Christian History. From this time he remained at Marburg, becoming emeritus in 1951.

At Marburg there was a considerable exchange of ideas among the professors. Marked differences of opinion were expressed within the faculty and by visiting lecturers. Bultmann speaks of the tension between himself and the philosopher of religion Rudolf Otto, who had succeeded Wilhelm Herrmann and who represented a position which Bultmann considered to be irrationalistic. There was also lively discussion during the visits of outside lecturers. Bultmann was strongly attracted to the new so-called dialectical theology. He agreed with it that Christianity was not simply one religion among others but was the response to the Word of God as it encounters man. He himself contributed toward its advancement and shared many of its positions. Although he continued to feel close to Gogarten, he became, as time passed, more and more estranged from Karl Barth, and a visit of Barth to Marburg would stir up excited discussion. Within the Marburg faculty itself there was a lively interchange between the theologians and the philosophers. This,

Bultmann writes, was particularly true when the philosopher Martin Heidegger taught at Marburg from 1922 to 1928. Bultmann entered into a particularly close relationship with him and began to draw heavily upon his ideas. It seemed to him that Heidegger's philosophy had a special relevance to the study of the New Testament. Together with Bultmann's professor, Wilhelm Herrmann, Heidegger has had a decisive influence upon Bultmann's thought.

In addition, Bultmann has also drawn heavily upon the thought of Søren Kierkegaard. Although he occupies his own distinctive place in theology, Bultmann is within that circle of theologians who, like Barth, Brunner, Niebuhr, Tillich, and Gogarten, are the spiritual heirs of the reaction to idealistic liberalism which was prepared by the literary effort of Kierkegaard in the nineteenth century and which gained a hearing during the Kierkegaard renaissance between the first and the second world wars.

More particularly in his own field of New Testament, Bultmann has been one of the foremost representatives in Germany of the scientific, radical criticism of the Bible. Coming out of the historical-critical school, he co-operated in developing a distinctive approach to the New Testament which is called "form criticism." He has an intimate acquaintance with the New Testament and also with classical literature. He has intensely pursued the study of primitive Christianity, examining its relationship to the Old Testament and Judaism as well as to the religions of its contemporary world.

II. EXPOSITION

The Program Of Demythologization

The name of Bultmann is most often linked with his famous program of demythologization. Itself much older, this program began to receive widespread attention during the second world war, when Bultmann published his article, "New Testament and Mythology."[2] This writing provoked widespread discussion, and the program it set forth has been a focal point of attention, particularly on the European continent. Some believe that this program is indispensable if the Church is to speak to the contemporary world; others hold that it means the destruction of the Christian message. What is this program and what does it entail?

According to Bultmann the message of the New Testament is expressed in mythological terms. Its materials are drawn from the myths of Jewish apocalyptic literature and from the Gnostic myths of redemption. Naturally sharing the world view current in their time, the New Testament writers thought in the framework of a three-level cosmology, a heaven above, an earth beneath, and a hell under the earth. This view takes for granted that nature and human life are influenced by supernatural agents (Satan, demons, angels, God), which can invade and affect the course of nature and history. The New Testament regards history as the battlefield of these super-mundane powers. Its Gospel is also couched in mythological terms. The drama of human salvation unfolds against the background of a celestial history. Salvation is conceived and planned in the eternal counsels of the pre-existent God. A heavenly being is sent to earth in order to accomplish man's salvation. He influences nature, performing miracles which attest and authenticate His heavenly origin. In a sacrificial death, a substitutionary atonement, He overcomes the powers of the demons. In a final triumph He rises from the dead and ascends into heaven. The early Church expected His imminent return on the clouds of heaven. The New Testament views history as proceeding to a literal, cosmic end, an event of the same order as the events of our daily lives, though of much greater proportions. According to Bultmann all these teachings of the Bible and the Church are mythical.

Bultmann's criticism is not piecemeal. It involves the entire framework of the biblical message. The world view of the Bible is mythological and is as such impossible for the modern man honestly to believe.

As a type of thinking characteristic of primitive peoples, mythology has been displaced as a whole by the modern scientific world view. Whatever specific form this modern view may take, it does not allow for the possibility that our world can be invaded by supernatural powers. Worldly processes are controlled by purely immanent forces and operate according to law. It is impossible for man to assume the uniformity of nature by using modern apparatus like the radio and methods like that of modern medicine and yet honestly to believe in the biblical world view.

Bultmann's negative criticisms arise in part out of his concern with what the Church is to preach to our time. He wants to avoid coming to our generation with the demand that it accept what he believes is an outworn view of the world in which the biblical message has been encapsulated. To demand this belief of it is forced and unnatural. Modern man can accept the biblical world view only by a sacrifice of the intellect.

When one views Bultmann's program of demythologization, however, one must see it in its positive as well as its negative aspects. Bultmann holds that there is a biblical message (*kerygma*) which need not be jettisoned along with the framework in which it is expressed. It can be removed from its mythological setting.

By this Bultmann does not mean that certain mythological accretions should be pared off, leaving as the gospel message a hard core of rational or moral truths. His program does not mean a simple elimination of the thought-world of the New Testament. His program depends upon the idea that there is an alternative to demanding the literal acceptance of the biblical world view or rejecting it out of hand for another world view. The key, he thinks, is to view the New Testament literature, which is thoroughly impregnated with myth, with an eye for the self-understanding of the primitive Christian community expressed in it. This self-understanding is supposed to express the true intent of the biblical writers behind their mythological pattern of thought. The demythologization program has the purpose of setting free this biblical message, which is able to speak to man as he understands himself today.

Bultmann, however, does not regard demythologization as his own private undertaking nor even as something recent. It has been carried out, he thinks, in all so-called periods of enlightenment, in the criticism of myth among the Greeks and more particularly in modern times with the rise of science and the ascendancy of a naturalistic attitude to the world. Even within the myths themselves there is the beginning of demythologization.

With regard to the latter point the thought-world of the New Testament is no exception. The tensions within it give rise to criticism. Bultmann discovers such a contradiction between the ideas of the Virgin Birth and the pre-existence of Christ. Especially significant, he thinks, is the contradiction he discovers between the sovereignty of God and the appeal for human decision.

Demythologization within the New Testament appears to some extent in the writings of Paul and thoroughly in the writings of John. The decisive step was taken, Bultmann avers, when Paul declared that the transition from perdition to salvation was not reserved for the time of a final catastrophe but had already taken place in the coming of Jesus

Christ. A concern with a literal end is transmuted into the concern for the meaning of the event of Jesus Christ here and now.

Within the mythological framework itself of the New Testament there is, therefore, the suggestion that the true meaning of the myths is not found in their literal (what he calls their "objective") form. This point is of the greatest importance for Bultmann. Myths reflect man's understanding of himself in his world.

Critique Of Liberal Demythologization

The twofold orientation of Bultmann's program of demythologization is reflected in his attitude toward the older liberalism. Although his theology has arisen in reaction to liberalism, it is not a return to orthodoxy. Bultmann appreciates the critical spirit which inspired liberalism's own demythologization program. What he criticizes is liberalism's view of the Gospel message.

Liberalism sought to reinterpret the Christian faith, in order to square it with the modern, humanistic view of the world stemming from the Renaissance and the Enlightenment. In a long history of Bible criticism it tried to remove the husk of a primitive, mythological world view in order to retrieve the kernel of moral truth which comprised the message of the historical Jesus. Bultmann does not at all object to these criticisms. On the contrary, he welcomes them as being indispensable to honesty and clarity. If anything, his caveats are even more radical than those of the majority of the liberals. Although it is not the whole of his program, criticism is one of its major pillars.

Bultmann objects, however, to the positive interpretation of the Christian faith which liberalism sought to rescue from the critical flames. In its various forms liberalism believed that it could penetrate beyond the picture of Jesus given by the primitive Church to the real Jesus, the Jesus of history. The religious liberals viewed Jesus as the prophet of a kingdom of moral righteousness. He was the teacher of general human values. His impact upon history was ascribed to the strength of His towering personality. This reconstruction of the Christian message, though difficult, was carried on with the confidence that the methods of modern critical research would eventually bear fruit.

Even within the older liberalism itself Bultmann discovers tendencies which led to its dissolution. One example is the contribution of the New Testament scholar Johannes Weiss. His research convinced him that a purely "historical" Jesus, the teacher of moral truths, could not be disengaged from the supposedly mythological and more particularly the eschatological elements in the Bible. Far from being a disposable wrapper, they belonged essentially to Jesus' teachings. After the labors of Johannes Weiss, Bultmann concludes, it was no longer possible to think of Jesus' message as the expression of general human truths. Jesus' teaching focused on the expectation of a future coming of the Kingdom of God, not by the moral efforts of man but by a "supernatural" incursion of the power of God.

The shift away from the older liberalism cannot be understood, however, in terms of one or another single person or influence. The change of theological insights depended upon a change of mood which resulted in the breakdown of the idealistic philosophy upon which liberalism depended. The older liberalism fell when the general truths in which it thought it could find a transcendent key to the meaning of human existence were declared to be "human, all too human." On this background it is possible to understand why the dialectical theology entered the scene with a definite "no" to everything general. No longer able to discover the key here, it had to look beyond.

Bultmann is confronted on one side by a vanquished idealism. On the other side is a victorious philosophic realism, which brought the transcendent ideals to earth, viewing them as the projection of material human needs. Bultmann acknowledges this victory. He does not attempt to reverse it. Instead, his approach is to disqualify both idealism and realism. They are, he says, both "general." Idealism is general because it finds the key to man's life in general ideals. Realism is general, because it finds the explanation of man's life in general terms, as the expression of some specifiable motivations. Bultmann's answer, like that of the existentialists, is that the key cannot be found in anything general. That is to say, it cannot be located in anything that can be set over against one's self and viewed from outside. The ultimate is not anything general nor anything that can be understood in general. Everything falling within this scope is immanent. The transcendent is beyond.

The repudiation of the older liberalism must be seen therefore against the background of a shift in the idea of transcendence itself, which is most sharply expressed in the transition from idealistic to existentialistic philosophy.

We have now reached the vantage point from which the critique by Bultmann of liberal demythologization can be understood. While he agrees completely with liberalism's negative attitude toward the biblical world view, he objects that the older liberalism failed to rise above what is general. It sought to replace the mythological world view of the Bible with another world view, with an interpretation in general terms of the meaning of man's life. Such a program conflicts, he says, with the contemporary self-understanding of man. Here Bultmann is completely in line with existentialism. With it he maintains that any such general or "cosmical" interest only veils the true nature of man and of the human predicament. The critique extends not only to the interpretation of human existence but also to the interpretation of Jesus Christ. Bultmann's major criticism is that liberalism, remaining on the level of generality, has missed or at least has seriously distorted the biblical message (*kerygma*), which centers in the once-for-all event of Jesus Christ. This is the crux of his often-repeated attack.

A good illustration of Bultmann's position is his attitude toward his former professor, Wilhelm Herrmann. He discovers tendencies in this liberal theologian which go beyond liberalism. These he has taken up into his own theology. Herrmann is lauded for his idea of the purity of faith. Faith is not a state which can be described from outside, nor is it founded on anything outside of itself. Faith is inherently a directedness (an intention) toward something beyond it. Nevertheless, Bultmann thinks, Herrmann has fallen short of his own view; he has not entirely abandoned the standpoint of the older liberalism. He still regards faith as being anchored in something which can be viewed apart from faith. According to Herrmann, Bultmann writes, faith is respect and trust in moral goodness and power. What redeems us is the impressiveness of the person of Jesus. He is the embodiment of personal goodness who impresses man as being a revelation and who induces him to trust in the power of the good over the stubborn realities of life. This moral goodness and power, Bultmann retorts, is a general human possibility. Herrmann has not risen in the last analysis above the level of general human goodness. With the older liberalism therefore he cannot see the true profile of the once-for-all (*einmalig*) event in Jesus Christ.

General History And True History

Bultmann's rejection of the older liberalism for having stayed on the level of generality has a positive goal in mind. It is to affirm that the focus of Christian faith is the once-for-all event of Jesus Christ, the act of God which encounters man in the moment of decision. What this positive side of Bultmann's program means, however, depends upon the important distinction between general history and true history. This distinction, a legacy of Kierkegaard's view of time, pervades contemporary theology. It is regarded as a means of criticizing the older liberalism without falling back into what is thought to be an outworn, myth-ridden orthodoxy. This distinction is most important for Bultmann. Here the many strands of his thinking come together. What he once said about the theology of Barth and Gogarten could also be applied to his own thought. What the slogan "dialectical theology" means, he wrote, is, briefly stated, the insight into the true historicality of human existence.[3]

Bultmann uses the word "history" (*Historie*) to refer to the science of history or to the events on the ordinary level of history, which are as such open to investigation by the scientific historian. In the fashion of the modern naturalistic historian, Bultmann views history as a drama of human interaction, the product of human planning and accomplishment, without the intervention of any supernatural agency. It is the domain of the all-penetrating historical understanding, which seeks to grasp the course of events in a neutral, objective way. Any hope of obtaining an over-all view of history, which could disclose its direction and meaning, is however abandoned. Ordinary history is not a source of ultimate values and meanings.

In answer to the ultimate meaninglessness of history, Bultmann does not appeal, as Lessing did, to a super-historical source of meaning, a "timeless truth." Together with the existentialists, Bultmann would regard such an appeal as a disengagement, a flight out of existence. Instead, he vigorously sets forth the existentialistic idea of true historicality (*Geschichtlichkeit*).

Geschichte refers to a level of true occurrence, a decisive time or time of decision. It can be understood only by distinguishing it carefully from both the particular event (on a certain calendar date) of ordinary history and the timeless principle or meaning which is supposed to be above history. For Bultmann, both of these are general, because they are in principle available to anyone provided he can satisfy the proper conditions. Their truth is "objective," true apart from the riskful commitment of the self. Man's existence, on the contrary, is true or concrete history. It is not established beforehand, in effect already decided. It is not given in general, not anywhere and everywhere available. Instead, man is always involved in projecting his possibilities in terms of a particular understanding of himself and his world. What he is depends upon his decisions, in which he may either gain himself or lose himself.

With the existentialists, Bultmann does not wish to discover his final reference point in anything general, that is, in anything that can be set over against the subject and be viewed by it. That was the thrust of his criticism of Herrmann, that the ultimate was found in something that was objectifiable. What can be objectified is for a subject. And the subject can also be viewed from outside. Both subject and object, Bultmann claims, are general. As such they must be distinguished from the true selfhood of man.

In true history, one does not set his world, himself, and the other as objects over against himself as a subject. In the spirit of Martin Heidegger, Bultmann seeks to go beyond this distinction of subject and object. Heidegger has said that the very possibility of making this distinction is dependent upon something more fundamental, one's being-in-the-world. In brief, I do not *have* my being, which I then relate to my world; my being is itself being-in-the-world. I do not exist as an isolated self, which is then related to the other; my being is being-for-the-other. Bultmann has applied this existential thinking to his theology. At the heart of his criticism of generalizing thought is the idea that I am not related to myself as to something outside of myself, for example, an ideal to be attained for a true explanation or understanding of myself; I am myself only in relation to what is absolutely and completely concrete-historical, even as my being is also exhaustively concrete-historical.

Only in the context of this existentialist-inspired battle against generalizing thought can one understand adequately Bultmann's repudiation of the supposedly mythical framework of the proclamation of the New Testament. It is his intent to interpret all of the objectifying, non-concrete-historical elements in the Scriptures, discovering behind them their true intent, the existential self-understanding which is itself part of man's concrete-historical existence.

This struggle has also the positive goal of disclosing the message of the Gospel as Bultmann understands it. As we have pointed out, this message has to do with an event, an event of the peculiar kind that we have described. It is not an event of general history but the once-for-all event of Jesus Christ. To this event, Bultmann says, one is related not by generalizing thought but in faith.

KERYGMA AND FAITH

For Bultmann, as for Kierkegaard, the final reference point for the Christian is what is ultimately concrete-historical, the invasion of the eternal into time in the moment. The proclamation of this event, and not of any true statements about it, is the biblical message which is to be disengaged from the mythical framework which envelopes it.

The event of Jesus Christ is not open to the neutral historical investigator; it is only for faith. What this means for Bultmann cannot be altogether clear at this point. An implication, however, is that the event itself cannot be separated from the reception of the event by the believing individual, but primarily by the believing community, the Church. The Gospels witness more to the faith of the early Church than to any historically verifiable events.

The fact that Bultmann regards the Gospels as a witness to the faith of the early Christian community does not prevent him from asserting that there is a primary stratum of history in the Gospels which biblical criticism should seek to recover. There is now an adequate method, he claims, to distinguish the early strata of tradition concerning Jesus from the later ones. Besides being famed for his program of demythologization, Bultmann is also renowned for his contribution to the development of this method, known as form criticism.

The method of form criticism claims to be able to distinguish certain stylized forms which the primitive Christian community employed in expressing its faith in Jesus Christ. Applying carefully worked-out criteria of development, form criticism believes that it has an adequate means of distinguishing earlier from later Gospel traditions. In this way it uncovers a thin stratum of tradition which it believes is very close to the actual sayings of Jesus, if it is not identical with them.

Whatever historical stratum can be discovered in the biblical writings is, however, of secondary importance to Bultmann. In the entire body of the New Testament, he thinks, it is only an insignificant part. He agrees with Wrede that the Gospels may not be taken seriously as historical records of Christ. Together with Wellhausen, he regards them as the expression of the faith of the early Christian community. So far are they from the historical Jesus that they do not even reflect primarily the faith of the Palestinian church. They are for the greater part the expression of the preaching of the Hellenistic church, which was the earliest preaching to represent Christ as a cult deity whose death and resurrection are the basis of salvation. The message of the Gospels is that of the Christ-myth. Matthew and Luke are more mythical than Mark. In John the mythical has prevailed.

Bultmann is not dismayed at this scepticism. It is not necessary, as the liberal theology supposed, to reconstruct a life of Jesus. He is ready, he says, to let the entire edifice of the quest of the historical Jesus burn down quietly. All that is burned is the imaginative picture drawn by a theology which believed it could base faith upon history. Such reconstructions can let us know only a Christ after the flesh. Concerning such a Christ he has little or no interest.

Bultmann's unconcern rests upon his conviction that it is the faith of the Christian Church and not historical tradition or knowledge that brings it into contact with the saving event in Jesus Christ. What little we can salvage of historical value concerning the life of Jesus portrays him only as a rabbi and a prophet who made certain ethical and eschatological statements. It is faith that sees the event of Jesus Christ in its saving significance.

For Bultmann, this awareness – that the Christ event is for faith – is more important than any calculation of the proportion of historical to non-historical elements in the Scriptures. In fact, on the background of Bultmann's view of *Geschichte*, the entire question of the historical (*historisch*) and the non-historical (*unhistorisch*) becomes of secondary importance. The kerygma indeed refers to an event, but not to an event on the level of ordinary event. The message itself is made up of a tightly knit composite of historical and non-historical elements, so tightly knit that it is irrelevant for faith to discriminate between them.

Part of this message, for instance, concerns the historical event of the crucifixion of Christ. This event is not part of the kerygma, because it occurred on a calendar date of history. As a simple historical event it was, he says, repugnant to the early disciples. It was a scandal. It was only as the historical event of the death of Christ was joined with the triumphant faith in the non-historical resurrection of Christ from the dead that it attained its status as part of the kerygma. In its kerygmatic significance, having to do with man's salvation, it is only for faith. For faith the kerygma is that Jesus has died and is risen again. Bultmann is certain that it is an actual historical occurrence that Jesus was crucified. He is just as sure that Jesus did not actually rise from the dead. In the kerygma there is the intertwining of the historical and the unhistorical. They are both present in what is the object of faith.

The center of attention therefore is the correlation of faith and the kerygma of the saving event in Jesus Christ. In this correlation it is quite impossible to distinguish what is the foundation and what is the superstructure. As there is no objective (subjective) basis for the Christ event, either in a (general) eternal truth or a (general) individual fact, so there is no objective (subjective) ground for faith. Both are concrete-historical. Faith is a total orientation of man's being toward salvation in Christ. At the same time the Christ event is unthinkable apart from the faith of the believing community. It is just as possible to say that the faith produces the event as it is to say that the event produces the faith. The faith and the event are in strict correlation.

Nevertheless, Bultmann wishes to give the event in Christ a kind of priority. Within the correlation it is faith that is oriented to the event of Christ, and not the event to faith. Bultmann expresses this relationship in various ways. He says that faith is possible only from the "time" of Jesus Christ. He also says that the event of Jesus Christ is always coming, always impinging upon the believing community from beyond. He says that faith is openness to Christ.[4]

When Bultmann says that the event is coming and that it is on the boundary, he expresses its eschatological character. His eschatology, however, is also demythologized.

It is clear that no simple event in the past is theologically relevant. It is relevant only as it is taken up in faith. The same is true of the simple event in the future. A known event of the future is as irrelevant to faith as a known event of the past. Simple occurrences in the future or the past, even though they be of overwhelming magnitude, are equally indifferent theologically. To think of the end as a literal event on the plane of ordinary occurrence is itself mythological. Even as there must be a demythologized view of faith, there must also be demythologized view of eschatology.

ESCHATOLOGY

Bultmann agrees with the New Testament scholars who came to regard eschatology, the doctrine of the last things, as at the heart of Jesus' teachings. Jesus looked to the future. He expected the Kingdom of God to come as a literal end of world history in a cosmic catastrophe.

As we have indicated, however, Bultmann holds that this literal expectation of Jesus and of the primitive Church began very early to be demythologized. This occurred in the thought of Paul and especially in that of John. For Paul the Kingdom was not only a future occurrence but also a present reality. In John the demythologization process has been carried on much further. The Kingdom is regarded even more strongly to be a present reality in the believer's life of faith.

What we have observed about the foundations of Bultmann's thought applies in a telling way to his views on eschatology. It too must be demythologized. For modern man it is impossible to think of the end of the world as Jesus and the primitive Church thought of it. They viewed it in mythological terms as an end catastrophe resulting from the incursion of supernatural powers. Indeed, modern man is more inclined to think of a possible end of the world, especially since the invention of the atom bomb. If he does so, however, this end is the result of purely immanent causes, perhaps the result of an atomic chain reaction or the leveling off of usable energy. Such events would be purely contingent, without any reference to man's eternal destiny.

Demythologized eschatology does not refer to a future supernatural invasion of time nor even to a simple occurrence in the future with a decisive meaning. The idea of the end has become demythologized when it has lost its supposedly objective character altogether and has become contemporaneous, referring to the here and now. Demythologized eschatology is completely existential, having to do with the ultimate meaning of one's existence. It is that which confronts man from beyond himself, bringing him to a decision. It regards the end not as a *finis* but as a horizon of human life which gives it its final perspective.

From what we have said it is clear that Bultmann's distinction between the historical (*Historie*) and the concrete-historical (*Geschichte*) is more basic than any distinction between the past and the future in ordinary time. To speak of the last things as literal events in history which bear upon one's eternal destiny is mythological. It is an objectivizing manner of expression. Eschatology does not have to do with something that will come sometime. Even to speak of the event of Jesus Christ as a simple event of the past is also objectivizing. Together with Herrmann and Kierkegaard, Bultmann holds that the event of Christ must be contemporaneous. Hence the event of Christ is not a simple event in the empirical world; it is eschatological, bearing upon our existence here and now and establishing a horizon of meaning for our entire lives. For Bultmann therefore the simple event of the past or future, even though it be of the greatest magnitude, can have no decisive significance for one's self. Only as it relates concretely to one's decision, only as it is contemporaneous, is it theologically significant.

In his interpretation of the eschatological expectations of Jesus, therefore, Bultmann must distinguish between the outward, objectivizing expression and the inner meaning or intent. Like the liberals of the old school, he must distinguish the kernel from the husk. The difference is that in the older liberal thought he could extricate rational and moral truths from the husk of mythical expression. On his part, Bultmann interprets the mythical itself for the concrete-historical, existential truth behind it. In spite of their differences both methods demand a demythologization and reinterpretation of Jesus' sayings.

Although Jesus believed that there would be a literal end of history, Bultmann claims that this was not His true intent. According to Jesus, he says, the present has meaning not because there will be an imminent world catastrophe and judgment. Instead, the objectivizing idea of a literal end of history arose because the present was regarded to be filled with meaning. The present was of decisive significance. It was a time of decision.

As we have said, Bultmann regards the event of Jesus Christ to be eschatological because it is decisive. It is transforming. It sets man before a decision. The moment of the appearance of eternity in time is the eschatological "now" because in it falls the decision between life and death. The Church is regarded as the eschatological community because it has its being only in relationship to the once-for-all event of Jesus Christ and the new life which comes to it through him. In the eschatological present one is set before the decision whether to continue in his natural, fallen existence or (what is not within the scope of his own powers) whether he is to be truly open to the future.

Sin

To be in the eschatological present is to be faced with most basic decision. This is, Bultmann says, not a decision of the will. Such a decision is on the surface of one's life. The intended decision is a basic decision that underlies all other decisions. This is the decision between sin and salvation.

What these distinctions mean can be grasped only in terms of Bultmann's understanding of the New Testament view of man. Here, he says,
man is described in terms of body (σῶμα), soul (ψυχή), spirit (πνεῦμα),
and flesh (σάρξ). These distinctions do not refer to parts or levels of
his make-up.

Bultmann rejects a dichotomy (body and soul) or a trichotomy (body,
the feeling soul, and the thinking spirit). Instead, each of these terms
refers in its own way to man in the totality of his being. Man is body as
he exists in a relation, either normal or abnormal, to himself. He is related
to himself either in harmony or in inner conflict. He is soul as the specifically human state of being alive, which inheres in him as a striving,
willing, and purposing self. *Psyche* refers to the full human life, the natural life of earthly man. As purposefully active he is also one who knows
and judges (νοῦς) and one who has conscience (συνείδησις).[5]

All the above designations have a neutral coloring that is replaced by
a dark hue in Paul's use of "flesh." Again "flesh" does not refer to a part
or a layer of man's being. It designates a total orientation, a total self-
understanding, of man as a concrete-historical being. It is what is most
characteristic of man as he exists in the world. As "flesh" man's entire
being is conditioned by his having chosen a false direction and having
fallen short of his own true self. In Pauline usage "flesh" has become
nearly synonymous with "sin."

In terms of his anthropology Bultmann believes that he can attain
a view of human sin and salvation that is deeper than that either of
the older liberalism or orthodoxy. That is because his idea of human
sinful existence, like the other aspects of his thought, is dominated by
the idea of concrete-historicality. One is not a sinner because he has a
sinful human nature or because he has committed an act of transgression. Man's sinfulness is a total orientation. His existence before faith is
qualified entirely by being a sinner, by being fallen on the world.

The latter expression indicates that Bultmann, like the existentialists
in general, ties in the idea of sin with that of objectification. At its heart,
sin is the attempt of man to escape his concrete-historicality by seeking
objective guarantees. As concrete-historical, one's being is not pre-established. It must always be decided. Sin is the human attempt to escape
the uncertainty of one's being by reliance upon what is at hand, upon
what is at one's disposal. Man seeks to pre-establish his own life and its
values. As such he is oriented to the past. His life is already decided.

This state is a fallen one, because in seeking guarantees man takes himself to be what he really is not. His sinful existence is a veiling of his true selfhood.

The state of being fallen Bultmann takes to be a possibility for man. At the same time it is the elimination of possibility, because one considers his existence in effect to be already completed. One who is fallen can say only that he has possibility, not that he, in truly concrete-historical fashion, *is* possibility.

The above is the description of human fallenness as Bultmann conceives it, disengaged from the supposedly mythical conceptions which have surrounded it. It views man in a total self-understanding, a total dependence upon his past. In Bultmann's thinking the past is identical with what is at hand and at one's disposal. In this sense the past can even include the future, insofar as it falls within the scope of human knowing and intending. For as known it is already pre-established and at one's disposal.

Completely mythological, however, is the idea of the fall as a lapse at a certain calendar date of ordinary history. Mythological also is the idea of the fall as the transgression of the law of God. In his natural existence man is already fallen.

Dependent upon his past, man becomes dependent upon the powers of the world. It is these powers which it is possible for him to represent in an objectivizing, mythological way. As powers they are subject to the mythical imagination. They become represented as objectivized, mythological entities. Since they are temporal and transitory, one who is under their sway is fallen on what is ephemeral, on death and anxiety.

It is from this veiling of his true selfhood and from the attempt to establish his own value and worth that man must be saved. It is, Bultmann says, possible for man to gain insight into his condition of being fallen. But of himself he cannot overcome this bondage to the world. The more he seeks to establish his own righteousness, the more he is involved in sinful pretension. Man can overcome the world only from a source that is beyond himself. Salvation is not within the limits of what is at man's disposal; it is a salvation by grace.

SALVATION

What is impossible for man of his own volition becomes actual in an encounter with God's forgiving grace in Jesus Christ. In this encounter one breaks with his dependence upon the past – that is, upon that which is at his disposal – and becomes open to the future. That is, he becomes open to his true self, not as one who has possibilities but as one who is the possibility of being and who is always set before decision.

It is only faith that can orient us to the future. Salvation is an attitude of faith. Authentic life is that which lives out of the unseen, that which is not at man's disposal. It gives up all of its self-created securities.

Bultmann does not intend, however, to absolutize faith. Faith is always directed toward the object of faith. Apart from this orientation it would be no faith at all. It is only as one listens to the revelation of the Word of grace that faith exists and the possibility of the future is opened up. The life of salvation is possible in faith in God's grace, that is, in the faith that precisely the invisible, that which comes to man from beyond the scope of his powers of command, means for him not death but life. This grace is forgiving grace; it frees man from the past which holds him in bondage. This faith is faith in Jesus Christ, through whom is made possible the obedience in love which allows one to live authentically in the present.

Openness to the future does not mean that the past is eliminated. Indeed, the past is sinful. It can be in the authentic present, however, as forgiven. Openness to the future means that man is free from the temporality and the ephemerality which imprison him. He is free from death and anxiety. He no longer seeks to establish himself and guarantee his existence.

Authentic life is a complete devotedness. One is completely committed to the forgiving love in Jesus Christ. Devotion to Christ, however, cannot be produced. Faith is not a work. Devotion of faith is possible only in an encounter with God's own devoting love. Only the one who is already loved can love.

The life of faith is not a state or a condition. The encounter with the forgiving grace of Christ is concrete-historical. It must continually be renewed. One is always set afresh before the decision whether he is to be saved or lost, whether he is to be fallen in the world or whether he will grasp the new life of faith in Jesus Christ.

Considering the unbreakable connection which Bultmann sees between faith and the event of Jesus Christ, it is not surprising that this ever-newness also applies to it. Faith in Jesus Christ is not faith in an event that is simply past and finished. The event of Jesus Christ is ever coming, ever impinging upon our present. It is, to use Bultmann's expression, a truly eschatological event. This ever-recurring encounter takes place in the obedient listening to the preaching of the Church, which is the eschatological community.

PROCLAMATION AND THE CHURCH

Bultmann's program of demythologization has one of its roots in his concern for the proclamation of the Church. He was concerned how the witness of the Gospel could relate to contemporary man with his modern self-understanding. There are, however, other and more theological reasons why preaching and the Church are central in Bultmann's thinking. The Church is regarded by him to be the eschatological community. The eschatological event happens within the Church as the Word is preached. Where this moment occurs in the Church there is salvation.

Bultmann's position here again dovetails with what we have observed about concrete history. The Word of God has not come as a once-for-all-event on a particular calendar date of history. It is not an event whose significance touches us as it is passed down by memory and tradition to later generations. It is a continuing thing. There is nothing to stop Bultmann from saying that the event of Jesus Christ, His death and resurrection, happens over and over again in the life of the Church. In fact, this is exactly his position. The event of Christ is event in the preaching of the Church. In preaching, Jesus comes again. It is as faith is awakened in the Church that Jesus rises from the dead. What has happened in the resurrection occurs in all who believe.

The following are identical: the eschatological proclamation of the Word impinging on the Church, the saving act of Christ, and the resurrection of Christ. The Church is part of the resurrection.

Is there then a true proclamation of the once-for-all events, the life, death, and resurrection of Jesus Christ? Or have these unique events become reflections of the ongoing life of the believing community?

Bultmann certainly does not believe that his position dissolves the events of holy history into the subjective life of the Church. He says that as the content of faith (*quae creditor*) is preached, the event of revelation and salvation occurs. He says, further, that this eschatological event, the presence in the Church of judgment and of life, is not at the Church's disposal but is present only by the revelation of the Spirit of God.

It is important to remember, however, that Bultmann's rejoinder to the charge of subjectivism depends entirely upon his particular view of the structure of faith. Faith is intention. That is, faith is directed to the object of faith and is impossible apart from this directedness. Within the correlation of faith and the event in Jesus Christ, the accent must be on the event.

Whatever truth there may be in this general description of the nature of faith, it is undeniable that Bultmann gives a creative role to the faith of the community and that he regards the Christ event as concrete-historical, in the eschatological present. So great is the place he gives to the believing community that it is possible for him to say that it is not the resurrection which engenders the belief of the early Church but the belief of the Church which gives being to the resurrection. Further, the only event having significance for salvation is the ever-recurring event of Christ in the proclamation of the Church.

Bultmann has not dissolved the Christian faith into supposedly timeless ideal values. He has nevertheless dissolved the once-for-all event of Jesus Christ into a recurring, paradoxical contemporaneity of Jesus Christ in the preaching of the Church. This is indeed a different kind of dissolution but just as effective.

III. EVALUATION

The majority of contemporary theologians view revelation as event. Revelation is a holy history, centering in the event of Jesus Christ. They attack the older liberalism not only for eliminating the once-for-all-ness of the event in Christ but also for denying its true nature as event.

In some respects this emphasis is a wholesome corrective. It is true that God's plan of salvation depends upon a series of events which may be called a holy history. Salvation is not attained by way of a mystical withdrawal into oneself, away from the outside world. Whether in anticipation or in retrospect, faith is oriented to Jesus Christ, who lived, died, and rose again from the dead. It is also true that there is a once-for-all-ness to this revelation. Salvation is the issue of faith in the finished work of Christ. Christ is once for all delivered for our sins, the Just for the unjust, that He might bring us to God. Salvation is not anywhere and everywhere available to all. There is also a "too late," a passing of the day of God's call to the sinner. It is perfectly acceptable to speak of God's revelation thus in dynamic fashion.

As we have observed, however, Bultmann does not simply emphasize revelation as event. His view of revelation depends on a particular view of what a real event is. This understanding, in turn, depends upon the distinction between the historical and the concrete-historical. This distinction, finally, is a legacy of Søren Kierkegaard's idea of the moment filled with eternity. The paramount question is whether the saving event in Jesus Christ is truly understood in these terms or whether they distort it by pressing it into a false mold.

THE CORRELATION OF FAITH AND THE CHRIST EVENT

In Bultmann's thought the correlation of faith and the saving event in Jesus Christ is sharply set in contrast to the ordinary event in history, which is as such open to the historian. That is, the meaning of the saving event in Jesus Christ, in its correlation with faith, is not itself dependent upon an historical foundation. This certainly implies that faith and the Christ event cannot have an adequate ground in history, as the result of a neutral historical investigation. Technically put, they cannot find their legitimation in history. It is clear, however, that Bultmann's position involves more than this. It implies that the saving truths should not be dependent upon genetic questions – for example, concerning the origins of belief in the resurrection of Jesus Christ. The resurrection has meaning for Bultmann only within the correlation of event and faith in the kerygma. In contrast, the event occurring on the purely historical level is contingent. It may not be regarded as having cosmic significance. That is, it may not be thought of as having significance for the "eternal" destiny of man.

Bultmann's framework of thought demands that the correlation of faith and saving event be strictly distinguished from the level of history. A close look at his thinking discloses, however, that his view of the kerygma has embarrassing historical consequences.

Bultmann's Christology appears to be an improvement over that of the older liberalism in important respects. As we have seen, he has helped to form the attitude of the newer biblical criticism, which has more of an eye for the unity of the biblical message. He sees that a supposedly human teacher of ethical truths cannot be disengaged from the portrayal of the supernatural Savior of the world. It is artificial and wrong to attempt to separate out a kernel of moral truth in Jesus' teaching from the husk of an outworn mythical world view. These are bound up with each other, so that more particularly the eschatological teachings of the New Testament have been found to belong essentially to its message.

As we have observed, however, Bultmann holds that there was never a literal fulfillment of whatever kind of these expectations and that there will never be one. Under the pressure of the continued postponement of the end, the Church resorted to a demythologization, which related the future expectations more and more to the eschatological present. Christ was now thought to have come already, being present in the Church in the person of the Holy Spirit.

On the purely historical level, the creative role which Bultmann ascribes to the Christian community runs into difficulty. In an exceedingly short while after the death of Jesus there is supposed to have arisen in the consciousness of the primitive Church a picture of Jesus that was a blend of historical reports and mythological elements drawn from Jewish apocalyptic and Hellenistic cults. The time lapse is, however, far too short to allow for the memory of the Church to be molded by its spiritual environment, in whose thought-forms it is supposed to have expressed its sense of the importance of Jesus. Furthermore, it is difficult to discount the influence of the immediate disciples of Jesus. It has been said that if the method of form criticism were correct the disciples would have had to be translated into heaven immediately after the crucifixion.

In terms of Bultmann's theory the problems surrounding the resurrection of Christ are particularly difficult. As he himself recognizes, the resurrection is most certainly a part of holy history as understood by the Scriptures. Jesus Christ was delivered for our offenses and was raised again for our justification (Rom. 4:25). If the resurrection had not occurred, Paul argues, the witness of the Christians would have become meaningless and they would have been proved to be liars (1 Cor. 15:14). The good news of the resurrection of Christ was at the heart of the preaching of the early Church.

What has happened to the resurrection in Bultmann's theology? Because it would mean an interruption of the natural course of events, a breaking of the chain of cause and effect, a literal resurrection could not have happened. Even if it had occurred as a simple event in the past, it would have no significance of a saving kind for our lives at present. As a simple event, the resurrection would be purely contingent, altogether removed from the sphere of what is relevant to us. The resurrection becomes tied into the proclamation of the early Church as an expression of the constant awakening in its midst of the new life of salvation. It has significance only in terms of the faith of this primitive community. As we have seen, it is the faith of the early Church that gave rise to the resurrection and not the resurrection to the faith of the Church.

Even stressing as he does the creative power of the Church's faith, Bultmann cannot escape the problem of how this central and powerful belief originated. If Christ did not truly rise from the dead and if the story of the resurrection is a myth, how did this myth originate? It would have had to come into being in a very short while, perhaps only a few days, after the death of Jesus Christ. This would have involved a very radical change in the thoughts and attitudes of the disciples to their dead master. As Herman Ridderbos says: "To think of this as the mythical formation of the significance (*Bedeutsamkeit*) which the disciples abruptly ascribed to Jesus' crucifixion without any new fact as its basis, a fact which originated outside of themselves, is a postulate which is dictated by Bultmann's concept of reality but which is at the same time absolutely unintelligible from an historical point of view. It is especially incomprehensible if one remembers that this resurrection witness, in the primary sense of an eye witness (compare Acts 1:21, 22ff.), was the starting point and center of the Christian proclamation and formed the foundation of Christian certainty."[6]

From a somewhat different point of view the historical consequences of Bultmann's position are equally puzzling. In terms of his comparative-religions method, one would expect that there would be a foundation in the Jewish or the Greek milieu for the belief in the resurrection. It is precisely at this point, however, that Bultmann's theory runs into profound difficulty. The disciples were Jews; but, as Ridderbos says, "... it is an undeniable fact that to Judaism the figure of the dying and resurrected Messiah was entirely alien."[7] There is no point of contact in the current Jewish ideas in which to discover the origin of the belief in Jesus' return from death to life. Yet, some point of contact is required by Bultmann's presuppositions and method. Such a point might be sought in the Greek conceptions of the dying and rising gods. It is clear, however, that the faith of the Jerusalem Church could not have had its origin in such myths. Before any such invasion of outside influences could have occurred, the early Church was living in the faith that Christ had risen from the dead.

There is a further problem of a psychological nature. If one grants that there was a change of attitude on the part of the disciples from profound discouragement to assurance, how could this new faith have taken the form of a belief in the resurrection? This so-called "myth" is related to an historical person whose death had been experienced three days before. If it is denied that an actual resurrection took place, it is not enough to point by way of explanation to the supposed gullibility of men of this time or to the inadequacy of their conception of the world. It would be necessary to explain the origin of this belief in terms of profound psychological impressions, perhaps hallucinations. It is a psychological puzzle how the Christian proclamation could have been built upon such a foundation.

There are also considerations of a theological nature which relate to Bultmann's view of the correlation of faith and the event in Jesus Christ. Viewed from within the framework of his own theology, these questions far outreach the genetic problems we have already mentioned.

There is indeed a great difficulty in accounting psychologically for the subjective belief of the primitive Church in the resurrection if no actual bodily resurrection took place. It must also be observed that the certainty and power with which the early disciples preached the Gospel of the resurrection depended upon their subjective belief that it had occurred as a matter of fact, as an event of history with a before and an after, involving an empty tomb, various appearances, and eyewitnesses to these appearances. These disciples could not have preached with assurance and yet have delivered up the object of their faith to a view of nature and history that would rule out the possibility of the resurrection's having occurred. It can be objected, of course, that this anomalous situation could not have been that of the disciples, since in their mythological way of thinking they did not yet distinguish between the realm of faith and that of scientific understanding. However proper such a rejoinder might be from within the framework of Bultmann's thought, the same antinomy must apply to anyone who, like Bultmann himself, does make confession of the resurrection while denying from a critical, historical point of view that it ever occurred. This antinomy threatens what Bultmann should be very interested in retaining, the intentional directedness of faith.

Faith depends upon the conviction of the truth of that to which it is directed. It need not be argued at this point whether faith is based upon adequate evidence. The relationship of faith to evidence is complex. All we must ascertain at this juncture is that faith cannot exist side by side with the awareness of the untruth of that in which it is vested. With reference to Bultmann's position, it can be said that faith cannot be maintained in Jesus Christ if at the same time there is the awareness that what his faith refers to is explainable in purely immanent terms, perhaps as the result of profound psychological impressions or even hallucinations. It is not sufficient to object that faith is directed to the truth but not to truth of an objective kind. Such a rebuttal does not at all diminish the force of the observation that in such a dialectical situation the commitment of faith is impossible.

Contemporary theology is not unaware of this problem. It recognizes the fact that the so-called neutral understanding dissolves faith. It is sometimes said that it "de-divinizes" the world. In the thought of some theologians this antinomy is taken up into the structure of faith itself, when the claim is made that faith depends upon a constant purification by the acids of criticism if it is not to be objectified.

Equally difficult problems attach also to Bultmann's view of the saving event in Jesus Christ, particularly with regard to its uniqueness. It is not sufficient to say that Bultmann regards holy history as a chain of events in history which do not have historical analogies as do other historical events. Bultmann agrees with Ernst Troeltsch that the mere recital of events of the past is not history. Historical facts must be seen in an historical nexus. Any fact of history has at least possible historical analogies. It also has a possible immanent historical explanation. If this is the case, the historical fact is purely contingent, having as historical fact no possible relationship to man's eternal destiny. The implication is clear. Even though Bultmann should accept the historicity of the resurrection of Christ and of other biblical miracles, they would, as contingent events of history, still have no cosmic significance. That is to say, they would have no significance for our present life of salvation. They would be swallowed up in the unrelatedness of the brute facts of history.

We must conclude that, in the context of the neutral understanding of history, the event of Jesus Christ is lost in the abyss of the unrelated. Indeed, this unrelatedness need not imply that it, as an historical event, would have no relationship to other events. Any historical event, as we have seen, has at least possible analogies with other events. It would be unrelated in the sense that it could not relate to the center of man's being, to his self. It would have no significance for his here and now except insofar as its historical consequences might figure as an irrational quantity in his situation.

Bultmann rejects the attempt to overcome this contingency by seeking a trans-historical source of meaning and value in a timeless ideal. He likewise rejects a "historistic" position, which would discover ultimate meaning within the historical process itself. Such a view would be fundamentally mythical. As we have seen, Bultmann attempts a solution in terms of the concrete-historical event of Jesus Christ occurring in the eschatological present. Here, in an antinomic fashion, the uniqueness which is denied as such to any (general) historical event is supposed to characterize the encounter with the saving event in Christ. At the same time, however, this "once-for-all" event is anomalously thought of as recurring in the life of the Church. It occurs again and again in the preaching of the Word and its reception by the believing community.

Indeed, the Church takes a most important place in Bultmann's thinking. It has been said that all of the powers that Bultmann takes from Jesus Christ he gives to the primitive Church, so that its faith is even constitutive of the Gospel message. In his thought the fulcrum has shifted from the events of holy history, rightly conceived, to events in the consciousness of the Church. In reply to the charge of subjectivism Bultmann might point to his effort to maintain the priority of the event in Jesus Christ. It is eschatological, impinging from beyond on the present life of the believer. No one can produce salvation; it is a gift. Nevertheless, Bultmann's position must always provoke the question, whether the events of holy history have not become symbols of the existential experience of the believing community. If so, they have lost their uniqueness and Bultmann has been unmasked as a liberal, with no true place for the saving acts of God.

The above discussion uncovers a dilemma that is acutely felt by contemporary theology. It is involved in the contemporary view of *Geschichte* itself, which tends to disintegrate in either of the two directions it has been devised to avoid. The attempt, on the one hand, to express the significance of Jesus Christ tends to reduce Him to the symbol of something else, either of a timeless ideal or of a human existential experience. The attempt, on the other hand, to do justice to the uniqueness of Christ tends to make him sink into the abyss of the unrelated. To avoid this dilemma, we think, it is necessary to take an altogether different standpoint, forsaking the distinction between history and concrete history and listening more closely to the witness of the Scriptures to Jesus Christ.

THE REVELATION OF JESUS CHRIST

The most sensitive nerve of any theology is its answer to Christ's question, "Who do you say I am?" If Bultmann's answer in terms of the idea of *Geschichte* is inadequate, how can the true profile of Christ be allowed to appear?

Any adequate approach to the question of the identity of Jesus Christ must take into consideration the ongoing revelation of God, and more particularly the witness of Christ Himself. The Bible recognizes the importance of this testimony. Any claim to speak for God, for instance, must be authenticated. In the Old Testament the true prophet is sharply distinguished from the false by the fact that he has received his message from Jehovah. This is authenticated by his prophecy's coming true and by the agreement of his words with the Divine revelation which has been given before (cf. Jer. 28:9 and Deut. 18:21f.). Any event of divine revelation has to be seen in the context of the divine revelation concerning the event.

Jesus thought of Himself as being anticipated in prophecy and confirmed by it. To the Pharisees He gave the advice to search the Scriptures, because they testified of Him (John 5:39). The early Church was also convinced of this connection. It was conscious of preaching nothing else than Moses and the prophet had said (Acts 26:22). Christ chided the Jews for seeking a sign. No sign would be given them, He said, other than the sign of the prophet Jonah. The Son of man would be three days in the bowels of the earth and would rise again (Matt. 12:39f.).

Within the framework of his idea of *Geschichte* Bultmann allows for a correlation of revelation and event. The event of Jesus Christ is identical with the revelation of the significance of the event. At the same time, however, this history is sharply distinguished from the level of ordinary occurrence. Here there is no such correlation. Any event supposed to witness immediately to God is rejected as being mythical and a faith-producing miracle. Under the attack of criticism this gives way to a neutral, secular history where no miracle is possible and where no event can witness to God. In the context of the neutral view there is no God and no revelation.

The effect is sharply to set off event from revelation. Instead of the idea that the events of holy history – for example, the death and resurrection of Christ – have their meaning proclaimed and confirmed in divine prophecy, the events on the level of *Historie* become altogether ambiguous. Christ comes *incognito*. The death of Jesus becomes a complete surd, a brutal end to His disciples' illusions. It comes into the orbit of revelation only paradoxically, by being joined to the unhistorical idea of the resurrection in the faith and proclamation of the early Church. Instead of being interpreted as the shock and discouragement of the disciples, the result of their having misunderstood and forgotten what Christ Himself prophesied concerning His death and resurrection, the death of Jesus is wrenched entirely out of the context of prophetic interpretation and becomes a brute fact, an irrational shattering of the disciples' expectations.

The central issue is whether anything in the life of Christ, of the nature of ordinary or extraordinary event, can be considered in isolation from the witness which the Scriptures give of Him and from His own witness to Himself. It is only in the context of divine prophetic interpretation that the events surrounding Christ were brought into focus. It is useless to consider these facts "in themselves" and to declare that they themselves are ambiguous. They have their place and their meaning in the context of God's revelation, and to see them otherwise is to distort this meaning in unbelief. It is likewise useless to denature these facts by giving them over to a neutral, critical understanding of history and then paradoxically to incorporate them in a holy history within the life of a believing community. The events surrounding Christ, including His miracles, have their meaning in the light of what they were disclosed to be by divine revelation. They establish the identity of Christ as Savior and point to His saving work only in the context of the revelation of what that saving work is.

Indeed, it is true that the Christian faith is not the conclusion of a process of reasoning. It is not the end product of historical research, let us say, faith in a reconstructed Jesus of history. Christianity is indeed a faith; but it is a faith that may not be divorced from the events of holy history culminating in Christ and from the prophetic witness to the meaning of those events. It is only in terms of this prophetic witness, of the Scriptures as a whole and of Christ to Himself, that the true identity and uniqueness of Christ can be understood.

What Moses and the prophets said was that Christ would suffer and that He would be the first to rise from the dead (Acts 26:23). "And without controversy great is the mystery of godliness: God was manifest in the flesh, justified in the Spirit, seen of angels, preached unto the Gentiles, believed on in the world, received up into glory" (1 Tim. 3:16).

Whatever mysteries remain in the Word of the Gospel, the ultimate question is whether the Church receives the witness of Christ or puts stumbling blocks in the way by a false confidence in a supposedly neutral science. A most central question is that of ultimate authority.

THE QUESTION OF AUTHORITY

It might be objected that our very method of approach indicates that we have misunderstood Bultmann. According to our interpretation, his theology is dominated by the idea of *Geschichte*. Our approach itself, it might be objected, is abstract and generalizing. Does not Bultmann want to avoid interpreting the Bible in terms of a general principle? Does he not want to let the New Testament speak for itself? Is not his interest theological instead of philosophical?

Bultmann's viewpoint, however, rests upon a specific view of the relationship between philosophy and theology. His idea of concrete, true historical events depends upon a particular view of what an event is. To see the concrete-historical nature of the biblical message one must revise completely his natural way of understanding. This does not mean that a natural, childlike attitude must be regained after having been spoiled by abstract scientific or theological reasoning. What he means is that our ordinary way of looking at things is objectivizing. The natural attitude must be transcended by grace.

The implication of this position is that Bultmann's concrete-historical view of the saving event in Christ and of the kerygma cannot be reached or understood apart from a wide sweep of the critical broom to clear the way. His positive program depends upon the negative impact of demythologization. That is recognized by commentators. Bultmann, as we have observed, criticizes the biblical world view in terms of the modern one. Indeed, he does not advocate the modern world for its own sake. Myths themselves are supposed to indicate in a pre-critical way man's awareness that his world is bounded by powers that are not at his disposal. Nevertheless, as Heinrich Ott correctly observes, Bultmann gives the modern world view a critical function.[8] It is, Bultmann judges, incompatible with this world view for one to believe in any literal way in a host of biblical doctrines.

Anything that is an invasion of the supernatural or anything that "confuses" the saving activity of God with a literal event either past or future is eliminated as being mythological. The result is the denial of an entire list of historic Christian doctrines. Rejected as mythological are the pre-existence of Christ, the sinlessness of Christ, the idea of a sacrificial atonement, the resurrection, the ascension into heaven, the intercession of the exalted Christ, the coming judgment of God, and many other cardinal truths. "Mythological" becomes in this fashion little more than another term for "supernatural."

The evangelical critic of Bultmann must be careful not to criticize him simply in this or that respect – for example, with respect to his denial of the substitutionary atonement – while he lets him go uncriticized with respect to the general structure of his thinking. Bultmann's acceptance or rejection of particular doctrines of the Christian faith is controlled by the general principles with which he works. These involve such a basic transformation of the biblical message that what Bultmann emerges with may not rightly be called Christianity. His thought is a total reinterpretation of the Gospel in terms of an existentialist-inspired philosophy.

When one enters into discussion with such a theology, the issues are broad and inclusive. Involved is nothing less than the acceptance or rejection of the authority of the Word of God. One cannot have both the Bible and the theology of Bultmann, because Bultmann places the critical reason of man next to the Scriptures. He does not see them truly through the eyes of faith but through the spectacles of rationalistic and naturalistic commitment.

The once-for-all of the Scriptures is altogether different from that of Bultmann. Bultmann holds paradoxically that the once-for-all event of Jesus Christ is an eschatological event happening again and again in the life of the Church. According to the New Testament, the Church is built upon the foundation of the apostles and prophets, Jesus Christ being the chief cornerstone.

REFERENCES

1. Bultmann's own short biographical reflections are found in Schubert M. Ogden, ed., *Existence and Faith: Shorter Writings of Rudolf Bultmann* (1960).

2. This article, which appeared first in 1941, was based on an address delivered in the same year at Alpirsbach, Germany, before the Society for Evangelical Theology. The article has been republished as the leading selection in Hans-Werner Bartsch, ed., *Kerygma und Mythos*, I (1948).

3. Rudolph Bultmann, *Glauben und Verstehen*, I (1933), 118.

4. Cf. Rudolf Bultmann, "Neues testament und Mythologie," *Kerygma und Mythos*, I (1954), 29, 31.

5. See *Theology of the New Testament*, Vol. I (1951), 190ff.

6. Herman Ridderbos, *Bultmann* (1960), 34 (altered).

7. Ibid. 35.

8. Heinrich Ott, *Geschichte und Heilsgeschichte in der Theologie Rudolf Bultmanns* (1955), 36, 115.

PART FOUR

AN ASSESSMENT OF
HERMAN DOOYEWEERD

TRANSCENDENTAL METHOD
IN DOOYEWEERD[1]

In his "Zum Geleit" to the dissertation of Michael Fr. J. Marlet,[2] Herman Dooyeweerd praised him for having succeeded in penetrating into what is the heart of his method. They share, he said, the common ground of a transcendental criticism of theoretical thought. His own philosophy, Dooyeweerd continued, must be understood as a Christian transcendental philosophy.

Although Dooyeweerd criticized his own earlier work as not being transcendental enough, his philosophy from the outset was transcendentally oriented. What this means is not readily grasped; nevertheless, it is significant and worthy of painstaking study.

One of the major considerations behind Dooyeweerd's use of a transcendental method was his concern, on the one hand, for the structure of law which God has placed in his creation, a structure that is universally valid and that must be taken into account by everyone, and his conviction, on the other hand, that this law-order comes to its focus in the center of human existence in its relation to its transcendent origin, God.

The great turning point in his own thinking, Dooyeweerd said, came when he realized that all thought has a religious root. Originally, he was strongly under the influence of neo-Kantianism and then of the phenomenology of Edmund Husserl. He broke definitively with these positions when it became clear to him that theoretical thought is not neutral but is religiously oriented, being dependent upon a taking of position with regard to considerations lying outside of that thought, namely, to God as the Origin of all things, to the positioning of human existence in relation to him, and to an order of the cosmos in which thought is embedded and which provides the foundation of its very possibility.

Dooyeweerd then began to take a stance against "immanence thinking," i.e., thinking that proceeds on the assumption that the starting point of thought resides within thought itself.

A question then arises with force: How is this transcendent religious orientation related to those concerns which are proper to theoretical thought? Considering the same question from a somewhat different point of view, we might formulate it thus: How is this transcendent taking of position, which is obviously not agreed upon by all, related to the universal structure of things, which is common to all, no matter how diverse their religious orientation? The question arises, namely, concerning the relationship of the immanent concerns of theoretical thought to the transcendent taking of position with respect to the origin. This relationship and the method by which it was brought to expression Dooyeweerd began to call "transcendental."[3]

PART I

In his three-volume work of 1935-1936, *De Wijsbegeerte der Wetsidee* (*The Philosophy of the Idea of Law*),[4] in which he brought to systematic expression his developing philosophical insights, Dooyeweerd expressed the lack of self-sufficiency of all things, including thought, in relation to their origin (God) by declaring that the being of everything that exists is *meaning*. That is to say, everything in the cosmos points to everything else and also to its origin in the sovereign will of the Creator-God. In keeping with biblical revelation, he said that man was appointed to be the viceregent of God in the creation. All of the diverse rays of meaning in the cosmos focus on man and through him on their origin.

Where all the strands of meaning come together, in what Dooyeweerd has called the "heart," there is a fundamental, religious taking of position with respect to the origin. Either one is rooted in the transcendent God as he is revealed in the Scriptures or he is related to an idol, worshipping what is a fabrication of his apostate and distorted imagination, namely, a myth. At any and every point one is turned in his heart either to the right or to the left, either to the true God or to an idol. Because it is of a central, radical kind, this orientation manifests itself in all human activity.

This transcendent orientation does not allow itself to be grasped theoretically. It is the hidden player, Dooyeweerd said, on the instrument of thought, establishing its direction and determining its deepest religious sense. Thought, however, can be brought to reflect on this transcendent taking of position. Indeed, it turns inevitably in this direction.

Again, the direction that this reflection takes and the method of bringing it to expression Dooyeweerd called "transcendental." One who is engaged in theoretical thinking can, as it were, look back over his shoulder, to the religious motive that is driving his activity and establishing its orientation.

Transcendental method is that method which, allowing fully for the God-given, universally valid structure of reality, nevertheless brings thought to reflect on its own presupposita.[5]

Part II

Thought is not self-sufficient; it is dependent upon a divinely created order of reality, which manifests itself in experience. Within this experience Dooyeweerd distinguished horizons, as it were, three proscenium arches, within which experience appears; 1) the transcendent horizon (the heart); 2) the transcendental horizon (the ways in which our experience is qualified); 3) the "plastic" (*plastisch*) horizon (the level of concrete, individual things, events, persons).

In our attitude of naive experiencing, we relate to individual things, persons, and events without abstracting from their concreteness, as we would in the theoretical attitude of thought. In this naive experiencing there is a typical subject-object relation. The "subject" is subject to the law. On the subject side, i.e., on the side of what is subject to the law, there are both subjects and objects. For example, a man may gaze at a sunset and declare that is beautiful. The sunset itself cannot observe and make aesthetic judgments; it has, however, an objective aesthetic quality for the subject who observes and judges aesthetically.

Naive experience takes place within a horizon. That is, we can extend our experience indefinitely in every direction, while our experience yet remains of one kind, that of the experience of concrete, individual things, events and persons. This Dooyeweerd called the "plastic" horizon, thus indicating its immediate and concrete character.

Implicit already in our naive experiencing is the fact that the meaning of reality is expressed in various ways, which Dooyeweerd called "aspects" or "modes." The unity of meaning of the cosmos is diffused in a number of aspects which are interrelated in an unbreakable coherence of meaning. Dooyeweerd distinguished fifteen such modal aspects: arithmetical, spatial, kinematic, energetic effect, biotic, psychical, logical, historical, symbolical, social, economical, aesthetical, juridical, ethical, and pistical. In each there is a law-structure peculiar to the individual sphere, and subject to the law there is a specific expression of the subject-object relationship. This diversity of meaning is already present in naïve experience; however, the aspects are articulated and set over against one another only in the theoretical attitude of thought.

Dooyeweerd called this modal order the "transcendental horizon" of human experience. Each of the aspects is transcendental in character. That is to say, each aspect has a unique, underivable, generic sense that lies at the foundation of the possibility of the variable phenomena which it qualifies.

The modal aspects lie at the foundation of the possibility of human experiencing, including the possibility of thought. The aspects, however, are not of the nature of thought. They cannot be distinguished from each other by means of simple analytical distinctions. Neither can their meaning be exhausted in theoretical concepts. Instead, these aspects in their inter-relationships provide the abiding framework which lies at the foundation of the possibility of all thought.

Each of the modes is a unique aspect of experience, with its own nucleus of meaning, which holds for its own sphere. One cannot confuse the meaning of one sphere with that of any other without falling into antinomy.

Part III

The various aspects of reality are articulated and set over against one another in the theoretical attitude of thought.

An act of theoretical thought is an act of the entire person; nevertheless, as an act it is qualified by a setting up of the analytical aspect of the act of thought over against (in antithesis to) a non-analytical aspect of reality. This involves also setting up one aspect over against the others.

Every individual science deals with things, events, persons from a particular "functional" point of view. Thus physics does not deal with an event in its totality; it deals with an event as to its kinematic (movement) aspect. Psychology will not deal with events from their ethical but from their sensitive (feeling) aspect, etc.

How then does a scientist go about studying the phenomena from the point of view of his own speciality? Every science must seek to develop a concept of its own field of specialization. It will then deal with the variable phenomena within this aspect.

This concept must grasp the structure of the aspect in question, setting it off from the other aspects. This attempt strikes a limit, however, in the nucleus of meaning of the aspect. As we have suggested, this cannot be grasped in a theoretical concept; instead, it qualifies all of the conceptualization within its own sphere.

When theoretical thought seeks to gain a concept of a particular field of investigation, it bumps into the subsidiary moments of meaning within the aspect, which Dooyeweerd calls "analogies."[6] This is the case because none of the aspects is isolated from the rest. Each points to all the others. Thus the nucleus of meaning of every aspect is, as it were, ringed with its analogies. When one forms a concept of his field of investigation, he must view the analogies in their proper relationships to each other and to the nucleus of meaning which qualifies them.

In its concept-formation, theoretical thought is, therefore, inevitably brought into the position where it must ask concerning the coherence and the deeper unity of the aspects of experience. If the aspects are to be set off from one another, there is need for a background against which they can be viewed and for criteria by which they can be distinguished.

As a means of grasping the relationship of the aspects one might 1) take a particular aspect as the material source (origin) of meaning, or 2) seek to arrange the aspects in a purely formal way under a logical common denominator according to genus and species.

Because of their transcendental status, the nuclei of meaning of the various aspects cannot be established by way of definition according to *genus proximum* and *differentia specifica*. That is, one cannot define the aspects by ranging them under a common denominator and then distinguishing them by specific characteristics. This is shown by giving careful attention to the concept-formation as it is actually carried out in the special sciences.

The question of the coherence, the deeper unity, and also the origin of meaning of the cosmos is not simply a matter of a philosophical interest which may safely be ignored in the actual conduct of scientific investigation; it is involved in the formation of scientific concepts themselves. It is a question the answer to which affects the process of concept-formation in the special sciences.

Part IV

Forming a concept in a particular field of investigation involves distinguishing the appropriate aspect of experience. This concept-formation is, however, led by a theoretical *idea* of the coherence, the deeper unity, and the origin of the cosmos.

This idea remains theoretical in nature. It is immanent in theoretical thought. Nevertheless, the idea points beyond what is within the reach of theoretical thought. It guides theoretical thinking in a direction determined by a content that has its source beyond all theory.

The idea is transcendental precisely because, while remaining within the framework of the theoretical attitude of thought, it points nevertheless beyond its limits. Dooyeweerd writes, "... while maintaining the antithetic relation, the theoretical idea relates the theoretical concept to the presuppositions of all theoretical thought but itself remains theoretical in character, remaining thus within the limits of philosophical thought. Precisely in this resides what we have called its transcendental character."[7]

A crux of Dooyeweerd's transcendental method, therefore, is the relationship of the *concept* to the *idea*.

The idea guides thought in opening up the cosmos. This opening process takes place either in the true or in an apostate direction.

The nature of the idea furnishes a key to understanding the distinction between *presuppositions* and *presupposita*. A presupposition is a point of view that one holds prior to theoretical reflection, irrespective of whether he has given a theoretical account of the structure of the cosmos. The presupposita are the generally valid *a priori's* to which theoretical thought, paying attention in the strictest way to the structural questions, will inevitably be drawn back.

These *apriori's* should not be thought of, therefore, as if they were on the order of theoretical axioms.[8] The presupposita are encountered in the course of the investigation of the sciences themselves.

Because of his understanding of the nature of the *a priori's*, it is not surprising that Dooyeweerd placed such emphasis on philosophy's relating to the special sciences. Philosophy is obliged to remain in fruitful contact with the on-going work of science. His method was not to come to science with presuppositions of a metaphysical (e.g., theological) character. It was, on the contrary, to relate, along transcendental lines, the presupposita uncovered in the course of theoretical inquiry to the transcendent presuppositions.

Dooyeweerd's method, therefore, may be called "empirical-transcendental" in contrast to "transcendent-metaphysical."[9]

PART V

After the publication of his three-volume work *The Philosophy of the Idea of Law*, Dooyeweerd gave much thought to the further development and sharpening of his transcendental critique of thought. This attempt came to expression in a number of smaller publications; it took a more definite turn, however, with the publication in 1953 of the first volume of the English translation of his *magnum opus*, *A New Critique of Theoretical Thought*. Here Dooyeweerd criticized his former work as not being transcendental enough.

The question has naturally arisen as to how far this was a departure from his earlier position. Our analysis suggests strongly that the shift was not a major one. In the later work Dooyeweerd defines transcendental criticism as follows: "By this we understand a critical inquiry (respecting no single so-called theoretical axiom) into the *universally valid conditions which alone make theoretical thought possible, and which are required by the immanent structure of this thought itself.*"[10] Our analysis shows that what is indeed new in Dooyeweerd's formulation, namely, that transcendental criticism is required by the structure of theoretical thought itself, simply carries on with greater emphasis a line of approach he had from the beginning, that there is a divinely given law-structure of the cosmos, possessing general validity, which must be taken into account by any thinker. Dooyeweerd insisted throughout – even in his later period – that this accounting cannot be accomplished truly apart from the presuppositions of the Christian faith.

Dooyeweerd presented his transcendental critique with variations of detail. Representative, however, is the form it took in his work *In the Twilight of Western Thought*.[11] Here Dooyeweerd distinguished three questions which must be posed by any truly critical philosophy, that is, by any philosophy that does not allow any theoretical axiom to slip by without having given account of it: 1) What is the continuous bond of coherence between the logical aspect and the non-logical aspects of experience from which these aspects are abstracted in the theoretical attitude of thought? And, how is the mutual relation between these aspects to be conceived? 2) What is the central reference-point in our consciousness from which this theoretical synthesis can start? 3) How is the concentric direction of theoretical thought upon the ego possible, and whence does it originate?

Such critical analysis shows that all theoretical thought is dependent ultimately for its direction upon fundamental motives of a religious character.

REFERENCES

1. This is a revised version of the abstract of a paper delivered at the Intensive Seminar on the Philosophy of Science, sponsored by the American Scientific Affiliation, at Wheaton College, Wheaton, Illinois, December 15-19, 1969. The notes have been added in connection with its appearance now in printed form.

2. Michael Fr. J. Marlet. *Grundlinien der kalvinistischen 'Philosophie der Gesetzesidee' als christlicher Transzendentalphilosophie* (München: Karl Zink, 1954).

3. Cf. Herman Dooyeweerd, *A New Critique of Theoretical Thought* (Philadelphia: Presbyterian and Reformed Publishing Co.), I (1953), 88, where Dooyeweerd discusses the relationship between "transcendent" and "transcendental." Cf. 37-38.

4. Herman Dooyeweerd, *De Wijsbegeerte der Wetsidee* (Amsterdam: H. J. Paris, 1935-1936), 3 vols.

5. The distinction in Dooyeweerd's thought between presuppositions and presupposita has been little noticed and understood. It roots in the attitude Dooyeweerd took from the beginning of his philosophizing, that ultimate presuppositions of thought are not on the order of theoretical axioms. The latter, far from being able to serve as ultimate, metaphysical starting points, are themselves dependent upon the divinely given cosmic order of law and must be examined as to the religious motives underlying them.

6. Herman Dooyeweerd, *De analogische grondbegrippen der vakwetenschappen en hun betrekking tot de structuur van den menselijken ervaringshorizon* (Amsterdam: Noord-Hollandsche Uitgevers Maatschappij, 1954). Tr. Robert D. Knudsen, *The Analogical Concepts* (mimeographed, 1968).

7. Herman Dooyeweerd, *Encyclopedie van de Rechtswetenschap: Inleiding* (SRVU edition, mimeographed, 1967), 45. The translation is taken from Robert D. Knudsen, *Philosophia Reformanda: Reflections on the Philosophy of Herman*

Dooyeweerd (mimeographed, 1971), 15.

8. Again, too little attention has been given to the fact that Dooyeweerd's discovery of what he called "the religious root of all thought" meant for him an abandonment of the theory of presuppositions held by his predecessors, like Herman Bavinck, for whom presuppositions were on the order of theoretical axioms. Although he held these men and their thought in highest esteem, Dooyeweerd of all the original representatives of the reformational philosophy made this break most cleanly. This had much to do with his striking out from the first in a transcendental direction.

9. His break with his predecessors' view of presuppositions and his movement in a transcendental direction tied in with the broad empiricism Dooyeweerd advocated, also from the beginning of his philosophizing. His philosophy has rightly been called "empirical-transcendental." A general employment of this method, heavily slanted towards mathematics, is found in D. F. M. Strauss, *Wijsbegeerte en vakwetenskap* (Bloemfontein: Sacum, 1969). For an application in physics, see M. D. Stafleu, "Quantumfysica en Wijsbegeerte der Wetsidee," *Philosophia Reformata*, XXXI (1966), 126-156. A brief application in the field of economics is found in R. L. Haan, "Wegen in de economische wetenschap," *Philosophia Reformata*, I: vol. XXXVII (1972), 124-155; II: vol. XXXIX (1974), 1-40. For a description of the method and an extensive application of it in the field of jurisprudence, see H. J. van Eikema Hommes, *De elementaire grondbegrippen der rechtswetenschap: Een juridische methodologie* (Deventer: Kluwer, 1972); and Hommes, *De samengestelde grondbegrippen der rechtswetenschap: Een juridische methodologie* (Zwolle: W. E. J. Tjeenk Willink, 1976). Cf. the reviews of the last two works by Robert D. Knudsen in the *Westminster Theological Journal*, XXXIX (1976-1977), 192-195; and XL (1977-1978), 202-205.

10. Herman Dooyeweerd, *A New Critique*, I, 37. In the above quotation, the word "respecting" may not clearly reflect Dooyeweerd's meaning. What he intends to say is that no so-called theoretical axiom whatsoever has a privileged position that would exempt it from such a critical inquiry. Every theoretical axiom must be examined as to the religious motives underlying and already at work in it. Cf. Knudsen, *Philosophia Reformanda* (1971), 23, et passim.

11. Herman Dooyeweerd, *In the Twilight of Western Thought* (Philadelphia: Presbyterian and Reformed Publishing Co., 1960).

THE RELIGIOUS FOUNDATION OF DOOYEWEERD'S TRANSCENDENTAL METHOD

D ooyeweerd's philosophy is a Christian transcendental philosophy. Various important commentators on Dooyeweerd have understood that it must be interpreted in this way.

The transcendental orientation of Dooyeweerd's philosophy is clearly brought to expression in the well-known dissertation of Michael Fr. J. Marlet, *Grundlinien der kalvinistischen "Philosophie der Gesetzesidee" als christlicher Transzendentalphilosophie* (München: Karl Zink, 1954). There is also a clear presentation of this orientation in the dissertation of Vincent Brümmer, *Transcendental Criticism and Christian Philosophy* (Franeker: T. Wever, 1961). I myself have said that Dooyeweerd's thought must be understood, first of all, as transcendental. I made this point in my 1962 lecture presented at the annual philosophy conference at Wheaton College, Wheaton, Illinois, "Dooyeweerd's Philosophical Method." This lecture is incorporated, with some minor changes, in my *Philosophia Reformanda: Reflections on the Philosophy of Herman Dooyeweerd* (mimeographed, 1971). The first Ph.D. dissertation in America on Dooyeweerd was that of Roy A. Clouser, *Transcendental Critique, Ontological Reduction, and Religious Belief in the Philosophy of Herman Dooyeweerd* (dissertation, University of Pennsylvania, 1970), which presents Dooyeweerd consistently as a transcendental thinker. This writing almost immediately underwent revision; thus, one should, if possible, obtain the latest version. Clouser has now obtained recognition for his recent book *The Myth of Religious Neutrality: An Essay on the Hidden Role of Religious Belief in Theories* (Notre Dame/London: University of Notre Dame Press, 1991). Dooyeweerd's successor at the Free University of Amsterdam, H.J. Van Eikema Hommes, also interpreted Dooyeweerd consistently as a transcendental philosopher, e.g., in his *Major Trends in the History of Legal Philosophy* (Amsterdam/ New York/Oxford: North Holland Publishing Co., 1979).

That Dooyeweerd's philosophy must be understood as Christian transcendental philosophy certainly relates to his idea of transcendental critique. He himself stated that transcendental critique is the key to understanding his philosophy.[1] At the same time, it is also clear that the transcendental thrust of Dooyeweerd's philosophy, even though it is very much related to transcendental critique, is by no means identical with it. The transcendental orientation of Dooyeweerd's thought does not depend on the transcendental critique; instead, his program of transcendental critique depends on the transcendental orientation of his philosophy as a whole.

A. The Deepest Foundation of the Transcendental Orientation of Dooyeweerd's Philosophizing

It has often been said that Dooyeweerd's philosophy is heavily influenced by Kantianism. Some say that its problematics are those of neo-Kantianism. On this view, the transcendental orientation of Dooyeweerd's philosophizing likely stems from influences from outside. According to some, therefore, this transcendental orientation can be set aside as one considers what is intrinsic to Dooyeweerd's Christian philosophy.

Indeed, Dooyeweerd went through a phase where he was strongly under the influence, first, of neo-Kantianism and, second, of phenomenology. He states this himself. In the foreword to his *A New Critique of Theoretical Thought* (the English revised edition of his *De Wijsbegeerte der Wetsidee*), Dooyeweerd writes concerning his own development, "Originally I was strongly under the influence first of the neo-Kantian philosophy, later on of Husserl's phenomenology."[2]

It would have been strange if Dooyeweerd had not been confronted with Kantianism and phenomenology. Neo-Kantianism was being presented, even in the circles in which Dooyeweerd moved, as a "spiritual" philosophizing, in contrast to the "materialistic" tendencies of naturalism. Even Herman Bavinck was content with a distinction between spiritual and non-spiritual philosophizing. Dooyeweerd also came strongly under the influence of the phenomenology of Edmund Husserl. Of this it could also be said that it was "spiritual" as opposed to "materialistic" philosophizing. In his intellectual milieu, it was almost inevitable that Dooyeweerd would come into contact with these philosophical movements, even though it may not be thought inevitable that he would be influenced by them.

Dooyeweerd himself writes that he broke with these movements after his attempts to reconcile them with the Christian (more specifically, the Calvinistic) world-and-life-view had issued in failure. As he himself says, his critique of neo-Kantianism and phenomenology was, first of all, a critique of his own philosophical development. His critique of them was self-critique.[3]

No matter how much Kantianism and phenomenology may have turned Dooyeweerd's thinking in a transcendental direction, neither of these provides sufficient explanation for his position. Rather, Dooyeweerd's transcendental orientation can be understood, finally, only in terms of the radical view of religion to which he came, and which, in turn, led him to break with these movements. His view of religion provides the only sufficient explanation for the transcendental thrust of his philosophizing as a whole and for his method of transcendental critique.

The importance of this religious turnabout is shown by what Dooyeweerd goes on to write in the passage quoted above from the *New Critique*: "The great turning point in my thought was marked by the discovery of the religious root of thought itself, whereby a new light was shed on the failure of all attempts, including my own, to bring about an inner synthesis between the Christian faith and a philosophy which is rooted in faith in the self-sufficiency of human reason."[4]

In the light of this new understanding of the religious root of all thinking, Dooyeweerd had to reject as failures his earlier attempts at synthesis. Dooyeweerd came to the position that religion is not one terrain in distinction from others, e.g., as a clergyman is sometimes called "a religious," or as "religious" teachers are distinguished from "lay" ones. Such designations root in an almost universally accepted distinction between the "religious" and the "secular." According to Dooyeweerd, in contrast, religion underlies and is foundational to everything.

On this understanding, religion is not on the order of something one can pick up and use or set aside; rather, in everything one is and does religion is *already at work*. It cannot be fixed directly in one's gaze, therefore; it can be discerned only in depth, by way of reflecting on what is already present and is exerting influence on what one is doing. It is what Dooyeweerd calls "the hidden player" behind all thought.[5]

The reflection of which I speak will be transcendental. That is, it will relate all our activities to that which underlies them and provides the foundation for them. This reflection will be transcendental in that it will relate our immanent concerns to their transcendent religious root.

This view of religion implies that everything must be analyzed (critiqued) as to what underlies it, moves it along, guides it, and gives it its meaning. Thus, the religious orientation of Dooyeweerd's thinking is also the key, in general, to his method of transcendental critique and to the central place it has in his philosophy.

In saying this, I am using the term "transcendental critique" in the general sense of the word. In this sense it must be distinguished, though not separated, from the articulated transcendental critique as we find it in Dooyeweerd's later writings.

Before going on, I must observe that it does not invalidate Dooyeweerd's philosophy that he passed through Kantianism and phenomenology and continued to relate to them. That he did this does not imply that he was ever basically favorable to either of them. Apostate thinkers, Dooyeweerd says, can discover states of affairs in the created cosmos, even ones that escape the attention of Christian thinkers. Apostate thinking, however, is unable to give a true account of these states of affairs.

Dooyeweerd did not challenge the transcendental orientation of the philosophy of Kant. He says that Kant's thinking moved in a proper direction when it took a transcendental turn.[6] Dooyeweerd's criticism, indeed, was not that Kant's thinking was transcendental but that it was not transcendental enough. Kant was unable to carry out successfully the program he himself initiated. The same may be said of neo-Kantianism and the phenomenology of Edmund Husserl.[7] Even though Kantianism and phenomenology developed valuable insights, they were unable to capitalize on them or to give a proper account of the states of affairs that they had uncovered. Both were vitiated at a deeper level by a religious orientation that threw their insights out of focus.

If, then, the transcendental thrust of Dooyeweerd's thinking can be understood in terms of his view of religion, then how and against what background did this transcendental orientation take shape?

B. The Transcendental Orientation of the Idea of Law
1. The Law-Idea as Organon

As he began his philosophizing, Dooyeweerd looked for a way to make the Calvinistic world-and-life-view relevant to philosophy and science. He found the instrument (*organon*) for this in the *law-idea* (*wetsidee*). Every philosophical position, indeed, every enterprise in the realm of science, is controlled and directed by a law-idea. In everything one does, in philosophy and science, a law-idea is *already at work*.

Dooyeweerd's philosophy developed as a philosophy of the law-idea. That is to say, everything we are and do is embraced in a divinely established order. This order is discernible in a *reflection* on what is *already at work* in everything we are and do.

The Christian law-idea is grounded on the biblical teaching concerning the Creator-creature relationship.

2. The Sovereignty of God as the Creator, and the Creation as Subject

Dooyeweerd's philosophy developed with the understanding of the full sovereignty of God over the creation[8] and of the complete dependence of the creation on God's sovereign will as Creator.

One of the fundamental insights developed by both Dooyeweerd and his co-worker D. H. Th. Vollenhoven was that the created cosmos is *subject*. That is to say, the source of meaning of the created cosmos does not reside within this cosmos itself. The cosmos has its meaning only in its relation to God, who is the sovereign law-giver. In contrast to God, who is *above* the law, the created cosmos is *under* the law, *subject* to it. This relationship is so intimately entwined with the very existence of the created cosmos that it and everything in it are said to be *subject*. Everything in the created cosmos has its meaning in being subject to the divinely given law-order (*lex divina*).

3. The Law as the Boundary between God and the Creation

Both Vollenhoven and Dooyeweerd expressed the above idea by saying that the law is the *boundary* between God and the cosmos. God is above the law. The order that holds for the creation does not hold for him. Dooyeweerd often expresses this idea with the use of the Latin formula *Deus legibus solutes est*. God is free from the law. By the same token, everything in the cosmos is under the law. Thus, the law is a *boundary*. It stands on the boundary between God and the cosmos.

One confuses things if he thinks that this "law" is something that stands between God and the cosmos so as to erect a barrier between them. This misunderstanding has led to the complaint that according to Vollenhoven and Dooyeweerd the created cosmos does not stand in direct relationship to God, the Creator, but to the law. On this view, it is objected, the law has the effect of screening off God from his creation, so that the personal relationship to God, in which humankind stands, is replaced by a relationship to an impersonal law-order.

One can express the idea that the law is the boundary between God and the cosmos, however, in a way that helps to avoid this misunderstanding. I have found it helpful to express this idea by using a double negative: There is *nothing* in the created cosmos that is not subject to law. Using this double negative helps to bring out the transcendental thrust of Dooyeweerd's philosophy.[9]

As one experiences, Dooyeweerd says, one has an implicit awareness of the law-order undergirding his thought and life. Even in our ordinary experience, we have an implicit awareness of this law-order; but it is not articulated in ordinary experience.

4. The Law-Idea as a Boundary Idea

That the divinely given law-order is already present in everything we are and do means that we can approach it, reflectively, only in a transcendental *idea*. The boundary idea implies the orderedness of all things; at the same time it implies the lack of self-sufficiency of the law-order in regard to its origin. The law, then, truly stands at the boundary between God and the cosmos, as a dynamic orderedness that displays its lack of self-sufficiency. Dooyeweerd's view of the law as boundary complements, therefore, his idea of the created cosmos as meaning. In its restlessness it points beyond itself to the origin, in which alone it can find rest.

The law as boundary cannot be grasped in a theoretical concept, which would bring it under control of the human intellect, in the theoretical process of concept formation. It cannot be grasped by a person, in a relationship of control, even logical control. In every relationship of control, the law-order is already present and operating, providing the constant (ever-present) backdrop for all one's activity.

As an idea, the law-idea is theoretical. As a theoretical idea, however, it cannot be grasped in a theoretical concept. It itself cannot be conceptualized; rather, it accompanies and guides all our conceptualization. The law-idea stands at the boundary. All theoretical thinking points beyond itself and must come to reflect on what underlies it, motivates it, and gives it its direction. In his view of the relationship of the theoretical idea to the theoretical concept, the transcendental thrust of Dooyeweerd's philosophy comes to expression.

5. REFLECTION AS RELIGIOUSLY MOTIVATED

Throughout I have emphasized the role of reflection. One must reflect transcendentally on what is already at work in what he is and does. If it is to focus on what lies at the center (or heart), this reflection must be *total*. It must embrace the entire created cosmos in what Dooyeweerd called its temporal diversity.[10] Thus the question arose as to what stands out from this temporal diversity, as to the point where this total reflection comes to a focus.

The idea of total reflection depends on the understanding that created reality, in its totality, is religiously oriented. As one says, it is "covenantally" oriented. This is an insight that is characteristic of the Reformational Philosophy as a whole. That the reflection is total means that it is *religious*.

Dooyeweerd provides for *total* reflection of humankind on itself. In religion, there is a reflection on humankind standing in covenant relationship with God. This is the only basis for a total reflection. All other bases fall short.

As we saw, religion cannot, therefore, be limited to a particular sphere or perspective. It is impossible, therefore, to call religious reflection "theological" reflection, if by "theological" one has in mind something other than that everything is related to God.

At first, as we have seen, Dooyeweerd held that the law-idea is twofold. All theorizing, whether it be Christian or not, is controlled by an idea of the *origin* and the *coherence* of meaning of the created cosmos. Was this sufficient to account for where reflection comes to its focus?

C. Dooyeweerd's Modification of His Position in Line with its Transcendental Thrust

1. The Modification of the Idea that Humankind's Existence is Qualified by the Aspect of Faith

Dooyeweerd ascribes to Abraham Kuyper the discovery of the insight that faith is a function of human existence. That is to say, faith cannot be understood as something that one may have or not have. Everyone is led by a faith, whether one is aware of it or not. One may not accuse someone of being prejudiced simply because the person is led by a faith. Everyone is led by a faith. It is impossible to retreat from faith to a terrain ruled not by faith but by autonomous reason. Everyone is led by a faith, whether in the true or in an apostate direction.

Dooyeweerd accepted Kuyper's view from the beginning, and he continued to hold that everyone is guided by a faith. Faith is a function of human existence, which cannot be set aside any more than humankind's biotical function can be set aside.

In the course of time, Dooyeweerd came to a different view of the relationship of the faith function to human existence. Once he held, along with Kuyper, that human existence is qualified by faith. Later he came to the position that this faith itself is dependent on a deeper "level," namely, the "level" of *religion*. In doing this he departed from the notion that human existence is qualified by the aspect of faith. Faith is indeed an aspect of every human act, but this faith is informed by a religious orientation. Dooyeweerd came to the position that human existence is not qualified ultimately in terms of any function; it is ultimately religious.

What was the significance of Dooyeweerd's shift from the view that faith is the leading function to the view that human existence has no leading function? It certainly means that every tenet of faith must be examined as to the religious motive behind it. This shift also relates to Dooyeweerd's understanding of the nature of presupposition. It implies that a principle not only guides and controls but also underlies and impels.

This shift accentuated the idea that one must reflect on what is already at work in his life and thought. Religion is a power that is already at work, also in faith, giving it direction. As I see the matter, the rejection of the idea that faith is the leading function was in line with the transcendental thrust of Dooyeweerd's thought. This transcendental orientation was already present; rejecting the idea that humankind's life is qualified by faith accentuated it.

2. THE ADDITION OF A THIRD TERM TO THE LAW-IDEA: THE SELF

The transcendental direction of Dooyeweerd's thinking was also accentuated by his adding a third term to the law-idea, namely, the deeper unity of the cosmos as understood in reflection on the self.

To be sure, the addition of this term did not materially alter Dooyeweerd's position. It was a shift, however, that underlined the transcendental orientation of his thinking as a whole.

The transcendental orientation of Dooyeweerd's thinking, as I said, can be understood in terms of the view he developed as to religion. It took shape in his view of law. It found expression in the ever-present ideas of the coherence and the origin of the cosmos. It might still be thought, however, that presuppositions are on the order of theoretical axioms, which one can, as it were, reach up and appropriate. The addition of the third term pointed to the fact that the cosmic coherence and the origin of meaning are understood only in a reflection on the self, which in its activity is already embraced in a law-order, which, in turn, is already under the influence (control) of a religious orientation. In all that we say and do there is an implicit understanding of what the self is, as it stands *coram deo*. Dooyeweerd's adding a third term made it more difficult to misunderstand the meaning of the transcendental ideas, as if they were something "objective" that could be appropriated and used somewhat as one might use a rake or a hoe.

D. DOOYEWEERD'S SYSTEMATIC WORK, *De Wijsbegeerte der Wetsidee*

By the time Dooyeweerd published his *magnum opus*, his three volume *De Wijsbegeerte der Wetsidee* (1935-1936), he had incorporated the above changes into his thinking. He thought in terms of a tripartite law-idea. He said that human life does not have any finite qualification. These changes accentuated the transcendental thrust of his thinking.

Dooyeweerd developed the theory that all of our experience takes place under a number of horizons. As horizons, these qualify experience. They are always there, but not as static things. They continue to expand as experience grows.

The first horizon is that of concrete things and events. This Dooye-weerd calls the "plastic" horizon. Another horizon is that of the modal qualification of all things. This Dooyeweerd calls the "modal horizon." All of our experience is qualified in that it is temporal. This Dooyeweerd calls the "transcendental" horizon. All of our experience is accompanied by and rooted in the self. This Dooyeweerd calls the "transcendent horizon."

The transcendental thrust of Dooyeweerd's philosophy is expressed in his view of the modal aspects. This has not been emphasized enough.

A modal aspect qualifies thought. It establishes a field of investigation. As one develops concepts within one's field, his investigation is led by the meaning-kernel of the aspect, but this recedes as the investigation progresses. It is discerned transcendentally in the process of concept-formation itself.

The theorist must obtain a logical concept of the law-sphere which is being investigated; nevertheless, as one forms a concept of a particular sphere, he cannot grasp theoretically its fundamental sense, what Dooyeweerd variously calls its "nucleus" or "kernel" of meaning. The modal nuclei of meaning can only express themselves in *analogies*, i.e., in subsidiary moments of meaning which group around the nuclei of meaning and which point to the other aspects. The theorist will encounter the analogies "legal power," "social life," "aesthetic feeling," etc. These must be sorted out. These "analogies" are intrinsically multivocal concepts which refer to the other modal aspects. In sorting these out, one must take into consideration the original (nuclear) meaning of the aspects involved. But the meaning-kernel of the aspect itself cannot be construed conceptually. As the investigation proceeds, the meaning of the nucleus of meaning recedes. It qualifies all of the concepts used in the field. It itself cannot be grasped in a concept, nor can it be grasped in an adequate intuition.

Dooyeweerd describes as follows the nature and limits of theoretical definition in connection with his own field of jurisprudence:

The basic concept of law must embrace the modal sense of the juridical lawsphere. *And this modal sense can only be grasped in connection with the entire temporal coherence of the modalities.* At the same time, however, we strike against the inner limits of all definition in theoretical concepts. In the theoretical analysis of the modal structure of law we can never do more than set apart theoretically the various structural moments which are qualified by the *modal nucleus of meaning* of the juridical aspect. When we unify these moments synthetically into the fundamental concept of law, we inevitably strike against the *irreducible nucleus of meaning* which controls the meaning of the analogical and anticipatory moments. It is impossible to analyze logically this nucleus of meaning with any greater precision, because in it the *modal sovereignty in its own sphere* of the juridical aspect asserts itself over against the logical aspect. Every attempt to reduce this irreducible nucleus moment to something else produces completely indeterminate and therefore *theoretically valueless concept-formation. The modal nucleus of meaning of the aspect to be defined is thus the limit of all theoretical definition of concepts.*[11]

There is no adequate intuition of the meaning of the nuclei of the modal aspects. This is a major point in Dooyeweerd's criticism of phenomenology.

If we observe the nuclei of meaning against a receding horizon, we must be constantly aware that these are not under our control but that they, as a divinely given law-order, control human activity. Failure to respect the boundaries leads to antinomies, or inescapable contradictions. In this investigation, one is led by certain principles, e.g., the principle of the exclusion of antinomies, which serves to avoid confusing one aspect with the other. One must position oneself so as to exclude antinomy.

Theory involves a reflection on the self. For this reason all scientific investigation involves an implicit anthropology. If theory is to be carried on successfully, it must be possible to reflect on the self in its integrality. Dooyeweerd maintains that the assumption of neutrality in thought – the assumption that theory can rest in itself –brings with it the impossibility of reflecting on the self in its integrality. This reflection is impossible so long as theory is dominated by an apostate ground motive, which drives it in opposed directions. Reflection on the self is truly possible only on the foundation of the true Origin as revealed in the Scriptures.[12]

Various interpretations have been given of the modal aspects in their order within the created cosmos. One is that these are *perspectives* from which things can be viewed. According to Dooyeweerd, however, the aspects are *not perspectives on things*; they are *aspects* of things, *modes* in which things appear. In their diversity they raise the questions as to their deeper unity. Another is that these are *metaphysical* levels. According to Dooyeweerd, however, the aspects are not levels, which would suggest that they have an identity apart from each other. They are certainly not *metaphysical* levels, which would separate them from ongoing human experience. The aspects are present implicitly in all human experience. They are abstracted out in theoretical thinking, but even here they are dynamic, constantly going *before* thought and *undergirding* it without being brought under its control. This is especially significant because control is an essential element of theoretical thought, in its concept-formation.

Yet another position fails to distinguish between theory and pre-theory. In this there is a tendency to theoreticize reality. Theory is regarded to be the source of meaning in the cosmos. If this is so, then it is impossible to look transcendentally at that which underlies theory and accounts for its possibility. It is impossible to discern the modal structure which underlies theory and provides its qualification. According to Dooyeweerd, theory depends on pre-theory; understanding it involves reflecting on what underlies it and establishes its very possibility.

E. REFLECTION AS A PROBLEM IN CONTEMPORARY PHILOSOPHY AND THEOLOGY

Immanuel Kant thought of people's reflecting on themselves in ethical terms. In one's ethical act, he said, one constitutes oneself as an ethical being and a free personality.[13] Subsequent thought judged, however, that the reflection described by Kant was not deep enough. He had not found a truly transcendent reference point. Contrary to his expectations, his ethical self still belonged within the "world," within what can become an "object" of theoretical inquiry. [14] It became necessary, therefore, to penetrate deeper. What Kant placed at the center became external, a matter of conventional willing. This trend was present immediately after Kant in German idealism. In idealism we detect a distinction between a more superficial ethic, an ethic of conventional willing, and a deeper ethic, that of the idea. It was even present in Kant's later work, in his aesthetics, for which morality had become external and in which artistic creation stood at the center.

The effort to go beyond Kant was carried further in the phenomenological movement. Here there was an effort to penetrate deeper than before, so that the starting point of philosophy would be free from all partiality. It assigned Kant's ethical self, contrary to his own intentions, to the level of naturalistic thinking. It sought to provide a deeper basis for reflection on being human.

Existential thinking has also attempted to provide a deep reflection on human existence. This was to be attained by way of transcending, as the self was confronted with ultimate meaninglessness, the ultimate surd of the situation. Existential thinking is famous for its "encounter with nothingness." In this encounter all partial positions were to be transcended. Reflection took place as one bounced, as it were, off of the impenetrable wall of the situation. In this way reflection was supposed to avoid all partiality; it was supposed to be total.

Existential and phenomenological thought criticized their forebears for not having been able to attain a total reflection on the self. Instead, they said, earlier positions failed to transcend the subject-object relation. They could not do this because they were under the influence of a prior objectification.

Dooyeweerd concludes, however, that none of these efforts were successful. That is the case, because each of them committed the basic error of beginning within theoretical thought. In such a fashion, the possibility of total reflection was eliminated.

In theoretical thought, there is a reflection on that which precedes it and makes it possible. This reflection is not possible if one thinks that theoretical thought is sufficient to itself, or even if one thinks that theoretical thinking lies along a spectrum, so that it develops only gradually.

CONCLUDING REMARK

In evaluating Dooyeweerd's philosophy, one must keep in mind the difference between its philosophical conceptualization and the religious orientation that is crucial to it as a whole. On the one hand, Dooyeweerd was confident that faithful, painstaking inquiry into the created order of things could bear much fruit; he himself was very much aware, on the other hand, of the humanness and fallibility of the results of his philosophizing. He said freely that over the years all of the philosophical superstructure of the cosmonomic idea philosophy might well fall to the ground and be superseded. He never suggested, however, that God's creation could ever be understood properly apart from its religious foundation.

In writing this paper I have tried to illuminate the central place that religion has in Dooyeweerd's philosophy. I have argued that the final explanation of the transcendental orientation of his thinking resides in his view of religion. Dooyeweerd's view of religion played a central role in the development of his transcendental method, and this method itself can be understood finally only in relation to his view of religion.

References

1. Vincent Brümmer, *Transcendental Criticism and Christian Philosophy* (Franeker: T. Wever, 1961), 15, note. 7. Brømmer refers to Dooyeweerd's discussion with Van Peursen, "Van Peursen's critische vragen bij 'A New Critique of Theoretical Thought'," *Philosophia Reformata*, XXV (1960), 97. Cf. Dooyeweerd's "Calvinistische wijsbegeerte," which appeared in *Scientia*, vol. I (2nd ed., 1956), and was taken up in *Verkenningen in de wijsbegeerte, de sociologie, en de rechtsgeschiedenis* (Amsterdam: Buijten en Schipperheijn, 1962), 9-66. (It also appeared in the *Collected Works of Dooyeweerd*, The Edwin Mellen Press, 1996, Series B, Volume 1.) On p. 15 Dooyeweerd calls transcendental critique "the key to understanding the Philosophy of the Law-Idea" ("de sleutel ... tot het verstaan van de wijsbegeerte der wetsidee ...").

2. Herman Dooyeweerd, *A New Critique of Theoretical Thought*, vol. 1 (Philadelphia: Presbyterian and Reformed Publishing Co., 1953), The *Collected Works* of Dooyeweerd, The Edwin Mellen Press, 1997, A Series, Volume 1.

3. Cf. ibid. viii.

4. In the original, Dutch edition the entire passage reads as follows: "Aanvankelijk sterk onder den invloed eerst van de Neo-Kantiaansche wijsbegeerte, later van Husserl's phaenomenologie, beteekende het groote keerpunt in mijn denken de ontdekking van den religieuzen wortel van het denken zelve, waardoor mij een nieuw licht opging over de doorloopende mislukking van alle, aanvankelijk ook door mijzelf ondernomen, pogingen een innerlijke verbinding tot stand te brengen tusschen het Christelijk geloof en een wijsbegeerte, die geworteld is in het geloof in de zelfgenoegzaamheid der menschelijke rede." Herman Dooyeweerd, *De Wijsbegeerte der Wetsidee* (Amsterdam: H. J. Paris, 1935-1936), I, v.

5. Dooyeweerd uses an illustration to portray the idea that religion underlies everything and can be seen only indirectly. He calls religion the "hidden player" behind all thought. The illustration is drawn from the practice in certain Dutch churches where the organ console is hidden behind a screen. One hears the effects of the organist's manipulating the stops, keys, and pedals, but one does not see him. Analogously, one sees the outworkings of religion, but one does not observe religion itself directly. It is discerned by way of *reflection*.

6. In *A New Critique*, II (1955), 432, Dooyeweerd says of Kant, "In his doctrine of the theoretical Ideas, he was certainly led by a truly transcendental motive," but he proceeds immediately to criticism. In other places criticism overshadows the recognition of the truly transcendental orientation of Kant's thought. See Dooyeweerd, *Transcendental Problems of Philosophic Thought* (Grand Rapids: Wm. B. Eerdmans Publishing Co., 1948), 20.

7. In my 1962 Wheaton lecture, "Dooyeweerd's Philosophical Method," I described his philosophizing as "phenomenological," "transcendental," and "critical." In doing this, I was aware that there is danger in typifying positions in this way. I warned that each of these terms must be understood within the context of Dooyeweerd's philosophy itself. It may not be concluded from my use of these terms that I thought of Dooyeweerd's philosophy as a blend of phenomenology and Kantianism. This lecture and a set of endnotes, which were prepared after the lecture had been delivered, were included in my *Philosophia Reformanda: Reflections on the Philosophy of Herman Dooyeweerd* (mimeographed, 1971).

8. In his inaugural oration, *De betekenis der Wetsidee voor Rechtswetenschap en Rechtsphilosophie* (Kampen: I. H. Kok, [1926]), Dooyeweerd said that the law-idea of Calvinism rests on the twin pillars of all Christian thought, the confession of the divine sovereignty of God as the Creator and the confession of the divine plan for the world upheld by God's providential care. As Marcel Verburg writes, "... stelde hij dat de wetsidee van het calvinisme geworteld is in de *beide* elementen van alle christelijk denken: de belijdenis van de goddelijke schepperssouvereinheit en de belijdenis van het goddelijk voorzienig wereldplan." Marcel Verburg, *Herman Dooyeweerd: Leven en werk van een Nederlands christen-wijsgeer* (Baarn: Ten Have, 1989), 97. Verburg speaks of "beide elementen"; Dooyeweerd uses the words "beide fundamenten."

9. Using this double negative helps to avoid thinking of the law as if it were "something" between God and the created cosmos. Vollenhoven expressed the boundary idea in terms of a triad: God/law/cosmos (*God/wet/kosmos*). This formulation of itself does not imply that the law is "something" between God and the created cosmos. Vollenhoven does indeed contribute to the misunderstanding, however, as he goes on to describe these three factors as the necessary parts of a complete ontology. In his view, one or more of these "parts" can be disengaged from the rest, so that one can attempt to satisfy himself with an *incomplete* ontology. If one puts matters in this way, he runs the risk of suggesting that in order to have a complete ontology one must interject something between God and the created cosmos. On such a view, it is objected, one relates to the *law* and not directly to God himself. In speaking about the law as boundary, we should try to avoid this misunderstanding. We must emphasize that humankind, created in the image of God, stands in immediate relationship to God. Humankind stands immediately before God (*coram deo*) in covenant obedience or disobedience. The ideas of the law as boundary and of humankind's immediate relationship to God are not at all incompatible. One is immediately related to God, but this is a *structured* relationship.

10. In a deposition written in defense of his philosophy, Dooyeweerd made this point clearly: "De radicale breuk van de Wijsbegeerte der Wetsidee met de immantiephilosophie ligt toch ... hierin, dat de eerste bij het licht der Schrift tot den *religieuzen wortel* van het denken doordringt en heel het

tijdelijke menschelijk bestaan in zijn uitgang uit *dien religieuzen wortel*, het *hart* in den zin der Schrift, vat." (English translation: "The radical break of the Philosophy of the Law-Idea with immanence philosophy resides ... in the fact that it penetrates by the light of the Scriptures to the *religious root* of thought and conceives human temporal existence as a whole and as to its origin in terms of *its religious root*, the *heart* in the scriptural sense of the word.") Quoted from Verburg, op. cit., 213-214. (English version mine).

11. Herman Dooyeweerd, *Inleiding encyclopaedie der rechtswetenschap* (stenciled), 53 (English version mine). Quoted in Robert D. Knudsen, "Dooyeweerd's Philosophical Method," endnote no. 2. Cf. the discussion as a whole in *Philosophia Reformanda: Reflections on the Philosophy of Herman Dooyeweerd* (mimeographed, 1971).

12. "... both self-knowledge and knowledge of the absolute origin or pseudo-origin, exceed the limits of theoretical thought, and are rooted in the 'heart' or the religious centre of our existence.... Theoretical thought, too, is concerned in this central knowledge, in the transcendental process of self-reflection, in the concentric direction of the theoretically separated aspects of the gegenstand relation to the thinking self ... without veritable self-knowledge the true starting-point of theoretical synthesis cannot be discovered, and ... theoretic self-reflection in thought presupposes this central knowledge, since the concentric direction of theoretical thought can start only from the ego ... [God] has expressed His image in [the hu]man [being] by concentrating its entire temporal existence in the radical religious unity of an ego in which the totality of meaning of the temporal cosmos was to be focused upon its Origin. The fundamental dependence of human self-knowledge upon the knowledge of God has consequently its inner ground in the essence of religion as the central sphere of our created nature." Herman Dooyeweerd, *A New Critique of Theoretical Thought*, I, 55.

13. Dooyeweerd says that in Kant's position there is a "religious absolutizing of morality." *New Critique*, I, 49, note 1.

14. This shift is discussed both in Robert D. Knudsen, *Dialectic and Synthesis in Contemporary Theology* (1967) and in the companion writing "Roots of the New Theology" (1965), which appeared in John H. Skilton, ed., *Scripture and Confession: A Book about Confessions Old and New* (Phillipsburg, NJ: Presbyterian and Reformed Publishing Co., 1973). This shift was reflected in the attempt in philosophy and theology to surpass the ethical, resulting in positions that are called "transmoral." Transmorality is present in the thought of Friedrich Schelling, G. W. F. Hegel, Søren Kierkegaard, Friedrich Nietzsche, Karl Marx, Paul Tillich, among others.

DOOYEWEERD'S PHILOSOPHICAL METHOD [1]

To the present there is no full-scale discussion of Dooyeweerd's method. Two noteworthy studies, that of Michael Fr. J. Marlet, *Grundlinien der kalvinistischen 'Philosophie der Gesetzesidee' als christlicher Transzendentalphilosophie*, and that of Vincent Brümmer, *Transcendental Criticism and Christian Philosophy*, are extended discussions of what Dooyeweerd himself has been placing in the focus of attention, his transcendental critique; but there is as yet no study which treats Dooyeweerd's method in full detail as to its various facets. What we say here in this paper, therefore, will be preliminary and exploratory. We shall cover some relatively undiscussed territory as well as traversing well-known paths. Dooyeweerd's philosophizing has posed questions of method which will have to be discussed for a long while before they are brought clearly into view.

We shall group our own discussion around three major heads. Without claiming too much either for the divisions or for the order in which they are presented, we can say that Dooyeweerd's method is phenomenological, transcendental, and, in a negative sense, dialectical.

I. PHENOMENOLOGICAL

Dooyeweerd avers that the phenomenological movement is a most dangerous adversary of a truly Christian philosophy. A careful viewing of his philosophy reveals, however, that there are many points of similarity between his interests and methods and those of the phenomenological school. Without minimizing the definite stand he takes against phenomenology as it has actually been developed, there is a broad though real sense in which his method may be called phenomenological.[2]

Both Dooyeweerd and the phenomenological school have interests and goals in common. They are both interested in the so-called crisis of European science and the contribution that this crisis has made to the crisis of our Western civilization. Both are interested in rescuing Western philosophy from the various "isms" – psychologism, historicism, etc. -- which have stranded it on the crag of relativism. Both are interested in overcoming "naturalism," as Husserl conceives it, the attempted reduction of the phenomena of experience to the physical and the psychical. Both are interested in mounting a more radical critique of science than that of Immanuel Kant. They are both interested in a closer examination of the concepts with which science operates. Both the rationalistic phenomenology and Dooyeweerd have in common that they think of philosophy as being scientific in character, the science which lays the foundation for the particular sciences (*scientia scientiarum*).

What we have said thus far does little more than show that Dooyeweerd is concerned with problems which have busied the continental philosophical mind. There are, however, more significant similarities which bear mention. Though he does not give intentionality as wide a scope, Dooyeweerd holds that the theoretical attitude of thought is an intentional relatedness, a mental directedness to a *Gegenstand*. Like phenomenology Dooyeweerd is opposed to phenomenalism, which distinguishes between appearance and a thing-in-itself behind appearance. Dooyeweerd retains the orientation to the phenomena which Husserl epitomized in his slogan, "Zu den Sachen selbst." In Dooyeweerd, as in phenomenology, the problems of epistemology are not ignored; nevertheless, they are thought to depend upon prior ontological foundations.

Significant for our comparison is the fact that Dooyeweerd limits himself to what appears, viewing everything within the horizon of human experiencing. He radically excludes metaphysics, which pretends to deal theoretically with that which is beyond the range of any possible experience. In a broad sense his thought is empirical. Like the phenomenologists, for whom intuition of essence (*Wesenschau*) is non-sensory, Dooyeweerd is interested in an empiricism which is broader than the traditional kind. With Meinong and Husserl he recognizes phenomena other than physical and psychical. Experience, he says, may not be limited to what he calls the psychical-sensory aspect of our experiencing.

In every-day experiencing, Dooyeweerd says, there is a concrete living-with reality, which one experiences in its fullness and coherence as basically his own. This naive experiencing (which includes naïve thinking) is not itself a theory. It is a primary datum which underlies theoretical thought and which may not be ignored or replaced by it. In the theoretical attitude of thought we abstract from the coherence in time of our naive experiencing and we articulate certain aspects or modes – the arithmetical, the spatial, the physical, energetic effect, the biotic, the psychical, etc. Each of these aspects reveals a structure peculiarly its own. Each has a sovereignty in its own sphere by virtue of an irreducible nucleus of meaning – discrete quantity, for the arithmetical aspect; unbroken extension, for the spatial aspect; life, for the biotic aspect; feeling, for the psychical aspect, etc. This meaning is expressed in a law-side and a subject-side. Each of the aspects also expresses the coherence of the temporal order, anticipating later aspects and referring back to earlier aspects by way of subsidiary moments of meaning, which Dooyeweerd calls "analogies." Dooyeweerd speaks of grasping the structure of these modal aspects in the theoretical concept. As we shall discover later in more detail, however, the modal nucleus of meaning appears in the course of the analysis of the structure of the modal aspect; but it itself is not subject to logical analysis. In the process of the rigorous analysis of the structure of the modal aspect the modal nucleus of meaning, in terms of which the modal aspect has its peculiar qualification, is laid bare or disclosed.[3] It is brought to appear, to reveal itself. There is a definite parallel here to the phenomenological method.

It must be observed, however, that Dooyeweerd himself repeatedly warns against confusing one or another of his positions with that of the phenomenological school, and indeed he offers sharp opposition to it. His most obvious objection to phenomenology of the Husserl type, which he calls rationalistic phenomenology, is that it seeks a neutral, completely autonomous method in philosophy. It has aimed to open up broader vistas of experience. It has sought a unitary layer of human experience beyond all the antitheses (e.g., that of subject and object) which characterize our natural attitude of thought.[4] It has failed nevertheless, Dooyeweerd claims, to discover reality in its fundamental, unbroken unity, as it is given to us in naïve experience. It does not avoid viewing reality within the framework of an ultimate antithesis, for it sets a method of *Wesenschau*, an immediate intuition of reality as it appears to us, in contrast to an objectivizing method of the natural sciences. Furthermore, Dooyeweerd objects, Husserl's method of *Wesenschau* seeks for an ultimate, thus denying the lack of independence of the various sides of reality and becoming in a real sense metaphysical. Dooyeweerd also holds that Husserl's transcendental subject, in reference to which the field of phenomena appears, is also a construct of the theoretical attitude of thought and is not something given.[5]

According to Dooyeweerd, the phenomenologists miss the truly transcendental direction of thought.[6] The nucleus of meaning of a modal aspect of reality, he says, is not a static *eidos*. It may not be grasped in the theoretical concept but may only be approached in a transcendental direction, in the *idea*. A proper view of the human subject is also gained only by way of a truly transcendental reflection, which while remaining within the confines of theoretical thought points beyond it to the deeper unity of all experiencing.

Considering the basic criticisms Dooyeweerd has to offer of phenomenology, criticisms which involve the foundations of his philosophy, one must proceed with great caution in interpreting such parallels as we have drawn. Particularly in view of his broad empiricism, however, Dooyeweerd's method overall may be called "phenomenological." He himself writes that he was at one time deeply influenced by the phenomenological movement. Undoubtedly he retains many of its problems and attitudes. It is not that Dooyeweerd objects to a broadly phenomenological method; it is that he believes that the pretended neutrality of the phenomenologists has forced them to absolutize theoretical thought and has caused them to fail in their program. They fail to attain a truly transcendental direction of thought and they fail to grasp reality in its unity, which can be intended theoretically only in a transcendental direction.

II. TRANSCENDENTAL

Dooyeweerd's method is also transcendental. In recent years his efforts have been concentrated on developing a transcendental critique of theoretical thought. Earlier, he says, his criticisms of non-Christian philosophy were too transcendent. More recently it has been his intent to develop a truly transcendental critique, an investigation into the universally valid conditions which make theoretical thought possible, and which are required by the very structure of this thought itself.[7]

Dooyeweerd does not attempt to prove to another that Christianity is true or that Christian presuppositions must be accepted. Neither does he wish, primarily, to criticize the methods and the results of philosophic thought in terms of the doctrines of the Christian faith. Such critique, which he calls "transcendent," is not altogether out of place; but theoretically it is useless because it does not lay bare the inner, intrinsic connection between the theoretical attitude and Christian faith.

Dooyeweerd's method is to meet his opponent where he is, with his philosophical problems and results, seeking to confront him with undeniable states of affairs with regard to his own method of philosophizing, making him face up to the ultimate religious presuppositions of his own thinking, and challenging him with the claim that these presuppositions themselves can be truly understood only in terms of the Christian faith.

Such a critique is possible because of a radical tendency within thought itself towards an origin of meaning, what Dooyeweerd calls the concentric direction of theoretical thought. In the theoretical attitude of thought the logical aspect of our thought is set up over against a non-logical aspect of our experiencing in an antithetic, intentional relationship, seeking to grasp the aspect in a theoretical concept.[8] As Dooyeweerd describes this relationship more fully, we discover that the concept is a unity in a multiplicity of moments, which indeed grasps the structure of the particular modal aspect, but which has its limit, as we have already observed, in the nucleus of meaning which gives the structure of the aspect its peculiar qualification. Essential to Dooyeweerd's view of method is the idea that the fullness of meaning of the modal nucleus cannot be grasped in the theoretical concept but only approached transcendentally in a theoretical idea.[9] In his doctrine of ideas Kant is supposed to have struck out in the truly transcendental direction. His mistake was not that he was transcendental but that he was not transcendental enough.

True to his viewpoint that epistemology involves an ontological foundation, Dooyeweerd finds that this transcendental, concentric direction of thought is rooted in the restlessness of the created cosmos itself as it points beyond itself. It is to this restlessness and lack of self-sufficiency that he refers when he says that the cosmos is meaning. Meaning is the being of all that is. The transcendental direction is a direction in reality itself, expressing the created structure of the cosmos as meaning, its radical lack of self-sufficiency in relation to its origin.[10]

The idea that reality is meaning is reflected in Dooyeweerd's attempt to be radically critical, even more than Kant. He radically rejects metaphysics, which posits a fundamental identity of thought and being. There is, Dooyeweerd says, no stopping place within thought. The absolutization of any product of thought must be rigorously avoided. The concepts of theoretical thought demand a continual clarification of their meaning.

Dooyeweerd regards himself to differ markedly from phenomenology in that he regards this clarification to be ultimately unfinishable. In a remarkable passage he writes,

> Suppose the Idea phenomenologically conceived of as the eidos [εἶδος] of a modal aspect could be *fully realized* in theoretical insight, as the result of an adequate intuition of its essence, then this insight would have to grasp the fullness and the totality of meaning adequately.
>
> It should not only *intend* this fullness and totality in the transcendental direction of time; a mere referring to it as to the transcendent root of all temporal meaning, would not suffice. It should *possess* this fullness as an immanent datum of phenomenological consciousness. But as soon as this condition had been fulfilled, the modal meaning, as such, would have been cancelled. For this condition can only be realized in the transcendent identity of all temporal modal meaning."[11]

The fullness of meaning, the source of meaning which transcends all meaning, is not grasped metaphysically in the theoretical concept nor intuited in a phenomenological *Wesenschau* but is only intended in the transcendental direction of thought in the theoretical idea.

It is within this framework of the distinction between the theoretical concept and the theoretical idea that Dooyeweerd views the methods of the special sciences and philosophy. Particular sciences, like arithmetic, biology, economics, and ethics, deal with the variable phenomena within their respective fields. In order to do this, however, it is necessary for them to develop a well-defined concept of their field in distinction from others.

In order to distinguish the various aspects conceptually, however, one needs a basis of comparison (*grondnoemer*). If they had no such point of contact, they would be completely incommensurable, and it would be altogether impossible to discover in what respects they differed. Dooyeweerd claims that the immanence philosopher, who takes his point of departure within the antithetic relation of theoretical thought, is forced to discover this basis in an absolutized aspect. The concept of the aspect is extended, becoming an idea of the origin, the deeper unity, and the coherence of meaning of the other aspects of reality. Thus it is possible, for instance, for the psychologist to become psychologistic, viewing jurisprudence, e.g., as if it were fundamentally psychical in nature. Such a psychologistic view might claim that positive law has its only source in the sense of justice in human society. The attempt has also been made in jurisprudence to reduce law to a phenomenon of the historical national spirit. Such views involve reductionism, making the various spheres of reality phenomena of a single absolutized aspect, thereby destroying their sovereignty in their own spheres and distorting their structures.

It does not avail, Dooyeweerd says, to avoid the genetic[12] direction and to attempt simply to classify the various modal aspects according to the pattern of genus and species. In such a method one seeks to range the various aspects under a merely formal generic concept, a *genus proximum*. Then the aspects are distinguished from each other by specific differences. Thus under the generic concept, "norm of action," there has been made a distinction between the moral norm, which is supposed to regulate the inner attitude, and the legal and social norms, which are supposed to regulate external acts. Under the concept of the regulation of external acts, the legal norm is then distinguished as compulsory from the social norm as non-compulsory.[13] When such classification is employed to distinguish the various modal aspects, it is forgotten, Dooyeweerd says, that such terms as "compulsion" are ambiguous, being analogical in character. [14] There is social compulsion, economic compulsion, pistical compulsion, etc., as well as legal compulsion. Who is to say that compulsion is to be restricted to a so-called legal sphere and denied to the social sphere? The original meaning of compulsion is in the aspect of energetic effect, but it recurs in an analogical sense in all of the other aspects of reality. In its analogical senses it needs to be qualified by the nucleus of meaning of the aspect in which it functions. Without this qualification it remains ambiguous.[15] To distinguish one aspect of experience from another by way of the method of *genus proximum* and *differentia specifica* is to deny the universality in its own sphere of every aspect of reality and to employ concepts whose meaning remains ambiguous, leading to confusion within the concept formation of the particular sciences.

From the preceding discussion it is possible to grasp what Dooyeweerd means when he says that the very formation of concepts by the special sciences occurs under the leading of a theoretical idea. This idea, which Dooyeweerd calls a cosmonomic idea (*wetsidee*)[16] is threefold. It is composed of an idea of the mutual relationship and connection of the various aspects of reality, an idea of what Dooyeweerd calls the deeper root unity of these aspects, and an idea of their ultimate origin.

The Christian cosmonomic idea finds the absolute origin in the sovereign creative will of God, which guarantees the sovereignty within their own spheres of the various aspects of reality. Furthermore, it discovers the deeper unity of the aspects in the transcendental direction, in the human heart, which is nothing apart from its concentration of all temporal life towards a true or pretended origin. Finally, it discovers a coherence in diversity of the various aspects of reality, in their sovereignty and in their universality within their own spheres.

For Dooyeweerd the transcendental direction of thought is inseparably bound up with reflection on the human selfhood or heart. It is through the transcendental idea that the transcendent choice of position by the human heart with reference to the absolute origin of all things exerts an influence upon the immanent course of philosophic thought and upon the investigations of the special sciences.[17]

Dooyeweerd himself sketches the relationship of the concepts and the idea thus:

> The *theoretical idea* is always a philosophic (*wijsgerig*) idea of the totality and unity of the aspects which have been articulated in the antithetic (*gegenstand*) relation. Contrariwise, the theoretical concept as such is oriented to the theoretical distinguishing of the separate aspects. The theoretical idea is not able to eliminate this conceptual *distinguishing*; it simply relates the latter to the connection, the root unity, and the origin of the distinguished aspects. And theoretical distinction is only possible upon the foundation of such a theoretical idea. For without an idea of the whole a concept of the parts is not possible.

Thus, while maintaining the antithetic relation, the theoretical idea relates the theoretical concept to the presuppositions of all theoretical thought but itself remains theoretical in character, remaining thus within the limits of philosophic thought.

Precisely in this resides what we have called its transcendental character.[18]

Philosophic thought, on the other hand, which takes its point of departure within theoretical thought, is by reason of the antithetic relationship forced to elevate some aspect of reality to be the origin, thus missing the truly transcendental way of thought and distorting the coherence of the various aspects of reality, as they are given to us in naïve experience. The absolutization of one aspect of reality evokes the resistance of the others, Dooyeweerd says, leading to insoluble antinomies of thought.

III. DIALECTICAL

Because of his use of antinomy, we can say that Dooyeweerd's method, in a negative sense, is dialectical.

In Dooyeweerd's usage dialectic refers to an opposition (what others sometimes call a "polarity").[19] He speaks therefore of theoretical dialectic because in theoretical thought the logical aspect of thought is set over against a non-logical aspect of our experiencing. Such an antithesis is bridged over in theoretical synthesis.

On the contrary, immanence philosophy, which starts within the framework of theoretical thought itself, becomes involved in antinomy.

According to Dooyeweerd, the antinomy is not simply a contradiction which could be eliminated by further logical clarification. It is indeed a contradiction but only with reference to its logical aspect. In contrast to the merely logical contradiction the antinomy has an inter-modal character and depends upon the inevitably false attempts at synthesis which arise from the false choice of position by the heart with respect to the absolute origin. It is an indication that the boundaries of meaning of the modal aspects have been transgressed and that the attempt has been made to reduce one to the other. Antinomy has fundamentally a super-theoretical origin and therefore cannot be overcome by purely theoretical means. It involves a religious antithesis or dialectic, i.e., one which cannot be bridged over by theoretic synthesis.[20]

As is well known, Dooyeweerd says that it is not simply the individual human selfhood which is the Archimedean point of philosophy. The human self participates, according to whether it is turned to the true or to a false origin, in a super-individual spiritual community dominated by a true or an apostate religious motive. Only the Christian motive is integral in character. The apostate motives – the motive of form and matter, which dominated Greek thought, and the motive of nature and freedom, which has dominated our humanistic Western culture – are dialectical, in reality being composed of two religious motives which are in irreconcilable antagonism to each other.

Fundamental to Dooyeweerd's thought is that the Christian motive of creation, fall, and redemption in Christ excludes a religious dialectic. It involves neither antinomy in the formation of philosophic concepts nor the dualism inherent in the apostate motives of thought.

Dooyeweerd does not use antinomy therefore in a positive sense, which is characteristic of Hegelian philosophy. He employs it in a negative, critical way. A cornerstone of his method is the religiously founded principle of the exclusion of antinomies (*principium exclusae antinomiae*), as a foundational cosmological principle of thought. As he writes,

> In the new critique of philosophical thought, ... the tracing of theoretical antinomies has been elaborated into a systematical method of immanent criticism of the philosophical systems. This method may be used to test every philosophical total view of our experiential horizon by the structural data of the latter within the temporal order.[21]

A typical argument employing the method of antinomy is that an aspect of the cosmos cannot be thought both to presuppose and to found another aspect. Logististic thought has tried to reduce the mathematical to the logical aspect, claiming that logical multiplicity is the origin of number. Logical multiplicity, however, is a mathematical analogy within the logical sphere, which presupposes number and which therefore cannot found it. [22]

Further, it is argued that the reduction of one aspect to the other destroys meaning. Logistic thought, he says, attempts to construe space in a purely logical fashion in terms of a continuous logical progression from thought-point to thought-point. In this way it has elevated logical thought-space (the logical analogy of space) to be the origin of geometrical space. Thereby the modal boundaries between number, space, movement, and logical analysis have been eliminated, resulting in antinomy. The spatial point has no extension. If one wishes to construct a continuum logically out of points, the points are eliminated in the process.[23]

We cite further an extended example concerning juridical causality:

> In the modal sense of law there is an analogy of motion, which manifests itself as to the *law side* in the legal consequences of a legal fact, which are qualified by the legal norm, and as to the subject side in the *subjective*, i.e., the subjective-objective, causality of this fact.

According to a naturalistic view of reality, the subjective juridical causality was viewed in a natural scientific fashion.

When this natural scientific concept of causality was consistently applied, human acts falling within the causal nexus were placed on a line with natural events such as a bolt of lightning or the falling of a stone. These acts were simply put side by side in this causal chain as the indispensable conditions of the effect, apart from which it would not have occurred (the so-called theory of *conditio sine qua non*).

This naturalistic conception of causality, however, must of necessity lead to antinomies in jurisprudence, because it destroys any and all grounds for juridical accountability. If, for instance, the intentional discharge of a pistol by a murderer is simply a link in the causal chain leading to the death of the victim, and as such stands on one line with the mechanical motion of the projectile and the fortuitous presence of the victim in the line of fire, then it is no longer possible to say that the death was caused by a murderer. His deed is then simply one of many conditions for the occurrence of the effect. On what grounds is he then regarded to be juridically accountable for what has happened? In the causal sequences of natural science stock must be taken of an entire series of 'conditions' which are equivalent to each other.

Juridical imputation is possible only when a human act can be viewed as a *free cause* of an occurrence but never if this act as such forms only a link in a natural-causal chain. *If causality in a juridical sense were identical with causality in the sense of physics*, then this foundation for juridical imputation would be *eliminated*. That juridical causality, however, can exist only in unbreakable coherence of meaning with juridical imputation is evident from the so-called *causa omissionis* in jurisprudence.

By way of pure negligence, by sitting still, by doing nothing when one should act, one can cause damage in a juridical sense. Think only of a railroad man who falls asleep and does not change the signals, through whose negligence a train wreck is caused. This is not simply a *question of blame* which falls outside of every *causal nexus*.

We still have to observe how *guilt* in a juridical sense presupposes the *juridical causality* of the guilty act. But [already we can say that] the causality concept of physics can take only *positive* functions of motion into consideration. Negative conditions can never be causal in a physical sense.

> Undoubtedly, juridical causality cannot exist, has no mean-
> ing, *without the foundation* of causality in the original sense of
> physical movement. But it is only an analogy linked with the
> subjective meaning of law and as such remains qualified by
> the meaning-node of law.
>
> When the modal boundaries of meaning between this jurid-
> ical causality and causality in the original sense of physical
> movement are wiped out, antinomy is unavoidable.[24]

Turning in the final place to Dooyeweerd's basic ground-motives, it is clear that the oppositions of form and matter and of nature and freedom have been prominent both in philosophy and in theology. Contemporary philosophy is much concerned with the problem of objectification and depersonalization. Concern is expressed that a man not be viewed according to patterns taken from nature but that he be given the opportunity of developing his free personality. Similar interests are expressed in theology, particularly that which has been influenced by existential philosophy.

It is a superficial view, however, which leaves matters at this point. There must also be an eye for the antinomies within many current ideas of freedom. If we look at the thought of Karl Jaspers, for instance, we discover that the self is thought of first of all in antithesis to the world. The self must be freed from the necessities of the general, where it is regarded to be an instance of a general rule, and where it is regarded to be of value in terms of its function, and it must be seen in its freedom, which rises above all generality. Human freedom must be placed in antithesis to any generally valid criterion.[25] The meaning of one's existence is not given, either in fact or in principle.

Jaspers holds, however, that such a bare antithesis leads to nihilism. To be, I must be something or other. In the anxiety that I experience in breaking away from all support in the world lurks also the concern that I not lose myself. I can become myself, however, only when I no longer view everything, in lofty detachment, as simply one possibility among others but when I am altogether taken up with something by reason of a transcendent necessity.[26]

Here the generality which has been eliminated on one level, that of the world, returns on another level, that of the transcendent. The transcendent necessity cannot simply be a necessity for me, else it would lose its transcendent character and its power to grasp. It must be general, with a kind of objectivity; it must be the one in contrast to what is simply one thing among others.[27] There is, however, no criterion for discovering what is such a transcendent necessity, nor for distinguishing between its generality and that of the general validity of scientific statements. Jaspers believes that this transcendent generality in some unexplained fashion is able to be squared with man's freedom, while general validity is not.

REFERENCES

1. A slightly revised form of a lecture delivered at the Annual Philosophy Conference, Wheaton College, Wheaton, Illinois, October 13, 1962.

2. Various persons commenting on this paper have been struck by the fact that I indicated parallels between Dooyeweerd's thought and the phenomenological philosophy. Had I known that this facet of my presentation would catch the attention of the hearers as it did, I might have subdued it or have eliminated it entirely. I do not retreat from my position that in a broad though real sense Dooyeweerd's method may be called "phenomenological"; nevertheless, I must emphasize again that the statement in my lecture to this effect was ringed with a battery of qualifications and warnings. I must also reiterate that Dooyeweerd's method is first of all *transcendental*. The middle section of the paper, therefore, is the most important one. That I discussed Dooyeweerd's method under three heads at all was largely for the sake of convenience. Already in the introduction to the paper I made this clear, where I said that little weight should be placed on the divisions or on the order in which they were presented. The important thing is to penetrate and grasp the philosophy in its inner tendencies. For this a grasp of its transcendental thrust is indispensable.

3. The position of Dooyeweerd and of the other major representatives of the cosmonomic idea philosophy is that the cosmic order is not logical in character. The cosmos is indeed subject to a structure of law. This is demanded by the idea advocated by this philosophy that the law is the boundary between God and the cosmos. But not all cosmic law is logical law. The logical (analytical) is only one aspect of the cosmic order. Apart from this order logical thought would not even be possible. Dooyeweerd maintains that to think that the cosmic structure of law is logical is out of keeping with the fundamental thrust of his philosophy. "According to the transcendental basic Idea, on which our philosophic thought is founded," he says, "temporal reality cannot be of a logical nature ...; it is not even capable of being contained in a concept." (Dooyeweerd, *A New Critique*, II, 5. Hereafter cited as NCTT.) Later with an obvious reference to Kant, he remarks that the law-order is not transcendental-logical (NCTT II, 5). Dooyeweerd maintains nevertheless that the theorist seeks to obtain a

logical concept of the particular law-sphere he is investigating. However, as he builds up a concept of a particular sphere, he cannot express in a theoretical concept its most fundamental sense, what Dooyeweerd variously calls its "nucleus" or "kernel" of meaning. The modal nuclei of meaning can only express themselves in analogies, i.e., in subsidiary moments of meaning which group around the nuclei of meaning and which point to the other aspects of meaning. Examples of such analogies are "legal power," "social life," "psychical space," "aesthetic feeling," etc. Cf. Herman Dooyeweerd, "The Analogical Concepts" (mimeographed), trans. Robert D. Knudsen. Original Dutch title: *De analogische grondbegrippen der vakwetenschappen en hun betrekking tot de structuur van den menselijken ervaringshorizon. Medelingen der Koninklijke Nederlandse Akademie van Wetenschappen, afd. Letterkunde. Nieuwe reeks*, deel 17, no. 6 (Amsterdam: Noord-Hollandsche Uitgeversmaatschappij, 1954). Dooyeweerd describes as follows the nature and limits of theoretical definition in connection with his own field of jurisprudence: "And thereby at the same time the only possible method is pointed out by which to place juridical concept-formation on a basis that is truly fruitful and that escapes arbitrariness. The basic concept of law must embrace the modal sense of the juridical law-sphere. And this modal sense can only be grasped in connection with the entire temporal coherence of the modalities. At the same time, however, we strike against the inner limits of all definition in theoretical concepts.

"In the theoretical analysis of the modal structure of law we can never do more than set apart theoretically the various structural moments which are qualified by the modal nucleus of meaning of the juridical aspect. When we unify these moments synthetically into the fundamental concept of law, we inevitably strike against this irreducible modal nucleus of meaning which controls the meaning of the analogical and anticipatory moments. It is impossible to analyze logically this nucleus of meaning with any greater precision, because in it the modal sovereignty in its own sphere of the juridical aspect asserts itself over against the logical aspect. Every attempt to reduce this irreducible nuclear moment to something else produces completely in-determinate and therefore theoretically valueless concept-formation.

"The modal nucleus of meaning of the aspect to be defined is thus the limit of all theoretical definition of concepts." (Dooyeweerd, *Inleiding encyclopaedie*, 53. Hereafter cited as IERW.)

The specialty of meaning of the modal nuclei cannot be bridged over in a logical concept which could serve as a common denominator of their meaning. As Dooyeweerd says, the modalities themselves are "... ultimate genera of modal meaning under which are to be subsumed only typical and individual manifestations of the modalities within the different aspects" (NCTT II, 14). Thus no one of them is able to serve as a denominator for the other. Each one is unique and sovereign in it own sphere. In the process of forming the concept of an aspect, the modal nucleus of meaning is opened or laid bare (NCTT II, p. 485) as that which qualifies all of the moments of meaning within its own aspect.

Although there is a parallel here with the phenomenological philosophy, Dooyeweerd, as we shall observe more fully later on, maintains that what is laid bare is not a quiescent essence but an aspect of the meaning of the cosmos which in its restlessness continually points to its origin in the sovereign will of the Creator-God.

4. In NCTT, 546, Dooyeweerd allows that in the thought of Edmund Husserl and Max Scheler there is a break with the identification of the empirical with sensory experience that characterized Kantian philosophy. Cf. NCTT II, 477, 495; III, 32. This move opened the way to an empiricism broader than that of Kant. It is because Dooyeweerd has proceeded even farther along this path that we can call his method "phenomenological." For Dooyeweerd the empirical extends to all the modal aspects. In every concrete experience every aspect is present. His criticism of phenomenology as a philosophical position is, among other things, that in spite of its pretensions it has not been able to arrive at a concept of integral experience. It still suffers from the same type of dualism as the philosophy of Kant.

5. NCTT II, 546. Cf. Dooyeweerd, *Verkenningen in de wijsbegeerte, de sociologie en de rechtsgeschiedenis* (Amsterdam: Buijten en Schipperheijn, 1962), 17f. (Hereafter cited as VWSR.) Even more than earlier philosophies phenomenology has insisted on the universal application of neutral reason. It has removed some of the last roadblocks to its complete dominance. It will not allow reason to be limited, to stop short at a boundary. Thus even Kant's ethical self, which he thought to preserve from the inroads of theoretical understanding, falls and is included within the scope of the natural attitude of man which must be bracketed if one is to penetrate to the origin-al level of experience. On the contrary, it is part and parcel of Dooyeweerd's view, which shares Abraham Kuyper's objections to the weakening of boundaries (*verflauwing der grenzen*), that theoretical thought itself is bound to the law-structure of reality which provides the foundation of its very possibility.

The extension of the scope of theoretical understanding in the phenomenological philosophy is, as we have suggested, in the interests of allowing concrete experience in its radical unity to appear. Dooyeweerd says that this effort is a failure. The effort also fails to bring to appear the unitary "subject" of this experience. Johan Vander Hoeven, following closely in the line of Dooyeweerd, maintains that the transcendental subject of the phenomenologist is a construct, a fabrication of theoretical thought, instead of being the underlying unity which gives it its meaning. Cf. Johan Vander Hoeven, *The Rise and Development of the Phenomenological Movement*

(Hamilton, ON: The Association for Reformed Scientific Studies, 1965).

6. Dooyeweerd does not deny that phenomenology develops a transcendental philosophy. The concrete level of experiencing is supposed to be the transcendental level which gives to theoretical thought its meaning. Nevertheless, as we point out, Dooyeweerd maintains that phenomenology misses the truly transcendental direction. It could discover it only if it had a way of breaking through to the veritable concrete level of experiencing. As we point out, this possibility is closed to it because it is bound to the dogma of the neutrality of thought. It is forced to set up an immanent source of meaning (in rational phenomenology the eidos). We have already pointed out how Dooyeweerd maintains that it is impossible to grasp the nucleus of meaning of an aspect in a theoretical concept. The nuclei are dynamic, pointing to the fullness of created meaning. The nuclei in their character of meaning form the transcendental framework within which theoretical thought is possible. As the presupposition of theoretical thought they themselves cannot be adequately grasped by it.

7. Between the publication of his *De wijsbegeerte der wetsidee* (*The Philosophy of the Idea of Law*) in 1935 and the publication of the revised and enlarged English version from 1953-1958, Dooyeweerd moved in his thinking towards a critique of theoretical thought as such -- hence the change of the title to *A New Critique of Theoretical Thought*. A truly transcendental critique has to examine the theoretical attitude of thought itself (NCTT I, 35). He then goes on to define more fully what he means by such a critique: "By this we understand a critical inquiry (respecting no single so-called theoretical axiom) into the universally valid conditions which alone make theoretical thought possible, and which are required by the immanent structure of this thought itself" (NCTT I, 37).

In the above quotation the word "respecting" may not clearly reflect Dooyeweerd's meaning. What he intends to say is that no so-called theoretical axiom whatsoever has a privileged position which would allow it to be excluded from such a critical inquiry.

8. It is important to observe the exact terms in which Dooyeweerd expresses his idea of the anti-thetical character of theoretical thought. What is set up over against a non-logical aspect of reality is not the act of thought. For Dooyeweerd the act of thought as a real, concrete act involves in some fashion all of the modal aspects. In the theoretical attitude of thought it is the logical aspect of this act of thinking that is set up over against a non-logical aspect.

This anti-thetical relationship is not present structurally in reality as a matter of fact, i.e., in Dooyeweerd's terminology, "ontically." This is the erroneous supposition of the great majority of philosophers, who introduce a primary distinction between thought and being, ego and world, etc., as if they were fundamental oppositions which inhered in the very structure of reality. According to Dooyeweerd the anti-thetic relationship is not ontical; instead, it is the result of an active setting-up-over-against-each-other of the logical aspect of the act of thought and a non-logical aspect of experience. This is what is meant by Dooyeweerd when he calls this an "intentional" relationship to distinguish it from an ontical one.

The word "intentional" is used in phenomenology with an analogous meaning. It refers here to the idea that in the knowing situation there is not a passive reception of sense-impressions but an active going-out-towards the object. Phenomenology, however, sets up this active intending as the original attitude in contrast to the natural attitude of mind in which one is bound to the subject-object relationship. For Dooyeweerd, as we have already intimated, this opposition of a level of intentional act and the objectivized level of subject and object is a product of theoretical thinking and involves the antithesis that is inherent in the theoretical attitude of thought.

According to Dooyeweerd, the theoretical antithesis arises because of the non-logical character of that over against which the logical aspect of thought is set. Theoretical thinking seeks to gain a concept of its field of investigation; but in constructing its concepts, as we have seen, it works with the analogical concepts which cluster around the nucleus of an aspect but it cannot gain an adequate logical concept of the nucleus of meaning itself. The nucleus can only be disclosed in its original sense as that which qualifies all of the concepts used within its sphere. The modal aspects form the transcendental framework within which thought is possible. In dealing with them thought is inevitably turned in a transcendental direction.

9. Dooyeweerd says that one cannot logicize the modal meaning of an aspect (NCTT II, 485; cf. 506, 508). It cannot be grasped in a theoretical logical concept; it can only be approached in the idea. Only in the transcendental direction, in the idea, is it possible to reflect on the coherence of the modal aspects, their deeper unity, and their origin. Of cosmic time Dooyeweerd writes as follows: "Of cosmic time in its trans-modal continuity theoretical thought can have only a transcendental limiting concept, an idea, which must remain theoretically open, because it is nothing more than an approach to, and a pointing towards, the trans-modal horizon of time within the modal boundaries of the logical, a critical orienting of the movement of thought to its cosmic temporal boundary which cannot be circumscribed in a theoretical-logical fashion" (Dooyeweerd, "Het tijdsprobleem en zijn antinomieen op het immanentiestandpunt," *Philosophia Reformata*, IV, 6-7). A transcendental idea inevitably guides investigation in the special sciences. For his own field of jurisprudence, Dooyeweerd maintains that the concept of law is dependent upon the idea of law, etc. Cf. Dooyeweerd, *Encyclopaedie der rechtswetenschap* (Amsterdam: Drukkerij D. A. V. I. D., n.d.), I, 13. (Hereafter cited as ERW).

In Dooyeweerd's thought the theoretical idea is not sufficient to itself. Making it self-sufficient was a fault of idealism. Instead, the theoretical idea, and with it the transcendental direction of thought, are dependent for their content on a supra-theoretical stance vis-à-vis the absolute origin of all things.

10. The transcendental direction of thought is dependent upon the transcendental direction of cosmic time, as in its self-insufficiency the cosmos points beyond itself. From its inception Dooyeweerd's philosophy has maintained that meaning is the being of everything that is. In its character of meaning everything in the cosmos points in some fashion to everything else and then to its absolute origin in the sovereign will of the Creator-God.

Although Dooyeweerd has sharpened his critique, it would be a mistake to suppose that his thought has only recently moved in a transcendental direction. In our estimation the statement to which we have referred about the meaning character of reality, which occurs already on the second page of the prolegomena of his *De Wijsbegeerte der wetsidee*, demands a transcendental method. In the original the sentence reads as follows: "De zin is het zijn van alle creatuurlijk zijnde, de zijnswijze ook van onze zelfheid, en is van religieuzen wortel en van goddelijken oorsprong" (6). In the English translation it reads, "Meaning is the being of all that has been created and the nature even of our selfhood. It has a religious root and a divine origin" (NCTT I, 4).

11. Herman Dooyeweerd, *A New Critique of Theoretical Thought*, II (Philadelphia: Presbyterian and Reformed Publishing Co., 1955), 486.

12. By "genetic" we mean here the direction in thought to an origin. This can occur in a true direction, or in a false direction as illustrated in the various "isms" such as psychologism, biologism, and historicism. We do not have in mind a common usage of the word "genetic" to refer to a method of causal, mechanical explanation in terms of isolated causal factors. A "genetic" method in the latter sense is often contrasted with a method of empathetic understanding (*Verstehen*), a sphere of meaning, etc. The latter distinction is foreign to Dooyeweerd's thinking.

13. The method of classification according to *genus proximum* and *differentia specifica*, which Dooyeweerd thinks is properly applicable within a field of investigation qualified by the nucleus of meaning of an aspect of experience, he totally rejects as a means of distinguishing these modal aspects from each other. In biology there is a legitimate method of classification into genus and species. One cannot use this method of concept-formation, however, to describe, e.g., the difference between the biotic and the psychical aspects of experience. This hangs together with the transcendental status of these modal aspects. H. J. Hommes points out correctly that for Dooyeweerd each one of the modal aspects has a transcendental status. H. J. Hommes, *Een nieuwe herleving van het natuurrecht* (Zwolle: Tjeenk Willink, 1961), 224, 227, 228, 210, 239,

14. The analogical concept is multi-vocal in character, i.e., ambiguous. It requires the qualification of a particular nucleus of meaning. Thus "feeling" as an analogical concept is indeterminate as to its meaning; it must be qualified as "aesthetic feeling," "moral feeling," etc. 15. In his monograph on the analogical concepts Dooyeweerd says the following: "... in the various

branches of science there is no such thing as an unambiguous employment of these basic concepts.

"On the contrary, these concepts display an ambiguous or analogical character that cannot be laid at the door of an unfortunate use of words.

"As soon as we attempt ... to subject the modal sense of [the] aspects to a theoretical analysis, they manifest a strongly analogical structure.

"That is to say, every aspect of experience expresses within its modal structure the entire temporal order and connection of all the aspects. Only the central moment (kern-moment) of its modal structure, what we may call the nucleus of meaning (zinkern) of the aspect, manifests here an original and univocal character. But it can express this irreducible nucleus of meaning of the aspect only in connection with a series of analogical moments of meaning, which, on the one hand, refer back to the nuclei of meaning of all the earlier aspects and, on the other hand, point forward to the nuclei of meaning of all the later ones. It is to these analogical moments in the modal structure of the various aspects of our experience that the analogical concepts of the various special sciences are related. They express therefore an inner interrelatedness between the various fields of science, but they cannot do away with their modal diversity of meaning. They must receive their modal qualification from the irreducible nucleus of meaning of that aspect of experience which establishes the general characteristic of the particular scientific field in question.

"This state of affairs is expressed intuitively in the very terminology of the special sciences, in that to avoid misunderstanding one prefaces the terms referring to analogical concepts with an adjective, which indicates the general modal nature of the particular area of investigation" (Herman Dooyeweerd, *The Analogical Concepts*, mimeographed, tr. Robert D. Knudsen, 1-2).

16. The theoretical investigation of any field leads inevitably to the posing of transcendental questions. It is guided by an idea which is three-fold in character, having to do with the coherence, deeper unity, and origin of the cosmos. This three-fold idea dominating every philosophical system was called by Dooyeweerd a *wets-idee*, i.e., an *idea of law*. Thus his philosophy was called "The Philosophy of the Idea of Law" (*De wijsbegeerte der wetsidee*). A more recent designation is "The Philosophy of the Cosmonomic Idea." This was coined by H. De Jongste, who co-operated in the translation into English of several of Dooyeweerd's works, including his three-volume magnum opus. This designation was received with some hesitation by Dooyeweerd, but it has stuck and has been used frequently.

The notion of a three-fold idea is not new with Dooyeweerd. It is present in Kant's doctrine of the ideas. His triad of God, the soul, and the world compares roughly with Dooyeweerd's three ideas. Nevertheless, for Kant the ideas were deprived of any constitutive significance for theoretical inquiry. They were allowed to have only the status of heuristic or limiting concepts. According to Dooyeweerd, on the contrary, the triad of ideas in a law-idea dominates the formation of concepts in philosophy and in the special sciences. The ideas come to view as thought turns in a transcendental direction. They themselves are dependent for their meaning on a transcendent source, which through them dominates the immanent course of philosophical development. Every philosophy, whether it is aware of it or not, is led, therefore, as a matter of fact by a three-fold transcendental idea; nevertheless, the meaning of this idea – the particular content which it obtains – is determined transcendently in terms of a stance vis-à-vis the fullness of the truth.

17. It is most important to see that the transcendental method throws the bridge over between the immanent course of theoretical thought and the transcendent religious attitude, the fundamental "set of mind" which rules our lives. It is completely contrary to Dooyeweerd's intentions that the transcendental method as a method should be isolated and should be considered in any of its parts to be independent of the transcendent source of meaning. This he states explicitly in one of his recent writings: "This radical criticism of thought has brought to light in terms of the inner structure and nature of the theoretical attitude of thought itself the in-self-sufficiency of theoretical thought, its necessary dependence upon the central and supra-theoretical *dynamis* of the religious ground-motive.... It is to no avail to attempt to escape the transcendental critique of thought by making an appeal to the generally valid structure of our experience and of our theoretical thought. Indeed, this structure is the same for all; but it is oriented to the main focal point of the theoretical activity of thought apart from which the structure cannot be actualized, a point that it itself cannot bring into being.

"In the meanwhile, it is here that the transcendental critique itself comes of necessity in the grasp of the central fundamental motive that directs its theoretical investigation. As long as it limited itself to the formulation of the transcendental problems which were thrust upon it by the intentional structure of the theoretical attitude of thought itself, the transcendental critique could still appear to proceed from the very immanence standpoint whose illusory character it itself had brought to light.

"... The philosophy of the idea of law appeals indeed to generally valid states of affairs, when it initiates an investigation into the intentional structure of the theoretical attitude of thought. But at the same time it makes abundantly clear that these states of affairs of necessity remain hidden to one's theoretical view so long as the theoretical attitude of thought itself has not become a critical problem. Therefore its transcendental problematics are already dominated from the outset by the supra-theoretical presuppositions which are laid bare only in the last stage of the transcendental critique. On the contrary, immanence philosophy continues to hide its necessary presuppositions behind the dogma of the autonomy of theoretical thought. And yet its problematics, too, are fundamentally conditioned by a central, supra-theoretical starting point." (Dooyeweerd, VWSR, 44-46).

Thus the transcendental method is religiously conditioned from the outset, though in the course of theoretical investigation itself these presuppositions come to view only in the final stage of the argument. Dooyeweerd takes the position, therefore, that the immanent course of theoretical investigation is never neutral; it is always dominated by a *cosmonomic* idea, even though one may not be aware of the fact. Dooyeweerd maintains that one is even more completely under the control of such an idea if he is not aware of it and has not given therefore a theoretical account of it.

18. Herman Dooyeweerd, *Inleiding encyclopaedie der rechtswetenschap* (mimeographed), 39.

19. In Dooyeweerd's thought dialectic is the polar opposition of two moments of meaning, i.e., a relationship in which two moments of cosmic meaning are set up over against each other. Theoretical dialectic is the polar opposition of two moments of meaning in an antithetical relationship which requires a synthesis between them. Theoretical analysis demands theoretical synthesis. This synthesis is truly possible only if there has been no transgression of the boundaries of the law-order of reality. When there has been such a transgression, an opposition arises which cannot be resolved in a theoretical fashion. It has a more basic, a religious character. Religious dialectic, then, is the polar opposition of two moments of meaning in an antithetical relationship where it is impossible to reconcile the opposing poles because the opposition arises from a false taking-of-position vis-à-vis the origin. As a result the opposing moments of meaning propel human life religiously in opposite directions. Such religious dialectic can be overcome only by assuming a proper religious stance.

Dooyeweerd's view of dialectic differs from that of humanism as it is represented, e.g., by the philosophy of Hegel. The latter did not remain with the position of Kant, for whom the antinomy was a signal that the legitimate boundaries of the understanding had been transgressed, a warning to retreat from speculation into the domain proper to the understanding. Hegel enlarged the view of reason to include a dialectical logic which embraces antinomy, passing through opposing moments of meaning (thesis – antithesis) to a synthesis which both preserves them and which brings them to a higher unity. Thus antinomy, far from being set aside, is made the instrument of a self-unfolding speculative reason.

Indispensable to this dialectical movement is that it proceed immanently, i.e., that the movement from thesis to antithesis and then to synthesis proceed not from an external compulsion but from a necessity arising out of the moments themselves. For Hegel's dialectical thinking the necessity with which the thesis moves to the antithesis and then to the synthesis is an expression of rational autonomy. The immanence of the movement is that it is autonomous, having its law in itself.

For Dooyeweerd as well as for Hegel the absolutization of a moment of meaning calls forth of necessity the reaction of another moment of meaning – but for a different reason. For Dooyeweerd this reaction is a reflection of the integrality of the created order of meaning which, as it were, will not allow itself to be tampered with and protests the transgression of the boundaries of its law-structure. For Dooyeweerd the antinomy is not characteristic of theoretical thought; it is a sign that theoretical thinking has strayed and has become enmeshed in a dialectic which stems ultimately from a false religious stance. The "necessity" involved in the reaction of one moment to the absolutization of another is not a reflection of rational autonomy. Thus Dooyeweerd's notion of "dialectic" takes on a different hue from that of humanistic dialectical thinking. In Dooyeweerd's view the notion of "polarity" is the most prominent.

For Hegel, on the contrary, the idea of inner necessity as opposed to external necessity is a reflection of the humanistic ideal of personality with its ideas of rational autonomy and freedom. Hegel's position does not involve an abandonment of the humanistic confidence in reason; instead, contradictory thinking is employed in the service of the humanistic ideal of autonomous rationality. Hegel does not at all make a distinction between religious and theoretical dialectic. In his philosophy they merge.

20. For Dooyeweerd antinomy as opposed to contradiction has an inter-modal character. Unlike the contradiction, which is logical, antinomy does not occur within the boundaries of a single modal aspect of reality. It arises because the boundaries between two or more modal aspects has been transgressed. It arises because the true sovereignty in their own spheres of the aspects has been violated. Since the appearance of antinomy is a sign that there has been a transgression of boundaries, the exclusion of antinomy can be of service in distinguishing the aspects from each other.

The use of antinomy, therefore, becomes part of Dooyeweerd's method. He does not consider it to be an independent method, however, one which is divorced from the religious root of thought. Dooyeweerd maintains that the idea of the systatic unity of the cosmos is founded on the religious conviction that God is the creator and has spoken his divine judgment of approval over his creation. It is assumed that this approval ("divine complacency," as Reformed theology would say) involves that in its created estate the law-order of the cosmos is an integral unity. Since it is inter-modal in character, an antinomy cannot be a simple contradiction. Dooyeweerd says, however, that antinomy has a logical side. As to its logical side, antinomy is a contradiction; but as antinomy it transcends the confines of mere logical contradiction, which is amenable to further logical clarification.

21. Herman Dooyeweerd, *In the Twilight of Western Thought* (Philadelphia: Presbyterian and Reformed Publishing Co., 1960), 58-59.

22. Herman Dooyeweerd, *Inleiding encyclopaedia*, 59.

23. Ibid.

24. Ibid. 60-61.

25. This distinction is characteristic of consistent existentialism. Dependence upon anything that can be established in general is supposed to be destructive of human responsibility and freedom. This distinction

appears clearly in Jaspers' elucidation of human existence, when he says that it is not in general but is *geschichtlich* ("concrete-historical," or "historic"). There is a fundamental antithesis between these two terms. *Historicness* is not general. Cf. Robert D. Knudsen, *The Idea of Transcendence in the Philosophy of Karl Jaspers* (Kampen: J. H. Kok, 1958), 95. It is of no consequence that he, following Kierkegaard's idea of the double movement of infinity, introduces a wider and deeper meaning into the term "historicness." The fundamental antithesis remains.

26. It is true that Jaspers does not remain with the idea of the *historicness* of freedom as the bare negation of meaning. He seeks a source of meaning in a necessity that transcends natural necessity, one that is identical with one's freedom but that overarches it as well. This "dialectical" necessity, as it is often called, is a component of the full sense of *historicness*. Cf., ibid. 94-97, 114-126.

27. Having made the typical existentialistic distinction between generality and concrete-historical existence, Jaspers is not rid of the problem of objectivity. He realizes that in an existential relationship to the transcendent, bereft of all objectivity, the transcendent would be nothing more than a projection of one's subjectivity, just one possibility among others without any power to grasp one ultimately. His wrestlings with the antinomy involved in his position are most interesting to observe. Cf. ibid. 131, 132-140, 165-166. He reintroduces a generality of a special type into the transcendent, one in which the antinomy is lodged. Cf. ibid. 165-166, 176.

PHILOSOPHIA REFORMANDA: THE IDEA OF CHRISTIAN SCIENTIFIC ENDEAVOR IN THE THOUGHT OF HERMAN DOOYEWEERD[1]

Just 27 years ago in the year 1926 Dr. Dooyeweerd assumed his professorship at the Free University of Amsterdam. He had already had experience as a successful lawyer, and in seeking the theoretical foundations of his own field, he was driven to broader ontological and epistemological questions. The result was his effort to develop a distinctively Christian philosophy, which has come to be known as the Philosophy of the Idea of Law. This system is deep and thoroughgoing and it demands the attention of the Christian philosopher. It is of significance for the Christian working in the special sciences as well as to the Christian philosopher especially since it was conceived while Dooyeweerd was grappling with the problems of jurisprudence and since it has always sought fruitful contact with the special sciences.

Other thinkers are associated with this movement, men of no mean philosophical ability; however, I have chosen to limit myself to the philosophy of Dooyeweerd himself because of limitations of time and also because I believe his thought is especially significant for us in America as we try to develop a Christian approach to scientific endeavor. I shall then outline Dooyeweerd's position as it bears on the problem of Christian scientific thought.

In everyday life, Dooyeweerd says, we have a living contact with concrete reality in its manysidedness. The world with all its aspects is experienced in its wholeness and undividedness. The various sides of reality are not articulated. This attitude of naïve experience is not a theory about reality, a *naïve realist* theory of knowledge. We only develop theories when we assume the theoretical attitude. This attitude is quite different from that of naïve experience. In it we create a distance between the logical aspect of thought and one of the aspects of reality. In theoretical thought these aspects, which are unarticulated in everyday experience, are abstracted from the unity of cosmic time and are set over against each other as the fields of investigation for the special sciences, such as biology, physics, and psychology.

That there are various aspects of experience may become clear if we use an illustration. Let us suppose a fruit-grower has a shipment of apricots that he wishes to sell to a cannery. He meets with the cannery agent to talk business. This agent has $1,000 in bills, which he will use to pay for the shipment. These bills are *physical* things, which have various symbols printed on them. Now the fact that the cannery agent has bills with the face value of $1,000 does not determine the economic worth of these bills. He agrees to pay this sum, while several years before the shipment might have been worth only $500. The apricots are of the same quality and quantity, but inflation and devaluation have decreased the buying power of the dollar. But we are not finished. The apricots themselves are not simply valued at an absolute figure. The cannery can take perhaps only a portion of the grower's apricots because its market is not large enough to handle all the fruit produced in this good season. If no market for the other apricots can be found they are economically worthless, and they will be allowed to rot on the trees and fall off. The *location* of the apricots is also of significance. If the orchard is far removed from the cannery and the consumer, the apricots will be less valuable than those of a grower who is more conveniently located. Without going into a full analysis of the problem we see at least that *economic value* is something different than the face value of money and the apricots as physical objects. In order to assess economic worth one must look beyond the things that are the most obvious, the physical apricots and the dollar bills. By the time our seller and buyer have agreed on a price and have signed a *legal* document many factors have come into play. What we wish to note is that in this short sketch we have already distinguished a *physical*, an *economic*, a *spatial*, and a *legal* aspect of reality. Dooyeweerd now differentiates fifteen aspects of the cosmos: the mathematical, the spatial, the physical, physical effect, the biological, the psychical, the logical, the historical, the linguistic, the social, the economic, the aesthetic, the legal, the moral, and the pistical. In every concrete act all these aspects are included in some way or other,[2] though in naïve experience they are not theoretically distinguished.

In theoretical thought these aspects are articulated, abstracted from the unity of cosmic time, and they become the fields of investigation for the special sciences. In the theoretical attitude, therefore, there is an abstraction from full, concrete reality. Theoretical thought is characterized by "... an *antithetical relation* in which the *logical aspect of our thought* is opposed to *non-logical aspects of reality*."[3] In this antithetic relation the non-logical aspect presents a *problem*, which offers resistance to solution. The non-logical aspect stands over against thought and offers resistance to it as its *Gegenstand*. In this relation the theoretical problems are first raised which are met in the special sciences.

Philosophy is also theoretical in character. It is broader than the special sciences, however, and lies at their foundation. Dooyeweerd defines philosophy as *theoretical thought directed to the totality of meaning of our cosmos*.[4] While the special sciences limit their attention to the variable phenomena within particular aspects of reality, philosophy investigates the nature of these aspects in their diversity and mutual relationships.[5] This unity can be found only by referring to the origin of the cosmos. Dooyeweerd says that the cosmos is *meaning*. By this he intends to express the insufficiency of the cosmos with relation to its origin. No aspect of the cosmos is sufficient to itself. Each part points beyond itself and finally to the origin. There is an inner restlessness in all being, which Augustine expressed in his famous saying, "Thou hast made us for thyself and our soul is restless until it finds it rest in thee." Philosophy seeks on the theoretical plane this direction to the origin. It is thought *out* of and *to* the origin. All philosophic thought is led by a transcendental idea of the origin, unity, and the relation of the aspects of the cosmos. This idea Dooyeweerd calls the *Wetsidee* (Idea of Law), the term from which his philosophy gets its name.

Philosophy is not external to the special sciences. It is not bare speculation apart from sober investigation of the facts. It is not merely a *summa* of the results of the special sciences. In order to get a clear idea of any field of investigation it is necessary to see it in its relationship to the other sciences.

This is not merely a luxury but is necessary for successful scientific endeavor. A deep study of any special field must lead to philosophical questions.

At the core of Dooyeweerd's Christian philosophy is his transcendental critique of thought. He uses the term "transcendental" in the sense Kant used it, to refer to the direction of thought which seeks the theoretical foundations of its own possibility. Dooyeweerd claims, however, that he has put the critique of thought on a broader and deeper basis than did Kant. Though he initiated a critique of thought, Kant was dogmatic and uncritical in his starting point.[6] The problem of Kant is that of all *immanence philosophy*, which seeks to proclaim the autonomy of theoretical thought as the starting point of philosophy. It does not allow that thought be influenced by revelation. It sees no problem in the theoretical attitude itself, but seeks there the starting point which it assumes is the only guarantee for a truly undogmatic and critical way of thought.[7] But Dooyeweerd sees an inner problem in the theoretic attitude itself. His critique is directed at theoretic thought itself, seeking its presuppositions.

There is room for a true transcendental critique only when "... in a *radical-critical* attitude we can fix our *theoretical thought itself* on its necessary *presupposita*, ... which are postulated by this structure."[8] *Presupposita* differ from subjective *presuppositions*, which are the subjective view of the presupposita, and which vary from system to system. The presupposita are the universal and necessary conditions of theoretical thought as such.

That there is a problem hidden in the theoretical attitude is seen, Dooyeweerd says, from the fact that it has been conceived of in different ways. For instance, in Greek metaphysics *theoria* was presented as the way to the true knowledge of Divinity in contrast to the popular *pistis* (faith) and *doxa* (opinion).[9] In Thomist thought *theoria* was conceived as a natural base for the higher supernatural knowledge of revelation, and *pistis* was conceived as a gift superadded to the natural reason. To say that theoretical thought is autonomous is to fail to see its problematic character which makes it unsuited to be the starting point for a critique of thought.[10]

As we saw, Dooyeweerd claims that the theoretic attitude is characterized by an antithetic relation between the logical aspects of thought and particular non-logical aspects of reality. We also saw how the various aspects of reality are linked in the hierarchy of cosmic time, and that only in the theoretic attitude are they abstracted and become a *Gegenstand*. Now the central question in Dooyeweerd's investigation of thought is this: from what standpoint is it possible to apprehend in a synthetic view the various aspects of the cosmos which are articulated in the theoretic attitude?[11] In answering this problem immanence philosophy is inescapably involved in an embarrassment. It takes theoretical thought as its unproblematic starting point; but by its very nature theoretical thought is bound to the non-logical aspects of reality. It must effect a theoretical synthesis; however, there are as many possible theoretical syntheses are there are aspects of reality. One can have a synthesis of a biological nature, a psychological nature, etc. Because it takes its starting point in theoretical thought immanence philosophy will be forced to elevate one aspect of the cosmos, a particular synthetic view, to the absolute *arche* of all the rest. Dooyeweerd sees this embarrassment as the true source of all the *isms* in philosophy, which war against each other and which seem irreconcilable by purely theoretical debate. In the *Lebensphilosophie* as it expresses itself in Bergson in the opposition of the living force (*élan vital*) and the petrifaction of conceptual thought we find an absolutization of the biotic aspect. In Leibniz, with his application of the infinitesimal calculus to the realm of philosophy, we find an absolutization of the mathematical aspect. These isms are by no means limited to philosophy; they crop up also in the exact and empirical sciences. Among the mathematicians we have the formation of opposing schools, according to whether the thinkers find the origin of mathematics in logical thought, sense perception, an intuition of time, or a complex of linguistic symbols arising from convention.[12] One's position with respect to these problems determines one's appreciation of whole branches of mathematics.

The elevation of one of the aspects to the absolute *arche* involves an attempted reduction of the other aspects to it. This can take place with a show of success because the aspects are truly related to each other. But just because of this interrelatedness the false absolutization of one evokes the protest of the others and thought is enmeshed in theoretical *antinomies*. These are a study in themselves. We can mention, however, the famed antinomies of Zeno. Dooyeweerd says that these are the result of the attempt to reduce *motion*, which is the central meaning of the physical aspect, to space, and that thought of as a series of infinitely small mathematical points. It would be truly impossible for Zeno's arrow to move if the meaning of motion were to traverse an infinite number of spaces. However, motion has its own meaning, which is irreducible to space and number.

Synthesis of the logical aspect of thought with non-logical aspects of reality is possible because the aspects are not divorced from each other but are related in cosmic time. To establish the possibility of theoretical thought, however, we need also a transcendental idea "... of the deeper root unity of the distinguished aspects, an idea which can be gained only when we choose our standpoint above their theoretical diversity."[13] "The starting point, the Archimedean point, that first makes the theoretical synthesis possible, must lie *per se* above the theoretically articulated aspects."[14] Dooyeweerd says that this standpoint can be found only in relation to the self. Self-knowledge is necessary for a truly transcendental critique of thought. It is one of the presupposita of theoretical thought. Kant also realized the necessity of this direction to the self, and through it he tried to find a standpoint above the *isms* of philosophy. However, he found this point in what he called the transcendental unity of apperception, the *I think* which accompanies every act of thought but which can never become the *Gegenstand* of any possible experience. But this self is not the concrete self which thinks; it is merely the subjective pole of the antithetic relation. If one takes his starting point in the logical there is no way of bridging the gap between the logical and the non-logical aspect.[15] The true starting point must be above both the logical and the non-logical aspect if one is not to be absolutized at the expense of the other, and if the theoretical attitude is not to be annihilated.[16]

The self which transcends the poles of the antithetic relation is not the *I think*, but the concrete self which acts. Knowledge of this self is necessary for the transcendental critique. But self-knowledge is never possible in a purely theoretic way.[17] Self-knowledge is necessary for theoretical thought, but it is not gained by theoretical thought itself. This is apparent in that self- knowledge is always correlative to knowledge of God.[18] By an inner law of its own nature, which Dooyeweerd calls the "law of religious concentration," self-knowledge seeks its divine origin.[19] Theoretical thought is not apart from self knowledge, nor is self-knowledge apart from a religious commitment as to the origin, the unity, and the relationship of the various aspects of reality. All philosophy is led by such a transcendental idea (*Wetsidee*), which though theoretical in character is religiously conditioned.

The starting point of philosophy can not be purely individual. Dooyeweerd finds that the superindividual starting point is the religious root-community of humankind, in which the individual has a part, but which is of superindividual character. The self is not isolated but exists within a community, which is ruled by a motive force which brings it into being and gives it its form. Dooyeweerd distinguishes four such communities and motives in our Western world: 1) the motive of form and matter which dominated Greek thought; 2) the Christian motive of creation, fall, and redemption; 3) the motive of nature and grace, which found its high point in the thought of Thomas Aquinas; 4) the motive of nature and freedom, which rules modern humanistic thought. Behind all the logic and systematizing of the philosophers these fundamental motives are at work. Kant's distinction of theoretical and practical reason, for instance, is not just the result of logical reasoning, but is the expression of the covert dualism in the religious motive ruling his thought, that of *nature* and *freedom*.[20]

Dooyeweerd finds all of these motives except the Christian one to be composed of two antagonistic motives which battle against each other. Modern humanistic thought is dominated by the motive of *nature* and *freedom*. Nature is the sphere of the externally conditioned. Freedom is man's self-determination. The ideal of science is to construe experience as a concatenation of causal relationships; this leaves no room for the self-determination of free personality. In our country this problem comes to very clear expression in the thought of Reinhold Niebuhr, especially in his earlier writings.[21]

Thus, according to Dooyeweerd, theoretical thought is not autonomous. It is carried and formed by the motive of one or the other religious community. It is only the Christian motive which can give an integral view of reality, because it has a starting point in which it is possible to account for the origin, diversity, and the relation of the various aspects of the cosmos.

The claim that theoretical thought is not neutral but is dependent upon a religious commitment is of immense significance. It would provide an integral, internal relation between faith and scientific endeavor. It opens the way for a *Christian* scientific activity. If theoretical thought is neutral with respect to the Christian faith, then it is not possible to have *Christian* scientific endeavor. There is then but personal Christian faith and neutral scientific attitude. If an internal relation between the Christian faith and scientific endeavor exists, it will be possible also to have science under the kingship of Christ.

But does not the idea that science is religiously conditioned open the door to a flood of subjective prejudices that would destroy the objectivity of scientific endeavor and erase the possibility of fruitful communication between opposing positions? That such might happen is undeniable. But Dooyeweerd says that such would be a misunderstanding of the true nature of his critique. He claims that thought, while obeying the most rigid canons of procedure, must come to the conclusion that it has necessary religious commitments. The recognition of these presuppositions does not destroy the critical character of thought. That the critical investigation of thought is dependent on a super-theoretic starting point would injure its scientific character only if thereby a really scientific problem should be eliminated by an authoritative dictum.[22] His critique shows that thought which refuses to recognize its religious presuppositions and which holds to the independence of theoretical thought is dogmatic and uncritical in its starting point. Failure to see the religious root of thought has resulted in a fruitless battle of the various *isms* in philosophy, without the possibility of true communication between the opposing systems. Only when the source of the mutually destructive *isms* is uncovered is there again the possibility of fruitful contact between systems.

In stressing the antithesis between Christian and non-Christian also in the realm of *theoria*, Dooyeweerd follows in the footsteps of Abraham Kuyper. We should not interpret their views of the religious *apriori* subjectively, however, as if the Christian investigator were to come simply laden with subjective prejudices. Such would really destroy the scientific character of his effort. But to establish the fact that a true critical investigation of thought uncovers a religious apriori in all thought opens the way to establishing an organic relationship between faith and science. The way is then prepared for showing the fruitfulness of the Christian world view for science.

Seeing such an organic connection of faith and science will save the Christian from various pitfalls. It will free him, in the first place, from binding science to the proof of the Bible. The Christian is sincerely interested in the trustworthiness of the Scriptures, and he will be engaged in defending them from unbelieving attacks. He should not, however, confine the meaning of science to the support of biblical passages. Whether or not it is their conscious intent, many orthodox Christians give the impression that this all that science means to them. The Christian must establish the possibility of working at the sciences from a distinctively Christian point of view. He must in a positive way try to show the fruitfulness of the Christian world view for scientific effort. In the second place, it will save Christians from using scientific information just to find analogies to spiritual truth in nature. That there is some analogy between nature and the Christian life may be supposed from Christ's use of parables from nature. However, it is a mistake to assume that the "Christian" in Christian scientific endeavor is the discovery of some such analogies, perhaps *vestigia trinitatis* in the structure of the universe. In the third place, it will save the Christian from assuming that there is a neutral factuality that can be grasped and understood alike by Christian and non-Christian. A neutral factuality is almost bound to push religion back into the corner of the subjective. On the other hand, to see an organic connection between faith and science will make the Christian faith fruitful in every aspect of life, subjecting all to the kingship of Christ. The Christian can deepen himself in the sciences with the confidence that the earth is the Lord's and the fullness thereof.

Dooyeweerd does not see *theoria* as the sole way to truth and to true humanity, as did the Pythagoreans with their idea of the *bios theoretikos*. He does not degrade naive experience into an impossible theory of reality. In naive experience we encounter reality as it is given. It is the theoretical attitude that is strange to reality, because it breaks the original unity of the cosmos and seeks to regain it again in a theoretical synthesis. There are many activities in a developed culture for which theoretical activity is necessary, however. Theoretical thought itself is a deepening of thought as used in everyday life, and it is an instrument in the development of culture. Though it is not the calling of all Christians, it is a necessary task for the Christian community. Some members of the Christian community who have been endowed with particular gifts for thought should engage in theoretical activity on a distinctively Christian foundation. This will be one form of obedience to the command to subdue the earth. As the secrets of God's universe are unlocked, and as its potentialities are developed, it will be a testimony to the honor and glory of Him by whom, through whom, and to whom are all things, in heaven and on earth.

REFERENCES

1. A slightly revised form of a paper read to the 8th annual convention of the American Scientific Affiliation, Winona Lake, Indiana, September 1-3, 1953. This article in its original form appeared in the *Journal of the American Scientific Affiliation*, VI, #2 (June, 1954), 8-12.
2. Dooyeweerd, *Transcendental Problems of Philosophic Thought*, 30. (Hereafter designated, TPPT.)

3. TPPT, 29.
4.. Dooyeweerd, *De Wijsbegeerte der wetsidee*, I, 6.
5. Dooyeweerd, *Inleiding encyclopaedie der rechtswetenschap*, 13. (Hereafter designated, IERW.)
6. TPPT, 20.
7. IERW, 15.
8. TPPT, 25.
9. TPPT, 23.
10. TPPT, 24.
11. TPPT, 36.
12. TPPT, 39.
13. IERW, 14.
14. IERW, 14.
15. IERW, 14-15.
16. IERW, 14. ·
17. TPPT, 55.
18. TPPT, 53.
19. TPPT, 54.
20. TPPT, 24.
21. See his *Does Civilization Need Religion?* (New York: Macmillan, 1927), 6, 19, et passim.
22. TPPT, vi-vii.

BIBLIOGRAPHY OF THE WRITINGS OF ROBERT D. KNUDSEN

1947 Review: *Carl F. H. Henry: Remaking the Modern Mind*. Grand Rapids: Eerdmans, 1946. Westminster Theological Journal, IX (May, 1947), 250-55.

1949 Review: *H. Henry Meeter: Calvinism, An Interpretation of its Basic Ideas*. 2nd ed., revised. Volume one: *The Theological and the Political Ideas*. Grand Rapids: Zondervan. *Westminster Theological Journal*, XI (May, 1949), 176-78.

1951 Review: *Paul Tillich: Systematic Theology*, I. Chicago: University of Chicago Press, 1951. *Westminster Theological Journal*, XIV (November, 1951), 55-59.

1952 *Symbol and Myth in Contemporary Theology, With Special Reference to the Thought of Paul Tillich, Reinhold Niebuhr, and Nicolas Berdyaev*. Unpublished dissertation for the degree of S. T. M., Union Theological Seminary, New York, 1952. (See entry, 1963).

1953 "Calvinism in the Arena." *Calvin Forum*, XVIII, #7 (February, 1953), 139-42. "Toward a Reformed Philosophy." *Torch and Trumpet*, III, #1 (April-May, 1953), 24, 32. "Philosophical Miscellanea." *Journal of the American Scientific Affiliation*, V, #2 (June, 1953), 20-21.

Paths to God-Centered Living. Syllabus for course Christian World View, Rockmont College, Denver (mimeographed).

"Existentialism." *Journal of the American Scientific Affiliation*, V, #3 (September, 1953), 14-15.

"Husserl." *Journal of the American Scientific Affiliation,* V, #4 (December, 1953), 16-17.

Review: Gordon H. Clark: *A Christian View of Men and Things.* Grand Rapids: Eerdmans, 1952. *Westminster Theological Journal,* XV (May, 1953), 159-64.

Review: Charles W. Kegley and Robert W. Bretall, eds.: *The Theology of Paul Tillich.* New York: Macmillan, 1952. *Westminster Theological Journal,* XVI (November, 1953), 92-96.

Review: William Young: *Toward A Reformed Philosophy: The Development of a Protestant Philosophy in Dutch Calvinistic Thought Since the Time of Abraham Kuyper.* Franeker: T. Wever and Grand Rapids: Piet Hein, 1952. *Westminster Theological Journal,* XVI (November, 1953), 127-31.

1954 "Life-Philosophy." *Journal of the American Scientific Affiliation,* VI, #1 (March, 1954), 33-34.

"The Idea of Christian Scientific Endeavor in the Thought of Herman Dooyeweerd." *Journal of the American Scientific Affiliation,* VI, #2 (June, 1954), 8-12.

"The History of Science." *Journal of the American Scientific Affiliation,* VI, #2 (June, 1954), 26-27.

"Christianity and Culture." *Journal of the American Scientific Affiliation,* VI, #3 (September, 1954), 26-27.

"Josef Bohatec." *Journal of the American Scientific Affiliation,* VI, #4 (December, 1954), 17-18.

1955 "Reinhold Niebuhr on Faith and Culture." *Journal of the American Scientific Affiliation,* VII, #1 (March, 1955), 27-28.

"Introduction to Philosophy." *Journal of the American Scientific Affiliation,* VII, #2 (June, 1955), 18-20.

"Natural Law." *Journal of the American Scientific Affiliation*, VII, #4 (December, 1955), 31-32.

Review: R. Schippers: *De Gereformeerde zede*. Kampen: J. H. Kok, 1954. *Westminster Theological Journal*, XVIII (November, 1955), 88-91.

1956 "Karl Heim and the Transformation of the Scientific World View." *Journal of the American Scientific Affiliation*, VIII, #2 (June, 1956), 10-14.

Review: George F. Thomas: *Christian Ethics and Moral Philosophy*. New York: Charles Scribner's Sons, 1955. *Westminster Theological Journal*, XVIII (May, 1956), 202-6.

Review: Hans Hoffmann: *The Theology of Reinhold Niebuhr*. New York: Charles Scribner's Sons, 1956. *Westminster Theological Journal*, XIX (November, 1956), 88-91.

1957 "Beyond Existentialism?" *Journal of the American Scientific Affiliation*, IX, #1 (March, 1957), 16-17.

"Crisis of Science." *Journal of the American Scientific Affiliation*, IX, #2 (June, 1957), 19-20.

"Sputnik and the Philosophy of Education." *Journal of the American Scientific Affiliation*, IX, #4 (December, 1957), 19-20.

Review: Paul Schrotenboer: *A New Apologetics: An Analysis and Appraisal of the Eristic Theology of Emil Brunner*. Kampen: J. H. Kok, 1955. *Torch and Trumpet*, VI, #9 (February, 1957), 20-23.

Review: A. C. Drogendijk: *Man en vrouw en in het huwelijk*. Kampen: J. H. Kok, 1955. *Torch and Trumpet*, VII, #6 (November, 1957), 20.

1958 "Karl Jaspers on the Meaning of Science." *Journal of the American Scientific Affiliation*, X, #1 (March, 1958), 25-26.

The Idea of Transcendence in the Philosophy of Karl Jaspers: Academisch Proefschrift ter verkrijging van de graad van Doctor in de Letteren en Wijsbegeerte, Vrije Universiteit te Amsterdam. Kampen: J. H. Kok, 1958.

Translation: Gerrit C. Berkouwer: *Faith and Perseverance*. Grand Rapids: Eerdmans, 1958.

"Karl Jaspers on the Meaning of Science," II. *Journal of the American Scientific Affiliation*, X, #3 (September, 1958), 18-19.

"Karl Jaspers on the Meaning of Science," III. *Journal of the American Scientific Affiliation*, X, #4 (December, 1958), 23-24.

"Visit to a Dutch Synod." *Presbyterian Guardian*, XXVII, #3 (March 15, 1958), 37-38.

"One Message Only." *Presbyterian Guardian*, XXVII, #9 (October 15, 1958), 134-35, 144.

1959 "Milton's Paradise Lost." *Christianity Today*, III (February 16, 1959), 14-16.

"The Glory of the Ministry." *Presbyterian Guardian*, XXVIII, #13 (July 25, 1959), 195-98.

"Come, Holy Spirit." *Presbyterian Guardian*, XXVIII, #20 (December 5, 1959), 307-10.

"The Third Man." *Presbyterian Guardian*, XXVIII, #6 (March 25, 1959), 85.

"Ride On." *Presbyterian Guardian*, XXVIII, #5 (March 10, 1959), 73.

"A Faith that Redeemed." *Presbyterian Guardian*, XXVIII, #11 (June 25, 1959), 178.

"The Knockout Blow." *Presbyterian Guardian*, XXVIII, #16 (September 25, 1959), 256.

"The Resurrection of Theism." *Journal of the American Scientific Affiliation*, XI, #3 (September, 1959), 15-16.

Review: Paul Arthur Schilpp, ed.: *The Philosophy of Karl Jaspers: The Library of Living Philosophers.* New York: Tudor, 1957. *Westminster Theological Journal*, XXI (May, 1959), 179-82.

Review: Stuart Cornelius Hackett: *The Resurrection of Theism.* Chicago: Moody Press, 1957. *Westminster Theological Journal*, XXII (November, 1959), 49-52.

1960 "Adorning the Gospel." *Presbyterian Guardian*, XXIX, #4 (March 25, 1960), 53.

"Grace Abounding." *Presbyterian Guardian*, XXIX, #10 (October, 1960), 150.

"What Do You Confess?" *Presbyterian Guardian*, XXIX, #12 (December, 1960), 181.

Review: *Karl Barth: Protestant Thought from Rousseau to Ritschl: being the translation of eleven chapters of Die protestantisch Theologie im 19. Jahrundert;* translated by Brian Cozens. New York: Harper, 1967. *Christianity Today*, IV (February 15, 1960), 41-42.

Review: Walter Leibrecht, ed.: *Religion and Culture: Essays in Honor of Paul Tillich.* New York: Harper and Bros., 1959. *Westminster Theological Journal*, XXII (May, 1960), 183-85.

Review: Austin Farrer: *The Freedom of the Will.* New York: Charles Scribner's Sons, 1958. *Westminster Theological Journal*, XXIII (November , 1960), 94-97.

Review: Paul Tillich: *Gesammelte Werke.* Band I: Frühe Hauptwerke. Stuttgart: Evangelisches Verlagswerk, 1959). *Westminster Theological Journal*, XXIII (November, 1960), 127.

Review: Hendrik Van Riessen, et al: *Christian Perspectives*, 1960. Pella, IA: Pella Publishing Co., 1960. *Presbyterian Guardian*, XXIX, #6 (May 25, 1960), 86.

1961 "Heavenly Manna." *Presbyterian Guardian*, XXX, #2 (February, 1961), 40.

"Modern Thinkers." *Journal of the American Scientific Affiliation*, XIII, #1 (March, 1961), 23-24.

"Demetrius." *Presbyterian Guardian*, XXX, #3 (March, 1961), 60.

"Modern Thinkers, II." *Journal of the American Scientific Affiliation*, XIII, #2 (June, 1961), 56-57.

"Nature and Freedom in the Development of Reinhold Neibuhr's Idea of Myth?" *Perspectief: Feestbundel van de jongeren bij het vijfentwintig jarig bestaan van de Vereniging voor Calvinistische Wijsbegeerte*. Kampen: J. H. Kok, 1961. 183-89.

"Symbol and Reality in Nicolas Berdyaev." *Westminster Theological Journal*, XXIV (November, 1961), 38-47.

Review: Thomas H. L. Parker: *Calvin's Doctrine of the Knowledge of God*. [Rev. ed.] Grand Rapids: Eerdmans, 1959. *Christianity Today*, V (January 30, 1961), 35-37.

Review: Michael Alexander Vallon: *An Apostle of Freedom: Life and Teachings of Nicolas Berdyaev*. New York: Philosophical Library, 1960. *Westminster Theological Journal*, XXIII (May, 1961), 234-37.

Review: "For Collegians." Ed. David H. Freeman: *International Library of Philosophy and Theology: Modern Thinkers Series*. Philadelphia: Presbyterian and Reformed Publishing Co., 1960. *Presbyterian Guardian*, XXX, #8 (August, 1961), 142-43.

Review: Edward John Carnell: *The Kingdom of God and the Pride of Life*. Grand Rapids: Eerdmans, 1960. *Westminster Theological Journal*, XXIV (November, 1961), 109-11.

1962 "Let the Church Be the Church." *Presbyterian Guardian*, XXXI, #2 (February, 1962), 25.

"How to Conquer Your Neighbor." *Presbyterian Guardian*, XXXI, #9 (October, 1962), 144.

"Ethics and Birth Control." *Journal of the American Scientific Affiliation*, XIV, #1 (March, 1962). 7-11.

"A Question of World View." *Journal of the American Scientific Affiliation*, XIV, #1 (March, 1962), 28-29.

"Philosophical Anthropology." *Journal of the American Scientific Affiliation*, XIV (September, 1962), 90.

Review: Ian Ramsey, ed.: *Prospect for Metaphysics; Essays of Metaphysical Exploration.* New York: Philosophical Library, 1961. *Westminster Theological Journal*, XXIV (May, 1962), 227-29.

Review: Vincent Brümmer: *Transcendental Criticism and Christian Philosophy: A Presentation and Evaluation of Herman Dooyeweerd's Philosophy of the Cosmonomic Idea.* Franeker: T. Wever, 1961. *Westminster Theological Journal*, XXV (November, 1962), 113-16.

Review: ["Dooyeweerd's Thought"] Ronald Nash: *Dooyeweerd and the Amsterdam Philosophy.* Grand Rapids: Zondervan, 1967. *Presbyterian Guardian*, XXXI, #11 (December, 1962), 172.

1963 *Symbol and Myth in Contemporary Theology, With Special Reference to the Thought of Paul Tillich, Reinhold Niebuhr, and Nicolas Berdyaev.* 2nd, slightly revised edition of the thesis for the degree of S. T. M., Union Theological Seminary, New York, 1952. Mimeographed, 1963.

Review: Robert C. Tucker: *Philosophy and Myth in Karl Marx.* Cambridge: Cambridge University Press, 1961. *Westminster Theological Journal*, XXV (May, 1963), 190-93.

Review: June Bingham: *Courage to Change: An Introduction to the Life and Thought of Reinhold Niebuhr.* New York: Charles Scribner's Sons, 1961. *Westminster Theological Journal*, XXVI (November, 1963), 88.

Review: Philip S. Chen: *A New Look at God.* South Lancaster, MA: Chemical Elements Publishing Co., 1962. *Westminster Theological Journal*, XXVI (November, 1963), 110.

1964 Edwin H. Palmer, ed. *Encyclopedia of Christianity*, Vol. I. Wilmington, DE: National Foundation for Christian Education, 1964. Articles: "Althaus," 159-60; "Apologists," 369-70; "Aulön," 494-95; "Berdyaev," 634-35; "Bergson, Henri," 637-38.

"The Nature of Regeneration," Carl F. H. Henry, ed.: *Christian Faith and Modern Theology.* New York: Channel Press, 1964. 305-21.

Review: George H. Tavard: *Paul Tillich and the Christian Message.* New York: Charles Scribner's Sons, 1962. *Westminster Theological Journal*, XXVI (May, 1964), 220-22.

1965 Review: Paul Tillich: *Morality and Beyond.* Ruth Nanda Anshen, ed. New York: Harper and Row, 1963. *Westminster Theological Journal*, XXVII (May, 1965), 204-5.

"Rudolf Bultmann." Philip E. Hughes, ed.: *Creative Minds in Contemporary Theology.* Grand Rapids: Eerdmans, 1966. 131-62.

Sociology. Evidences Syllabus, part VIII. Mimeographed, 1966.

1966 Translation: Herman Dooyeweerd: "The Secularization of Science," *International Reformed Bulletin*, no. 26 (9th year; July, 1966), 2-17. Translated with notes from "La sécularisation de la science." *La revue Réformée*, V (1954), 138-57. (See entry, 1979).

1967 *Dialectic and Synthesis in Contemporary Theology.* Mimeographed,

1967."The Ambiguity of Human Autonomy and Freedom in the Thought of Paul Tillich," I. *Philosophia Reformata*, XXXIII (1967), 55-67.

"What Evangelicals Can Learn from Abraham Kuyper and Herman Bavinck as to Theological Methodology." Lecture delivered at the 19th Annual Convention of the Evangelical Theological Society, Toronto, Ontario, December 27-29, 1967. Mimeographed, 1967.

Review: James M. Robinson and John B. Cobb, eds.: *The New Hermeneutic.* New York: Harper and Row, 1964. *Westminster Theological Journal*, XXX (November, 1967), 67-71.

1968 *The Analogical Concepts.* Translated by Robert D. Knudsen from Herman Dooyeweerd: *De analogische grondbegrippen der vakwetenschappen en hun betrekking tot de structuur van den menselijken ervaringshorizon.* Amsterdam: Noord-Hollandsche Uitgeversmaatschappij, 1954. Mimeographed, 1968.

"The Ambiguity of Human Autonomy and Freedom in the Thought of Paul Tillich," II. *Philosophia Reformata*, XXXIII (1968), 32-44.

Philosophia Reformanda: Reflections on the Philosophy of Herman Dooyeweerd. Mimeographed, 1968. (See entry, 1971).

Gary G. Cohen, ed. *Encyclopedia of Christianity*, Vol. II. Wilmington, DE: National Foundation for Christian Education, 1964. Articles: "Blondel, Maurice," 117-18; "Bohatec, Josef," 128; "Buber, Martin," 204-7.

Review: Paul Tillich: *Perspectives on 19th and 20th Century Protestant Theology.* New York, Evanston, London: Harper and Row, 1967. D. Mackenzie Brown, ed.: *Ultimate Concern: Tillich in Dialogue.* New York, Evanston, London: Harper and Row, 1965. David Hopper: *Tillich: A Theological Portrait.* Philadelphia, New York: J. B. Lippincott, 1968. Kenneth Hamilton: *The System and the Gospel.* Grand Rapids: Eerdmans, 1967. *Westminster Theological Journal*, XXX (May, 1968), 246-49.

Review: Hebden Taylor: *Evolution and the Reformation of Biology.* Nutley, NJ: Craig Press, 1967. *Westminster Theological Journal*, XXX (May, 1968), 249-50.

Review: Robert L. Reymond: *Introductory Studies in Contemporary Theology*. Philadelphia: Presbyterian and Reformed, 1968. *Westminster Theological Journal*, XXXI (November, 1968), 127-28.

Review: Robert F. Evans: *Pelagius: Inquiries and Reappraisals*. New York: Seabury Press, 1968. Christianity Today, XIII (November 8, 1968), 26.

1969 "The Ambiguity of Human Autonomy and Freedom in the Thought of Paul Tillich," III. *Philosophia Reformata*, XXXIV (1969), 38-51.

History. Evidences Syllabus, part VII. Mimeographed, 1969. (See entry, 1976).

"Transcendental Motives in Karl Jaspers' Philosophy." *Philosophia Reformata*, XXXIV (1969), 122-33.

Where to Now? Lecture delivered to the meeting of the Middle-Atlantic Chapter of the Association for the Advancement of Christian Scholarship, Philadelphia, May 15, 1969. Mimeographed, 1969.

Review: *Calvin Seerveld: A Christian Critique of Art and Literature*. Toronto: Wedge Publishing Foundation, 1968. *Westminster Theological Journal*, XXXI (May, 1969), 224-25.

Review: Eric C. Rust: *Science and Faith: Towards a Theological Understanding of Science*. New York: Oxford University Press, 1967. *Westminster Theological Journal*, XXXI (May, 1969), 230-32.

1971 "Progressive and Regressive Tendencies in Christian Apologetics." *Jerusalem and Athens: Critical Discussions on the Theology and Apologetics of Cornelius Van Til.* E. R. Geehan, ed. Philadelphia: Presbyterian and Reformed, 1971. 275-98.

Translation: J. A. Mekkes: "Knowing." *Jerusalem and Athens: Critical Discussions on the Theology and Apologetics of Cornelius Van Til.* E. R. Geehan, ed. Philadelphia: Presbyterian and Reformed, 1971. 306-19.

Review: André Malet: *The Thought of Rudolf Bultmann*. Garden City, NY: Doubleday, 1971. *Christianity Today*, XVI (November 5, 1971), 21-26.

1972 *Psychology.* Syllabus for the course, "The Encounter of Christianity with Secular Science," part VI. Mimeographed, 1972. [The "Secularization" course was formerly called "Evidences."]

"Anathema or Dialogue?" *Westminster Theological Journal*, XXXIV (May, 1972), 137-51.

Sociology. Syllabus for the course, "The Encounter of Christianity with Secular Science," part VIII. Mimeographed, 1972. [The "Secularization" course was formerly called "Evidences."]

"The Ambiguity of Human Autonomy and Freedom in the Thought of Paul Tillich," IV. *Philosophia Reformata*, XXXVII (1972), 3-25.

Philip E. Hughes, ed. *Encyclopedia of Christianity*, Vol. III. Wilmington, DE: National Foundation for Christian Education, 1964. Articles: "Conceptualism," 81-82; "Croce, Benedetto," 250-51; "Dostoevsky," 449-50; "Dualism," 465-66.

Philip E. Hughes, ed. *Encyclopedia of Christianity*, Vol. IV. Wilmington, DE: National Foundation for Christian Education, 1964. Articles: "Fénelon," 189-190; "Fichte," 192-93.

Review: Ernst Troeltsch: *The Absoluteness of Christianity and the History of Religions*. Richmond: John Knox Press, 1971. *Westminster Theological Journal*, XXXIV (May, 1972), 255.

1973 "Crosscurrents." *Westminster Theological Journal*, XXXV (Spring, 1973), 303-14.

"Roots of the New Theology." *Scripture and Confession: A Book about Confessions Old and New.* John H. Skilton, ed. Philadelphia: Presbyterian and Reformed, 1973. 247-73.
"Moral Theology." *Baker's Dictionary of Christian Ethics*. Carl F. H. Henry, ed. Grand Rapids: Baker Book House, 1973. 433-34.

Review: Oswald O. Schrag: *Existence, Existenz, and Transcendence: An Introduction to the Philosophy of Karl Jaspers*. Pittsburgh: Duquesne University Press, 1971. *Philosophy and Rhetoric,* VI, #3 (Summer, 1973), 196-97.

1974 "Introduction." For the general syllabus for the course "The Philosophy of Herman Dooyeweerd." Mimeographed, 1974. (See 1993 entry).

1975 Merrill C. Tenney, ed.: *The Zondervan Pictorial Encyclopedia of the Bible.* Grand Rapids: Zondervan, 1975. Vol. V. Articles: "Reconciliation," 44-45; "Redeemer, Redemption," 49-51; "Regeneration," 52-57.

1976 *History: The Encounter of Christianity with Secular Science.* Cherry Hill, NJ: Mack Publishing Co., 1976.

"To Our Readers." *Westminster Theological Journal,* XXXVIII (Spring, 1976), 279-80.

Translation (with Ali M. Knudsen): Jan Dengerink: "The Idea of Justice in Christian Perspective." *Westminster Theological Journal,* XXXIX (Fall, 1976), 1-59.

Review: Ronald J. Sider, ed.: *The Chicago Declaration.* Carol Stream, IL: Creation House, 1974. *Westminster Theological Journal,* XXXVIII (Winter, 1976), 218-25.

Review: William R. Coats: *God in Public: Political Theology Beyond Niebuhr.* Grand Rapids: Eerdmans, 1974. *Westminster Theological Journal,* XXXVIII (Winter, 1976), 242-45.

Review: Roger A. Johnson: *The Origins of Demythologizing: Philosophy and Historiography in the Theology of Rudolf Bultmann.* Leiden: E. J. Brill, 1974. *Westminster Theological Journal,* XXXVIII (Spring, 1976), 395-403.

Review: Ronald H. Stone: *Reinhold Niebuhr: Prophet to Politicians.* Nashville: Abingdon Press, 1972. *Westminster Theological Journal,* XXXVIII (Spring, 1976), 429-32.

Review: H. J. Van Eikema Hommes: *De elementaire grondbegrippen der rechtswetenschap: Een juridisch methodologie.* Deventer: Kluwer, 1972.

Hoofdlijnen van de geschiedenis der rechtsfilosofie. Deventer: Kluwer, 1972. *Westminster Theological Journal,* XXXVIX (Fall, 1976), 192-95.

Review: D. Kempff: *A Bibliography of Calviniana, 1959-1974. Heiko A. Oberman, ed. Studies in Medieval and Reformation Thought,* XV. Leiden: E. J. Brill, 1975. *Westminster Theological Journal,* XXXVIX (Fall, 1976), 203-5.

1977 Review: *Paul Tillich: The Construction of the History of Religion in Schelling's Positive Philosophy.* Lewisburg, PA: Bucknell University Press, 1974. *Mysticism and Guilt-Consciousness in Schelling's Philosophical Development.* Lewisburg: Bucknell University Press, 1974. John J. Carey, ed. *Tillich Studies,* 1975. North American Paul Tillich Society, 1975. *Westminster Theological Journal,* XVIX (Spring, 1977), 399-402.

Review: H. J. Van Eikema Hommes: *De samengestelde grondbegrippen der rechtswetenschap: Een juridisch methodologie.* Zwolle: E. J. Tjeenk Willink, 1976. *Westminster Theological Journal,* XL (Fall, 1977), 202-5.

1978 "Analysis of Theological Concepts: A Methodological Sketch." *Westminster Theological Journal,* XL (Spring, 1978), 229-44.

"Modal Aspects." *Anakainosis,* I, #1 (September, 1978), 2-6.

Review: Robert F. Brown: *The Later Philosophy of Schelling: The Influence of Boehme on the Works of 1809-1815.* Lewisburg, PA: Bucknell University Press, 1977. *Westminster Theological Journal,* XL (Spring, 1978), 366-68.

Review: John Elbert Wilson: *Gott, Mensch und Welt bei Franz Overbeck.* Bern/Frankfurt am Main/Las Vegas: Peter Lang, 1977. *Westminster Theological Journal,* XLI (Fall, 1978), 217.

Review: Stefan Schnitz: *Sprache, Sozietät und Geschichte bei Franz Baader.* Bern: Herbert Lang and Frankfurt: Peter Lang, 1975. *Westminster Theological Journal,* XLI (Fall, 1978), 218.

Review: Manfred Kwiran: *Index to Literature on Barth, Bonhoeffer and Bultmann. Theologische Zeitschrift,* special number, VII. Basel: Friedrich Reinhardt, 1977. *Westminster Theological Journal,* XLI (Fall, 1978), 218-19.

1979 "Enkapsis." *Anakainosis*, I, #2 (January, 1979), 4-5.

"Transcendental Method in Dooyeweerd." *Anakainosis*, I, #3 (April, 1979), 2-8.

"Introduction," Herman Dooyeweerd: *The Secularization of Science*. Memphis, TN: Christian Studies Center, 1979. i-iv. Translated with notes from "La sécularisation de la science." *La revue Réformée*, V (1954), 138-57. (See entry, 1966).

"Dooyeweerd's Doctrine of Science." *Journal of the American Scientific Affiliation*, XXXI, #4 (December, 1979), 209-13.

1980 *Psychology: The Encounter of Christianity with Secular Science*. Memphis, TN: Christian Studies Center, 1980.

1981 "Apologetics and History." *Life is Religion: Essays in Honor of H. Evan Runner*. Henry Vander Goot, ed. St. Catherines, ON: Paideia Press, 1981. 119-33.

Sociology: The Encounter of Christianity with Secular Science. Memphis, TN: Christian Studies Center, 1981.

Review: John Murray: *Select Lectures in Systematic Theology. Collected Writings of John Murray*, II. Edinburgh: The Banner of Truth Trust, 1977. *Westminster Theological Journal*, XLIII (Spring, 1981), 406-7.

1982 "Calvinism as a Cultural Force." *John Calvin: His Influence in the Western World*. W. Stanford Reid, ed. Grand Rapids: Zondervan, 1982. 13-29.

1986 "The Transcendental Perspective of Westminster's Apologetic." *Westminster Theological Journal*, XLVIII (Fall, 1986), 223-39.

1987 Co-author (with John M. Frame): "Van Til, Cornelius, 1895-1987." *Fundamentalist Journal*, VI (Spring, 1987), 36-37.

1988 "The Significance of Cornelius Van Til." *The Outlook*, XXXVIII, # 5 (May, 1988), 13-14.

Sinclair B. Ferguson and David W. Wright, eds.: *New Dictionary of Theology*. Leicester/Downer's Grove: InterVarsity Press, 1988. Articles: "Dooyeweerd, Herman," 206-7; "Images," 329-30; "Symbol," 669-70.

1990 "May We Use the Term 'Theonomy' [for our Application of Biblical Law]?" *Theonomy: A Reformed Critique*. William S. Barker and W. Robert Godfrey, eds. Grand Rapids: Zondervan, 1990. 15-37.

"Witness and Dialogue in Missions." *New Horizons*, 11, # 2 (February, 1990), 15-16.

"Do Christians Have a Political Agenda?" *New Horizons*, 11, #5 (May, 1990), 19-20.

"Salt and Light." *Trinity Topics* (September, October, 1990), 1-2.

1991 "The Defense of the Faith in the Early Church." *New Horizons*, 12, #10 (December, 1991), 19-20.

1992 "Foundations." *New Horizons*, 13, #8 (October, 1992), 26.

Lightning Source UK Ltd.
Milton Keynes UK
UKOW05f2129110717
305131UK00002B/417/P